Leadership and Management Development

Leadership and Management Development

Jan Carmichael
Head of Division of Human Resource Management,
Huddersfield University Business School

Chris Collins
Senior Lecturer in Human Resource Management,
Huddersfield University Business School

Peter Emsell
Senior Lecturer in Strategic Human Resource Management,
Huddersfield University Business School

Jon Haydon
Senior Lecturer in Human Resource Management and Human
Resource Development, Huddersfield University Business School

OXFORD
UNIVERSITY PRESS

OXFORD
UNIVERSITY PRESS

Great Clarendon Street, Oxford OX2 6DP

Oxford University Press is a department of the University of Oxford.
It furthers the University's objective of excellence in research, scholarship,
and education by publishing worldwide in
Oxford   New York

Auckland Cape Town Dar es Salaam Hong Kong Karachi
Kuala Lumpur Madrid Melbourne Mexico City Nairobi
New Delhi Shanghai Taipei Toronto

With offices in

Argentina Austria Brazil Chile Czech Republic France Greece
Guatemala Hungary Italy Japan Poland Portugal Singapore
South Korea Switzerland Thailand Turkey Ukraine Vietnam

Oxford is a registered trade mark of Oxford University Press
in the UK and in certain other countries

Published in the United States
by Oxford University Press Inc., New York

British Library Cataloguing in Publication Data
Data available

Library of Congress Cataloging in Publication Data
Data available

Typeset by Techset Compostion Ltd., Salisbury, UK
Printed in Great Britain
on acid-free paper by Ashford Colour Press Ltd.

ISBN 978-0-19-958087-3

3 5 7 9 10 8 6 4

Brief Contents

Detailed Contents

List of Case Studies

List of Boxes

List of Figures

List of Tables

How to use this Book

Introduction to leadership and management development

CHAPTER 1

The aims of this chapter are to:

● set the scene for the rest of the book, by setting out the general approach and philosophy taken by the authors, as well as to outline aspects of both the content, structure and features of the book. It seeks to make clear the rationale for the book and its intended audiences.

● consider the contemporary importance of leadership and management development.

● discuss the varied potential audiences for the book.

● outline the key themes, structure, and features of the book.

Learning objectives
Each chapter opens with a bulleted outline of the main concepts and ideas. These serve as helpful signposts to what you can expect to learn from each chapter.

Case study 1.1: Nando's

The legend of Barcelos (Barci)

And so the legend goes that back in the 14th century in Barcelos, a village in Portugal, a pilgrim was wrongly accused of theft—the penalty was death! The pilgrim appealed for justice to Our Lady and St James, the patron saint of protection. The judge who would decide the pilgrim's fate was also about to eat a roast cockerel supper and so the pilgrim pleaded, 'If I am innocent may that cockerel rise and crow!' To everyone's astonishment, and luckily for the pilgrim, the cockerel did rise and crowed heartily!! We love this legend and so we decided that Barcelos or Barci as he is more commonly known in Nando's should be our ambassador because of the association with faith, justice and good fortune.

http://www.nandos.co.uk

It all started in 1987, when Robby Brozen and his friend, Fernando Duarte, visited a restaurant called Chickenland in Rossettenville, South Africa, and fell in love with PERi-PERi flamed grilled chicken. They bought the restaurant and changed the name to Nando's. Five years later, Nando's moved to the UK, where Robby Enthoven opened the first Nando's restaurant in Ealing, London. Robbie's vision was not just to build another chain of restaurants that serve chicken-based meals, but to create something unique that was based around the many aspects of the South African–Portuguese culture which had played a big part in the formative years of his life. He wanted all restaurants to be individual and reflect their location and characteristics. Together with an engaging and inspiring style of people management and a quality product, the Nando's brand was born.

Case studies
The book is packed with case examples which provide an excellent forum to compare practices of different organizations, and encourage reflective learning.

Reflection point 2.3

● Which of these influences do you think are likely to have the greatest influence, either by offering new opportunities or becoming threats in the next five to ten years in an organization you know and why?

Reflection points
These invite you to pause and reflect on various aspects of leadership and management development.

Summary of section

So far we have seen how strategy is influenced by the strength of conviction of leaders in organizations. Their personal values, the power they hold, the culture they are surrounded by and their own personal characteristics and talent. We now move along the pathway to effective strategy formulation by looking at how strategy is formulated in different organizational settings.

We have also seen some different perspectives on the concept of capability and competence. This section is designed to get the reader to contemplate whether leadership capability can be structured and learned in a process approach to leadership development. Or should there be a greater consideration of the concept of playing to peoples' natural 'talents'. Alternatively, have both concepts a part to play in leadership and management development?

End-of-section summaries

Summaries are provided at relevant points to structure the chapter and consolidate your learning before you move on.

Questions

1 What are the implications for the manager working overseas of Hofstede's model for comparing cultures?

2 Identify key economic and social events that have occurred within your culture during the last decade. (This may include other countries' interventions, economic circumstances, technological changes, and educational advances.)

3 What support is needed before, during, and after expatriation?

4 In what ways are the skills needed by international managers different from traditional management skills?

5 What is cultural intelligence? Specify what it involves.

6 Are there conditions that create universal responses from employees regardless of culture?

7 What is the predominant leadership style within your organization and how does this reflect cultural influences?

8 What do you feel are the key barriers to women gaining international assignments in your organization?

9 What are the benefits for international organizations in recruiting a diverse workforce?

10 What are your views regarding convergence/divergence of management practices?

Knowledge and discussion questions

Questions have been included at the end of every chapter to test your grasp of the key concepts and provide you with an opportunity for discussion.

Suggestions for further reading

Classical leadership: www.infed.org/leadership/traditional_leadership.htm
This website helps to bring a lot of the theories together. Michele Erina Doyle and Mark K. Smith explore some of the classical models of leadership. In particular they look at earlier approaches to studying the area via the notions of traits and behaviours, and at what has become known as contingency theory. From there they turn to more recent transformational theories and some issues of practice.

Finkelstein, S., Hambrick, D., and Cannella, A. (2008) *Strategic Leadership: Theory and Research on Executives, Top Management Teams, and Boards*, USA: OUP.
This book integrates and assesses the vast and rapidly growing literature on strategic leadership, which is the study of top executives and their effects on organizations. The basic premise is that in order to understand why organizations do the things they do, or perform the way they do, we need to deeply comprehend the people at the top: their experiences, abilities, values, social connections, aspirations, and other human features. The actions—or inactions—of a relatively small number of key people at the apex of an organization can dramatically affect organizational outcomes.

Further reading and online resources

An annotated list of recommended reading on each subject will help guide you through the literature and key websites provide online hubs of information for writing essays or researching projects.

How to use the Online Resource Centre

http://www.oxfordtextbooks.co.uk/orc/carmichael/

For registered adopters of the text

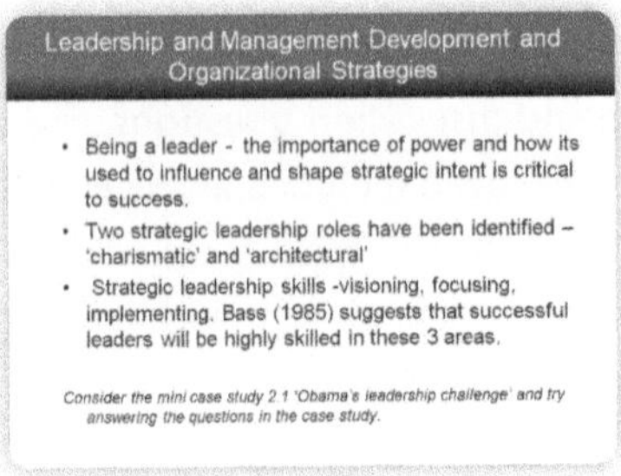

PowerPoint® lecture slides

A suite of PowerPoint slides has been designed by the authors for use in your lecture presentations which highlight the main points from each chapter. These can be easily customized to match your own lecture style.

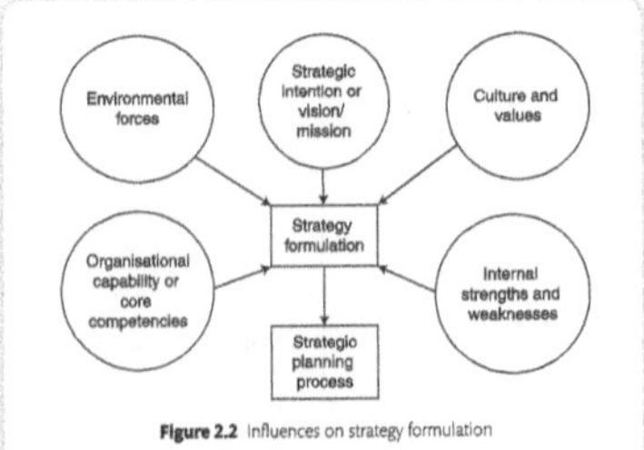

Figure 2.2 Influences on strategy formulation

Artwork from the book

Figures and tables from the text are provided in electronic format, for you to use in your teaching.

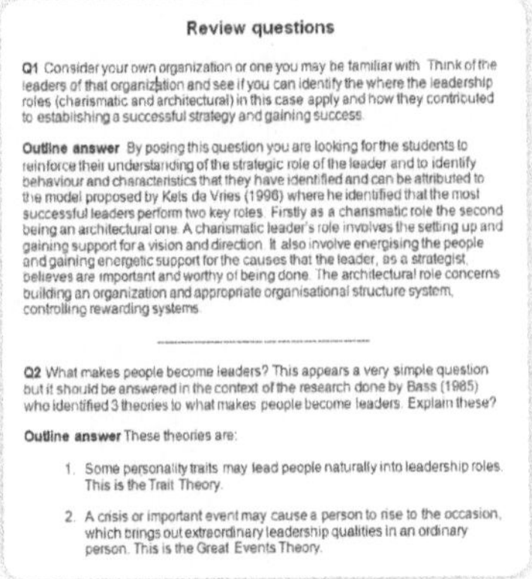

Review questions

Q1 Consider your own organization or one you may be familiar with. Think of the leaders of that organization and see if you can identify the where the leadership roles (charismatic and architectural) in this case apply and how they contributed to establishing a successful strategy and gaining success.

Outline answer By posing this question you are looking for the students to reinforce their understanding of the strategic role of the leader and to identify behaviour and characteristics that they have identified and can be attributed to the model proposed by Kets de Vries (1996) where he identified that the most successful leaders perform two key roles. Firstly as a charismatic role the second being an architectural one. A charismatic leader's role involves the setting up and gaining support for a vision and direction. It also involve energising the people and gaining energetic support for the causes that the leader, as a strategist, believes are important and worthy of being done. The architectural role concerns building an organization and appropriate organisational structure system, controlling rewarding systems.

Q2 What makes people become leaders? This appears a very simple question but it should be answered in the context of the research done by Bass (1985) who identified 3 theories to what makes people become leaders. Explain these?

Outline answer These theories are:

1. Some personality traits may lead people naturally into leadership roles. This is the Trait Theory.
2. A crisis or important event may cause a person to rise to the occasion, which brings out extraordinary leadership qualities in an ordinary person. This is the Great Events Theory.

Suggested answers to case questions, reflection points, and discussion questions from the book

Suggested answers to the case study questions, ref ection points, and discussion questions in the book succinctly highlight the main points students should be covering in their answers, to help with your seminar preparation.

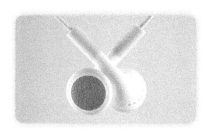

For students

Audio podcasts

Learn more about the issues raised in the three longer case studies in the book by downloading these audio podcasts, which enable you to listen to business leaders' thoughts on the issues surrounding each topic area. The organizations featured are Nando's, West York Fire and Rescue Service, and a strategic health authority.

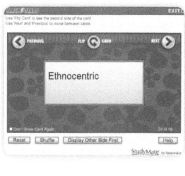

Multiple choice questions

Multiple choice questions for each chapter provide a quick and easy way to test your understanding during revision. These self-marking questions give you instant feedback and provide page references to the textbook to help you focus on areas which need further study.

Flashcard glossary

Learning the jargon associated with the range of topics on leadership and management can be a challenge, so these online f ashcards have been designed to help you memorize the key terms used in the book. Click through the randomized def nitions and see if you can identify which key term they are describing. You can even download them to your iPod for revision on the move!

Sample exam questions and suggested answers

Sample questions and answers help to reinforce your learning and act as a great revision tool.

Annotated web links

Links to relevant websites direct you towards valuable sources of information, as well as professional associations.

Introduction to leadership and management development

The aims of this chapter are to:

- set the scene for the rest of the book, by setting out the general approach and philosophy taken by the authors, as well as to outline aspects of both the content, structure and features of the book. It seeks to make clear the rationale for the book and its intended audiences.

- consider the contemporary importance of leadership and management development.

- discuss the varied potential audiences for the book.

- outline the key themes, structure, and features of the book.

Introduction

This book aims to provide an evaluation of the current understanding about leadership and management development, taking account of the historical background to leadership and management development and the recurring themes developed from this legacy. It takes both a theoretical and a practical approach, underpinned by a number of mini case studies throughout the chapters.

It considers leadership and management development (L&MD) in terms of its context in organizations; its links and possible integration with human resource management and human resource development (HRM and HRD), organizational development, and strategic choices within organizational strategy, and the role that the wider environmental context has on its processes and practice at work. The major contemporary factors influencing L&MD are considered within the book, including globalization and the need for global understanding and competence of managers, ethical imperatives, and diversity in the workplace.

Time is given to consider factors that influence individual managers and leaders in terms of impacts on their learning as well as evaluating a range of well-known and less-used processes and interventions in developing managers for their personal careers and for the organizations that employ them.

The notions of leadership and management are themselves, of course, contested and much discussed concepts. Although a consideration of ideas associated with leadership and management would fill an entirely different book, we broadly take the view that (although the notions overlap in reality and are described variously by different academics and organizations):

- Leadership is strategic, focused on vision, and involves a strong element of building trust and emotional engagement with 'followers'.

- Management is operational, focused on goal achievement, and more directive of those managed.

These issues are developed in part one, particularly in Chapter 5.

Leadership and management development, therefore, involves the development of individuals and of organizational capacity in respect of these dimensions—the strategic/operational, the visioning/goal achievement, and the trust/direction elements. It is largely uncontested that it is possible to develop managers and to seek to ensure a continuing supply of managerial talent within organizations—managers can be supported to develop managerial skills and behaviours of various kinds. Where leadership is concerned, this is slightly more problematic, and there is a strand of thought which suggests leaders are born rather more than they are made. It is our contention that—whilst there may be some truth in that—it is, nevertheless, also possible to support the development of some leadership skills and behaviours in individuals, and to seek to develop a continuing cohort of potential future leaders within an organization. The development of leadership competence may require, in some instances, different approaches to those involved in management development but there are also many areas of overlap between them.

When we consider leadership and management development, we take a broad view which encompasses all the activities and processes making up the organization's attempts to create an ongoing supply of appropriate leadership and management capacity, to enable it to achieve its objectives, to sustain itself, and to transform itself as necessary.

There are, inevitably, overlaps between leadership and management development and other ideas, concepts, and processes involved in the management and development of people. These include, for example, aspects of resourcing, succession planning, talent management and development, reward, and employee learning and development. Dependent on one's definition of these concepts, and the context in which they are applied, it is not always apparent where the borders may lie, or even which might be considered a subset of which.

These ideas are discussed mainly within part three, particularly Chapters 8 and 9.

Why leadership and management development are important today

The history of management development is long and although that of leader development is probably shorter, the importance of both cannot be underestimated. Since two major reports (Handy *et al.*, 1987 and Constable and McCormick, 1987) identified that the UK had the lowest number of 'qualified' and degree-educated managers when compared to our major competitors of the time and that there seemed to be a relationship between productivity or organizational success and educational achievement of managers and leaders (Constable and McCormick, 1987), the development of leaders and managers has grown in importance.

Handy *et al.* (1987) found that most managers had little higher education and when a manager got a new managerial role they generally learned about the new job through gaining experience at work. These reports led to the professionalization of managers in the UK and to the realization that leaders were not just heroic characters who appeared in an organization's hour of need, much as Winston Churchill did in the Second World War, but that there was a diversity in leadership and that individuals could be assisted to develop leadership and management skills. Debates about the connections between leaders' and managers' similarities and differences are one of the key sections discussed in the book.

Since the need for developing leaders and managers was recognized, an increasing range of approaches with different interventions has developed, some focusing on education of managers, others on the training and development of skills and behavioural elements of roles, and still others on holistic approaches to personal development within the workplace. The array of methods and interventions available continues to grow, along with the different types of developers, from in-house generalists, through educational institutions, and to externally outsourced experts. Still, whatever interventions are used, each must be appropriate to the environment and individuals who want to learn.

Within organizations, leadership and management development has grown, often in isolation, from the remainder of personnel and HRM, and sometimes even as a separate function from employee training and development. Whilst there may have been good reasons for such separation, however, it is important that clear links are made within the major human resource management and development areas—and that these, in turn, are able to contribute to and be part of business strategic planning to secure an organization's future senior managers and leaders. The importance of horizontal and vertical integration of business strategy, organizational development, and the management and development of human resources (HR) has never been more obvious as organizations, from all sectors struggle for survival in an increasingly difficult national and international environment.

The growing importance of continued development of those who are future leaders and managers can be recognized by reviewing changes in the external environments in which organizations operate. Within the UK, there are major changes and debates about the nature of work and the working population, with increasing diversity, changing opportunities, and increased external political, economic, environmental, and social influences. Globally, changes and influences are very easy to identify through new developing economies and cultures. Recent crises help to demonstrate that all nations and economies are critically linked and that survival of each is reliant on all. Managers and leaders therefore have to learn how to work in such organizational and international environments, taking account of diversities within. For organizations, there are more opportunities due to greater employee mobility, but with technological development there are requirements to manage increasingly distant and diverse employee groups through technological networks.

Therefore, with all of the changes briefly outlined above, it is an appropriate time to take stock and ask:

What are the key current theories and features that provide good practice and will these continue to do so looking ahead?

This book attempts to draw together what is known in the key areas of leadership and management development, and to critically analyse its contribution to date and its potential for the future. Gaps in knowledge and performance are identified and questions posed, with suggestions to help to apply current understanding to provide solutions. However, the authors are aware that leadership and management development does not stand still—there are constant new challenges identified and innovative ideas to overcome them. In many ways, this is the main attraction of the study of leadership and management development—there are no definite correct solutions, just many different options that lead to a greater understanding, both of ourselves, and of organizational leaders and managers.

Readership and ways of reading the book

This book is based on the writers' long experience of involvement in the education and development of managers. It is intended to be used for teaching students about the topics of leadership and management development and also as a reference for anyone whose work involves the development of managers and leaders. There are four main groups of individuals who will find the book of benefit:

- Those studying Human Resource Development as part of a post-graduate qualification within Higher Education.
- Tutors and final year undergraduates interested in current thinking and practice in development.
- Practitioners who wish to challenge and inform current practice.
- Managers and leaders who wish to create a greater understanding of their personal development.

In higher education (HE), there are a number of courses on which this book may be used: as part of a Masters in Human Resource Management or Development as the key book to support a module on Leadership or Management Development; or on a more general Masters, in which Development of People in organizations is a key subject. To support its use on Masters programmes in HE, it is mapped against these Management Benchmarks.

This book has also been mapped against the new Chartered Institute of Personnel and Development (CIPD) elective standards in management and leadership development and, indeed, against the compulsory module entitled 'Leading, Managing and Developing People'. Please see Table 1.1 for further details of how our chapters relate to the modules. It is, therefore, useful to anyone studying such a subject, as part of an HR Masters programme, whether to gain CIPD accreditation or purely for higher-level study.

The book may also be used by those teaching final year undergraduate programmes in which there is a need to encourage practical application of key concepts and to encourage higher study.

For readers who wish to use the book to inform their practice there are numerous examples of how different L&MD interventions and processes may be used, along

Table 1.1 CIPD standards and book chapters

CIPD outcomes: leadership and management development (L&MD)	Book chapters	CIPD outcomes: L&MD people
1. Explain and critically analyse the concepts of leadership and management and their application in an organizational, social, environmental, and multicultural context	3 Contextual factors in leadership and management development 4 The history of leadership and management development 5 The nature of leadership and management	3 Debate and critically evaluate the characteristics of effective leadership and the methods used to develop leaders in organizations
2. Evaluate, select and apply a range of approaches to identifying leadership and management development needs in differing organizational contexts	2 Leadership and management development and organizational strategies 9 Design and delivery of leadership and management development interventions	3 Debate and critically evaluate the characteristics of effective leadership and the methods used to develop leaders in organizations
3. Critically analyse and evaluate approaches to the formulation and implementation of leadership and management development strategies to meet current and future organizational needs	2 Leadership and management (L&MD) development and organizational strategies	6 Assess the contribution made by HRM and HRD specialists in different types of organizations
4. Design, critically evaluate, and advise on a range of leadership and management development interventions to implement leadership and management development strategies and plans	8 Leadership and management development processes to add value 9 Design and delivery of leadership and management development interventions	
5. Work collaboratively, ethically, and effectively to support a partnership approach to leadership and management development	11 Developing leaders and managers for a diverse workforce 12 Developing ethical leaders and managers	7 Promote professionalism and an ethical approach to HRM and HRD practice in organizations
6. Explain and evaluate the role of leadership and management development in enhancing and developing organizational competence	8 Leadership and management development processes to add value 10 Evaluation of leadership and management development	4 Contribute to the promotion of flexible working and effective change management in organizations.
7. Critically assess and evaluate approaches to the development of leadership and management in international and global contexts	13 Developing leaders and managers with a global competence	

with coverage of key issues that need to be addressed practically in any organization that takes the development of leaders and managers seriously.

A number of the figures and discussion questions can be used by practitioners in helping senior managers to understand the current situation in their organization, and how changes can help them to improve opportunities for developing staff. The reflection points can be utilized by individual practitioners or for use with a group of managers, to help them to understand their own personal development and opportunities to improve capability.

Any manager or those in leadership positions for whom personal development has not been, to this point, a key priority will find help in the book from a personal perspective and also help to encourage other managers to understand the need for continual development for survival in organizations.

There are two aspects to the book that will be of benefit to all potential readership groups:

- *Reflexivity*. Involves asking readers to contemplate frequently what the recently outlined concepts mean to them in their own experience. We then suggest that they discuss their thoughts and findings with others in order to come to a deeper understanding of what L&MD means for them, and how they can contribute to developing others in organizations.

- *Mini case study examples*. The writers have included a wide range of different cases to encourage discussion and practical application of concepts addressed. This aims to encourage readers to use current experience and to challenge information provided, to begin to develop managers and leaders who are both knowledgeable and also capable of action. There are cases of differing lengths in all the chapters throughout the book—all are based on real organizations, though anonymity is often used for a variety of reasons, not least to avoid too many reader preconceptions. Some are constructed as composites of more than one organization in order to illustrate a point.

There are three longer case studies that link to the online resources associated with the book. These are presented at the beginning, middle (Chapter 6), and end of the book, but they are designed to be used flexibly to consider either specific aspects of the case, or in a more integrated and holistic way.

The authors are all based in the UK, and have a wide range of experience of developing managers within organizations and teaching on educational programmes so that this book takes many ideas from leadership and management development in the UK. We are, however, committed as far as possible to ensuring that the book has an international flavour—and we have included mini case studies and examples throughout the text from a variety of international contexts. We have also drawn upon literature and research from around the world, not restricting ourselves to British and American viewpoints.

Structure and overview of the book

This section provides an overview of the book's structure, followed by a brief synopsis of the chapters and additional features within the book and additional support available.

Structure of the book

The book is structured along a number of key parts which are outlined briefly in the introduction. Within each part are a number of chapters, covering particular issues associated with the part. The key parts within the book are as follows.

Leadership and management context and strategy are explored in the first part, which provides an overview of ideas about organizational leadership and management, from a historical to a present-day perspective, and attempts to predict some of the key issues for leaders and managers to come. The important and reciprocal links between organizational development and strategy and leadership and management development are explored. There are examples of strategy formulation that both impact on and require contribution from organizational leaders.

The main environmental factors that influence organizations are outlined in order to provide an approach to understanding changes in the corporate environment and the crucial role of L&MD to support it. There is an introduction to two contemporary factors that influence organizational leadership and management: cultural diversity and globalization which will be further developed in a later part.

Chapters within this part are: Chapter 2, which considers the role of leaders—both in organizational life and elsewhere—in shaping strategy and promoting transformational change. It discusses the strategic leadership skills of visioning, focusing, and implementing before looking at strategy itself. Within this discussion, it considers strategic choice, influencing factors, strategy formulation, and different models within each of these areas.

Chapter 3 looks at the international contextual factors of globalization, the growth of the BRIC (Brazil, Russia, India, and China) economies, cultural diversity, and leadership and management development for international managers. It explores both theoretical aspects of these issues and aspects of practical application.

In Chapter 4, we discuss the progression of different management development approaches, locating the discussion within particular historical and global contexts. The final chapter in this section, Chapter 5, moves on to a consideration of the nature of leadership and management, and the similarities and differences between these two concepts.

The second part—understanding learning of leaders and managers—provides a rationale for the importance of encouraging all managers and leaders to appreciate the key role they play in any organization, whether to make profit or for organizational efficiency and effectiveness and survival. This part looks, in some detail, at what is known about individuals and how they learn, particularly focusing on learning through experience and the importance of individual learning as distinct from organizational training and development. We investigate what encourages managers to learn and how organizations need to provide appropriate situations for learning. Individual differences in learning are also evaluated to identify factors that explain why and how managers learn in different ways.

Within this part, Chapter 6 focuses on how managers learn, presenting the many debates, models, and concepts involved. It examines theoretical approaches and their practical applications, concluding that the complexities of learning suggest no single explanation or application will ever be satisfactory on its own. Chapter 7 concentrates on differences—in personality, personal characteristics, intelligence, and learning—and examining their impact on the behaviour of leaders and managers. This part leads onto the next one, which has a more organizational focus.

Part three considers learning processes, interventions, and evaluation. The commonly known processes and practices used in developing leaders and managers are reviewed. We distinguish between organizational processes—that are commonly part of HR departments' responsibilities—and the interventions that are used in helping managers to learn and develop. These interventions may:

- be performed by those within the organization who hold responsibility for L&MD.
- or simply be managed within the organization, with delivery outsourced to specialists.
- or be seen as part of the role of managers and leaders within the organization in taking responsibility for developing others.

Whoever has responsibility, and whoever carries out these roles, it is important that there is a coherent approach to supporting the learning of leaders and managers. They should be expected to add value to an organization, and such interventions should be evaluated so that their effectiveness can be assessed. The final chapter in this part discusses issues of evaluation within L&MD.

Within this part, Chapter 8 considers how planned leadership and management development processes can add value to organizations. It discusses a range of overlapping processes that are to be found under the guise of talent management, career management or succession management, as well as considers the identification of L&MD needs, and the use of competency frameworks and L&MD audits. Chapter 9 discusses a range of specific interventions to be found within the developers' toolkit, including well-known applications such as coaching, mentoring, action learning, and management education. It includes both planned, formal events and attempts to capture more informal learning.

In Chapter 10, we consider the question of evaluation, including the difficulties and constraints involved. A range of models are critically analysed in relation to their application for leadership and management development.

The final part, contemporary issues in leadership and management development, focuses on the main factors that influence the development of leaders and managers in all organizations. Earlier factors in the organizational environment are further elaborated in light of the changing needs of organizations and implications for developing future leaders and managers. Key issues addressed include:

- diversity of the workforce
- developing ethical managers and leaders
- developing managers in a global environment.

Chapters in this part: Chapter 11, which discusses aspects of developing managers for a diverse workforce. The advent of globalization, the development of trading blocs with fewer restrictions on the movement of labour, and other changing demographic factors, mean that many organizations around the world are experiencing an increasing diversity within their workforce. The chapter discusses the issues involved in both developing a more diverse cohort of managers, and in helping managers to work effectively with their more diverse workforces.

Chapter 12 considers the issues involved in the development of ethical leaders and managers, in the light of the growth of the concept of corporate social responsibility and concerns relating to trust within both public and private sector organizations. There is also discussion of the ethical dilemmas that might be faced by managers operating in an international context. Chapter 13 further develops the theme of global leadership and managerial competencies.

Finally, Chapter 14 summarizes key issues covered in the book, and considers how they may continue to influence leadership and management development in the future. We also identify what may be the hot topics for future consideration as organizations and the global environment continue to change.

Features of the book

This book has a number of features that are designed to support different groups of readers. There is a companion website that provides students with additional resources to aid study, mini case study analysis, and learning from the book. Tutors who adopt the book can also get additional information from the website to support the use of the discussion questions and to provide additional resources and activities that can be used to support learning.

There are also a range of features in the book that are designed to be used by learners, tutors, and development professionals. These are outlined below.

Support within chapters

This section provides the features within the book to aid understanding and the involvement of readers. All of the chapters are introduced with a mini case study or pertinent information regarding the main topic in the chapter to orientate the reader and provide thought-provoking appropriate discussion. Throughout each chapter, there are a number of features—listed below—to give an emphasis to the practical application of concepts and personal reflection for each reader.

Mini case studies of different lengths are used in order to provide activity to involve the reader and check understanding and application. There is a final mini case study in each chapter that attempts to pull together the main issues covered in the chapter. All the case studies are based on real organizational situations that the team has experienced and take most of the information from these situations. As mentioned above, in certain cases, a decision was made to keep the identity of organizations and people involved anonymous, whilst others were happy to include their identity. The cases all provide information to involve readers and it is intended that, where there is anonymity, sufficient background information is provided to give a context to the readers' discussions.

The aim of the mini case studies is to encourage readers to use their knowledge and experience to examine specific situations in leadership and management development. It may lead to identifying good practice that can be transferred into new contexts or to question and challenge current organizational practice. Both of these outcomes are intended to engage readers to develop a keen interest and an ability to review critically organizational situations that may be encountered and to formulate strategies and actions for successful outcomes through the integration of theory and practical business leadership.

A key aim of the book is to cultivate professionals with a good understanding of leadership and management development who can operate in different contexts with confidence to question and further develop personal and organizational knowledge and practice.

The companion website provides general guidance for students on case analysis, and the tutor website provides case information and key discussion points. Also to be found on the website are supporting audio and text resources linked to the three larger case studies that are found at the end of the introductory and concluding chapters, and at the end of Chapter 6.

Reflection points are included in each chapter at appropriate points in order to encourage readers to reflect on their own experiences, either as managers, leaders, and developers, or on experiences of seeing others in such roles. These reflections have numerous purposes for different readerships:

- Reflections may be built into assignments for students or could become part of a PDP process, supported by further information on the student and tutor website.

- Using reflections in a reflexive way to discuss their thoughts and findings with others who have gone through similar experiences to come to a deeper understanding of what leadership, management, and development means for them.

- Then applying double-loop learning to identify how the understanding can contribute to their abilities and organizational processes for developing leaders and managers in organizations.

Sections within each chapter are briefly summarized to aid recall and understanding, with two levels of questions included at the end of the chapters (see below). There is also a glossary at the end of the book to define key terms used throughout the text.

At the end of each chapter is a range of resources that are provided to support students' learning:

- Short knowledge questions. These encourage a brief review of the key points covered in a chapter which will help with immediate recall and preparation for examinations and will support personal learning about topics.

- Longer discussion questions. These are provided to encourage individuals or groups of students to consider the implications of the topics covered and would provide seminar activities or discussions as part of workshop activities. These questions may also be used by tutors to provide the basis of assignment topics. Additional briefing notes are provided on the tutor site.

- Suggestions for further reading. These are included to aid readers' further investigation into topics of particular interest and, although not intended to be exhaustive, will provide a good starting point.

Main issues and concepts

There are a number of ideas and issues discussed in the book that we have highlighted briefly below—either because we regard them as particularly important, and/or because they recur at different points in different contexts. As readers, you may have your own views as to what are considered important aspects of the book, and we encourage you to reflect upon those and to contact us with your thoughts in this respect.

- The need to integrate all development with business strategy and future direction and needs—for leadership and management development to be as effective as possible, there needs to be a clear and close link between development activities and the organization's direction of travel (but see also the issue of tension between individual and organizational needs).

- The need to take account of contextual factors in all development—all discussion of any aspect of leadership and management development needs to recognize its highly situational nature, since the individuals and organizations involved (and the wider context of time, place, etc.) will create a unique situation for which previous solutions may hold limited relevance.

- The possible tension between individual and organizational needs/beliefs—although the organization might seek to ensure congruence with strategic direction, a significant element of leadership and management development might be built around individual reflection and self-development. This might well produce tensions between the individual's developing objectives, needs, values, and beliefs and those of the organization, which will ultimately need to be resolved one way or another.

- The constant need for low-cost solutions and demonstration of added value as pressures grow for justification of all non-core organizational activities in the face of increasing competition.

- An increasing recognition of the reality that learning is integrated with work, perhaps especially in relation to leadership and managerial work—and that our approaches to development need to recognize this reality or face becoming ever more ineffective and marginalized.

- The increasing diversity in both the employed population, and the leadership and management talent pool—leading to a need for new approaches to leadership and management development within organizations, and to changing skill sets for leaders and managers.

- An understanding of the similarities and differences in leaders and managers, and the issues this raises in relation to development processes and interventions.

- An appreciation of the historical context of leadership and management development—American and British models predominate, and there is a need for an improved and more open approach to leadership and management development in the UK and elsewhere.

- The difficulties of trying to estimate future needs in a turbulent environment and different organizational types—one certainty is perhaps the need to develop leaders and managers with the ability to cope with or thrive on change, as this is the one constant that can be confidently predicted (and links well to the point below).

- The ongoing need for learning/reflective managers and leaders, not just (or rather than) learned ones—the ability to reflect and learn from personal experience and the environment around us is a key element in managing change productively. We would do well to heed the following, which is surely as good a recommendation for continuing development as you will find:

> In a time of drastic change it is the learners who inherit the future. The learned usually find themselves equipped to live in a world that no longer exists.
>
> Hoffer, 1973

The major case studies found in this book

Case study 1.1 is designed to be used for multiple reasons in support of student learning. It can be used as the basis for:

■ a summative assessment exam.

■ a work-based simulation project.

■ a formative assessment exercise.

■ class-based discussions.

Typical questions and answers can be found on the Online Resource Centre for this book or lecturers can design and develop their own to match preferred learning objectives.

In addition, there are two further cases based on public sector organizations which can be found in Chapter 6 and in the concluding chapter for similar purposes.

Case study 1.1: Nando's

The legend of Barcelos (Barci)

And so the legend goes that back in the 14th century in Barcelos, a village in Portugal, a pilgrim was wrongly accused of theft—the penalty was death! The pilgrim appealed for justice to Our Lady and St James, the patron saint of protection. The judge who would decide the pilgrim's fate was also about to eat a roast cockerel supper and so the pilgrim pleaded, 'If I am innocent may that cockerel rise and crow!' To everyone's astonishment, and luckily for the pilgrim, the cockerel did rise and crowed heartily!! We love this legend and so we decided that Barcelos or Barci as he is more commonly known in Nando's should be our ambassador because of the association with faith, justice and good fortune.

http://www.nandos.co.uk

It all started in 1987, when Robby Brozen and his friend, Fernando Duarte, visited a restaurant called Chickenland in Rossettenville, South Africa, and fell in love with PERi-PERi flamed grilled chicken. They bought the restaurant and changed the name to Nando's. Five years later, Nando's moved to the UK, where Robby Enthoven opened the first Nando's restaurant in Ealing, London. Robbie's vision was not just to build another chain of restaurants that serve chicken-based meals, but to create something unique that was based around the many aspects of the South African–Portuguese culture which had played a big part in the formative years of his life. He wanted all restaurants to be individual and reflect their location and characteristics. Together with an engaging and inspiring style of people management and a quality product, the Nando's brand was born.

From this point onwards, a remarkable and unique multinational business unfolded. Fast forward to 2010, the company employs 7,000 people in the UK, operates 228 restaurants, and is growing at a rate of 15 to 20 more restaurants on a year-by-year basis. Internationally, it has developed a portfolio of franchise agreements that, whilst staying close to the core values and culture of Nando's, allows flexibility for the culture of the countries they operate in to be incorporated. In March 2010, Nando's achieved first place in the *Sunday Times* Top 25 Best Big Companies to Work For (a 'big company' is classed as one with 5,000 or more employees).

In 2009, Nando's celebrated achieving the maximum three stars in the Best Companies Accreditation award. They were the only big company in the UK to achieve three stars. This award measures eight key areas, including personal growth, well-being, and leadership. In 2010, they again entered the *Sunday Times* competition, and once again received three stars, showing not only quality but sustained commitment to the leadership and management development across the organization.

National Training Awards are the most prestigious awards for training in the UK, and, at Nando's, they have achieved awards for five of their in-house training schemes. These are: buddy systems ('buddies' are staff who help train new staff); new restaurants opening training; working in management teams (team building); Nando's inductions; and coaching programmes. In addition, Nando's was first recognized as an Investor in People in 1998. They are now celebrating ten years of recognition.

So, what is behind this remarkable set of achievements? According to HR director Julia Claydon, 'It's not just one thing, it's a whole mix of different things.' At the heart of the business are a unique culture and a set of fundamental values and ways of doing things. Pride, passion, courage, integrity, and family are the five values that drive behaviours and decision making in the company. 'Fun, friendly, and different,' is the way one employee described the feeling of working at Nando's and the sense of belonging that is found within the company or 'family' as it is described. 'I wanted to be part of a success story and be with a family of like-minded people.' They even use different words, tone of voice, and language in everyday life at Nando's. The board of directors are referred to as 'the Full Monty', restaurant managers are called 'Patrao' ('head of the family' in Portuguese), 'Nandoca' is a waiter, 'Grillers' are the chefs, and the head office in Putney is referred to as 'Central Support'. All throughout the restaurants, on the menus, the walls, internal documentation, company website, and marketing material, you will see the same fun, funky, and different style of language. Barci the cockerel is the symbol of Nando's and the legend that goes with it.

They refer to CSR (corporate social responsibility) at Nando's as 'Do the right thing.' The spirit of Nando's is alive in each of their restaurants through the hand-selected, eclectic mix of global music and unique features to ensure you enjoy the Nando's experience. They have the largest collection of art by South African artists in the UK and the support and investment in this industry has changed many lives for the better in deprived areas of South Africa. On the green energy front, a new Nando's restaurant at Junction 27 on the M62 in West Yorkshire is an eco-restaurant, where heat from the grills is recycled to heat up the water and central-heating system. Also, frying fat is recycled for fuel. This approach will be rolled out gradually to all the Nando's group of restaurants. The staff are encouraged to participate in community projects in the locations of their own sites, and schools and colleges partnerships and the funding of community improvements, as well as the donation of staff time and effort is strongly supported and is also seen as a staff development opportunity.

Pride, passion courage, integrity, and family, the five company values drive the everyday ethical and honest behaviour, and this engaging culture results in an impressive level of 45 per cent of appointments that are filled through career succession within the businesses. The management ethos is to allow as much leadership responsibility and authority for decision making to be at the local restaurant level as possible, once the restaurant has been approved and signed off personally by Robby Enthoven himself. In essence, the leadership and management style is one that can be associated with a 'hands-on' action-orientated, situational, and contingency approach. There is a fairly tight framework, as you would expect, to ensure consistency around the product and brand, that is centrally controlled by the support functions of procurement, marketing, and distribution. Yet almost all else is down to the local leadership of the Patrao (manager/family leader). That is, the recruitment/selection, resourcing, motivation, training of staff, and the customer service and profitability of the restaurant. Coaching and facilitation in the Nando's way as well as developing the business profitability and the personal growth of the Patraos themselves, and spotting future talent, are provided by the next level up of management, the MDs (managing directors). Even below the conventional management level, all Nandocas are encouraged to challenge substandard quality and service in line with the company values.

There is a comprehensive development process to support career paths. There are some specific and technical courses that all must go on, such as food hygiene, licensed house, health and safety regulations, etc. Then also many other sessions—coaching, people management, finance, leadership development, etc. Staff can select as many as appropriate that have been identified in the success management process. In terms of speed of career progression, it usually takes approximately 12 to 18 months to get to first assistant position and a further similar period to get to be Patrao. As can be seen, investment in training is given high priority as this is considered a key enabler for business success. In fact, the training costs amount to approximately 75 per cent of the human resources budget.

Nando's HR department is challenged with improving the training and development evaluation systems and looking for continuous improvement methods that will really measure worth and added value of this level of training and development. Whilst there is a strong intuitive sense and informal evidence that this investment in training is linked to the success of the business, Nando's would ideally like stronger, more specific assessments.

Diversity is also a major way in which Nando's is different from other restaurant groups. It has always taken on all staff, regardless of their level of English. They are trained in ways that work best for that individual and provided with development opportunities. These staff are given opportunities to develop within Nando's to be the best they can and there are numerous stories and examples of employees from abroad who have fitted in well with the Nando's family culture and gone on to develop successful careers within Nando's.

Recruitment and selection are done by each restaurant itself and the team who work there are also heavily involved. Normally, a trial shift is done to see if a new person has the right skills and competencies, if they have the right attitude, and if they get involved in the fun and delivery of good service within the restaurant. Engagement and a high level of involvement by all staff are important to Nando's. It is a regular occurrence for conferences and formal get-togethers, where staff are consulted and included in introducing new working practices and processes. But it's not all work; they also like to enjoy themselves, and one thing about the people at Nando's: they know how to party!

Questions

1 Consider the approaches to leadership and development, both formal and informal, that are found in the Nando's organization. List them and discuss them in small groups.

2 Consider the leadership style, cultural issues, and the nature of the industry that Nando's operates in. How does this leadership style compare with other restaurant food chains you are aware of?

3 What are the contemporary issues and challenges related to leadership and development that are found in this case study? Pay particular attention to competition and the environment.

PART : 1

Leadership and management development context and strategy

CHAPTER

2

Leadership and management development, and organizational strategies

The aims of this chapter are to:

- explain the role of a leader in enabling the creation of strategy, facilitating the delivery of the chosen strategy, and releasing the potential of the workforce.

- understand how the strategic development process in organizations works.

- understand how organizations approach strategic decision making and plan for meeting the fundamental aims, mission, and vision of the organization, whilst keeping the way things are done aligned to the values and culture that are rooted in the organization's origins.

- provide an insight into the interplay between strategy and development of the organization's human resources.

- review some examples of where organizations have laid claims to sizeable gains in competitive advantage through human resources development (HRD) practices.

Introduction

Leadership and management development, whilst shaped to a large extent by the changing nature of the corporate business world and the associated strategies of businesses, is in itself a worthy pursuit for all those who hold an interest, for whatever reason, in the subject area. Therefore, in the early part of the chapter, you will see how some key leadership roles and skills are common, not only in the corporate business world, but also in other aspects of life too. The chapter then goes on to concentrate on the strategic development process that is employed in organizations and identifies the role of leaders and managers in creating strategy and then in delivering the outcomes of the chosen strategy. Towards the end of the chapter, we draw together lessons from the chapter and illustrate some examples of where leadership and management capabilities have been central in producing successful strategies for organizations.

Most leadership development books focus only on the professional skills required in an organizational setting, while books about personal growth concentrate on your needs beyond work. What this book tries to do is look at total leadership and combines both. After all, you don't leave your leadership characteristics and personality at the office gates: as humans, the process of learning and improvement is part of our biological and social makeup.

More than thirty years ago, Mintzberg (1973) made it clear that a requirement of management is that managers themselves take part in regular education. They need to learn and grow, and discover their future and potential as a leader. Mintzberg suggested that leaders need to have their own inner leadership, a transformational relationship with themselves in which they consciously dedicate time and resources to the education of themselves and continue to grow and develop in order to meet the challenges of the changing world in which they are operating.

Box 2.1 Being a leader

Leaders come in all types, shapes, and sizes, but looking through history there do appear to be some common themes. These gifted people have to be able to think clearly and wisely, make things happen, communicate well, and engage other people to follow their lead. Leaders have the gift to inspire people to perform beyond what they had previously considered to be their best and achieve outstanding results. This type of leadership is exemplified by many of the great political, military, and industrial leaders of the past. People like Ghandi, Churchill, Martin Luther King, Kennedy, Mandela, and so forth. Yet the gifts found in these leaders are not just confined to these social groups. Similar leadership traits have been demonstrated within organizations, witness the likes of Richard Branson (Virgin), Jan Carlzon (SAS), Sam Walton (Walmart), Anita Roddick (The Body Shop), and Alan Sugar (Amstrad).

Reflection point 2.1

- Think about or research the people mentioned in Box 2.1. In what ways do these people demonstrate leadership skills and characteristics?

There is no single 'right style' of personality to be a leader. There are many styles and characteristics found in leaders that are unique to the individual and the setting they work within. Some leaders are visionary and entrepreneurial, others are excellent at shaping and influencing others, role modelling values and developing people around them to deliver goals and deliver successful change on behalf of the organization they are employed by.

Perception is a powerful measure of a leader's effectiveness. Research by Bass (1990) identified that many people who worked with, or for, effective leaders describe their perception of the leader as follows:

They are people who make them enthusiastic about assignments, who inspire loyalty to the organization, who command respect from everyone through their actions, who have a special gift of seeing what is really important and as people who had a sense of mission.

Power is intrinsically linked with leadership. Strategic leaders, like the ones mentioned previously in this chapter, are prime examples of people who were put in, or had gained, a position of power and had the discretion of how they used this power. Some leaders will use the power to impose their own will and ideas. Other will choose to use the power to 'play in' others to share that power and responsibility. Much will depend on the levels of trust and relationships with others and the personality of the leader as an individual. However, what is clear is that in most cases, effective leaders are motivated by their power and exert this power by applying their own ideas and values at the very outset and origin of any transformational change situation; thus they become the key strategists and exert influence over that change.

Strategic leaders' roles

It is sometimes said that because strategy is about choices, it is difficult to separate strategy from strategists. Kets de Vries (1996) identified that the most successful

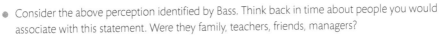

Reflection point 2.2

- Consider the above perception identified by Bass. Think back in time about people you would associate with this statement. Were they family, teachers, friends, managers?

leaders perform two key roles: the first, charismatic; and the second, architectural. A charismatic leader's role involves setting up and gaining support for a vision and direction. It also involve energizing people and gaining energetic support for the causes that the leader, as a strategist, believes are important and worthy of being done. The architectural role concerns building an organization and an appropriate organizational structure system, controlling rewarding systems.

In the business world, this could be growing the business from small origins to one much larger and more profitable. In other settings, it could be changing aspects of society that are worthy, through the eyes of the leader who personally believes something is worthy of change. These could range from global political changes to social injustices which an individual takes it upon themselves to change. Mini case study 2.1 highlights the impact that the leader has on the creation of strategy and the two roles of charismatic leader and architect of change that are keys to success.

Mini case study 2.1: Obama's leadership challenge

Along with billions of people around the world, I watched as Barack Obama was sworn in as America's first African-American President on Jan. 20. I wept at the possibility and promise that this monumental moment in history represents. I wept at the thought of the magnitude of the job this new leader faces.

The political pundits have all offered their observations about the legacy of the Bush years and the abysmal state of our nation's economy, which our new President must find a way to remedy. Some believe that it's a nearly impossible job. For certain, he's inherited the inbox from hell—a country that's fraught with crisis in every imaginable sector. There is enough stacked against Obama to prompt others to ask: 'How will he possibly succeed?' My perspective is different. I think the more important question is: 'Why will we as a nation succeed?' It's the very question that all organizations or countries fighting to overcome incredible odds must ask and be able to answer.

Obama, like any other organizational leader, must examine what he has working in his favour and determine the key levers that he can utilize to achieve objectives. From my vantage point, the most important leadership strategies that he can employ are as follows:

Engage the nation

Obama emerged as a relatively unknown Washington rookie and managed to snatch the Presidency from the hands of seemingly more experienced and better-connected contenders. Why? Because he, unlike any other candidate in recent history, has engaged Americans in the struggle to rebuild our country and regain respect on the world stage. He conveyed a strong sense of purpose that no other candidate did as convincingly.

Obama has accomplished that by setting a clear vision, communicating broadly, and inviting voters to share their views and ideas with him. He has been accessible in an unprecedented way, using the Internet as a tool to reach out to voters. Any leader trying to orchestrate a change of this magnitude cannot do so without engaging and inspiring the people, who will ultimately make change happen, be they employees or voters. To his credit, our new President understands this important step.

Demonstrate passionate leadership

Obama seems to understand the passions that he carries and how to utilize those passions to get results. In our work with executives, we've observed distinct passion patterns in great business leaders that I call Passion Archetypes. In the President's case, he would qualify as a Transformer, Healer, and Conceiver.

Conceivers are big-picture thinkers and innovators. They'll push the edges of the envelope and seek out new ideas and better solutions. Transformers thrive in change. The chaos of our current environment, which is a playing field that invites Transformers to construct a better future and empower others in working towards it, is a milieu in which Obama should feel quite at home. The Healer in Obama is the zone of passion that we saw frequently on the campaign trail. It allowed him to connect so deeply with voters—their pain, fear, and lost hopes—in such a profound and meaningful way that he cemented a place for himself in history.

Hire and empower talented people whose passions, skills, and values balance your own

The team the President builds around him will need to be equally passionate—and held to the same standard of high skills and strong values. Without this powerful combination, his Administration will be hard-pressed to overcome what it's up against. The team will need not only to complement the strengths of Obama's passions but also to help overcome his own vulnerabilities. Conceivers, for example, can at times explore possibilities for the pure joy of examining ideas, and fail to create a process that promotes action.

The President will need capable individuals on his team who are passionate about creating structure in the midst of chaos, and interpreting and digesting information to support decision making. Perhaps we'll see that passion in Cabinet members such as Rahm Emanuel and Tim Geithner, as they operate in their respective roles to establish appropriate structure for running the Oval Office and unraveling the mess that has become our economy.

As a Transformer, Obama will need capable Connectors on his staff—people who can assist him with tough negotiations both in the U.S. and abroad, while networking with others to keep the nation engaged in the process of change. The job of Secretary of State is an important position in which incorporating a leader with a Connector passion might make a big difference in Obama's success. It's the role for a consummate listener and bridge-builder, who can manage through differences without fraying relationships. We'll be looking for that passion in Hillary Clinton.

Along with the rapid rate of change that the nation will no doubt experience, we can expect more difficulty and pain as we work through issues. This is also the case in organizations undertaking large scale change processes. Having other Healers as part of his staff will keep Obama connected to the plight of average Americans. With their help, the rarefied air of the President's office will not cloud Obama's understanding of the impact that Washington's decisions have on those of us trying to do such things as earn a living or navigate through a broken healthcare system. In a heath-care czar or Surgeon General, a Healer and Altruist would be a positive addition to the President's staff.

Find the zone and hold everyone accountable

Ultimately, Obama will need the full range of Passion Archetypes to create a powerful, effective, and balanced team. Most important, he will need to create a work environment in which all can perform in a zone where their skills, passions, and values intersect. If he holds himself and others accountable to this robust way of operating, he'll have much better chance of engaging the nation for the long haul and creating a better future for us all.

Given the floundering economy, an unresolved healthcare crisis, two wars, a lagging educational system, a planet in ecological peril, an American public with deeply eroded faith in its government—and a gigantic bailout pill (bill?) that would choke an elephant—being invited to serve on Obama's team might seem more like punishment than a chance for glory. It will require every leadership ability that Obama and his team can muster … and the passion, prayers, and commitment of an inspired nation.

Question

1 Consider the challenge faced by Barack Obama on his election as President of the USA. Can you identify the three skills and abilities—visioning, focusing, implementing—that are required in the challenge ahead for the US government?

Extract from an article in *Business Week* (27 January 2009), 'Leadership and Teamwork', by Alaina Love. Permission to reuse given by *Business Week*. www.thepurposelink.com

There will be much more discussion later in the book about leadership and management and how the skills connected with these roles can be developed. However, it is important to understand the significance of the leader's/leaders' role at the inception of strategy as the strategist who makes it all happen at the very outset.

Summary of section

We have seen that leadership cannot be too sharply defined. There is no clear right or wrong way of going about being a leader; it is highly dependent on the personal characteristics of the individual. So far, we have seen some examples of what leadership 'looks like', which should give the reader a taster for some of the concepts that will follow in the chapter. The key point to understand, is that leadership is more of an art than a science and there are different leadership styles, depending on individual characteristics. What is more clearly defined

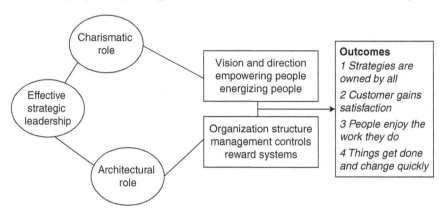

Figure 2.1 Strategic leadership roles

Adapted from Thompson and Martin, *Strategic Management Awareness and Change.*

is the 'role of the leader' and there is research to show what these roles are in order to create effective leadership.

Strategic leadership skills

As we have seen so far, the study of leadership and management applies on a historical, global, and political scale, as well as in organizational settings. History has shown us both good and bad examples of well-known people who portray great or not-so-great leadership skills. As students of this subject, we should seek to go beyond this one-dimensional approach and look for a deeper insight into what makes successful leaders and those that have the ability to transform situations.

Leadership is a process by which a person influences others to accomplish an objective and directs the organization in a way that makes it more cohesive and coherent. Leaders carry out this process by applying their leadership attributes and style. Bass (1990b), in his work on leadership, identified three basic ways to explain how people become leaders. The first two explain the leadership development for a small number of people. The third way explains how people become leaders of larger groups and in modern organizations of today. These theories are:

- Some personality traits may lead people naturally into leadership roles. This is the trait theory.

- A crisis or important event may cause a person to rise to the occasion, which brings out extraordinary leadership qualities in an ordinary person. This is the great events theory.

- People can choose to become leaders. People can learn leadership skills. This is the transformational leadership theory.

Transformational leadership theory is the most widely accepted theory today and the premise on which this chapter and large parts of this book is based.

This idea of strategic leadership styles and the notion that people can learn leadership styles and apply them in harmony with their individual personality characteristics is derived from the earlier work of Bass (1985). The basic premise of this work is that, in order to create a high-performing organization, leaders have to move from a more traditional transactional view—where a manager or supervisor had the positional power to control and 'boss people around'—to one of transformational leadership. Bass identified successful strategic leadership style as a combination of three different individual skills and abilities. A true transforming leader will rate highly in all three skills and abilities, which are:

- visioning

- focusing

- implementing.

From what has so far been written in this chapter, it is hoped that you can start understanding the pivotal importance of the leader in any organization and the complexities that are apparent in the context of the role of the leader as the 'strategist'. Evidence shows that leaders play unique roles in using the power afforded to them, overlaid with a unique mixture of personal abilities and skills. These combine together, giving transformational leaders a strong sense of how things should be done, often referred to as their own value set. All these facets combine to create uniqueness in the first stages of forming a strategic direction for the organization— the one they are leading, whether a social enterprise business or the United States government.

Many organizations take the approach that in learning what successful leaders do, a defined set of competencies can be derived and these then form the basis of development programmes. Once in place, these programmes develop leadership capabilities and thereby create a pipeline of successful leaders and managers. However, things are never so simple. Ulrich and Brockbank (2007) added to the argument by identifying that leadership competencies should be diagnosed from their results and the organizational impact, and not from some idealized competency template. Later in the book, in Chapter 9, a deeper look at the competency approach and whether 'cloning' of leaders and managers—which in a simplistic way the competency models purport to do—is either feasible or desirable.

Having learned about the critical role of the leader in the framing and initial shaping of strategic intentions, it is important now to examine what we understand by strategy and how the strategic development process works in organizations.

Strategy—what is it?

In its simplest form, strategy is about explaining what 'choices' have been made in determining what organizations and managers do. There is no single right answer and different strategies can and do lead to similar outcomes; and, along the way to forming strategy, some things have to be sacrificed and others have to be traded off in reaching a chosen strategic mix that meets the requirements and addresses the challenges being faced. Figure 2.2 illustrates the forces that are influential in making choices about the strategies organizations develop.

Environmental forces

Environmental forces often offer opportunities—and, considering the rapid pace at which the world is changing, this has created the need for strategists and companies to speed up their decision making. Otherwise, they get left behind by more agile competitors who do respond faster to changing circumstances and opportunities.

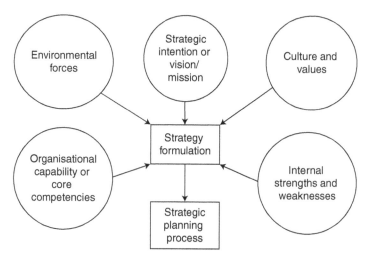

Figure 2.2 Influences on strategy formulation

The PESTEL framework (political, economic, social, technological, environmental, and legal) is often used to identify environmental forces of influence which might affect organizations. Table 2.1 shows some examples of environmental forces that can affect strategies in organizations.

Table 2.1 Environmental forces

Political
- Government stability and actions
- Social mobility
- Capital markets
- Social welfare policy
- Overseas trade agreements

Economic forces
- Economy of countries
- Competition: UK and global markets
- Suppliers of raw materials
- Unemployment
- Disposable income
- Interest rates

Sociocultural
- Labour markets
- Sociological changes, e.g. smoking ban, population demographics, and income distribution
- Education
- Lifestyle changes

Technological forces
- Research and development (R&D) policy
- New inventions
- Rates of obsolescence
- Investment of governments

Environmental forces
- Ecology protection laws
- Waste disposal methods and costs
- Recycling incentives
- Energy consumptions

Legal
- Competition legislation
- Health & Safety
- Employment law
- Consumer protection laws
- Product manufacturing standards

Reflection point 2.3

- Which of these influences do you think are likely to have the greatest influence, either by offering new opportunities or becoming threats in the next five to ten years in an organization you know and why?

Strategic intention or vision and mission

In its simplest form, the strategic intent—or, as it is alternatively referred to by others, the vision and mission of the organization, either way—is about what the organization does and the reason the organization exists. Moreover, it captures how the organization sees itself in the future. These matters are often articulated in a formal statement and these statements often take a customer-orientated view of the world and the words it uses to define this. Below, are a few examples to demonstrate how organizations articulate how they see themselves and what they do. As you will notice the label used, either strategic intent or vision and mission, is individual preference to a large extent and interchangeable. The important point to understand is that both approaches articulate where the organization sees itself and what it does.

Vision and mission statements

Box 2.2 is derived from a simple internet search that illustrates just a few examples of organizations' mission, vision, and strategic intent statements. More often than not, linked to this will be a statement about the culture and core values which have a combined to influence on the content and direction of the organizations strategy.

Box 2.2 Organizations' mission, vision, and strategic intent statements

Ford Motor Company (2009)

Vision: To become the world's leading company for automotive products and services.

Mission: We are a globally diverse family, with a proud heritage, that's passionately committed to providing outstanding products and services.

Barclays (2009)

Strategic intent: Barclays strategy is to achieve good growth through time by diversifying its business base and increasing its presence in markets and segments that are growing rapidly. The Group's ambition is to become one of a handful of universal banks leading the global financial services industry, helping customers and clients throughout the world achieve their goals.

Aviva Insurance (2009)

Mission: Our purpose is to bring prosperity and peace of mind to our customers.

We will do this by realizing our vision: One Aviva, twice the value. By working together across our businesses, we will optimize our performance in the global marketplace and maximize the value we can generate for all our stakeholders.

Santander Banking Group (2009)

Vision: The Santander vision is to become the best commercial bank in the UK. We want to be:

1) Best for service and 2) Best for customer loyalty

This means offering our customers a full range of financial products—from bank accounts, mortgages and credit cards, to finance for small businesses and large corporate organizations.

We are committed to offering our customers the best market-leading products and services. To do this, we need to be the most efficient bank in the UK too. The more efficient we become, the more we can pass back those savings to customers with value-for-money products and services. During 2008 we had more 'Best Buy' product recommendations in the national media than any other bank, something we aim to continue.

At Santander we also know our most valuable asset is our people. We want to be the best bank to work for through a culture of equality and opportunity, a bank where people are rewarded and recognized for their contribution to the business.

Reflection point 2.4

- Try surfing the web for other organizations you know of but across different sectors—that is, private sector, public sector, and the third sector (not-for-profit organizations). Review the visions, missions, and values, and examine the differences in approach.

Culture and values

There are many good books that are dedicated to understanding the importance of culture in the context of strategy formulation. In this book, we only aim to highlight how culture is influential alongside other forces and seek to gain an understanding of how this can be recognized and assessed in terms of its importance in the broader context of leadership and management development. Culture is a cacophony of complex issues, relationships, and sets of behaviours. In this chapter, we have looked at just two approaches that are useful in increasing our understanding. Handy (1976) made a meaningful contribution to understanding culture by characterizing it in terms of the relationship between the organization and individuals and also the

Table 2.2 Organizational culture and characteristics

Type of culture	Strategy driven by	Characteristics	
		Modus operandi	Suited to deliver
Role culture	Committees	Structure and systems	Efficiency and repetitive tasks
Task culture	Teams	Shared values and ad hoc procedures	Projects or tasks innovation
Power culture	Leaders	Command	Rapid response
Personal culture	Individuals	Personal creativity and expert power	Innovation

Source: Adapted from *Understanding Organizations* by Charles Handy (Penguin Books 1976, Fourth edition 1993) Copyright © Charles Handy, 1976, 1981, 1985, 1993, 1999.

importance of power and hierarchy. He identified four types of culture and the characteristics that underpin these.

When characterizing organizational cultures in this way, it is important to understand that there is no best or worst culture. The issue is that culture is likely to drive strategy towards a best-fit solution and therefore show a distinct alignment between the dominant cultural influences of the organization and the appropriate strategy being sought in the search for a successful formula and outcome.

Another useful approach to understanding culture is found in the work of Johnson and Scholes (2002) and the Cultural Web. In this approach, the underlying assumptions that are apparent in all organizations—which, although not instantly recognizable as an influencing factor in their own right—come together in a complex relationship to create a unique blend that is defined as organizational culture. This model is depicted in Figure 2.3.

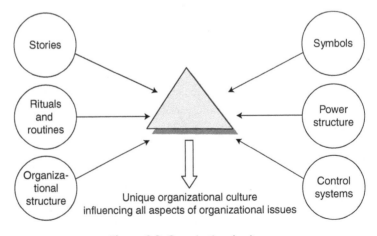

Figure 2.3 Organizational culture

Stories. Refer to such things as: what are the anecdotal stories—mainly from the past, mythical, or factual—that have been significant in the history of the organization; and which individuals have been classed as heroes, mavericks, or villains for their actions. This can be people in leaders, managers or sub-management roles; these stories can be about key events and instances that are remembered by the workforce as significant, or have gained notoriety in terms of strengths or weaknesses that have deviated from the norms. These stories have been passed down the ages and are seen to add 'fabric' to the organization and to play a small part in how it goes about its everyday business.

Symbols. Refer to things such as: what status symbols are found in an organization, what jargon or terminology is used, and what specific symbols are connected with the organization.

Power structure. Refers to such things as: the core beliefs and assumptions of the leaders; how strongly held are these core beliefs; and how power is distributed in the organization. These power-related issues are likely to have grown with the organization over the years and can be seen as blockages to change.

Organizational structure. Refers to such things as: how many levels there are in the hierarchy and what is the span of control. How formal or informal are the reporting lines and whether the structure encourages competition or collaboration. Where significant decisions are made in the organizations, are they central or decentralized?

Control systems. Refer to things such as: how the performance management systems work, what is measured, and how it is rewarded. These are facets which have an important influence on behaviour. Do the control systems promote teamwork or individual outputs? Also, how the organization's financial resources are controlled—are budgets delegated down the organization or kept to senior management level?

Rituals and routines. Refer to such things as: are there key rituals that are linked to the values and core beliefs of the organization? Are there ceremonies—internal or external—that the organization adopts to award for success? Are there rituals or routines that form part of the induction process for new entrants?

In summary, the above influences create a 'Cultural Web', which, when considered in a combined state, creates a dominant culture that is unique to an organization that is often taken for granted but when broken down into these headings, provides us with a useful understanding of an organization's culture. Johnson and Scholes carried out this evaluation project in a study of the National Health Service (NHS) in the 1990s. Now, try the following exercise to help cement a deeper understanding of organizational culture and of how powerful it can be.

Reflection point 2.5

- In small groups, consider an organization you are familiar with and evaluate its dominant culture in light of the above listed influences. How easy or hard would it be to change these influences?

Core values

The core values of an organization are those that are central to the way that organization functions, how it makes decisions, how it manages its people, and how it goes about its everyday tasks. Core values are only a few in number (between five and eight as a benchmark), but are key, inasmuch as they reflect the deeply held values of the organization and are independent of the current industry environment and management fads. One way to determine whether a value is a core value is to consider whether it continues to be supported if circumstances change and cause it to be seen as a liability. If the answer to that is that it would be kept, then it is a core value that is rooted in the DNA of the organization. It therefore follows that if an organization diversified into new industries and markets, it would take the core values with it, rather than adopt new values that may, on the surface, correlate with those you would expect in the new setting. For instance, consider the following examples of values that some organizations have chosen to be their core values.

- customer service excellence
- social responsibility
- embrace change
- technological innovation
- professionalism
- teamwork
- dedication to continuous improvement.

Having these deep-rooted values also avoids strategic drift, an important factor identified by Johnson and Scholes (2002). There are usually long periods of relative continuity in which strategies remain mainly unchanged or where the changes are small and incremental. In this situation, the pressure to compromise values is small as clear congruence is evident between missions, vision, and values and the focus for the organization and its leaders is in delivery of the strategic goals. There are also periods of flux in which strategies change but in no clear direction, again there is no real pressure to compromise on the organization's deep-rooted values. It is only when the organization faces transformational change where there is a fundamental change in strategic direction that things need to happen differently. This is most infrequent in the lifespan of an organization; but when this does occur, the values are challenged and the pressure to change 'the way we do things around here' is at its most likely as an answer, rightly or wrongly, in an effort to avoid strategic drift. Basically this entails abandoning the original paradigm and adopting a new one.

Summary of section

We have seen how an organization's strategic intent and the choices it makes in pursuit of its mission and vision is highly influenced by the people entrusted to lead it. The power given or owned by the leader, along with the style of the leader, has a massive influence on shaping an organization's strategy. Other factors include: how many stake-holders are involved; the constitution of the organization, and the culture and values of the organization that also shape strategy. Yet, arguably, it is the leaders' influence that determines the level of success of organizations. The high levels of remuneration awarded to leaders in both private and public sector organizations would seem to support this notion.

The capability and core competencies of organizations

Within a particular industry or market sector, it is an obvious fact that some organizations outperform others in terms of profitability, growth, and service levels. This superior vantage position is often referred to as having *competitive advantage* over rivals. When the competitive advantage is maintained over long periods of time, it is referred to as *sustained competitive advantage*. Two of the key building blocks of sustained competitive advantage are organizational capability and core competencies.

Organizational capabilities refers to the specific strengths that allow the organization to differentiate its products or services from those offered by rivals. This can be in the form of resources such as: the copyrights and patents it owns; the financial strength of its balance sheet; its research and development capability; and its management ability to change quickly the core competencies of the workforce such as

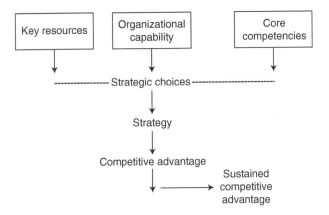

Figure 2.4 Enablers for sustained competitive advantage

Prahalad and Hamel, *The Core Competencies of the Corporation.*

marketing excellence, production efficiencies, vigilant brand management, and supply chain superiority. The important point that needs to be understood is that an organization's capability and core competencies greatly influence the strategic choices that are captured in a strategy and made enablers for success, and in turn lead to sustained competitive advantage.

Prahalad and Hamel (1990) have made a significant contribution to the understanding of organizational capability and core competencies and the influence these have in gaining sustained competitive advantage. What is most relevant to this book is the importance given by Prahalad and Hamel to collective learning in organizations and the coordination of skills. They made the point that core competencies are the source of competitive advantage. Organizations build competencies over a period of time that may at the outset support the products and services of a particular point in time in its evolution. As time moves on and external forces change and shift creating opportunities, these core competencies can then be tapped in a combination of different ways as both internal and external opportunities present themselves. Metaphorically, core competencies can be described as the glue that bonds business units or divisions within the same organization. You will see examples in later chapters of this book of how this coordinated learning within organizations manifests itself.

Internal strengths and weaknesses

We saw earlier in this chapter that internal strengths and weaknesses have influence on the strategic choices and the formulation of the chosen strategy of an organization. In this section, we explain how an evaluation of an organization's internal strengths and weaknesses can be as important as an external evaluation of markets and environmental issues in strategy formulation. To further develop and understand this, it is useful to refer to the work of Barney (1995), 'Looking Inside for Competitive Advantage'. Acknowledging that a traditional SWOT framework is a useful tool in surfacing issues that are worthy of consideration in the strategy formulation stage, the further consideration of Value, Rareness, Imitability, and Organization can surface issues that a traditional SWOT (strengths, weaknesses, opportunities, and threats) evaluation is blind to and therefore give a more complete picture of the influence of internal strengths and weaknesses in formulating strategy.

Resourced-based view of the firm

Resource-based strategy was succinctly described by Harrison (2009), as a firm's resources becoming valuable when they enable it to exploit opportunities and reduce threats. According to earlier work by Barney (1991) and in relation to Porter's (1980) work on value chains and adding value, firms with strong resource-based strategies do this by:

- meeting or creating a market need
- having uniqueness and sustainability
- being hard to copy
- being path dependent (that is to say, some things are so deeply embedded into the fabric of the business, that they cannot be poached by competitors).

VRIO evaluation

To begin evaluating the competitive implications of an organization's internal resources and capabilities, a good starting point is to review some key issues and ask a series of questions on value, rareness, imitablity, and organization (VRIO):

- *Value.* Do these resources and capabilities add value by neutralizing weaknesses or exploiting opportunities?
- *Rareness.* Does the organization have internal resources or capabilities that are different to its competitors and are therefore a source of competitive advantage in terms of its rareness?
- *Imitability.* Should the organization have resources and capability that is both valuable and rare, this gives a time span where it will enjoy advantage over its competitors. However, this may only last until it can be replicated by its competitors and is not, therefore, a source of sustainable competitive advantage. It is important then to consider and evaluate the complexities, difficulties, and costs of an organization following a strategy of imitating another in order to gain competitive advantage. Equally, it is important to reverse this evaluation process and consider how and what a competitor would need to do in order to imitate your own organization's internal source of advantage.
- *Organization.* An organization's potential for competitive advantage by exploiting the value, rareness, and inimitability of its internal resources and capability depends to a large extent on how it is organized in order to realize this potential. Although there are numerous components for how it goes about this, there are some key aspects that are worthy of evaluation. The following questions may be useful in surfacing issues that will help decide if an organization is a strength or weakness in terms of a source of competitive advantage.

Do the organization's management control and reward systems drive performance? Are they integrative? Do they relate to the VRI aspects in leveraging competitive advantage of the organization's resources and capabilities. See Mini case study 2.2 as an example of how this can be applied in a practical setting.

Mini case study 2.2: Workforce development at AFI-Uplift Ltd

AFI-Uplift Limited (AFI) is the second largest powered access company in the UK, hiring powered access booms and scissor lifts. It now employs 160 contracted staff across twelve national sites, both on a part-time and full-time basis. This flexible approach to employment works well for the company and keeps internal costs surprisingly low whilst achieving service levels for its customers. To achieve this balance, a lot of effort is required in the control of the organization's resources. Not only in controlling the shift patterns of the workforce, but also in ensuring that the plant and machinery is moved efficiently around the sites so that they are available for hire and downtime is minimized. 'Sweating the asset', as the management like to refer to it, is something they are excellent at doing on a day-to-day basis.

Since its formation, the company has grown its rental fleet to over 3,570 machines. This was greatly helped by the government's regulations regarding 'Work at Height', where employers have the duty of care to ensure working at heights is planned and carried out in a safe manner. It has also developed a successful Training Centre facility that runs courses for larger organizations operating in the construction industry. Historically, the board of directors took a positive decision to invest in the company's infrastructure, increasing its coverage across the UK—which was more in anticipation of growth, than as a response to it, particularly in terms of its personnel and core competencies. As a result, previous attention was given to finding qualified senior personnel externally, with the company providing only a small amount of financial resources in the training and development of its existing workforce. With all senior positions in the company filled through external sources, this left little opportunity for its junior members of staff to develop within the company. This has previously resulted in higher than national average attrition figures.

However, over recent years, particularly following a substantial £15 million financial investment through a well-known high street investment bank, the company's strategy changed, with its board making a conscientious decision to invest time and money in its entire staff and to address the particular issue of the development of its junior staff, as well as increasing the commitment and engagement to the company and its strategic plans. As a result, it has avidly promoted the working ethos that 'Work has to be fun' and has encouraged a proactive, teamwork approach to foster a 'well-being' and 'fun' culture amongst its employees. In turn, it is thought that a happy workforce will result in increased productivity for the company. This is quite a different approach from the industry norm, which tends to see the typical employee in a blue-collar job as a low skilled manual worker/driver who is low on self-motivation, earning a minimum wage, and someone who requires close supervision and control.

In line with this, in January 2007, AFI began seeking the Investors in People (IIP) Award, investing in training and developing of its staff. As a result of the geographic layout of the company, together with financial government incentives, it was advantageous to the company that the standard was sought independently by all thirteen sites, rather than applying for one standard as a whole. This was done on an ongoing, rolling process. In line with this new investment, AFI published its Training and Development Policy to all staff, publicizing and communicating its aims and objectives in relation to this investment and telling the workforce how it was going to spend the new money on their development. In part, this read:

We shall increase our market share through the ongoing investment in the training of our staff ... in IT systems and in the widest range of well-presented and maintained machines ... AFI will be acknowledged as the most knowledgeable and helpful in the industry ... surpassing our customers' expectations in delivering the right machines at the agreed time ... differentiating ourselves from our competitors through the attitude of teams within the depots.

A commitment to this process was given from the board downwards with two key areas being highlighted. First, all areas of management were made aware of the importance of their roles, not as traditional managers/supervisors, but as transformational leaders. Second, the company put time and money investment into increasing the capability of all areas of the workforce in terms of developing five core competencies: health and safety awareness; product technical knowledge; understanding customers' business challenges; teamwork; and customer service skills. These would be delivered within the next twelve months through the strategy of formal and informal training.

AFI were successful in obtaining the IIP Award across most sites in the summer of 2008, with the remaining sites following thereafter. However, the IIP Award can be withdrawn at any time if its guidelines and recommendations are not met. Yet, above the desire to gain this award, the Board were keen to make development and training an integral part of the company's values and strategic intent. Therefore, training and development of staff within the company continues to be an ongoing investment. The company is riding out the recession despite its relatively higher operating costs, whilst competitors in the industry are being forced to reduce their fleet sizes and/or 'run on' older machines, thereby increasing maintenance costs. Others, unfortunately, are going into administration.

Question

1 Consider the above case study and evaluate the internal strengths and weaknesses using the VRIO framework.

Copyright: Peter Emsell and Lisa Bailey, University of Huddersfield Business School

Hierarchical levels of strategy

Strategy can be formulated on three different levels:

- corporate level
- business or unit level
- departmental or functional level.

Whilst many books on strategy may be focused on gaining competitive advantage, not all organizations compete. Many organizations in the public sector voluntary organizations or charities also need strategies as a means of articulating the organization's intent, purpose, and values at the core of its existence. By wrapping up all these facets into a strategy, that organization has something that all its stakeholders can relate to and use in directing its contribution towards its goals, and doing so in an efficient and effective manner.

These three hierarchical levels of strategy are explored a little further below.

Corporate level strategy

Corporate level strategy is fundamentally concerned with the selection of industries and businesses in which the company should compete and with the development and coordination of its portfolio of businesses. Consider Virgin, which operates businesses in the airline, media, banking, rail transport, and telecommunication industries. In this example, corporate level strategy is concerned with exploiting new opportunities and ventures that Virgin should be involved in, identifying overall goals for the organization's businesses in terms of growth, market share, and profitability. Corporate level strategy is also concerned with identifying if there are any ways that businesses can be integrated and managed and if there are any core competencies that can be shared and leveraged in order to gain synergies.

Business unit level strategy

A strategic business unit may be a division, subsidiary, profit centre, or similar unit that can be planned independently from other business units in the organization. At the business unit level, the strategic issues are less about the common issues with other business units and more about its position in relation to its rivals, exploiting specific environmental opportunities and addressing issues that are appropriate to the business and industry it operates in. Porter (1980) identified three generic strategies that are appropriate to the formulation of business unit strategy:

- cost leadership
- differentiation
- focus.

These three generic strategies give a useful framework on which a business unit can build up and develop a strategy that best fits it individual set of circumstances and challenges.

Functional or department level strategy

Strategy formulation at the functional or departmental level of an organization is more likely to be concerned with business processes such as: the flow of work through the function or department; how it links up to other functions within the larger organization; and how it interfaces with its external relationships typically through contracts or service level agreements. It will also be concerned with the control of its specific resources, for example finance, human resources, R&D, and marketing and sales, and how these combine to create sustained competitive advantage. A strategic plan developed at this level should always have alignment or 'line of sight' with the higher-level business unit and corporate strategies that you would expect to see in an overall hierarchical framework.

Reflection point 2.6

- Consider an organization, business, or functional department you are familiar with and list the challenges and actions you would expect to see in its strategic plan.

Strategically successful organizations

It can be concluded that successful organizations seem to be distinguished from their less successful competitors by a common pattern of management practices:

- They identify more effectively than others the key success factors inherent in the economies of each business.
- They segment their markets so as to gain decisive competitive advantage.
- They carefully measure and analyse any competitive advantage. This requires a sound basis for assessing an organization's advantages relative to others or to its challenges.
- They anticipate the responses. Good strategic thinking in any type of organization implies that they understand how situations may change over time. Business and military is a matter of manoeuvring for a superior position and anticipating how others will respond and with what measure of success.
- They exploit opportunities more or differently than do their competitors. Seeking to keep ahead.
- They make priority investments in the form of finance, time, and other resources as part of their strategy in achieving success.

The capability of people involved in such successful organizations is the driving force in shaping strategies. The challenge is finding this raw talent and developing this capability that lies at the heart of leadership and management development and, as such, this is the focus of subsequent chapters in this book.

There are many variations among academics and business commentators as to how leadership capability can be harnessed and directed into performance outcomes and in turn become the making of successful organizations.

Strengths-based development

A contrarian's view, originally put forward by the Gallup Organization, which challenges the traditional leadership and management development approach and that is worthy of attention, is built around the paradigm of positivism and strengths-based leadership. The paradigm assumes that in order to gain a high level of performance in any organization, there needs to be engagement and the role of the manager is key in gaining and sustaining that engagement. The paradigm unfolds and explains that, to a large extent, we are all from an early age 'hardwired' as individuals to having certain strengths and talents in terms of carrying out tasks, management being such an example. It follows then, that the best gateway to sustaining organizational performance is first to identify the raw talent required for the task in hand or even to some extent alter the tasks and roles to fit the raw talent, then go on to develop the strengths of the people to get even better at delivering the outcomes. It argues that, in most cases, organizations concentrate the training and development investment on addressing weaknesses, which is claimed to be totally counter-intuitive.

The way organizations gain the greatest return on investment is to identify the ways in which people naturally think, feel, and behave as unique individuals, then build upon those talents to create strength and success. In contrast, the 'management competencies' approach that we have come to know from the classical schools of management adopts a paradigm that assumes that there is a set of descriptors that capture the skills, traits, and styles that make a generic leader and a manager. The assumption here is that these can all be identified, developed, and learned by people who have the basic intellect, time, and motivation to do so: almost in a military-style approach and to a large extent how armed forces organizations develop their officers.

The origin of this approach stemmed from the work of Buckingham, Clifton, and Coffman who were employed as consultants at the Gallup Organization in the 1980s. All have moved onto establish their own successful consultancy groups and in the 1990s researched this particular ideology of what makes a high-performing organization and the role of managers within this paradigm. They wrote the books, *First, Break All the Rules* and *Now, Discover Your Strengths*, both of which were influential in gaining support and creditability amongst corporate organizations for their strengths-based approach. Both books became best sellers in their day and like many high-quality researched management books, they stood the test of time and went on to become the foundation for further research of this particular underpinning ideology. Mini case study 2.3 gives a practical example of the strengths-based approach.

Mini case study 2.3: A hotel chain: Strengths-based selection—ABC Consultancy

Several years ago, a luxury hotel management firm operating 41 properties in six countries contracted ABC Consultancy to improve its business performance in key front-line and management positions. ABC recommended a long-term selection and hiring strategy aimed at hiring more associates with talents similar to those of the best associates and upgrading the levels of talent within the following roles:

- sales managers
- food and beverage managers

- food and beverage servers
- property managers
- front-desk staff.

Working closely with client management, ABC consultants created a 'strengths-based' selection profile for each position that was tailored to the client's business needs. The consultants began by studying the client's structure and business strategy. They reviewed the client's job performance criteria and studied the best performers in each role to identify the talents that contributed to their success. They then developed success models, which were used to construct customized, structured interviews to assess job applicants.

Follow-up business impact analysis determined that the process and systems delivered a higher success rate for new hires who achieved high scores on the selection interviews.

Sales manager hiring successes

Analysis of four years of performance data for sales managers who were hired using these processes showed, among other things, that:

- The interview total score predicts actual job performance as measured by how well sales managers met their goals for hotel-room bookings. Those sales managers who scored highly on the selection interview sold more room bookings relative to their sales goal than sales managers who scored much lower on the selection interview. In terms of revenue, on average, the highest-scoring managers outperformed lower-scoring managers by more than $300,000 in room bookings annually, and they outperformed the lowest-scoring managers by more than $1 million in room bookings annually.
- Although many factors can influence an employee's decision to leave a position or organization, the interview total score of sales managers who were hired using the system was shown to be predictive of voluntary employee attrition. Over the four-year period studied, Gallup's analysis revealed that 40 per cent of the lowest-scoring managers voluntarily left the company, compared with 15 per cent of the middle-scoring managers, and 14 per cent of the high-scoring managers.

Food and beverage manager and server and front-desk staff hiring successes

The selection interviews predicted a new hire's performance in these positions as well. Highlights of the business impact analysis included:

- High-scoring food and beverage managers outperformed lower-scoring managers by $33 per square foot in revenue; they also worked more efficiently, working fewer hours while serving more beverages and meals.
- Food and beverage servers with low scores on the selection interview had, on average, two to three times more health and safety incidents than did their high-scoring counterparts.
- Front-desk staff members with high scores on the selection interview produced, on average, two to three times more revenue—by selling upgrades in hotel services at the time of check-in—than their lower-scoring counterparts.

Question

1 What lessons can be learned from this case study and applied to an organization that either you work for or are aware of?

Summary of section

So far we have seen how strategy is influenced by the strength of conviction of leaders in organizations. Their personal values, the power they hold, the culture they are surrounded by and their own personal characteristics and talent. We now move along the pathway to effective strategy formulation by looking at how strategy is formulated in different organizational settings.

We have also seen some different perspectives on the concept of capability and competence. This section is designed to get the reader to contemplate whether leadership capability can be structured and learned in a process approach to leadership development. Or should there be a greater consideration of the concept of playing to peoples' natural 'talents'. Alternatively, have both concepts a part to play in leadership and management development?

Creation of strategy in different organizational settings

One very useful way of identifying how strategy is and has been created in different organizational setting is the typology in Figure 2.5. These organizations may be public sector, private sector, or voluntary organizations and found across different industries and economies. For large or small, new or established organizations, the model in Figure 2.5 will help in gaining an additional perspective and understanding.

Whittington developed this fourfold typology to help understand the complex nature of strategy and the influences that shape the decisions and final outcomes. When reading through the following descriptors of each quadrant, pause for a moment after each one and consider the core competencies and capabilities that the managers and leaders working in these organizations might have. The four types are:

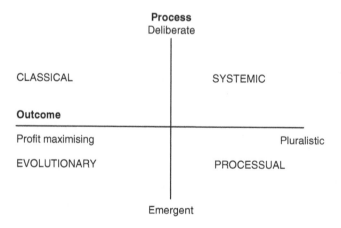

Figure 2.5 Strategy formulation

Adapted from Whittington, R. (1993) What is Strategy and Does It Matter? London: Routledge

Classical (quadrant: profit-maximizing + deliberate)

This quadrant shows that strategy is to be shaped to one of deliberate profit-maximizing that seeks to gain competitive advantage. This classical approach typifies an organizational setting where managers have nothing but the organization's interests in mind and who are above the day-to-day skirmishes that are prevalent in the lower levels of an organization's hierarchy. A small group of managers make decisions on behalf of stakeholders in a paternalistic, traditional management style. It assumes there is one best way to manage people and employment and leaves little room for choice when deciding the direction of the organization.

Evolutionary (quadrant: profit maximizing + emergent)

This angle shows strategy as a product of market forces in which the most productive organizations win in the end. This is similar in many respects to the Darwinism view of evolution built around the principle that the strongest will survive or win by constantly adapting and changing to meet the challenges of the external and internal forces it faces, thereby beating off its competitors.

Processual (quadrant: pluralistic + emergent)

This view stems from the assumption that people are too limited in their understanding of what strategy is ultimately to decide on the best set of choices. Strategy formulation with this backdrop setting advocates that a timely process of discussion and disagreement takes place. It involves managers at different levels in order to gain a wide variety of inputs and outputs as the way of arriving at the strategy. A feature of this approach is that strategy is never nailed down and committed to by all who have an input in its formulation. It is not unusual for different variations and interpretations of the strategy as well as the content, direction, and implementation plans for delivering the strategy to be derived in this kind of setting.

Systemic (quadrant: pluralistic + deliberate)

In this quadrant, strategy is shaped by social systems in which the organization is embedded. Culture is an important facet in this respect and 'how things are done around here'. That is, the country and history, the gender, class, legal regulation, and deep-rooted values shape the way employers behave and make decisions on what is considered important and less important in the organizations they operated within.

Reflection point 2.7

- Discuss this model in small groups and see if you can identify some of these traits in an organization you are familiar with. Has your perspective changed at all after consideration of this model in terms of how strategy is derived?

Alignment of organizational strategy and human resources development work practices

There have been many investigations in the 1990s into the importance of integration or 'best fit' between an organization's strategy and performance outcomes and the importance of its human resources development (HRD) practices. Three major contributions of research which built up in an iterative manner on each other's work were carried out: first, by Guest (1987); then by Huselid (1995); and later by Pfeffer (1998). All agreed and could prove a positive correlation between: the high performance of an organization, the commitment of its workforce, and the HRD work practices deployed in that organization. With such overwhelming academic evidence that supports the importance that human resources management (HRM) and HRD practices do add sustained competitive value, it comes as a surprise to learn that according to the CIPD Annual Survey Report (2005) only 44 per cent of organizations have formal HRD strategic plans in which are captured the organization's development needs and implementation plans.

Andrew Mayo (2002) identified a simple concept that can be applied to show how an organization can take business goals that arise from the corporate level, business level or functional/departmental level and convert these into HRD learning goals. An eight-step methodology forms the framework for achieving a strategic 'best fit'. A major benefit of this approach is that it encourages and challenges managers involved in this process to examine whether the development/training solution is the problem or the answer to the problem is a change required to the organization's processes and/or systems. This is often a common trap that managers fall into when linking or integrating business strategy to HRD strategies.

Summary of chapter

From what has been learned so far, it should by now be quite clear that the creation or formulation of an organization's strategy depends first and foremost on the leaders who are involved in choosing and deciding what and how things are to be done. Following the transformational leadership paradigm of Bass (1990b) and regarding leadership capability, it is highly feasible that people can be developed, and new skills can be taught and learned in an effort to create effective leaders. Then, what has to be done, the techniques used, and choosing the correct blend of leadership skills form the basis of the remaining chapters of this book.

With little exception, the need for competent and committed people comes high on the list of the critical success factors that contribute to the success of an organization. This is not at all to play down other functions; indeed, the IT, financial systems, and marketing functions play a key part in the makeup of a successful organization. Yet, it is the people, leaders, and managers, who determine the direction of the organization, shape the strategies, communicate and engage with the workforce, and make the decisions that shape all the functional areas of an organization. In simple terms, everything that an organization does, in the end, depends on its people.

Every organization is made up of separate teams, and the performance of those teams, no matter how successful the company may be, varies widely. What makes the difference? The manager. Managers play a significant role in creating an environment within which individuals can thrive, discover their talents, and use their best selves daily. Great managers help people to identify and leverage their unique strengths.

The challenge for an organization is first to understand its own influence, culture, internal processes, and strengths and weaknesses. Only when it has developed the competence to do this, will it be able to move on to the point where an appropriate and value-adding HRD strategy and courses of action can be put in place that recruits, develops, retains, and motivates top-class leaders and managers.

Reflection point 2.8

Using the case study on Workforce Development at AFI-Uplift Ltd (Mini case study 2.2), try to answer the following question:

- In what ways do you think the HRD practices are aligned with the business strategy?

Questions

1 What are the three main types of leadership theories?

2 Based on the work of Bass (1985), what are the three main skills and abilities of a successful transformational leader?

3 What are the common elements that you are likely to find in an organization's mission, vision, and values statement?

4 Considering the Cultural Web (Johnson and Scholes, 1992), what are the underlying assumptions that are not always obvious but do influence an organization's dominant culture?

5 Porter (1980) identifies three generic strategies that are appropriate to the formulation of business unit strategy. What are they?

6 What, in your own words, are the steps in moving from organization strategy to strategic leadership and management development?

7 How can Whittington's typology model aid in the understanding of strategic choices?

Discussion questions

1 Considering there has been so much written over the years about leadership and what makes an effective leader, why do you think it is such an elusive subject?

2 It is often said that strategy is about making choices. Why do you think, therefore, that strategic decision making has not become a computerized process?

3 We are told that many aspects of transformational leadership can be learned. If so, why are there so many different competency models and variations in leadership development and training programmes?

4 Consider an organization you are familiar with and, in small groups, identify and discuss examples of vision, mission, and values statements—what are the similarities and differences and how can you explain these?

Suggestions for further reading

Ulrich, D. and Brockbank, W. (2005) *HR: The Value Proposition*, Boston, MA: Harvard Business School Press.
This book provides a very useful insight into the practical application of how HR strategy must be linked to business strategy in order to have any value. Developing the workforce and in particular the leadership and management capability are explained very succinctly.

Buckingham, M. and Coffman, C. (2005) *First, Break All the Rules: What the World's Greatest Managers Do Differently*, 2nd edition, New York: Simon & Schuster.
This book was a ground-breaking piece of work that challenged the conventional approaches to the development of leaders and managers in organizations. Many organizations adopted the paradigm put forward and claimed high levels of success in its application.

Buckingham, M. and Clifton, D.O. (2001) *Now, Discover Your Strengths*, 1st edition, New York: The Free Press.
In some ways, this is an extension of the previous book. It builds on the concept of talent and provides practical solutions for L&MD practitioners to follow.

Thompson, J. and Martin, F. (2005) *Strategic Management: Awareness and Change*, 5th edition, Cengage Learning (formerly Thomson Learning).
This book has some excellent case studies and examples that demonstrate how strategic leadership works in practice and how important the role of the leader is in achieving this success.

Love, A. and Cugnon, M. (2009) *The Purpose Linked Organisation: How Passionate Leaders Inspire Winning Teams and Great Results*, McGraw Hill.

CHAPTER 3

Contextual factors in leadership and management development

The aims of this chapter are to:

- explore management development in the context of the growing economies of Brazil, Russia, India, and China—the BRICs, as they have become known. These being the economies that are forecast to overtake the USA, the UK, Japan, Germany, and the rest of Europe in the next decade.

- examine the key concepts of cultural diversity and globalization.

- analyse the contextual factors that will affect management development in the next generation.

- highlight the factors that will shape the future of management development for the next generation of global business leaders and managers.

Introduction

Brazil, Russia, India, and China (the BRICs) have no great history of management development and in the recent past have looked to US and UK business schools and writers for guidance and best practice. The signs are that this is changing and one can see that the BRICs with their own real-life experiences will further develop their own management ideologies and solutions on how best to develop their own leaders and managers of the future. This chapter provides an insight into these developments and highlights the factors that will shape the future of management development for the next generation of global business leaders and managers.

Mini case study 3.1: Operating with an overseas subsidiary

The Jamaican subsidiary

This case discusses a problem facing headquarters in running a subsidiary.

You are the CEO of a multinational company based in your home country. You receive this letter from the personnel manager in your Jamaican subsidiary addressed to your home.

Dear M_____,

Do you remember me? I am Sylvia S, your personnel manager in Kingston, Jamaica. I have worried a long time about this problem, but now I have decided to tell you.

You know that 18 months ago you appointed a new managing director here, Mr F, who came from our subsidiary in Panama. I have to tell you that we have not been a happy company since he joined us. The reason is that he is a good friend of Mr D, the marketing manager. [Mr D is a Jamaican.] They were friends before Mr F came here.

Often, Mr D says, 'You must promote this person or that person because they are loyal to me'. Mr F always does what he says. But Mr D's people are often not good for the company and one man, Mr H, was in prison for six months. (I do not think that Mr F knows that Mr H was in prison.) This means that the very good people leave because they are ashamed not to be promoted.

I know that Mr F has been reporting other reasons why we have such a high loss of staff. He says that some of them are not good, or are greedy for benefits, or are asking for training that is too expensive. Sometimes I have to sign these reports, but I know what the truth is and I am ashamed.

Now that you have read my letter, you perhaps think that I am a troublemaker. That is not true and I only want to serve the company. Even if you dismiss me, I shall know that I have done my best.

Yours sincerely

Sylvia S

You have made several tours to the Kingston subsidiary and you remember Sylvia well. Over ten years, she has worked her way up from filing clerk to her present position. She has always impressed you as a person of integrity, who has the company's best interests at heart. You do not think that she would report a story like this without good reason—but of course, you cannot be 100 per cent certain. If the story is true, it has serious implications for a very profitable subsidiary.

Questions

1 What do you need to know about the company before you can comment on this case?

2 What aspects are related to national culture?

3 What does the case tell us about communication in the company?

4 What would you do? And why?

Summary of section

Mini case study 3.1 illustrates the importance when working with an overseas subsidiary of ensuring agreement on the goals of the subsidiary, the choice of operating and control systems, and choice of management.

Making the business case

Diversity is about differences and there are many definitions of diversity. The diversity debate reflects definitions focused on power imbalances and historical disadvantages such as race and gender (Grossman, 2000; Linnehan and Konrad, 1999). All differences are embraced by other scholars (Rijsman, 1997), whilst yet others integrate aspects of both approaches (Fujimoto *et al.*, 2000). Cox bridges the gap in the debate by defining cultural diversity as: 'the representation, in one social system, of people with distinctly different group affiliations of cultural significance' (1994, p 6).

Legal requirements, equal employment opportunities, and positive action are often associated with diversity. Managers often focus on disabilities, age, ethnic background, and sexual orientation as part of their organization's diversity initiatives. However, managers also struggle with different views in responding to diversity (Wellner, 2000). Responses to diversity are led by an organization's tolerance for ambiguity, the demand for conformity, and the value placed on diversity, cultural fit, and acculturation (Carr-Ruffino, 1996). One of four strategies is often used to deal with cross-national and intra-national diversity:

- A narrow view of multiculturalism focused on openness to the positive nature of all cultures. This stance creates new and meaningful ways of interacting in the workplace.

- Separation, perhaps the least functional strategy, rejects all cultural values except one's own and leads to conflict between employees from different cultural backgrounds.

Reflection point 3.1

- Is diversity management a key issue in your organization?
- How can you progress the business case for diversity management within your organization/ workplace?

- Assimilation, the adoption of the organization's culture, is often seen by subordinate groups as conforming to the values of the dominant group and can lead to mistrust if there is no attempt to understand the values of the subordinate group.

- Deculturation, where all groups maintain their own values without trying to influence anyone else (Connerley and Pedersen, 2005).

A conceptual framework is provided by the multicultural perspective that recognizes the complexities of a plural society. However, shared concerns that culturally link individuals to one another are also recognized and can be used to aid in an understanding of ourselves and those who make up our workforce.

Organizational viability depends more than ever before on the knowledge, skills, abilities, and attitudes of an organization's whole workforce. Therefore, management development is required that encourages innovation, high performance, and a learning culture that embraces all employees (Macdonald, 1995). Managers need heightened multicultural awareness, knowledge, and skills to increase their power, energy, and freedom of choice in a fast-changing multicultural and diverse world. Countries, as individual organizations, are led to comply with international perspectives on managing diversity by an increasingly litigation-focused society. However, becoming more cross-culturally aware brings greater rewards than avoiding financial and reputational losses due to lawsuits and adverse publicity. Demographic changes will rapidly continue to affect us all and heighten needs for multicultural awareness for all workers. This is especially true for those who influence others in the workplace, whether on a formal or informal authority basis. In this way, more can be achieved from relationships in the workplace.

The complex nature of culture
Taylor defined culture in an anthropological and sociological context as 'that complex whole which includes knowledge, belief, art, morals, law, custom and any

Reflection point 3.2

- Has the need for multicultural skills increased from what it was a decade ago?

other capabilities and habits acquired by man as a member of society' (1871/1924, p 1). Cultural patterns of thought and action are set before our birth. These are inherited from our parents and teachers. Growing awareness of other people and cultures teaches us that our culture is one of many possible patterns of thinking and acting. Ethnocentrism gives a name to the belief that one's own culture is better than others and is a natural tendency. Multiculturalism provides a paradox of looking at how we are the same and different at the same time. That is our uniqueness and how our identity is shared with others. Powerful groups can impose their perspectives on others in the melting pot metaphor. The focus on differences can result in a stereotypical view in an exclusionary perspective. A shared and unique perspective provides a more accurate perspective. Pedersen (1999) identifies the positives to be gained by developing multicultural awareness:

- *Accuracy*. All behaviour is learned and acted out in a cultural setting, so accurate assessment, meaningful understanding, and appropriate interventions are culturally contextual constructs.

- *Conflict management*. If awareness is increased of shared positive values and expectations, then teaching and learning can occur of shared positive values and expectations in each cultural context.

- *Identity*. The relatives, friends, acquaintances, and enemies—the culture teachers who have taught us identity.

- *A healthy society*. Brought about by a healthy socio-ecosystem needing a diversity of cultural perspectives.

- *Encapsulation protection*. A culture-centred perspective prevents inappropriate use or imposition of our own culturally encapsulated self-reference criteria in the evaluation of others.

- *Survival*. Working and meeting with other groups provides an opportunity to practise adaptive functioning for our own survival.

- *Social justice*. An appreciation of social justice and moral development in a multicultural context enables the differentiation of absolutes from culturally relative principles.

- *Right-thinking*. Overemphasizing differences will erect barriers and provide hostile relationships. Overemphasizing similarities will result in a melting pot perspective. A culture-centred perspective provides a complementary view.

- *Personalized learning*. Learning and change involve a degree of culture shock of active learning that could not be learned in any other way.

- *Spirituality*. The culture-centred perspective enhances our understanding of a shared reality. The majority of cultures share the same questions as to how we come to exist and what occurs after our death.

Reflection point 3.3

- How do managers avoid overemphasizing differences and similarities at the same time?
- How can managers promote the adoption of a multicultural perspective at all times and not just after a diversity training workshop or other intervention?

■ *Political stability.* Pluralism is built as an alternative to authoritarianism or anarchy in society. Population growth, pollution, and use of limited global resources make learning to live together a preferred option for living with others.

■ *Strengthening leadership theory.* Making culture central rather than marginal to our choice of leadership theory will enable that theory to operate more effectively in a variety of different cultural contexts.

Pedersen provides the positive arguments for the multicultural perspective and illustrates why culture continues to be one of the key constraints in organizations and with strong implications for management development.

Summary of section

This section has considered the implications of various initiatives with regard to diversity in organizations. From both a practitioner and an academic viewpoint a great deal of work needs to be done in order to maximize the full potential of our human resources.

The meanings of culture

The multicultural perspective is central to understanding contemporary business and management. This is by no means a recent preoccupation. In the 1950s, Mead and Krocber and Kluckhohn identified unique patterns of values and behaviour in different societies. Their work was then applied within the field of business studies, in part because of growing Western interest in Japanese work practices and the emerging debates on globalization. Geert Hofstede's work in 1980 raised the profile of the cross-cultural perspective, and its influence on business and management continues today. There has also been a new focus on organizational or corporate culture and ways that this facet of culture can be used to effect change and improve business performance.

Earlier, Taylor's (1871/1924) definition of culture was provided to illustrate the complexity of culture. There have been a number of definitions of culture but an agreed definition has proved elusive and can be said to be an area of academic study in its own right. Existing definitions of culture focus on different elements of the concept. The links between culture and behaviour are inferential or speculative.

Macro-level culture plays out in individuals' behaviour and organizational arrangements in diverse and unpredictable ways. Similarly, in an organization, the same values are not shared to produce consistency in behaviour patterns.

In order to increase the validity of cross-cultural research in a management or business setting, it is vital to appreciate that cultures can change quickly and all age groups within a population are focused on. The complex linkages between organizational, professional, national, and regional settings should also be considered (French, 2007). The ideas, meanings, and values held by a culture's members provide an understanding of culture. This is reflected in Hofstede's work (2001, p 9), where he referred to 'the collective programming of the mind that distinguishes the members of one group or category of people from another'. This cultural perspective sees collective programming taking place through socialization, the processes by which values are transmitted from one generation to another. Hofstede recognized individual programming, whereby individual personality and abilities were allowed for as well as common behaviour patterns through collective programming.

Cross-cultural study has been focused at the individual or small group level following its inception as being manifested through the minds of individuals and expressed through attitudes and preferred behaviour, made real through communication. Trompenaars and Hampden-Turner applied research to the effects on business through questionnaires and surveys completed by individuals. The institutional level of analysis has provided the focus for other writers who have considered culture as having a range of institutional or society-wide factors that then combine with attitudes to feed into a country's culture. These factors include:

- the education system
- values/shared meanings
- political economic system
- religion/philosophical beliefs
- economic prosperity
- language.

Culture should be viewed as an idea that is shown at the level of individuals and social institutions to understand its true nature and potential effects.

Organizational culture

Organizational or corporate culture are not synonymous terms; Needle (2004, p 238) distinguishes between them thus:

Organizational culture represents the collective values, beliefs and principles of organizational members and is a product of such factors as history, product market, technology, strategy, type of employees, management style, national cultures, and so on. Corporate culture, on the other hand, refers to those cultures deliberately created by management to achieve specific strategic ends.

Writers such as Peters and Waterman and Deal and Kennedy identified a correlation between company-level culture and success. Excellent companies with strong cultures deliver success. This distinction provides an insight into the interest in the topic in the 1980s.

National and organizational culture–similarities

Culture is often portrayed as having different levels. Sathe (1985) compared culture to an iceberg or an onion. The outer level or layer is made up of artefacts, the readily apparent manifestation of culture. They are shown in logos, the layout of the office, and the role of stories in the organization's history, and they symbolize culture. Norms and behaviours comprise the middle layer, with values and core assumptions making up the bottom layer. Among these levels, cultural differences can provide contrasting ideas about what is meant by good management. French leaders must stand apart and be the expert. Scandinavian organizations prefer a more democratic and participative style of leadership.

A further common feature shared by national and organizational cultures is the presence of subcultures. Here, both levels of culture experience countercultures, where members actively seek to undermine the dominant culture.

Understanding models of culture

Previously, the concept of culture was considered and its effects at different levels reviewed. This provides the backcloth to allow the different models to explain cultural differences in order that different societies can be understood, in addition to considering how the models can then explain differences in management development in the workplace.

The nature of most businesses was mostly non-global until fairly recently, so that researchers in the cross-cultural field were mostly anthropologists. Their models and writings were mostly descriptive. A comparative approach has also been adopted by researchers in this field, whereby core dimensions of culture are identified and individual countries are plotted or scored along these dimensions. The core dimensions used by management scholars are shown in Box 3.1.

Reflection point 3.4

- What is the preferred style of leadership within your organization?
- How does this style reflect cultural differences?

Box 3.1 Dimensions of culture used by leading management scholars

Schein

Relationship with nature

Human activity

Human nature

Relationships with people

Time

Truth and reality

Trompenaars

Relationship with nature

Relationship with people

Universalism v particularism

Individualism v collectivism

Affectivity

Diffuse v specific

Achievement v ascriptive

Relationship with time

Kluckhohn and Strodtbeck

Relationship with time

Human activity

Human nature

Relationships with people

Time

Hall

Space

(personal/physical)

Time

(monochromic/polychromic)

Language

(high context/low context)

Friendships

Adler

Human nature

Relationship with nature

Individualist/collectivist

Human activity (being/doing)

Space (private/public)

Time (past/present/future)

Hofstede

Uncertainty avoidance

Power distance

Individualism/collectivism

Masculinity/femininity

Geert Hofstede, Fons Trompenaars, Andre Laurent, and Edward Hall—a US anthropologist—have been influential in challenging the universalism of management practices from the USA; and, in a globalized world, managers need to appreciate how national cultural differences might affect their organizations. A critical and evaluative view is required to go beyond what has previously been written, recognizing the importance of culture in organizational life and management development.

The focus of this text is management development and it is recognized that this is not the place to provide an in-depth critique of the relevant models. Rather, it is proposed to signpost the importance of comparing the culture-specific approach with a

Reflection point 3.5

- How might cultural differences make it difficult for a UK visitor to China to do business?
- Should an organization have fixed rules about the management of people that cover operations in all the countries it operates in? Should the rules be varied for the different cultures represented within the organization? Can the two views be reconciled?

consideration of similarities between global organizations and, where appropriate, the convergence between them. Texts such as those by French (2007) and Brewster *et al.* (2007) provide the critical stance that is necessary to appreciate the model's impact on management development.

The framework provided by these scholars gives managers an initial map showing the issues that they need to take into account when working in an international environment. On an individual level, the value orientations that people hold are indicated. By appreciating these helpful indicators and realizing their limitations, managers can avoid stereotyping and can try out appropriate behaviours and management styles that will lead to a more effective intercultural ability at individual, team, and organizational levels.

Academics show the impact of national culture by comparing managers who work in similar organizations across societies. Tayeb's 1988 study found similarities between Indian and English organizations on specialization and centralization dimensions but differences between them in the degree of consultation and delegation of authority. English managers consulted their workforce much more widely than did their Indian counterparts. English employees communicated more with each other than did the Indian employees. The samples' differences were consistent with the cultural differences between Indian and English peoples as a whole.

A comparative study of British and Chinese manufacturing organizations indicated that decisions within the range of supervisors in the British organizations were within the gift of senior managers in China (Easterby-Smith *et al.*, 1995).

Tayeb (1988, p 92) identified examples of the processes that form the basis of organizational life and the linkages to cultural traits. It is these dimensions that make up everyday life at work and are accepted as commonplace—until the manager goes to a foreign subsidiary, or there is an organizational merger or the formation of a joint international venture with a company from another country.

Reflection point 3.6

- How does national culture impact your organization's life with regard to human resources policies and practices, managerial values, leadership styles, teams, and cultural intelligence?

Table 3.1 Culture–organizational dimensions linked to cultural traits

Organizational dimensions	Cultural traits
Centralization	Attitudes to power and authority
Specialization and formalization	Ability to cope with uncertainty
Formalization and standardization	Attitude to control and discipline
Direction of communication	Attitude to information sharing
Span of control	Attitude to power and authority

The way forward

A great deal of cross-cultural academic work that has been applied to the business context and management development underlying business and management studies has been developed on the dimensions of culture and then the location of individual countries along these comparative scales, listing items such as Hofstede's 'uncertainty avoidance' or 'universalism'. In this way, societies have been categorized and then compared one with another.

A more evaluative approach that has been suggested would promote the understanding of the validity of these models and their application in real-life situations. New directions for future work could also be suggested. Fang (2003, p 364) emphasizes this point, noting: 'Geert Hofstede is a great scholar of our times; he has been inspiring us to catch up and move on. Culture is full of life, energy, complexity, diversity and paradox. Our cross-cultural theories should capture such dynamism.'

The work of Kluckhohn and Strodtbeck (1961), Hofstede (1980), Bond and Hall (1990), Schwartz (1992), Trompenaars (1993), and the GLOBE (Global Leadership and Organization Behaviour Effectiveness) research programme by House *et al.* (2001) provide the foundations of cross-cultural management theory. Earlier signposting to French (2007) and Brewster *et al.* (2007) enables the reader to identify the main contributions of these writers. French clearly identifies the main rationale of these writers as follows: 'that cultural differences are located in the ways that people think and in their preferred values and preferences for dealing with particular situations'.

Whilst understanding that individuals respond in particular ways to their own socialization, the main models indicate that there is sufficient 'collective programming'—Hofstede's phrasing—within different societies for the key focus to be on comparison, meaning the differences between cultures. This is not the only approach that can be taken, however.

Fang (2003) questions, for example, whether the analysis provided by Hofstede and Bond (1988) with the five dimensions of culture can reflect the complexity and depth of Chinese culture. Koen (2005, p 55) furthers this view by emphasizing:

the need to understand social systems from the inside and through the definitions of its members. It attempts to analyse the internal coherence of single examples and condemns any attempt at classification across cultures as denying the uniqueness of each culture.

Bond did, however, consider an Eastern focus by asking four Chinese colleagues from Hong Kong and Taiwan to draw up a list of ten fundamental values for Chinese people. Fang criticized Bond's approach as drawing too heavily on Confucianism, Taoism, and Buddhism, and in doing so, neglecting contemporary values and so producing an incomplete view of a specific culture. One clear omission was *guanxi*, about which Chen notes (2004, p 44):

> Anyone who has had experience in dealing with the Chinese could hardly fail to observe that Chinese people attach great importance to cultivating, maintaining and developing guanxi (connection or relationship). Anyone who has associated with the Chinese at even a minimum level would easily notice the Chinese sensitivity to [face] and renqing (humanized obligation) in their daily life. These traits are shared by the Chinese living not only in mainland China but also in Taiwan, Hong Kong and other overseas Chinese societies all over the world. Simply put, these three concepts of guanxi, face and renqing are the keys for understanding Chinese social behavioural patterns and their business dynamics.

The lack of commercial laws in China furthers the need for trust between parties and so provides a context where *guanxi* flourishes. It will be of interest to see if *guanxi* changes in importance in the future.

Different research methods

Hofstede focused his main research on IBM. He allowed for differences with the various country samples and so was able to claim that his research provided an accurate picture of the societies represented. Clegg *et al.* (2005) questioned whether the respondents were representative in terms of gender and age, and reflects on cultural changes that may be occurring in specific countries and societies.

Schuwartz's work was based on a sample of teachers and students and so focused on age differences and the educational sector. Trompenaar's sample was mostly based on management workshops and so allowed generalizations to apply. The approach used was to identify matched samples in different societies and then to compare these with similar populations in other countries and so indicate culturally based differences. This, termed the etic approach, identified by French (2007), suggests that a different methodological approach is more suited to the long-term observation of a single group from the anthropological discipline.

Thompson and Phua (2005) used Hofstede's cultural dimensions and impact on attitudes and values for a study of Anglo-Saxon and Chinese managers working in the Hong Kong construction industry. The researchers considered that senior managers might make up a distinct group, distinguishing them from other employee groups. Furthermore, actual decisions made by managers might focus on task and business imperatives as to the managers' cultural background. From their sample of

398 respondents, Thompson and Phua found no evidence of expected cultural norms, and concluded that:

> senior Chinese managers exhibit no significant differences from their Anglo-Saxon counterparts in terms of collectivism or cooperation, and even manifest significantly lower in-group identity than Anglo-Saxons. Moreover, Chinese managers, contrary to what Hofstede's categorizations would lead us to expect, are associated negatively with collectivism and intra-firm co-operation.

It may be that Anglo-Saxon managers' values have changed to take account of the new context that they are operating in. It could also be considered that Chinese society in Hong Kong has rapidly taken on a varied range of cultural influences; senior managers may take on a set of cultural norms different from those linked to countries or geographical clusters. A case may be made for a focus on ethnographic non-statistical work in the cross-cultural field of management to give meaningful data of use to practitioners.

Emerging theoretical approaches

Actual norms of behaviour emergent from value dimensions could be analysed. Fink *et al.* (2005) propose the idea of 'cultural standards', in which an individual reacts to a certain situation by considering the views and judgements of others, and that when doing so they will attempt to behave within the boundaries set by specific people and their own culture. This, Fink *et al.* consider, would be key to understanding the realities of cross-cultural working. They are critical of the existing models and the extent to which they capture the reality of practical situations. Critical incidents found in cross-cultural business interactions would need identifying and interpreting. This approach may well shed light on cross-cultural business.

Holden (2002) criticized the view that culture can be seen as having stable and consistent categories focused on values and norms which make up the cultural groups. Hoden (2002, p 28) questions the currency of this view:

> This essentialist or functionalist view can be valid if we want to understand the characteristics of a particular cultural system, such as a country or company, but when, as in everyday international business practice, cultures clash and fuse with each other in myriad ways, the concept is unhelpful: it is virtually programmed to exaggerate the differences between cultures and to generate criteria to rank them competitively.

Reflection point 3.7

- Provide an evaluation of the methods used in cross-cultural research.
- What are the limitations of existing frameworks for understanding culture and cultural difference?

Holden's view is that this has been a preoccupation with the identification and management of cross-cultural differences. Rather, he sees the importance of shared meanings and interpretations—meanings produced in patterns which are reproduced and continually changed by the individuals identifying with them and negotiated during social interaction. For Holden, knowledge transfer and continuous learning are important. Holden's work implies a key role for a manager's competencies and cultural know-how.

Convergence, divergence, globalization, and cross-cultural management

Globalization implies increased interactions between cultural groups and homogenization between cultures: a view of heightened convergence, economically, politically, and culturally, where national borders become less relevant and less of a driving force in modern business. This may be seen as a harmonizer between societies on the outer or surface layer of culture (Schein, 1985). In Asian countries, this can be seen as the trend for younger people to adopt Western dress. Business philosophies and techniques—for example, the quality assurance movement—can also be seen as spreading.

However, globalization is a speculative picture and is seen as referring to an increasing process of inter-connectedness across large sections of the world. For example, the global integration of financial markets shrinks time, enables instant financial transactions, and creates a competitive global environment, heightening the speed and accuracy of information flows. The reality of globalization is the interdependence of events in one part of the world with another. It is also the influence of events on economic and business life becoming more international and leaving a feeling of powerlessness in individual countries. The speed and richness of current global communications, linked with the mobility possible due to improved transport links, have led to the 'intensification of worldwide social relations' (Giddens, 1990).

The nature of culture, which may be deep rooted, means that norms, values, and ways of communicating may still vary across cultural groups in a relatively consistent way (French, 2007). A simplified and deterministic view of the connections between globalization and cross-cultural management is not possible because these are in practice multidimensional and unpredictable.

Diversity management

A further aspect of globalization is the flow of labour across the world, which may be professional, knowledge workers, or skilled manual workers filling labour shortages. This trend has led to an interest in literature on managing diversity. The concepts embraced reflect a desire to secure distributive justice for individuals and promote a sense of inclusiveness within organizations where individuals feel valued and then contribute their best. Pilbeam and Corbridge (2006) make the business case for managing diversity including enhanced customer relations, cost-effective employment relations, and enhanced creativity and innovation, whilst acknowledging that 'the business case for diversity is complex and difficult to quantify' (p 226). Multinational corporations regard workforce diversity as key to their success.

The impact of national culture

Approaches to the study of culture have been considered earlier in this chapter. However, the validity of studying national cultural differences is questioned by those who oppose the concept that culture is a key influence on behaviour. Such people argue that individual differences, and not cultural ones, explain why people act in the way that they do.

In questioning the interaction between culturally determined behaviours and individual personality differences, Hofstede (1991) contended that culture lies between human nature on the one side and individual personality on the other. Hofstede (1991, pp 5–6) unpicks the differences in the levels as:

> *Human nature is what all human beings ... have in common: it represents the universal level in a person's mental software. The human ability to feel fear, anger, love, joy, sadness, the need to associate with others, to talk about it with other humans all belong to this level of mental programming. However, what one does with these feelings, how one expresses fear, joy, observations, and so on, is modified by culture. The personality of an individual, on the other hand, is his/her unique personal set of mental programmes which he/she does not share with any other human being. It is based upon traits which are partly inherited with the individual's unique set of genes and partly learned.*

When working in intercultural situations, a problem that can occur is the tendency to confuse personality and culture. Personality and culture are both individual- and group-based concepts.

The new cultural paradigm research tradition attempts to study how key cultural values might impact on the individual level. Earley and Mosakowski (2002) argue that individuals from a particular culture can share a given cultural value or belief but measurement of scores at the individual level provides enough distribution of scores over the cultural scale for members from within a single country to register value orientations as having significant differences.

Human resources (HR) practices with regard to individual preferences and value-free preferences predictability at the individual level through knowing an individual's value orientations have been considered by Sparrow (2006). This issue has practical importance for manoeuvrability for international HR directions when transferring practices abroad. The values of an organization's workforce can predict significantly its preference for HR practices. Employee attitudes and mindsets to certain practices can be changed by communication and education and training processes. However, employee values are a great deal more resistant to change.

Studies by Sparrow and Wu (1998) and Nyambegera *et al.* (2000) found that choices as to whether a performance appraisal process should measure what is achieved, objectives, or how it should be achieved, competencies, could be predicted by individual-level cultural values. Cultural values at the individual level would then help to explain how HR practices to which employees are subjected are perceived. Sparrow (2006) acknowledged that other factors such as demographic issues—for example, age, service, gender, and grade—might also play a part. However, he considered that 10 to 16 per cent of the attractiveness or not of the various HR practices might be due to cultural values.

There has been growth in the amount of critical work in the field of international management. A large proportion of this work has been carried out by Western and mainly European writers. Bond's work on Chinese values, together with that of the Dentsu Institute of Human Studies 1996–2000, which focused on Japan, questioned some Western perceptions of Asian culture as well as showing similarities between Western and Asian respondents. The homogeneity assumption criticizes approaches that make categories of cultures which assume homogeneity of culture within any single country (Koslowsky *et al.*, 2002). Large countries such as Russia, China, Indonesia, and India, as well as smaller countries like Belgium and Switzerland, may contain different cultures within their borders.

Regional differences impact values and beliefs, as in the USA where different northeastern, midwestern, western, and southern brands of individualism can be identified.

Linked to the above argument is the idea that some societies are tight or loose (Gelfand *et al.*, 2007). Tightness indicates the strength of social norms—that is, how clear or pervasive the norms are within any society, and the degree of sanctions, the degree of deviation permitted. Accountability also plays a part in this concept.

Reflection point 3.8

In small groups consider the following:

- Can the existence of a single national culture be assumed?
- Is culture as a variable decreasing in importance with the growth of globalisation?
- How might cultural differences affect human resource management processes such as selection, appraisals, learning, and development, or employee relations in your organization and/or country?

Summary of section

This section has reviewed existing frameworks for understanding culture and cultural difference. Cultural convergence and divergence and the interplay between these forces and the implications of these issues have also been considered.

Leadership and management styles

An analysis of leadership styles in different countries provides a context for the ways in which HR policies and practices are developed. Leadership involves providing a vision, communicating it, and then motivating people to follow. Every manager should be a leader, but this is not always the case and this theme is reflected elsewhere in this text.

There are different levels of decision making and discretion and the ways that time is prioritized by managers. Bass (1990a) indicated that there had been more than 3,500 studies of leadership in the USA. These included:

■ situational and/or contingency theory/theories

■ Theory X and Theory Y

■ the Ohio State and University of Michigan behavioural theories

■ managerial grid theory

■ path–goal theory.

In spite of this spread of US-based theories, inconclusive support has been found for them (Yu Ki, 1994).

Cross-cultural studies tend to indicate a strong connection between culture and leadership styles (Lammers and Hickson, 1979, p 10). Specific cultural traditions, values, ideologies, and norms are 'bound to differentiate as much or even more than structural factors between societies'. This work has been taken further by the GLOBE Project (House *et al.*, 2001), in which variations in scores around leadership dimensions demonstrate that charismatic, team-oriented, and participative styles are the most effective styles. The GLOBE Project introduced a new cross-cultural framework and positioned societies in clusters which combined cultural background and preferred leadership styles.

It is important for managers to appreciate the role of culture and weave this learning into their solutions when working globally. Managers can be divided into:

■ the expatriate/international manager who may be an executive in a leadership role that involves international assignments across countries and cultures, with skills defined by the location of the assignment

■ the global/transnational manager who may be an executive assigned to positions with cross-border responsibilities, having practical experience and understanding of international business and competencies.

Leaving aside the issue of the range of competencies and skills, there are two key aspects to the global mentality:

■ attitudes and values

■ mindset (cognitive structures).

An international orientation is represented by attitudes and values, and correlates with the extent and the quality of international experience. Murtha *et al.* (1998) identified a core value as a set or logic that is associated with global operations. This included:

- a good mental model of how knowledge and information are shared across the people with whom they need to interact. This model covers the broker of knowledge role as well as an understanding as to how tacit knowledge spreads across top management teams. The boundary-spanning role puts them in touch with the varied networks inside the organization.

- a superior mental model of the organization. Graen and Hui (1999) argue the need for cross-national differences to be managed effectively by developing global leadership through transcultural skills, in this way addressing the complexity of cross-cultural management.

The multicultural team

Multicultural teams are used as a means of coping with the complex and dynamic nature of work. There can be several reasons why managers need to operate through such teams:

- Organizations seek to work locally in an attempt to reduce their reliance on expatriates in their traditional coordination and control role.

- The use of international joint venturing heightens the need to ensure that the organization learns from partnership.

- Globalized operations emphasize the need for international working at lower levels of the organization's hierarchy.

The above impact on the HR function to develop policies and practices that support the use of effective teams. This may include recruiting and selecting team players, using team reward systems, and developing mentoring and coaching behaviours for future leaders.

The multicultural team tends to be high performing or very low performing (Shapiro *et al.*, 2002). The difference in the teams lies in how their diversity is

Reflection point 3.9

- What do leaders have to do to go beyond national borders?
- How are the skills required by international management teams any different from the traditional team-building skills needed to cope with heterogeneous groups from within a single culture?

managed and is impacted upon by their task, stage of development, and the ways in which their diversity is managed. The complex nature of the different cultural perspectives of the team, assumptions made about the nature of the task, and process issues create a common reality and therefore shared ground rules for the development of the team.

Developing cultural intelligence

Earley and Mosakowski (2004) developed the concept of cultural intelligence. They considered this in the context of attitudes and skills which enable individuals to work effectively across cultures through interpreting unfamiliar and ambiguous gestures as a local would. Earley and Mosakowski consider that managers with global responsibilities can be socially intelligent in their own settings but ineffective in new cultures. Four components to cultural intelligence were identified:

- mind: learning strategies whereby people acquire and develop coping strategies

- knowledge: about different cultures

- heart: a desire to persevere in the face of a challenge when adapting to a new culture, and a belief in their own ability to master the situation

- body: developing a range of culturally appropriate behaviours in order to enter the world of a different culture and promote the development of trust.

Globalization and international management

Earlier in this chapter, globalization was described as a speculative picture, increasing the process of inter-connectedness across large sections of the world. There is a polarization of views between those who consider that national cultures, economies, and borders are dissolving (Korten, 1995 and Ohmae, 1990). Then there are those who consider this view to be exaggerated, for example Doremus *et al.* (1998), Hirst and Thompson (1999), and Zysman (1996).

The lack of agreed definition as to what globalization is and the use of the term to cover a range of concepts such as internationalization, liberalization, universalization, Westernization, and modernization causes confusion. Other uses of the word 'globalization' cover its implications for social structures, such as old or new capitalism, post-capitalism, cultural homogeneity, or heterogeneity.

Reflection point 3.10

- What does cultural intelligence involve?

A further complication in this ambiguity is the number of areas in which the term is used. Scholte (2000) highlighted these areas as being:

- global communications: air transport, telecommunications, electronic mass media
- global markets: products, sales strategies
- global production: production chains, sourcing of inputs
- global money: currencies, bank cards, digital cash, credit cards
- global finance: foreign exchange markets, banking, bonds, insurance business
- global organizations: governance agencies, companies, corporate strategic alliances
- global social ecology: atmosphere, biosphere, hydrosphere, geosphere
- global consciousness: world as a single place, symbols, events, solidarities.

The debates around the implications of the above are not within the scope of this text but are signposted. Global production, organizations, markets, and finance would seem to be the focus of the globalization debate, with economic arguments and their political consequences with respect to the implications for organizations and management being of key concern.

The host of definitions is split between those focused on the quantitative linkages between countries and the growth of these linkages, and the qualitative nature of these linkages. The former implies that the last quarter of the 20th century saw a step change in the pace of growth in the linkages between countries. The latter definitions emphasize the functional integration of national economies. Dicken (2003, pp 10–12) sees this as an important differential:

> Although in quantitative terms, the world economy was perhaps at least as open before 1914 as it is today—in some aspects, such as labour migration, even more so—the nature of its integration was qualitatively very different. International economic integration before 1914—and, in fact, until only about four decades ago—was essentially shallow integration, manifested largely through arm's length trade in goods and services between independent firms and through international movement of portfolio capital. Today, we live in a world in which deep integration, organized primarily within the production networks of trans-national corporations (TNCs), is becoming increasingly pervasive.

The interaction between the transnational corporations and nation states is key to an appreciation of the globalization debate. The rapid and recent process of economic globalization leading to a global economy which makes national economic management irrelevant is at the centre of the debate. Child (2002) saw a lack of sensitivity to particular nations or regions and a convergence between modes of organization as countries develop similar economic and political systems. Technological change, information, and communications technologies impact heavily on the design of effective organizations, and critics of this perspective consider that decisions reflect managerial preferences for control over the work process rather than technological influence. Oversimplification may well be at work here.

Psychological universalism links to the technological argument, in which it is considered that all human beings share common needs and motivational drives. This then impacts on the design of work organization, managerial practices, and employee reward systems.

The fall of the Berlin Wall in 1989 and the breakup of the USSR in 1991 led many to believe in a converging model of society as favoured by Western Europe and the USA, and Fukuyama's (1993) phrase, 'the end of history', probably most famously expressed this view. However, there are many such as Huntingdon (2002) who argue that there are still several societal systems dividing the world and therefore limits to convergence. Economic theory has fuelled much of the debate on globalization with the argument that free market economies will prevail and give a common ground for management. The Organisation for Economic Co-operation and Development (OECD), the World Trade Organisation (WTO), and the International Monetary Fund (IMF)—perhaps predictably—favour this view, considering that globalization will benefit most companies and consumers. Whitley (2000) assessed the globalization of economic activity and identified three specific ways that existing capitalist forms would be changed:

- Globalization may change the nature and behaviour of firms that engage in large-scale international coordination and control, which in turn could transform the characteristics of their home business system.

- Globalization implies inward foreign direct investment and capital market internalization which may alter the rules of the competitive game in host business systems.

- Globalization may generate a new supranational level of economic organization and competition that in time will come to dominate national and regional systems.

Whilst the globalization debate remains unsubstantiated, there would appear to be significant global influences on management through information technologies. Parts of the world that were closed off from the international economy are now becoming part of it, and sectors once subject to regulation and ownership restrictions are becoming liberalized and internationalized. The growth of multinational

Reflection point 3.11

In small groups, consider the following:

- What is meant by globalization and what evidence is there to show that it is taking place?
- Describe and assess the criticisms of the globalization theorists.

corporations (MNCs) with their chains of production and service provision has been a key feature of globalization (Edwards and Rees, 2006).

National systems and management action

The internationalization strategies of MNCs bring major changes in the internal domestic business systems of individual countries and host business systems. However, their influence is mediated by local institutions and agencies. If these are cohesive and resilient, then the system is less likely to change. Existing patterns of economic organization and competition reflect upon the emerging transnational business systems.

Cultural and institutional perspectives provide two analytical categories to give a context for the national dimension. The cultural perspective has been highlighted earlier in this chapter. Sparrow and Hiltrop (1994) observed that MNCs vary in the degree to which they recognize cultural diversity. If managers believe the impact of national culture to be minimal, then their policy will be to ignore the differences in employee values, norms, and preferences. Furthermore, if managers view all other ways of doing things as inferior, then their policy will be to minimize the impact of cultural diversity, for example by recruiting a homogeneous workforce. When managers recognize the potentially positive benefits of cultural diversity, then a truly international workforce will be created to build on the similarities and differences of the different nationalities, so creating new forms of management and organization (Edwards and Rees, 2006).

National cultural differences are important to international human resource management (HRM) as they have great potential for impact on organizational culture. They can be a source of competitive advantage and HRM practices are key to maintaining and promoting this advantage. The cultural approach is used to explain the ways in which MNCs adapt to the cultures of host country cultures. Hofstede has argued that culture is all pervasive. If this is so, then the comparative study of organizations across cultural boundaries using employing concepts and equivalent operational measures from only one culture creates issues in terms of validity. Child (2002) indicates that if meanings vary in different societies, then the concepts and their measurement have questionable equivalence.

Furthermore, there are considerable variations within countries according to regions, social classes, and ethic groups. Cross-national research addresses the societal origins of cultural differences and leaves institutional perspectives to explain managerial and business differences across countries. The state, legal and financial systems, and the family are the key institutions with regard to shaping national business systems. These institutions are liable to be slow to change in the light of economic and technological change. They can influence a country's ability to carry out production and economic activity efficiently.

Education systems and the way that social relations are structured affect the amount of ascription and achievement within a society and so the creation of economic wealth and innovation. Sparrow and Hiltrop (1994, pp 52–9) observe that 'the role of the state, financial systems, national systems of education and training, and labour relations systems combine to form a dominant logic of action in each country, and these will guide management practice'.

Employment law—which impacts on recruitment and selection, dismissal, educational qualifications, employee relations, health and safety, the working environment, employment contracts, and levels of consultation—then is the reflection of political traditions and restricts or provides the freedom for managers to respond to pressures in the workplace. Consultation is, for example, stronger in Europe than in the USA.

It is noteworthy that none of these differences is static. MNCs will look for advantages from national differences in order to gain competitive advantage. An important issue amongst institutionalists is the extent to which the dominant institutions across countries are converging on particular types. The two different approaches of accounting for and explaining national cultures have been considered. Both approaches might emphasize national factors and so underplay those that interact with global, regional, and organizational factors.

A more holistic way of viewing these rigid analytical categories has been considered by Child (2002) when drawing upon Max Weber's (1964) framework for the analysis of socioeconomic development. According to Child (2002, p 44), the Weberian framework:

> qualifies the current dominance that economic universalism enjoys in policy discussions by stressing the need to allow room for the influence of ideas and values. Equally, it cautions against any tendency to ascribe overriding explanatory power to national culture.

In Child's model the material forces represent the pressures arising from globalization and regionalization, and such effects can lead to changes in the nature of national systems. Ideational influences are linked to the national level and illustrate the way in which cultures and institutions are interrelated and interdependent. Child puts it thus (2002, p 44):

> when institutions change, people may adapt their values quite rapidly.

Reflection point 3.12

In small groups consider the following:

- In which ways do national cultures impact upon organizations and management?
- Does the culturalist or institutionalist approach offer a more useful way to understand national differences?

The differences in business systems give rise to management styles and employment practices that have their own identities. Such styles and practices are dynamic and change in response to external pressures. There is interaction between the global and the local, cultures and institutions, and management actions and social structures.

International management and development

Much of the writing about international management roles is centred on selecting employees with potential for expatriate assignments and then devising an international management development programme for them.

However other factors need to be considered. MNCs operate within different structures and are not simply headquartered in a home country with foreign operatives run by expatriates. The size of the operations often gives host and third-country nationals a management role. The career of the international manager will tend to be shorter, more varied, and uncertain as operations are switched between countries.

IMD should be included within the context of management learning and goes beyond training and development to include succession planning, performance management, and personal and family welfare.

Briscoe and Schuler (2004), Sparrow *et al.* (2004), and Tayeb (2004) provide insights into learning that has taken place in recent years:

- the importance of responding to individual learning styles
- the growing significance of informal and incidental learning that takes place through everyday work activities as opposed to formal off-the-job training sessions
- evidence that work experiences of a negative as well as a positive kind can be very important for individual learning and career development

Reflection point 3.13

The shorter, more varied career has implications for international management development (IMD):

- Should IMD be restricted to high-potential expatriates?
- Should development be extended to other managers in different roles and at different stages of their careers?
- What impact would there be for third-country nationals who might not previously have been included in IMD activity?

- linked to this, the growing awareness of the ways in which formal work-related activities can be harnessed as learning tools

- the growing interest in organizational and team learning as well as individual learning

- a growing awareness that the wider organizational culture and the specific learning culture of the organization can encourage or inhibit individual, team, and organizational learning

- the potential contribution of information and communications technology to individual, team, and organizational learning as well as knowledge transfer in particular; this underpins the enthusiasm for knowledge management and corporate universities.

The changing scope of international management development

Prior to the 1990s, the international manager tended to be assigned to a project for two years, was typically mid-to-late career, from a senior level corporate employee base, and had a trailing wife. Briefings were normally provided prior to departure, sometimes with the opportunity to visit the overseas site.

This neo-colonial model was seen to have flaws (Scullion, 1993):

- The rate of expatriate turnover costs was higher than similar management groups.

- There were replacement and development costs and other hidden costs to the organization, such as replacement and development of employees.

- The trailing spouse was becoming replaced by dual-career couples who demanded career development for both partners.

- The patterns of family life and women's employment were changing.

- There was a reluctance by expatriates to disturb their children's education.

- The repatriation process was often seen as not overcoming the culture shock, lost career opportunities, and even unemployment faced on return to the home country.

Short-term assignments are now increasingly used by European, Japanese, and US MNCs and draw on employees from a range of business functions.

Forster (2000) carried out a study of 500 expatriates in 36 UK companies, showing that a sizeable number experienced psychological difficulties on return. Rather than long-term overseas tours, cross-border job swaps, short assignments, or engagement in a virtual project team in a multicultural setting would become the norm.

> ### Mini case study 3.2: Contexts for leadership and management development
>
> This mini case study explores different contexts in which leadership and management development takes place and considers the needs of different managers.
>
> Think about the way that professionals are being developed in your organization and list what you see as the challenges facing developers in your organization.
>
> A prime challenge for developers may stem from the individualistic approach that professionals have towards their work. Professional work may be viewed as rewarding and intellectually challenging, and loyalty to the profession and its values may cause a dilemma within the organization.
>
> A personalized approach to professional development is embodied in the idea of continuous professional development (CPD).
>
> CPD is essentially continuous, owned and managed by the learner, with transparent learning objectives meeting both organizational and individual goals. Regular investment of an individual's time should be seen as an essential part of a professional life.
>
> **Question**
>
> 1 What arrangements have you made/are you making for your professional development to include management knowledge and skills?

The development implications

This change requires managers with international competencies who may be at different stages of corporate international development.

The growing use of international joint ventures and cross-border alliances provides a way of maximizing synergies and minimizing risks.

Middle-level technical and commercial employees may now be exposed to international responsibility and so there is a growing need for the provision of time- and cost-effective management development.

Sparrow (1999) developed role specifications for international management:

- the home-based manager who has a central focus on different markets and players

- multicultural team members who work on a series of international projects

- internationally mobile managers who undertake frequent but short visits to numerous overseas locations while remaining loyal to the parent culture

- employees in specialist non-management roles that involve international activity or transfer of knowledge from sales, training, buying, engineering, etc.

- expatriates who carry the parent organizational culture, but who undertake lengthy assignments representing the parent in a limited number of host countries

- transitional managers who move across borders on behalf of the organization, but are relatively detached from any organizational headquarters.

The variety of management roles shown above has implications both for the type of development required and for the skills to be developed.

Learning theory and international management development

A new interest in IMD has led to the implication of wider theoretical insights from academia.

These include that adults learn most effectively when the learning experience is located within meaningful experiences; that behavioural skills are improved through observation and practice and with feedback from others; that learning also requires the ability to search for and identify new patterns of thinking to allow new assumptions to be assimilated; that most learning is informal and incidental rather than planned and formal; that powerful learning can come from negative and challenging experiences.

The variety of international management roles combined with the reluctance of some managers to take on an expatriate career has led to a number of new initiatives in IMD programmes. These include:

- the identification of international leadership competencies as a basis for developing managers for international assignments
- cross-cultural awareness training
- multicultural team building and development
- IMD for women.

Identifying and developing international leadership competencies

Globalization, as shown previously, has shown how culture affects norms and values.

Yeung and Ready (1995) identified key differences in the national emphasis on leadership capabilities. Australians consider that global managers are required to lead change, whereas Korean and Japanese leaders disagree. US, German, Australian, Italian, Korean, and UK leaders do not value skills in internal and external networking as highly as French employers.

Morrison (2000) has shown that there is inconclusive and ambiguous evidence for agreed competencies, cultural differences, management style, and the impact of culture. The evidence itself varies from descriptive to analytical samples. A number of international businesses have developed their own company-specific models in response to the above. On occasions the models devised are in response to senior management preferences and are not built up in a rigorous way.

Neary and O'Grady (2000) and Connor (2000) have identified that whilst there is no agreement as to what global leadership competencies are, there is consensus as to the need to develop managers through such an approach.

Shortfalls in new international managers are perceived and corporate leadership programmes are now used earlier in managers' careers to provide this much needed development.

Multicultural team building and cross-cultural training may be added to the themes of global strategy, leadership style and behaviour, culture, and organizational capabilities.

In this way participants 'reframe their cognitive maps' and are able to reflect on their experiences and are exposed to colleagues from other cultures (Edwards and Rees, 2006).

The programmes are costly to provide and so may only be used for a proportion of an organization's international employees. However, whilst the number of employees involved in international work is increasing they are increasingly used by European, Japanese, and US organizations for short-term assignments. Such short-term work can involve stays in large international hotels with little opportunity to mix with host country nationals and so limited exposure to the culture of the country.

Cross-cultural awareness training

The last point, a protection or sheltering from full exposure to the culture of the host country linked to culture shock after an initial 'honeymoon' period on arrival overseas, can cause as Eschbach *et al.* (2001) estimated a 50 per cent curtailment of international assignment by US international managers. The curtailment, failure, of an assignment will incur the costs to the organization of transportation, housing/hotelling, family moving expenses, schooling and other allowances, the reward package, and hiring replacement employee costs in the home country. More intangible expenses such as loss of goodwill for those involved with the assignment, loss of self-esteem, loss of career, ill health, and domestic disruption will also be incurred.

Cross-cultural training is often provided by organizations to prevent the failure of an assignment and is more than the mere provision of factual information on the host country.

A cross-cultural training programme might include in its content:

- general and country-specific cultural awareness
- area studies, history, geography, politics, economics
- frameworks for understanding and valuing cultural differences
- planning for a successful international assignment
- intercultural business skills for working effectively in the local environment
- understanding cultural variations for those with regional responsibilities
- business and social customs in the host country
- international transition and stress management
- practical approaches to culture-shock management and lifestyle adjustment
- information on daily living issues
- special issues: partners and families abroad
- repatriation as a pre-departure issue.

Such a programme would be appropriate for home-based employees who are in frequent contact with nationals from other countries.

Multicultural team working, which can be virtual as well as face to face, also requires an appreciation of differences in organizational behaviour, including communication, motivation, and decision making.

International management development for women

Despite the growth of equal opportunities policies in the USA and Western Europe, this has not been reflected in the proportion of women working in international management. Barham and Devine (1991) show that women tend to be more culturally sensitive and are able to be more effective in their work with managers from other countries.

Stereotyping and prejudices held by senior management hinder international career development and succession planning.

Reflection point 3.14

In small groups consider the following:

- What do you think are the key competencies that international managers require?
- Which learning and development theories will be applicable to devising IMD programmes?
- Will the growth of technology mean that organizations will need to rely on international managers less in the future?

Mini case study 3.3: Organizational change; planning a turnaround

This case deals with planning in a crisis.

Lucia is the daughter of an important Brazilian entrepreneur. After studying in Europe and the United States for a number of years, she asked her father for a job. He suggested that she take responsibility for one of the family's many interests, a small company located in France. The company produced and sold soaps and shampoos. Profits were down and the company was beginning to lose money. 'See what you can do to turn it around,' said the entrepreneur. 'And if you don't have any luck, we'll sell.'

Lucia visited the factory. She found the plant in bad repair and the roof leaked. The general manager introduced her to the 80 employees, who were clearly demoralized. The older members were resigned to retirement; this was an area of high unemployment, and they were most unlikely to find other jobs.

On her way out of the meeting, one of the younger workers accosted her. 'It doesn't have to be like this,' he said. 'We used to make the best soap in France and we can make it again. The problem is, none of the sales staff know their job.'

'Back to your station,' said the general manager, and to Lucia's surprise, the young man obeyed.

'Pierre is a hothead,' the general manager explained.

'But is he right about the sales staff?'

'I'm sure they do their best,' came the defensive answer. 'And the real problem is our suppliers. The worse our problems, the more unreliable they grow. And the bank, of course. They say that as things are now, they can't lend us any more.'

Lucia returned to her hotel in thoughtful mood. She had two options. She could return home and propose the sale. The proceeds would cover recent losses, but her reputation would suffer in the family. Or she could plan a turnaround.

Questions

1 Outline the pressures for change, and the factors which will help the introduction of change into this company.

2 Consider at least one managerial technique which could help in this situation. Would adaptation of the technique be necessary in order for it to be successfully used?

3 In relation to a culture with which you are familiar, identify aspects which you think have changed. What do you think are the reasons for those changes?

4 To what extent do you think that education is a force for change in cultures, or a means of maintaining establishment domination? Outline and justify the reasons for your view.

Chapter summary

This chapter has provided a context to explore management development and to appreciate the issues faced by the growing economies of Brazil, Russia, India, and China as they increasingly take their place on the international stage and surpass the US and Western economies.

The nature of cultural diversity and globalization has been examined with reference to some of the main models and theories.

The notion of globalization has been reviewed to provide an appreciation of the increasing importance of the development of global strategy whilst adapting to local circumstances.

The development of international managers has been considered to provide a focus for the future of management development for the next generation of global business leaders.

The chapter links to Chapter 4, which will provide a history and background of management development and subsequently into Chapter 13 and the development of managers and leaders with global competence.

Questions

1 What are the implications for the manager working overseas of Hofstede's model for comparing cultures?

2 Identify key economic and social events that have occurred within your culture during the last decade. (This may include other countries' interventions, economic circumstances, technological changes, and educational advances.)

3 What support is needed before, during, and after expatriation?

4 In what ways are the skills needed by international managers different from traditional management skills?

5 What is cultural intelligence? Specify what it involves.

6 Are there conditions that create universal responses from employees regardless of culture?

7 What is the predominant leadership style within your organization and how does this reflect cultural influences?

8 What do you feel are the key barriers to women gaining international assignments in your organization?

9 What are the benefits for international organizations in recruiting a diverse workforce?

10 What are your views regarding convergence/divergence of management practices?

Discussion questions

1 In your organization, how is cultural diversity managed or ignored?

2 How does globalization affect your organization?

3 How do organizations measure success or failure of expatriate assignments?

4 Evaluate the learning and development opportunities provided by your organization, or one you are familiar with, to support short- and/or long-term international assignments.

Suggestions for further reading

Hamilton, L. and Webster, P. (2009) *The International Business Environment*, Oxford: Oxford University Press.
This text with online resources provides a context to global management development.

Lane, H.W., Maznevski, M.L., DiStefano, J.J., and Dietz, J. (2009) *International Management Behavior: Leading with a Global Mindset*, Chichester: John Wiley.
This book provides insights into global business perspectives through case studies. Its focus is on managing people from different cultures and managing global organizations to achieve effective results.

Mead, R. and Andrews, T.G. (2009) *International Management*, 4th edition, Chichester: John Wiley.
Provides insights into cross-cultural management and links management theories to practical global examples.

The history of leadership and management development

The aims of this chapter are to:

- reflect back on the history of management development.

- review the traditional approach to management development and explain and evaluate this with examples of how management development has been applied in various organizations in the public and private sectors.

- show how the emphasis has shifted to one where organizations are now increasingly focusing on the softer people skills that are essential to meet the challenges of the new business environment.

Introduction

Managers are increasingly facing business problems that require a pluralistic leadership and managerial style and a more solutions-centred approach. Competence in managing group dynamics and relationships will be discussed and evaluated in this chapter.

Managing in the traditional hierarchical organization will be contrasted and compared with the more competitive organizations that are flatter and structured in a matrix style. This chapter will identify the skills required in these different types of organizations in terms of empowerment, delegation, and allocation of responsibilities, achieving output results and how to go about developing these.

Included in this chapter is an evaluation of the value of the skills of utilizing personal power and influence, understanding, and managing change.

The opening activity will inevitably cause difficulties because it is difficult to reach agreement when specifying tasks, behaviours, and capabilities. Managing is also a political process which is influenced by personal values and interests rather than a rational activity. The processional view of management is similar to that of strategy, which sees it as emergent over time in an organization as unplanned, and planned actions are carried out to ensure the organization's survival into the future.

Management development is complex and problematic due to the lack of consistent or definitive meaning of management development.

Mabey and Salaman (1995) highlight four management agendas or purposes. Their view contrasts with the view that management development should be linked with the organization.

This view assumes a large organization that can afford to invest in a formal approach to management development.

Mabey and Salaman's four management agendas are:

- *Functional performance*. Focuses on knowledge, skills, and attitudes of individual managers. Assumes unproblematic link between management development and performance.

- *Political reinforcement*. Focuses on reinforcing and propagating skills and attitude valued by top managers. Assumes top managers are correct in their diagnosis and prescription.

Reflection point 4.1

- Produce a broad specification of management tasks required in your organization or one with which you are familiar.
- Identify the key difference in managerial skills and capabilities required in the organization of your choice.

- *Compensation.* Management development is seen as part of the reward system for managers. Assumes development is motivational and encourages commitment.

- *Psychic defence.* Management development provides a safety valve for managerial anxieties. Assumes competitive careers and associated anxieties.

Summary of section

This section focused on the growing emphasis on management development amongst professionals, and a growing tendency to professionalize such developments. However, there is a variety of purposes and benefits perceived by organizational stakeholders.

Approaches to management development

However, this view ignores the growth of the smaller organization (O'Dwyer and Ryan, 2002). The formalized view of management development excludes the contribution of 'accidental', 'informal', or 'situated' learning and development (Fox, 1997; Mumford, 1997). Additionally, there is a lack of recognition of wider life experiences in management learning (Watson and Harris, 1999).

There is then disagreement on the purpose of management development and exclusion of some contexts of application and learning and development opportunities.

Senior managers tend to receive more training than those at the bottom of the ladder. This partly recognizes the importance of leadership and management to both organizational and national economic success.

There has been a proliferation of management courses together with concerns about their quality, which led to the establishment of the Council for Excellence in Leadership and Management.

The lack of consensus of definition of 'management' and 'development' has heightened issues of concern. Mumford and Gold (2004, p 2) define 'management' as a description of managers' activities, but then what managers do is questionable.

Mumford and Gold (p 14) then define management as an 'attempt to improve managerial effectiveness through a learning process'.

The Chartered Institute of Personnel and Development (CIPD) (2007) go further in this debate by defining management as the 'structured process by which managers learn and improve their skills for the benefit of their employing organizations and themselves. The word "structured" is important because managers learn all the time from experience in doing their jobs. Only if that informal learning is picked up or used should it be counted as management development.'

The context in which management development is cast is that of the social and economic environment, with individual organizational settings focused on the individual development of managers making for a myriad of permutations.

Rapid, continuous, and increasing change overlays the management tiers—the tiers being set within a framework of varied levels and situations covering graduate entry and self-grown junior managers to senior managers and professionals in SMEs and multinationals, as well as developing diversity.

Organizations differ in their approaches to management development. Burgoyne (1988, p 41) sees six levels of maturity of an organization's provisions of management development:

1 *No systematic management development.* Reliance on natural, laissez-faire processes.

2 *Isolated tactical management development.* It is ad hoc, merely responding to problems or events.

3 *Integrated and coordinated structural and development tactics.* The use of career structure management and assisted learning are integrated and coordinated.

4 *Management development implements corporate policy.* This is achieved through HR planning, providing a strategic framework and direction for the tactics of career structure management and of learning, education, and training.

5 *Management development input to corporate policy formation.* It feeds information back into corporate policy decision making on the strengths, weaknesses, and potential of management, and helps with forecasting and analysis of manageability of proposed projects, ventures, and changes.

6 *Strategic development of the management of corporate policy.* Management development processes enhance the nature and quality of corporate policy formation processes, which they help inform and implement.

The planning of learning and development within an organization suggests that management and development should fit with the business strategy for the present and the future together with its values and ethics.

Mumford and Gold (2004, p 28) set organizational strategy in the external economic and social context, so providing guidance on managerial requirements. In this sustaining model, policy develops delivery and the outcomes are analysed and then provide feedback for the organizational strategy.

Thomson *et al.* (2001) highlight that organizations with a formal policy are more likely to undertake more management development than those without.

Maby (2002, p 1140) finds that the amount of priority given to management development compared with the less meaningful index of whether there is a written policy and the use of diagnostic-and-await processes are important, so highlighting that merely writing a policy does not guarantee provision of management development.

The wide range of demands placed on management development necessitate the use of different methods. These include formal education and training such as the

Mini case study 4.1: Core capabilities

Sunrise is a leading producer of cereals and manufacturer of convenience foods such as cereal bars, waffles, crackers, biscuits, and pastries.

Strategic direction and coherence are added to develop the organization by senior managers in the European operation through the identification of the organization and people components that they see as being important in building high-performing teams. They consider that the core capabilities that they require are:

- consumer understanding and brand development
- designing and delivering great products
- business planning and management
- customer management.

Six value statements then link these capabilities to a personal agenda for employees:

- We act with integrity and show respect.
- We are all accountable.
- We have the hunger and humility to learn.
- We are passionate about our business, our brands and our food.
- We love success.
- We strive for simplicity.

Questions

1 What do these core capabilities and values suggest for Sunrise's development agenda?

2 Compare these statements with those of an organization with which you are familiar.

MBA or undergraduate management degrees, internally or externally provided training courses, outdoor development, coaching, and mentoring as well as creative learning methods.

Historical perspectives of management development

The first text to set out the responsibilities of a manager, *The Duties of the Vizier*, was written 3,500 years ago in Ancient Egypt.

The first modern business school, set up for the purpose of teaching managers to do their jobs efficiently and effectively, was established by the East India Company in 1805, 104 years before the Harvard Business School.

History teaches us that each set of circumstances generates a managerial response. What is right for one time and place, and for one company in one set of circumstances, will not always work for others (Morgan, 2009).

In the mid 1980s the UK was emerging from the most significant recession since the 1930s and showing the signs of recovery that preceded the disastrous boom of 1989.

At that time in the post Peters and Waterman days the emphasis was on excellence. This was then superseded by the impact of the Management Charter Initiative and the concept of national standards for management qualifications.

By the 1990s the perspective had changed again. At that time an even deeper and longer recession than that of the 1980s was in place in the UK. Manufacturing in the UK and specifically in the south-east of England was particularly hard hit. Mobile young managers found themselves landed with the yoke of negative equity and management had moved on again. Organizations were 'rationalizing', 'downsizing', and 'rightsizing'.

Tom Peters's exhortation to managers to create fewer, flatter, structures and bash bureaucracy had become a regular feature of organizational life in an increasingly desperate bid for survival.

ICI was in the middle of splitting itself into separate businesses following the predatory bid from Hanson. IBM and General Motors had just recorded the largest corporate losses in history thus far, whilst Microsoft—founded, managed, and largely owned by Bill Gates, still under 40 and dismissed as 'nerdy' by a senior executive in a competitor company—had recorded a higher turnover than the once seemingly indomitable IBM.

The underlying assumptions and values of management development were at that time opened up to some serious questioning, as the organizations in which they were developed vied with one another to see which could operate with the leanest corporate office (Robinson, 1991).

The focus of attention had also begun to fall increasingly upon smaller and medium-sized enterprises (SMEs). This brought forward the question as to what management development had ever done for them. SMEs had always been important to Western economies, but it was only the failure of so many big organizations that had brought their smaller fellows to the interest of management development practitioners.

A series of booms and depressions marked the end of the 20th century, with 2001 marking the beginning of a new millennium and century and the first decade with a global economy. With the collapse of the Soviet Union in 1991 the nations of the world accepted the need to adjust their own economic structure and policies to the demands of the emerging global marketplace. The winds of change carried the swiftly changing advances in information and communications technology, 'informing millions of people everywhere of new possibilities for employment and consumption and thousands of firms of new opportunities for investment and growth' (Cameron and Neal, 2003).

Management development has long been considered an attempt to increase managerial effectiveness through planned and deliberate learning processes. Client managers as the customers for such processes have tended to be clear about management development within their organizations and were able to draw the distinction between management development and management training.

The latter has been seen as a process leading to the acquisition of skills whilst management development tended to be viewed as a broadening, educational process through which the individual is shaped to the attitudes, values, rites, and rituals of increasingly higher levels of management within the organization. Management development may or may not include formal training and it may be self-managed. Client managers would then link management training to a process through which the individual acquires the skills relevant to a specific management job or level.

They would regard management development as having much more to do with career development and progression. A sharper perspective of this is drawn in organizations where the responsibility for management training is seen as relating to the training or learning and development functions whilst management development is linked to the personnel or human resource management function. If these functions are not fully integrated into the organization, then there may be competition over which function is accountable for what and over where the senior status lies.

The main purpose of management development is to enhance effective management behaviour. It is not just about knowledge or attitudes, although these are significant. There are managers who are knowledgeable and have appropriate attitudes but are not effective.

Doing the right things in the right way is what makes for an effective manager. The effective manager is one who uses effective managerial behaviour, and maximizes on this through further effective development and learning.

Effectiveness in management development is best achieved when the three different aspects of effectiveness are brought together. Mumford (1991) refers to these as:

- a contingent definition of effective managerial behaviour
- a developmental process which emphasizes activities in which managers are required to be effective, rather than emphasizing the knowledge necessary for action
- the identification of learning processes which are effective for the individual or group, rather than economical and convenient for tutors or trainers.

Learning may be formal, from courses and training or outside the classroom and in the workplace, in communities of practice and maximized through, for example, learning sets, mentoring, personal development plans, and personal learning journals.

The classical view of management development stressed five headings summarizing managerial activities:

- forecast/plan
- organize
- motivate
- coordinate
- control.

Stewart (1976), Mintzberg (1980), and Kotter (1982) have shown through their research that the basis of these concepts is unscientific. These three researchers have argued that these headings have been unrealistic. Each writer has then developed their own statement of key managerial activities.

It is likely that any generalized statement about managerial activities for any particular manager or group of managers will be incorrect.

Variations in required managerial behaviour are to be found in different organizations; rather, effectiveness of the manager and their managerial activities will depend on the specific function and job of the manager with the manager's and others' interpretation of the job and role.

Kotter and Mintzberg stress the importance of interpersonal relationships and the effective use of networks and more organization-specific training, and management development has resulted.

However, training needs analysis is still relatively superficial and leads to the commissioning of management development whose content is largely similar from one organization to another.

A more rigorous analytical approach to the training needs analysis is often blocked by line managers not engaging in the analytical process. The actual definition of effective behaviour is often not carried through.

An alternative approach to management development has been that of management competencies. This approach, based on Boyatzis (1982), has been found useful by organizations in not requiring managers to start from scratch but assisted by a list of competencies produced by Boyatzis—or in the UK, that produced by the Management Charter Initiative.

Reflection point 4.2

- What methods of assessing development needs are used in your organization?
- How effective are these methods?

A consideration of the competencies has provoked thought about what managers need to be able to do, the appropriateness of the nationally agreed list to the organization, and so the content of the competencies.

Effectiveness in management has largely passed by training and educational institutions who are offering taught management development courses outside the organization. Rather, such institutions have remained in the areas which they understand: those of conceptual or theoretical knowledge. There have been shifts of perception of programmes designed and implemented for particular companies; this has not been reflected on open programmes.

Managers themselves have often, in a similar way to the argument above, become separated from the perception and reality of management development processes. Rather, a pragmatic judgement is made on a manager's effectiveness as to whether they can get things done. If effectiveness is about outcomes or results actually achieved rather than the knowledge possessed by a particular manager, then it would seem appropriate to help managers learn from actions carried out. By focusing on action rather than emphasizing knowledge provision, and interpreting and using that knowledge, success is more likely to be achieved.

The benefits to be gained by working with real past experiences were originally identified and developed by the work of Revans (1982), Morris (1991), and Mumford (1988; 1989).

Revans and Morris have often been misinterpreted as being about a defined project or a group of managers discussing their own projects. Increasingly management development has included projects as a central part of the content. However, this has not been an accurate representation of what is meant by using real-life experience.

Working on direct problem solving as a simulation of management effectiveness through building bridges with Lego blocks or outdoor experiences is more likely to be an argument for the provision of varied learning activities than using real work experiences for development.

Programmes devised through the rigorous analysis of an organization by the managers themselves and giving attention to skills involved in working with information technology and management skills such as interviewing, negotiation, or interpersonal relationships can improve managerial performance.

Management development activities and learning

Burgoyne's (1988) framework of the levels of maturity of organizational management development were highlighted earlier in this chapter. The model offers a framework for the formal processes of management development.

However, the natural management development progresses no further than Level 1. There is no attempt to build these often explicit and powerful potential building blocks into the model.

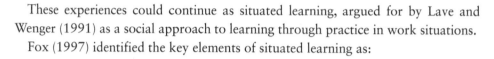

Reflection point 4.3

- Does your own learning experience relate to situated learning?
- How could you improve its effectiveness?

These experiences could continue as situated learning, argued for by Lave and Wenger (1991) as a social approach to learning through practice in work situations. Fox (1997) identified the key elements of situated learning as:

- People who perform work practice belong to a community of practice, and it is within that community that learning occurs 'naturally'.

- The community of practice has an apprenticeship system which may be formal or informal, and novices learn to participate by assisting more experienced members. Novices are 'legitimate' but on the 'periphery' of a community. They can observe skilled practitioners and then copy and learn.

- Communities are dependent on other communities and are part of a network of communities (Mumford and Gold, 2004, p 100).

The totality of management development in an organization should put in place both formal and informal learning activities and experiences.

Mumford's model (1987) reflects a concern for working on tasks which managers are largely responsible for. This then gives the first dimension: high concern for task versus low concern for task.

The second dimension focuses on learning and times when a manager's concern for learning is high when 'consciously and deliberately' attending to learning. At other times attention to learning will be low.

Mumford then related the two dimensions to the characteristics of Types 1, 2 and 3 or Informal Integrated and Formal Management Development.

Research leading to this model indicated some organizations at Level 1 in the Burgoyne (1988) model, whilst others were at Levels 4 and 5. The learning experiences that had been significant were often informal and unplanned experiences in and around the job.

Type 2 learning brings management development into the real world.

Manager-centred learning

Manager-centred learning will engage the attention of managers. Management development that is designed with content that is relevant to managers when they arrive on a course will lead to more effective learning. Listening, studying, reflecting, and

Reflection point 4.4

- Which of the following elements of manager-centred learning do you consider significant to your learning?
  - managerial reality
  - preferred approaches to learning
  - building on experience
  - using familiar learning processes
  - continued learning

generating new ideas are not enough; it is the transformation to real managerial life that makes for effectiveness.

For many programmes of learning it is valuable for the learner to continue to learn after the event or programme of learning.

Further reading or individual action plans are only partial ways of continuing with the learning process. Rather, providers of management development should enhance the capacity of managers to learn outside as well as on their courses. This suggests learning how to learn, which has been summarized by Mumford (1995) as:

- intuitive approach: unconscious natural process

- incidental approach: events trigger post-mortem

- retrospective approach: regular review process

- prospective approach: planning to learn from experience.

The emphasis on reflection and planning in the learning process is significant as the capacity to deal with these individual preferences is built in.

Informal and formally designed management development opportunities

Kolb (1984) drew up a model of a learning cycle indicating what should be happening when learning in and around the job as well as what should be happening in any learning experience. Honey and Mumford (1996) built on Kolb's original theory but had a practical difference from Kolb's in their planning of the next stages compared with Kolb's active experimentation.

Kolb's model involved action or having a concrete experience, which led to the learner reviewing the experience—the reflective observation. Replaying the event or abstract conceptualisation led to further thinking and planning—the personalisation to repeat the experience.

The difference implicitly considers that action takes place without planning as a result of a thoughtful learning process. Kolb's learning cycle was essentially an

Mini case study 4.2: Reflective accounts

The need to reflect upon the practice of work-based learning and use the process to identify strengths, weaknesses, and actions to be taken from your experiences is relevant when seeking work. Through reflective practice it is possible to answer most effectively questions at the interview and create a good impression.

In the workplace, reflection may be stimulated by responses to specific situations; this might be triggered by particular feelings such as:

- feeling uneasy about something
- feeling something is not right
- feeling that your existing knowledge is not appropriate
- feeling that you do not know what to do
- feeling that you have to do something differently.

Or reflection might be triggered by something significant that happened at work or even in a class discussion about something that happened in the workplace. This is often known as a critical incident, such as:

- something that went unusually well
- something that went badly or lead to problems
- something that you found especially demanding or challenging
- something that made a difference in your work.

Question

1 Using Kolb's model, select one of the following subjects and write a reflective account of what happened, what you felt, what you did, and what you have learnt from this feeling or critical incident, and what you would do differently next time:
  - a conflict
  - a moment of joy
  - a misunderstanding
  - a missed opportunity
  - an extremity of emotion
  - a dilemma
  - a celebration
  - a success.

experiential cycle, whereas the Honey and Mumford learning cycle suggests learning can occur, for example, from a conclusion in a lecture.

Emerging from the above is an emphasis on individual learning differences and preferences. Honey and Mumford's learning styles and their follow-up Learning Styles Questionnaire are considered in detail in the references which are listed in the bibliography.

In order to maximize the effectiveness of informal learning, managers need to be taught to go through the process of assessing and planning what to do about the learning experience.

Lave and Wenger (1991) similarly support the value of natural learning through the support of social relations of a community of practitioners.

There needs to be recognition that informal learning, which could include opportunities from the list in Box 4.1, can also include disadvantages.

These disadvantages include:

- idealisation whereby past experiences are valued to the exclusion of other learning opportunities

- narrowness where a manager's work experience is specific and blinkers the desire to widen the managerial perspective

- obsolescence: previously acquired experience may have become out of date. This may be exemplified by a manager from the public sector moving into the private sector.

Box 4.1 Informal learning opportunities for managers

- analysing mistakes
- managing changes
- attending conferences or seminars
- meetings
- being coached, counselled, mentored
- negotiating
- budgeting
- networking
- covering for others' absences
- performance appraisals
- dealings with colleagues and peers
- planning project work
- dealings with subordinates
- reading
- dealings with your manager
- same job with more responsibilities
- giving a presentation
- secondments
- interviewing
- solving problems
- job change in a new function
- unfamiliar tasks
- job change within the same function
- working in groups
- job rotation
- working with consultants
- making decisions

> ### Reflection point 4.5
>
> ● Can you identify learning opportunities which have proved to be effective for you?

Learning through an organized plan can be more effective and will often commence with an appraisal and individual development plan.

The list below indicates a range of different formal learning opportunities on and around the job.

Work-based formal learning opportunities:

- Changes in the job:
  - □ promotion
  - □ same job but in different function
  - □ secondment.
- Changes in job content:
  - □ extra responsibility and tasks
  - □ special projects
  - □ committees or task groups.
- Within the job:
  - □ being coached/counselled/mentored
  - □ monitoring and feedback by line management.

Location

Previously education was seen as a process focused on the whole person and total career whereas training, learning, and development were seen as helping managers to learn specific things to address particular circumstances within organizations or sectors.

This difference now seems to have become eroded. Training centres tend to be more practical and relate more to organizational needs, although they see themselves as also equipping a manager for life.

Education centres concentrate more on managers' development to address an organization's specific needs. University business schools now will undertake in-company work as well as offering the more knowledge-based MBA programmes.

Research by CEML (2002) indicated that management qualifications benefited individual managers and their careers but did little to improve organizational performance.

At the undergraduate level, business and management degrees make for more employable graduates but are not specifically required for management work.

Theoretical teaching and its application to management practice remain a concern (CEML, 2002). There are arguments that the complexities of the moral and political world should be addressed.

Summary of section

Managers and their organizations differ in their responses to learning processes, reflecting the growing range of theories of learning and development. It is likely that managers learn effectively in the context of practice and that they differ in the way they learn from experience and in the way they approach learning activities.

Management development policy

Throughout this text stress is made on the need to align human resources with the individual organization's business strategy.

A CIPD report (CIPD, 2002) argues that the focus of management development is to deliver the organization's current business model and to contribute to the development of future business models—business models here being synonymous with business strategy.

Current and future provision of managerial capability includes concern with individuals and their individual learning with a need to balance group needs. Current provision is concerned with the current behaviour of managers either as individuals or as a collective resource. Future provision is concerned with ensuring the availability of skills and experience to meet future demands.

This may mean preparing individuals for future promotion opportunities or could be focused on the organization as a whole by ensuring that there is a pool of managerial capability to fill senior positions as this becomes necessary.

There may be interconnection between the two demands since there is a concern to manage the organization's internal labour market through interventions in career progression.

However, tensions often arise between the two purposes and it can be difficult to meet both needs in a single management development programme (Hirsh and Carter, 2002). Indeed, Woodall and Winstanley (1998) refer to this tension as a need to balance integration and differentiation.

Management development becomes more effective through gaining purpose by linking to organizational strategy. Through an organization having a management development policy there is a translation of the organization's requirements into activities.

There may be disagreement within the organization about the management development policy and it may represent an espoused view rather than a reflection of what actually happens or will happen.

Research by Thomson *et al.* (2001) indicates that organizations which have formal management development policies are more likely to provide management development than those organizations who do not have such a policy in place.

The policy provides an opportunity to give management development a focus as a driver towards the organization's strategy and to devote resources and responsibility to it.

As Mabey (2003) showed, management development can contribute to a positive HR context and can include both formal and informal development.

Formal management development policy

The policy would normally include:

- a statement of the purpose of management development
- a statement indicating the processes to be used in identifying and developing managers.

Reflection point 4.6

- Does your organization have a formal management development policy?
- Does your organization's policy work effectively?
- What could be done to ensure that the policy worked more effectively or to convince your organization of the need for such a policy?

A typology of management development

The alignment of management development with the organization strategy is highlighted by Jansen and Van der Velde (2001). They review empirical research in the Netherlands indicating that management development was more prevalent in market or commercial organizations and that it became more prevalent in a turbulent environment and tighter labour market.

The public sector in the Netherlands was noted as showing a growing interest in management development as the sector directed such development at organizational development and personnel development.

Findings were that if management development is to amount to more than 'just a few educational activities, it should have broad support in the organization'.

Jansen and Van der Velde's research noted the variance in definitions of management development, but after surveying 92 Dutch companies concerning their management development policy and practice, they identified four types of development:

- administrative management development found in lifetime employment environments
- derived management development where in 'up or out' environments management development is strictly planned and linked closely to company strategy
- partner management development, mainly found in innovative and information technology environments where it is key to combine business development with human development
- leading management development in turbulent market situations.

A weakness was identified in the research of the need for an even greater linkage between management development and organization strategy and a systematic evaluation of management development practices.

Evaluation of management development

A managing director of an organization would be concerned to ensure that management development activities had contributed to increased organizational performance, whereas a finance director would probably be more interested in proving that the financial benefits for an organization were greater than the costs of providing the management development.

Proving the value of the investment made in management development as indicated above is necessary but it is difficult to achieve. A measure of performance is generally required which could be quantitative as well as financial. Such measurement could include:

- prior to participating in a management development event
- after participating in a management development event

Reflection point 4.7

- How is management development evaluated in your organization, or how should it be evaluated?
- Who is (or should be) responsible for the evaluation of management development in your organization?

- where a group of managers have undertaken a management development programme showing that the benefits achieved were due to the planned programme rather than by chance.

Kirkpatrick (1983) recommended evaluation at different stages or levels of the programme:

Level 1: Reaction of the learners following an activity

Level 2: Learning skills gained from the activity

Level 3: Behaviour of the learners in the workplace after the activity

Level 4: Results of the changes in performance at work after the activity.

Phillips (1996) modified Kirkpatrick's classic model to add a Level 5 whereby a cost–benefit analysis could be applied to measure the net programme benefits by calculating the programme benefits divided by the programme cost.

Formative (evaluation part way through a programme) and summative (evaluation on completion of the programme) evaluation if also applied would provide evaluation of the learning process itself rather than only focusing on the outcomes of the management development activities.

The main purposes of evaluation in management development are:

- proving that a particular outcome has been achieved as a result of management development activities

- improving activities carried out within the organization

- learning how data can be used by managers and others as part of the learning process with management development events

- controlling the content and delivery of the programme within defined boundaries (Easterby-Smith, 1994).

The choices of evaluation reflect the requirements in organizations to respond to a variety of different needs such as when a particular activity is under threat or there is a need to prioritize the interests of stakeholders.

Other issues that need consideration linked to purpose are what data is collected, who it is collected from, when and how it is collected, and the analysis and presentation of results (Mumford and Gold, 2004).

Transference of learning

Once a management development programme has been completed managers may need help to bring their newly acquired learning back into the organization. Transferring learning back into performance occurs when skills, knowledge, and attitudes are not only learned and retained but are reinforced by further practical

> ## Reflection point 4.8
>
> - What helps or hinders the provision of a positive learning climate in your organization?
> - How do organizational power and politics affect management development in your organization?

application over time in the workplace. Lack of motivation on the part of the manager (learner) or where there is no support from colleagues and line managers may inhibit the transference of learning.

A positive learning climate is then essential to make for an effective transference. Such a climate may well include:

- reviewing work so that it stretches or at least matches the learner's capabilities

- an ongoing dialogue with line managers to set objectives and review performance to take account of the development that has occurred

- the provision of ongoing coaching and informal support.

Summary of section

Management development can be seen as a strategic tool to implement organizational development and so improve business performance. Policies in organizations reflect this direction on a day-to-day basis and are a symbol of an organization's intentions and contribution to a positive supportive work environment.

Soft skills for managers

There is considerable overlap between leadership and management, which is considered elsewhere in this text. The study of leadership often brings with it many terms and metaphors from sporting and military contexts. However, the public, private, and non-profit organizations often use the term 'manager' synonymously.

There is a growing market in leadership studies, business development, and leadership. Indeed, the Management Standards Centre, the 2003 Investors in People UK, and the CIPD's leadership and management standards demonstrate this growing interest in leadership and management as traditional organizations with hierarchical structures become scarcer and all sectors become more flexible and task or client focused.

Handy's (1976) matrix organizations are now becoming more the norm in a highly fluid environment. The shamrock style of organization (Handy, 1989) indicates the move towards further operational flexibility.

Atkinson (1984) in his flexible organization model described how individual managers are now required to exercise a different form of authority and getting things done through other people.

> *The 2007 version of the CIPD Managing and Leading People Professional Standards recognises that soft skills are just as important as technical ones, and so these are better represented and thus reflect more fully aspects of leadership ... which appear at the higher levels of organizations.*
>
> Rayner and Adam-Smith, 2009, p 51

Theoretical frameworks have been developed by several theorists: Mullins (2007), Bloisi *et al.* (2003), Hersey *et al.* (2001), Huczynski and Buchanan (2007), Kreitner and Kinicki (2001), and Yuki (2006). These theorists identify seven main schools of thought:

- the qualities or traits approach: which identifies the significant features of acknowledged leader
- the functional or group approach: considers what leaders do to be effective
- the approach which sees leadership as a behavioural category: focuses on the effects which leaders have on the actual performance of groups by examining leader behaviours and relating them to outcomes
- the leadership styles approach: an analysis of differences in leadership styles
- the situational approach and contingency models: considers the organizational and environmental circumstances in which the leadership activity occurs
- transformational leadership: leadership considered in a society which no longer accepts authority as the basis for command
- inspirational leadership: leadership linked to the concept of trait theories and in particular charisma.

Against a backcloth of setting standards for managers in whichever sector, with social and political change encouraging a more individual and less obedient approach to traditional forms of authority, softer leadership and management skills are becoming more important.

Reflection point 4.9

- What do you think the main differences between leadership and management are?
- Do all good managers have to be good leaders?
- Do all business leaders have to be good managers?

A growing public interest in the standards of behaviour and ethics of managers, dealt with elsewhere in this text, impacts on the competencies required of managers.

The processes by which managers can acquire the softer skills are analysed by Routledge and Carmichael (2007), whilst theory and practice are interwoven by Porter and Stone (2003) and Whetten, Cameron, and Woods (2000) as they consider the softer people skills and their acquisition.

Management and development in uncertain times

The increasingly turbulent economic environment that is currently being experienced puts an even greater emphasis on the importance of management development in organizations across all sectors and globally.

Arguably it is when times become difficult that leadership and management are most required, especially leaders who can lead people through uncertainty, keeping employees engaged and focused on performance as organizations need to compete in the financial, customer, product, and labour markets simultaneously.

Notwithstanding the current turbulent economic climate since the 1970s, globally organizations have experienced major change. The pace and scale of these changes seem unlikely to abate and are altering existing structures, cultures, and technologies.

These transformational change contexts have seen the introduction of new working practices such as total quality management, business process re-engineering, continuous improvement, team working, lean production methods, and culture change.

Crucially the valuing of employees as unlocking an organization's strategic advantage in the market within which it is located and the linkage between high commitment or high performance practices and improvements in organizational performance require the honing of softer people skills by managers.

High commitment or high performance work practices, in contrast to scientific management, are often described as Japanese management practices. These work practices are characterized by:

- suggestion schemes, quality circles, problem-solving groups or other forms of employee participation in idea generation

- employee participation in decision making

- freedom of expression

- extensive teamwork, including self-managing teams

- reformulation of work to make best use of upgraded skills.

Political and power barriers can get in the way of the implementation of these practices. Managers may not wish to accept that previous approaches introduced by them have not succeeded, and middle managers whose roles often are most affected by the high-performance work practices often resist their introduction (Hobeche, 2002).

High-commitment practices are often more likely to be found in the public sector than the private, with the exception of the use of personality tests by human resources functions and incentive pay systems. This is based on the findings of Kersley *et al.* (2006).

Management development for change

An open mind on the future will be one of the most potent assets an organization's leaders and managers can have. However, an understanding of all the variables will not be enough as the pace of the change increases.

Rather, individuals will need to be able to provide leadership on:

- What should the organization's strategy be and how will the organization know if they have got it right?

- How will the organization know when the change strategy should be changed?

- Should quicker response times be identified when paradoxically there is a greater need for strategic consistency which also avoids crisis management? (Fricker, 1991)

Furthermore, as Buchanan and Boddy (1992) noted, a heavy responsibility falls upon the change management team. This is in terms of planning and overseeing the change project, motivating others, and dealing with issues. Reciprocally the change management team must also receive support to avoid them becoming demoralized and so losing the ability to motivate others.

On occasions change agents can be encouraged by the inducement of financial rewards, sometimes by the lure of promotion, but often the most effective method is through public and private praise of the individuals concerned.

> Change demands new knowledge, skills and competencies. Increasingly, managers are having to learn new leadership styles, staff are having to learn to work as teams, and all are expected to be innovators and improvers. This requires more than just training and retraining. It may also include on-the-job counselling and coaching. Consequently, organizations need to consider what is required, who requires it in a way that encourages rather than threatens staff.
>
> Burnes, 2009, pp 463–4

Carnall (2003) considered that change was complex and needed to be part of every manager's role. Carnall proposed four core managerial competences to be essential for the effective management of change:

- decision making: including intuition and vision, gathering and utilizing information, understanding and synthesizing conflicting views

- coalition building: gaining support and resources to implement views and to implement decisions

- achieving action: handling opposition, motivating people, providing support, and building self-esteem

- maintaining momentum and effort: involving team building, sharing information and problems, ensuring ownership of ideas, providing feedback and motivating.

These competencies reflect the need for new softer skills to successfully undertake change projects.

At a time when organizations are taking change very seriously with its rapid and radical agendas, management development and education are receiving a higher priority in most advanced countries. Entry into a managerial job often requires formal, university-level qualifications (Arnold *et al.*, 2005; Jones *et al.*, 2000).

Management development varies between countries (Keuning, 1998). For example, in Japan it tends to be a competitive process commencing with the recruitment of elite cohorts, whilst in Germany there is a greater emphasis on the apprenticeship system and the development of managers through a career path involving the attainment of higher degrees. France is similar to Japan in an elitist approach and the attainment of degrees in business or law.

The UK is more ad hoc in its approach to management development and education. Indeed for this reason in the 1980s and 1990s there was growing interest in this area from the government. This earlier development being abandoned, in 2002 the government established the Council for Excellence in Leadership and Management.

The Council considered that most leadership and management programmes lacked the ability to provide appropriate leadership skills and that this was detrimental to the UK's economic performance (Paton, 2003).

The management diplomas and MBAs in the UK have an important role in a large number of management development programmes but they are now being balanced with more individual and experientially based approaches. The emphasis is now more on individual development and in terms of aligning behaviour with the needs of the organization and society.

Traditional organizational hierarchy and the matrix approach

No organization is sheltered from the changing tides of economic, social, political, and technological trends. The placid socio-economic certainties of the 20th century are being eroded. Marketplaces are becoming very competitive as technologies, physical assets, and long-standing brands are challenged.

Sainsbury's underwent job losses in the UK during 1999 and Marks and Spencer radically restructured in 2001 in response to falling profits.

Globalisation has become a major influence when a decade ago the birth of the Euro manager was predicted.

The UK has seen the rapid development of information technology, financial services, and travel and tourism whilst manufacturing is now focused on the developing world rather than the developed world.

The workplace reflects these changes including tackling issues relating to corruption, inequality, fairness, and ethics through corporate social responsibility.

During the last 30 years, as trade unionism has declined alongside its power base in the manufacturing sector, so legislation has increased as protection for employees against some of the negative effects of modern working conditions.

Consumer demand has prompted a need for a greater degree of flexibility in the workplace and working patterns have changed as a result. Organizations are becoming increasingly reliant on different types of flexible worker. The nature of the employment contract is changing to facilitate the need for the flexible worker.

The need for leadership to lead the culture changes above is essential. Inappropriate leadership behaviours such as a disconnection between management rhetoric and practice will hinder the positioning of high-performance work practices and lower morale and employee engagement.

Many organizations have flattened management layers with an emphasis towards smaller, more flexible units with fewer levels of management.

Glynn and Holbeche (1998) commented on the changing role of the manager:

No longer are they expected to be the first among equals or the technical expert. The current trend in management thinking is to see the manager as a helper rather than a problem-solving hero. In all sectors managers are being encouraged to take on the role of coach, whether or not they have appropriate skills for this.

Managers are holding together workers of all kinds due to the flexible worker demands. Implicit in this is the nature of the individuals being managed changing. Highly skilled knowledge workers generally are critical of management and so need a different management style from the traditional worker.

Managers then have the task of managing performance, raising standards, and gaining commitment from people over whom they may have no direct-line reporting control and who may have technical skills than are higher than those of the manager.

Team working is more prevalent than in previous decades and cross-functional or cross-boundary working is increasingly common.

Virtual teams who come together for a specific business project are increasingly common.

Glynn and Holbeche (1998) indicate that 'relatively conventional command–and-control management styles in which managers believe that they have the solution to problems remain the order of the day'.

Reflection point 4.10

- How far does your experience confirm or deny the propositions advanced above?
- To what extent does your organization experience inappropriate leadership and management styles?

However, the need for key skills, including influencing, political, and strategic thinking skills, is apparent. Transformational leadership exercised by senior management will be vital to enable organizations to achieve innovative solutions to business problems. Leadership will continue to be important, as will the need to establish an environment in which innovation can flourish.

Management levels in the organizational hierarchy

A determinant of the manager's job is hierarchical level. The management levels are shown in Figure 4.1.

Top mangers are responsible for setting organizational goals and defining strategies for achieving them, monitoring and interpreting the external environment, and making decisions that affect the entire organization. They look to the long term and

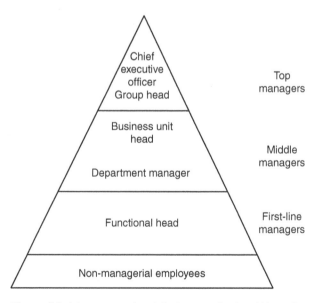

Figure 4.1 Management levels in the organizational hierarchy

must be able to communicate a shared vision of the future for the organization, shape the culture of the organization, and promote an entrepreneurial spirit to manage change.

Middle managers are concerned with the near future and establish good relationships with peers around the organization, encourage teamwork, and resolve conflicts.

They have a key role in facilitating change and responding to rapid shifts in the environment. Their personal power is based on good relationships throughout the organization and being versatile and adaptable with a high degree of emotional intelligence. An increasing skill of middle managers is project management.

First-line managers are directly responsible for the production of goods and services. Their main concern is the application of rules and procedures to achieve efficient production, provide technical assistance, and motivate managerial employees (Daft, 2006).

The matrix approach to management combines aspects of functional structure and divisional structures, and the approach evolved as a way to improve horizontal coordination and information sharing.

Here functional structure is seen as the grouping of positions into departments based on similar skills, expertise, and resource use. People, facilities, and other resources share a common function, being grouped into a single department.

In the divisional structure departments are grouped together based on organizational outputs, as in Figure 4.2.

In the functional structure managers and employees have similar training and expertise, rules and procedures are established, and the rights of managers higher in

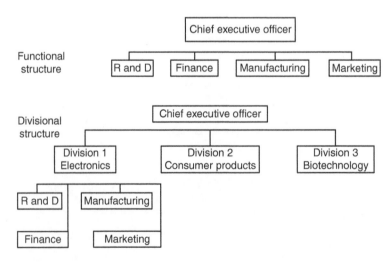

Figure 4.2 Functional and divisional structures in a matrix organization

the hierarchy to make decisions and give orders is accepted. Information flows up and down the vertical hierarchy.

In the divisional structure the chain of command from each function converges at a lower level in the hierarchy. Decision making is pushed lower down in the hierarchy, freeing the chief executive officer and other top managers for strategic planning.

Summary of section

There are predictable trends that are affecting the content and delivery of management development. Trends of globalisation require managers to work across cultural boundaries and be effective with regard to the growing importance of diversity at work and appreciating values and ethics. Softer managerial and people skills are a way of coping with the discontinuity in the workplace where change is the norm.

Summary of chapter

This chapter has traced the history of management development considering the pluralistic leadership and management styles that are emerging.

Management development approaches have been identified and ways of evaluating them.

Softer people skills and more strategic ways of working have been reviewed which meet the challenges of the business environment.

The increasingly turbulent economy has been identified as a driver of the changes in management development and trends for the future will be highlighted in the concluding chapter.

Questions

1 Through further reading identify three definitions of management development.

2 Keep a diary for a week noting all the new things that you learnt at work. How will you apply them to your practice?

3 What are some of the reasons that organizations invest in management development? What assumptions lie behind these reasons about how people learn, and what they should learn?

4 In what ways does your organization currently assist managers to learn from the opportunities created for them through formal and informal management development?

5 Why should an organization develop a formally stated management development policy?

6 Can evaluation be designed to prove the added value of management development?

7 Think of a recent management development programme in your organization. Write a description of the programme, striving to maintain independence as an evaluator.

8 What are the advantages and disadvantages of both formal and informal learning processes?

Discussion questions

1 Consider the implications for management development practice arising from changes in organization contingencies.

2 Imagine you are in charge of devising a management development programme for a large commercial organization. What topics would you include?

3 Should management development always serve the needs of the organization?

4 Management development should be aligned to corporate strategy. Discuss.

Reflection point 4.11

- Assist a fellow student, colleague or line manager to empower others and delegate effectively. Use your own examples which may take a coaching, teaching or any formal/informal approach with which you are familiar.

- Compile a shortlist of the managers and leaders that you respect. Identify the characteristics that they have in common. In what ways could you model your behaviour on them?

- Decide upon a short-term goal or plan that you want to achieve this year.

- Make it compatible with the top priorities in your life. Identify the steps, the reporting and accounting mechanisms, and the benchmarks for success and rewards.

- Identify a part of your work where you feel performance is below your expectations.

- Identify the obstacles that you are encountering to improved performance.

- Then formulate a plan for overcoming these obstacles, which should include getting commitments from others.

- Discuss your plan with the individuals affected by it and agree a range of actions that all parties can accept.

- Implement your plan for a set period of time and then review your achievements. How successful were you in making the changes you identified? Did your performance improve as expected?

Reflection point 4.12

Consider the questions below, which are the types of questions that employers may ask at interview or at a performance appraisal. They require that you provide examples of when you faced particular situations and demonstrated particular skills. This is designed to help raise self-awareness and improve the ability to articulate skills.

- *Achievement orientation*. This maintains and inspires a results-driven approach and focuses on results and critical performance indicators.
  - Recall an important goal that you were set in the past. What strategies did you use to achieve it? What was successful?
  - Think about a difficult task you have been required to undertake. What extra effort did you exert to achieve the goals set and accomplish the task?
  - Can you recall a time when you were effective on prioritizing tasks and so completing a project on time? How did you approach this and what was the outcome? What did you learn?
- *Analysis*. This relates and compares data from different sources, identifying issues, securing relevant information, and identifying relationships.
  - What are your considerations when presenting a solution to a work issue?
  - Think about a work problem you faced in the past. How did you go about finding a resolution?
  - How would you identify appropriate data sources to inform your decisions?
- *Creativity*. Generates and recognizes how best practice and imaginative ideas can be applied to different situations.
  - Think about a problem that you have solved in a unique way. What was the outcome? Were you satisfied with it?
- If you had an idea that you know might be considered unusual by your manager, how would you present it? Think about the most significant or creative presentation which you have had to complete. How did you approach it? What was the result?
- *Influencing*. Influences others by expressing themselves effectively in a group and in one-to-one situations.
  - Describe a time when you were able to convince a sceptical or resistant person to purchase a product or use your skills.
  - Think about a specific instance in which you were able to encourage others to take a chance with a new idea or project. What did you do?
  - Describe a situation in which you were able to positively influence the actions of others in a desired direction. How did you approach it? What happened?
- *Leadership*. Takes responsibility for the directions and actions of a team.
  - When working on a team project, have you ever had an experience where there was strong disagreement among team members? What did you do?
  - How have you recognized and rewarded a team player in the past? What was the situation? What did you do?

Suggestions for further reading

Wren, A.D., and Bedeian, A.G. (2009) *The Evolution of Management Thought*, Chichester: John Wiley.
Traces the origin and development of modern management concepts and enables a logical, coherent picture of the present state of management practice to be appreciated.

Drucker, P.F. (1999) *Management Challenges for the 21st Century*, New York: Harper Business.
A seminal text providing insights into future trends in management development.

Bailey, W., and Spicer, A. (2007) 'When does national identity matter? Convergence and divergence in international business ethics', *Academy of Management Journal*, vol. 50, no. 6, December, pp 1462–80.
Gives insights into the convergence/divergence debate and issues of national identity.

Alas, R. (2006) 'Ethics in countries with different cultural dimensions', *Journal of Business Ethics*, vol. 69, no. 3, December, pp 237–47.
Provides a cross-cultural view of ethical leadership and management development.

The nature of leadership and management

The aims of this chapter are to:

- make explicit the similarities and differences between leadership and management.

- appreciate and review the characteristics of the main theoretical frameworks that have been developed and which underpin these similarities and differences.

- appreciate how the concepts, models, and frameworks relate to current examples within organizations and in different sectors.

- assess the importance of leadership and management to organizational performance.

- appreciate how leadership is present at all levels in modern organizations, either consciously or unconsciously.

- understand how the shared characteristics of leadership and management have evolved and interact.

- understand the characteristics of the main theoretical frameworks of situational and contingency models.

- understand how within a framework of 'continuous improvement' leadership and management principles have been recast.

- understand and appreciate the action-centred leadership approach, task team, and individual model put forward by Adair and its usefulness in leadership development within organizations.

- understand what is meant by transformational leadership.

- appreciate the differences between the concept of transformational and transactional leadership.

- reflect on the appropriate styles of leadership and management to suit the fast-changing business environment.

- apply the concepts found in this chapter in a way that gives the organization the best prospects of understanding and developing leadership and management capability.

Introduction

In more contemporary times there has been a lot of discussion and debate about how organizations' approaches to leadership and management have changed over the years. If we were to draw a timeline in years from say 1900 to 2010 and plot the various approaches that have been derived it would make interesting reading. It would invariably show an earlier point along the timeline when hierarchical organizations prevailed, with strategic development being strongly linked to leadership and with leadership and management being associated with a command-and-control style. Towards the other end of the timeline we would see how leadership in organizations now very often consciously or unconsciously is reflected at a lower level in organizations where situational and contingency styles of leadership are an integral part of the managerial role. The Nando's case study at the introduction section of this book is a good example of how contemporary organizations place a lot of faith in the success of first-level managers in terms of the linkage to business performance. You will find other examples within this chapter that will reinforce this paradigm. This case study also highlighted how the demarcation lines between the characteristics of leadership and management have become blurred in the modern world. Junior first-line managers are expected to demonstrate leadership qualities that were the domain of senior managers in years gone by.

As a student of leadership and management development it is important that one first gains an insight into the paradox surrounding the subject and then goes on to gain a deeper understanding of how things have changed and how they have evolved. The paradox surrounding the subject is that on one hand nothing has changed much since time began in terms of how leaders emerge, have certain traits and take ownership for getting things done and achieving outcomes. On the other hand, the world around us has changed dramatically from the environmental, social, technological, and economic perspectives. Leaders and managers have consequently had to adapt and learn new skills and approaches in order to continue getting the best out of those they lead and achieve the desired outcomes for the organizations and businesses they represent.

With the Reflection point 5.1 in mind and in order to understand more about how the landscape has changed in relation to the nature of leadership and management

Reflection point 5.1

- Consider the work life and times of your grandparents and parents. Reflect on some of the stories they passed down to you about the type of work they did and the working relationships they had with colleagues, supervisors, and managers in the workplace. What is different and what remains the same in comparison to your experiences?

development, we will need to review and evaluate the characteristics of the main theoretical frameworks. This will hopefully provide organizations with the best prospects of achieving a formula for success, in an integrative and 'best fit' approach for their respective organizations—in other words, developing a sustainable level of leadership and management capability that adds value to the organization and is an enabler for overall business performance.

So first, what is the difference between leadership and management? It is a question that has been asked on numerous occasions and also answered in many different ways. Both subjects are well reported and topical. A simple internet search (3 November 2010) for 'leadership' brings back 112 million results and the same search for 'management' brings a result of 717 million hits. In day-to-day discussion the two can often be applied interchangeably, yet in other contexts are quite different.

Consider the following that seem to capture the differences.

Difference between leadership and management?

It appears that the biggest difference between managers and leaders is the way they motivate the people who work [for] or follow them, and this sets the tone for most other aspects of what they do. Many people working in organizations actually fulfil both roles. They have management jobs, but they realize that you cannot buy hearts and minds, especially to follow them down a difficult path, and so they need to act as leaders too.

Bass, 1985

Leadership and management are two distinct but complementary systems. While managers promote stability, leaders press for change. Only organizations that can embrace both sides of that contradiction can thrive in turbulent times.

Kotter, 1995

Box 5.1 sets out the differences and similarities between the nature of leadership and management activities. These two lists are derived from a combination of many sources that agree on the types of activities that are commonly attributed to each heading.

From a closer study and a practical reflection on this list it can be seen that the two lists are difficult to separate: for instance, if a manager is involved in an activity that

Reflection point 5.2

- Consider a manager or supervisor you have worked for, either in a part-time job whilst at school or in the early stages of your work life. Can you think of instances when they were acting in the capacity of a leader and the capacity of a manager?

Box 5.1 Differences and similarities between leadership and management

Management

Management focuses on work. We manage work activities such as money, time, paperwork, materials, equipment. Management's focus is on:

- planning
- organizing,
- controlling
- coordinating
- directing
- resource use
- time management
- logistics and the supply chain
- finance and money management
- budgeting
- strategy
- decision making
- problem solving.

Leadership

Leadership has an essential focus on people and how they can be influenced. Leaders focus on:

- vision
- inspiration
- persuasion
- motivation
- relationships
- teamwork
- listening.

One can add to the list activities such as:

- counselling
- coaching
- teaching
- mentoring.

involves planning, organizing and controlling—tasks that are commonly found in managerial project work. It appears impossible that this could be achieved successfully without applying some of the leadership activities found in the second column, such as team working, listening, and persuasion.

Hopefully from this it can be seen that activities from either list are used and also that in achieving a successful outcome, one would have to switch regularly and almost instinctively from activities on the management list to those found on the leadership list. This goes a small way to demonstrating the difficulty in the academic analysis of the subject.

Reflection point 5.3

- Consider a project you have been involved in at work or in a learning environment (school, college, or in your home life). Reflect on what was involved and the outcomes achieved. Now look down the lists headed leadership and management in Box 5.1 and decide which competencies or skills were deployed by you.
- What was the ratio of management to leadership activities you arrived at?
- Compare these with other people in your group and discuss these.

> ## Box 5.2 Leadership or management: which approach is best?
>
> The old proverb says that leadership is doing the right thing; management is doing things right. The difference between the two is not as clear as the saying would suggest, and both are required for effective corporate growth: leadership risk creates opportunities while management strictness turns them into tangible results.
>
> Leaders seize opportunities; managers avert threats. Both together progress more.
>
> Leaders amplify strengths; managers reduce weaknesses. Both together develop more.
>
> However, 'if your organization is not on a journey, don't bother about leadership—just settle for management' (Adair, 1985).
>
> *Action Centred Leaadership*, John Adair.

One of the major academic contributors in defining what managers do was Mintzberg (1973). In a piece of research that involved following managers around and charting exactly what they did, a list similar to the one on the left of Box 5.1 was constructed.

Such theoretical studies have contributed to give an ideology of management that has shaped processes within organizations. It is safe to say that most of the recruitment, selection, and formal training of managers that has taken place over the last 25 years has been grounded in this ideology, with the foundations being rooted in the work of Maslow (1943), McClelland (1961), Herzberg (1972), motivational theory, organizational productivity, and work study analysis. These theories were formulated in a time when the relationships between workers and managers were typically more autocratic and the demarcation lines between roles more defined. Indeed the psychological distance between managers and workers was far greater in the 1960–80 period than we find today in modern organizations. Later in the chapter we will discuss what brought about a change in approach to leadership and management development between the 1980s and the present day.

Adair (1985) advocated that management and leadership were distinctly different and could be split from each other when analysing the subject.

The point Adair makes is that there are valuable elements of management not necessarily found in leadership, e.g. administration and managing resources. Leadership on the other hand contains elements not necessarily found in management, e.g. inspiring others through the leader's own enthusiasm and commitment.

Differences and similarities: leadership and management; an alternative view

Over the years the philosophical terms 'management' and 'leadership' have, in the organizational context, been used both as synonyms and with clearly differentiated meanings.

There has been a history of debate about whether the use of these terms should be restricted or applied more loosely and interchangeably. This debate generally reflects an awareness of the distinction made by Burns (1978) between 'transactional' leadership (characterized by e.g. emphasis on processes, procedures, resource management, reward, and management by exception) and 'transformational' leadership (characterized by e.g. vision, influence, personal relationships, creativity).

That those two adjectives, transactional and transformational, are in fact used just as well with the noun 'management' as with the noun 'leadership' indicates that there is such a messy overlap between the two in academic practice that, according to Burns (1978), attempts to pontificate about their differences are largely a waste of time in the modern world. Therefore we move forward in this chapter with the acceptance that the terminology of leadership and management is used synonymously in the commerce and business world we find ourselves operating in today.

Theoretical frameworks of leadership

There is a broad range of leadership models and options for those who are interested in researching the subject. Here are just a few that we feel are critical to gain a deeper understanding of the subject. They will be reviewed in outline only, as a fuller review would be outside the scope of this chapter. The Further reading section of this chapter will give references to students who may wish to follow up with more research in this area:

- action-centred leadership
- trait theory of leadership
- situational and contingency theories of leadership
- transformational leadership theory.

Summary of section

We have seen so far that the terms and definitions of leadership and management have a high level of overlap and to some extent the pursuit of further clarity is futile. It may be better therefore to consider them as close and interchangeable.

Action-centred leadership

The action-centred leadership model is a significant theoretical model of leadership that was put forward by John Adair (1973) and is probably his best known work. The model consists of three elements: achieving the task; developing the team; and developing individuals—the last two being mutually dependent as well as separately

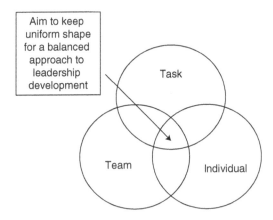

Figure 5.1 Developing managers using action-centred leadership

Adapted from Action Centred Leadership, John Adair.

essential to the overall leadership role. It is often presented in diagram format with three overlapping circles: task, team, and individual.

The focus for the development of managers and leaders in this model is to maintain a balance between the three overlaid circles and pictorially aiming to keep the centre a uniform shape. In practicality managers and leaders tend to focus most effort and time into the task at the detriment of the team's development and performance. Similarly with the individual circle that refers to time and effort with individuals on a one-to-one basis, including one's own time.

Importantly as well, Adair set out these core functions of leadership and says they are vital to the action-centred leadership model:

- planning: seeking information, defining tasks, setting aims, initiating, briefing, task allocation, setting standards

- controlling: maintaining standards, ensuring progress, ongoing decision making

- supporting: individuals' contributions, encouraging, team spirit, reconciling, morale

- informing: clarifying tasks and plans, updating, receiving feedback and interpreting

- evaluating: feasibility of ideas, performance, enabling self-assessment.

The action-centred leadership model therefore does not stand alone; it must be part of an integrated approach to managing and leading, and should also include a strong emphasis on applying these principles through training.

In particular, Adair's most significant contribution to the study of leadership and management was probably that he was the first to demonstrate that leadership is a trainable, transferable skill rather than an exclusively inborn ability. In this he was aligning with the 'nurture' side of the nature–nurture debate.

Adair's action-centred leadership model also advocates that leadership qualities can be exerted at all levels in an organization, not only by the leaders at the top. This makes the model very useful in the design and delivery of leadership and management development programmes in modern organizations, in that the core principles of the theory can be applied to improve all-round competence of managers from board of director level to first-line team manager.

What brought about the post-1980 change?

In many ways the mid 1980s were the change point for leadership and management theory in the corporate environment. The whole philosophy until then was in many ways supply driven—that is, looking for efficiencies but with managers' focus being on motivating the workforce to be better organized and produce higher levels of output. This was a mixture in thinking between the earlier Taylorist approach of the era 1900–50 and the later contingency approach of Fiedler *et al.* that became popular in the period 1960–80. Then came a dramatic paradigm shift that was based on customers, quality, elimination of waste, and competition. The momentum for this new paradigm was based on a philosophy of continuous improvement, and Japanese companies were the driving force behind this.

In the 1980s, manufacturing firms faced pressures that were to wipe out whole industries, let alone single organizations or businesses. In the USA, UK and other parts of the Western world, Japanese companies such as Honda, Fujitsu, Toyota, Cannon, Datsun, to name a few, brought a whole new meaning to the study of management and in turn grew market share and customer loyalty by producing high-quality, value-for-money products. They intensively examined their competitors and customers' needs, to determine what they needed to do differently to reduce cost, eliminate waste, and provide value for customers. To do this, management needs to cultivate 'a process-oriented way of thinking and developing strategies that assure continuous improvement involving people at all levels of the organizational hierarchy' (Imai, 1986). Such a system requires a new organizational culture that considers change, rather than stability being the norm, and involvement and engagement by everyone as a major focus. Under this ethic, complacency with the current 'way of doing things' is banished from the firm.

Modern history shows that the managements of UK manufacturing industries in particular found this difficult to adjust to. Tasks that managers typically did—controlling, organizing, planning, problem solving and decision making—were now tasks under the new paradigm that the workers on the shop floor would become involved in, while managers had to take on a new role that involved a lot of the activities that in the past had been under the heading of leadership: providing a vision, influencing, facilitating change, leading by example, and shaping change.

Providing this action-centred style of leadership required a new set of skills that could be taught and learnt in the way Adair (1985) proposed. They are based on the following strategies:

- identifying key stakeholders and including them in decision making

- gaining awareness of symbolic language and how to use it

- creating a culture that encourages and rewards continuous improvement

- demonstrating constancy of purpose

- managing several levels of change, intervening when and where necessary to make sure strategies work in unison.

With these in place, the facilitative leader/manager will guide their organization to greater productivity and profitability (Beer, 1990).

Senior managers also had a new challenge: to provide leadership by establishing a vision for a better organization. The action-centred approach advocates that this vision must then be communicated to all employees. In this regard, the role of senior management has changed from providing solutions to empowering others within the organization. According to Beer (1990), the most effective senior managers have come to realize their limited power to mandate corporate renewal from the top. So rather than insisting on specific solutions, which was the case prior to the 1980s, managers have come to define their job as one that creates a climate for change. As part of that role, it is their responsibility to reinforce communication and cooperation within and among the groups solving major problems, and to promulgate 'lessons learned', be they good or bad, expected or unexpected, successes or failures—in other words, to provide transformational and facilitative leadership.

In response to the successful approach to leadership and management adopted by Japanese companies, many competing companies in the USA and the UK copied and adopted similar approaches. Very soon the benefits of this approach were applied in new manufacturing industries such as logistics, customer service, financial, and the public sector.

A very important precondition for implementing a continuous improvement system is widespread dissatisfaction with the current way in which the organization functions. In the case of profit-making service organizations, it is relatively straightforward. Dissatisfaction is heightened by red ink or losing market share. However, with respect to non-profit service organizations such as government, education, and utilities, these kinds of competitive pressures are largely absent. Therefore, organizational dissatisfaction must be created from within.

Top management must provide leadership by establishing a vision for a better organization. This vision must then be communicated to all employees. Only by creating a high 'discomfort index' can non-profit service organizations hope to create

> ### Reflection point 5.4
>
> ● Working in small groups, try to pick out where you see similarities between the CIS approach to leadership and management and those of the Taylorist approach, situational leadership, the contingency approach, and the action-centred approach.

a desire, and thereby gain the necessary support, for organizational renewal and change. To sustain continuous improvement initiatives, top management should be aware of the pivotal role it plays in helping to formulate the vision and mission of the organization and setting a strategic direction to be followed.

Interestingly within the continuous improvement systems (CIS) approach described above, there are elements of the Taylorist approach, situational leadership, contingency approach, and action-centred approach.

Trait theory of leadership

The trait theory of leadership goes back a long way and is underpinned by the basic assumption that people are born with inherited traits. This has often been referred to as 'the leadership gene' and follows the school of thought that leadership is inherent within human nature and only a limited amount of capability can be nurtured. People who make good leaders have the right (or sufficient) combination of traits that are associated with leadership.

Early research on leadership was therefore based on the psychological focus of the day, which was of people having inherited characteristics or traits. Attention was thus put on discovering these traits, often by studying successful leaders, but with the underlying assumption that if other people could also be found with these traits, then they too could also become great leaders.

Stogdill (1974) identified the traits and skills shown in Table 5.1 as critical to leaders.

McCall and Lombardo (1983) researched both success and failure, and identified four primary traits by which leaders could succeed or 'derail':

- *emotional stability and composure*: calm, confident and predictable, particularly when under stress

- *admitting error*: owning up to mistakes, rather than putting energy into covering up

- *good interpersonal skills*: able to communicate and persuade others without resort to negative or coercive tactics

- *intellectual breadth*: able to understand a wide range of areas, rather than having a narrow (and narrow-minded) area of expertise.

Table 5.1 Traits and skills associated with leadership

Traits	Skills
• adaptable to situations	• clever (intelligent)
• alert to social environment	• conceptually skilled
• ambitious and achievement-orientated	• creative
• assertive	• diplomatic and tactful
• cooperative	• fluent in speaking
• decisive	• knowledgeable about group task
• dependable	• organized (administrative ability)
• dominant (desire to influence others)	• persuasive
• energetic (high activity level)	• socially skilled
• persistent	
• self-confident	
• tolerant of stress	
• willing to assume responsibility	

There have been many different studies of leadership traits and they agree only in the general qualities needed to be a leader.

There has been a period in time when the trait theory has taken a back seat in the study of leadership. For a long period, inherited traits were sidelined as learned and situational factors were considered to be far more realistic as reasons for people acquiring leadership positions. Only in more recent times, with the development of psychometric assessments and testing techniques, has there been a re-emergence of the trait theories. New methods and measurements were developed after these influential reviews that would ultimately re-establish the trait theory as a viable approach to the study of leadership. For example, improvements in researchers' use of the 'round-robin research design methodology', which is a recent acknowledged social research method, similar to 360° feedback rating systems, where data is collected from each person who interacts with or rates every other person in the group. It allows researchers to see that individuals can and do emerge as leaders across a variety of situations and tasks. Additionally, during the 1980s, statistical advances allowed researchers to conduct meta-analysis, in which they could quantitatively analyse and summarize the findings from a wide array of studies. This allowed trait theorists to create a comprehensive and quantitative picture of previous leadership research rather than rely on the qualitative reviews or alternative subject reviews of the past. Equipped with new methods, leadership researchers revealed the following:

■ Individuals can and do emerge as leaders across a variety of situations and tasks. Significant relationships exist between leadership and such individual traits as:

  □ intelligence

  □ adjustment

Reflection point 5.5

● Pause and think about the value that trait theory can have. What are the pros and cons of using trait theory in learning and management development?

☐ extraversion

☐ conscientiousness

☐ openness to experience

☐ general self-efficacy.

While the trait theory of leadership has certainly regained popularity, its re-emergence has not been accompanied by a corresponding increase in sophisticated conceptual frameworks. Specifically, Zaccaro (2007) noted that trait theories still:

■ focus on a small set of individual attributes, such as Big Five personality traits, to the neglect of cognitive abilities, motives, values, social skills, expertise, and problem-solving skills

■ fail to consider patterns or integrations of multiple attributes

■ do not distinguish between those leader attributes that are generally not malleable over time and those that are shaped by, and bound to, situational influences

■ do not consider how stable leader attributes account for the behavioural diversity necessary for effective leadership.

Regardless of these perceived shortcomings, trait theory has re-emerged as a useful framework for identifying and developing leaders in a variety of organizational settings.

Situational and contingency (behavioural and style) theory of leadership

The early management theorists followed the Taylorist school of thought that assumed there was one best style of leadership: that of scientific management. In this theory of management, analyses and syntheses of workflows are essential, with the objective of improving labour productivity and increased output.

Taylorism played a critically important part in the evolution of the business world in the early part of the 20th century. To a large extent the principles of Taylor's work drove industrialization and mass production in the USA and then later in the UK. The classic example is the Ford factory and the production of the Model T Ford motor car—the one where the customer could have any colour so long as it was black. Every aspect of the mass production process, specifically the human involvement factors, was analysed for efficiency gains, and the result was that costs were kept to a minimum in order that the sales price was within the reach of more customers. In his work entitled *The Principles of Scientific Management* (1911), Taylor began trying to discover a way for workers to increase their efficiency. He believed that decisions based upon tradition and 'rules of thumb' should be replaced by precise procedures developed after careful study of an individual at work. The paradigm of his work was contingent on a high level of managerial control over employee work practices and a deskilling of the work wherever possible.

Eventually there were criticisms of the Taylorist approach and the main ones were that the application of scientific management sometimes fails to account for two inherent difficulties that are behaviourally based:

- Individuals are different from each other: the most efficient way of working for one person may be inefficient for another.
- The economic interests of workers and management are rarely identical, so that both the measurement processes and the retraining required by Taylor's methods are frequently resented and sometimes sabotaged by the workforce.

Around 50 years later these flaws were addressed in a contingency approach. This was Fiedler's contingency model, which advocates that the leader's effectiveness is based on 'situational contingency', which is a result of interaction of two factors: 'leadership style' and 'situational favourableness'.

In the late 1950s and early 1960s, industrial and business psychologists such as Fiedler (1967) started to study the leadership and behaviour styles of managers. Before Fiedler's study, industrial psychologists focused on the personal traits of successful leaders on one hand and on the other believed in an ideal science of organization as advocated by Taylor (1911). They felt there was a best way to run a company or group which produced the best decisions and most effective business practices. The importance of Fiedler's contingency theory is that it has influenced almost all modern management theories by denying the existence of a singular ideal organizational approach.

The basis of Fiedler's contingency model involved assessing a potential leader with a scale of work style ranging from task oriented at one end to relationship oriented at the other. Then, contingent on factors such as stress level in the organization, type of work, flexibility of the group to change, and use of technology, a customized coordination of resources, people, tasks, and the correct style of management could be implemented.

Leadership portrayed as a wide spectrum of possible effective styles was a groundbreaking idea at the time. It is still central in a lot of modern management theories which reject rigid assumptions about ideal management.

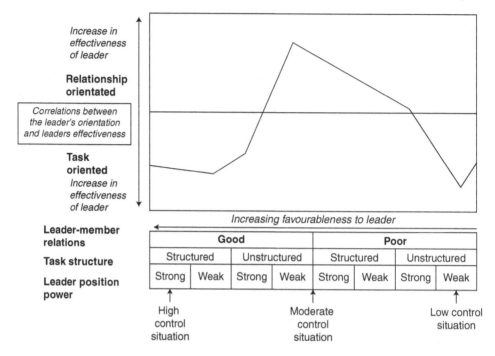

Figure 5.2 Contingency model

Note: Attention is drawn to the graph and the peak point on the traced line where high level of favourableness to the leader is present, taking into account all the variables in this model that are shown down the left-hand side.

Theory of Leadership Effectiveness, F. E. Fiedler.

The key to leadership effectiveness is viewed by most variants of contingency theory as choosing the correct style of leader. This style is dependent on the interaction of internal and external factors with the organization. For example, the ability to lead is dependent upon the perception of subordinates of and by the leader, the leader's relationship with them, and the degree of consensus on the scope of a given task.

Situational contingency theory agreed with contingency theories on the basic idea of there being no single correct solution to organization. This and other similarities led to its main ideology merging into mainstream contingency and situational theories, such as those of Vroom and Yetton (1973), who followed the principle that group effectiveness requires a match between a leader's style and situational demands.

Fiedler's theory further adds that most situations will have three hierarchical aspects that will structure the leader's role:

■ the confidence and loyalty a group feels towards the leader

■ the ambiguity or clarity of the structure of the group's task

- the inherent authority or power of the leader, which plays an important role in group performance.

Transformational leadership theory

Transformational leadership is a type of leadership style that leads to positive changes in those who follow. It is said that transformational leaders are generally energetic, enthusiastic, and passionate. Not only are these leaders concerned and involved in the process; they are also focused on helping every member of the group succeed as well. This type of leader is exemplified by many great military, political, and industrial leaders of the past—people like, Ghandi, Churchill, Kennedy, Mandela, and so on.

The concept of transformational leadership was initially introduced by leadership expert and presidential biographer James Macgregor Burns. According to Burns (1978), transformational leadership can be seen when 'leaders and followers make each other advance to a higher level of morale and motivation'. Through the strength of their vision and personality, transformational leaders are able to inspire followers to change expectations, perceptions, and motivations to work towards common goals.

The term transformational leadership is now used in organizational psychology. Burns related to the difficulty in differentiation between leadership and management and claimed that the differences are in characteristics and behaviours. He established two concepts: 'transformational leadership' and 'transactional leadership'. According to Burns, the transformational approach creates significant change in the life of people and organizations. It redesigns perceptions and values, changes expectations and aspirations of employees. Unlike the transactional approach, it is not based on a 'give and take' relationship, but on the leader's personality, traits, and ability to make a change through vision and goals.

Later, Bass (1980) expanded upon Burns's original ideas to develop what is today referred to as Bass's transformational leadership theory. According to Bass, transformational leadership can be defined based on the impact that it has on followers. Transformational leaders, Bass suggested, garner trust, respect, and admiration from their followers.

The components of transformational leadership

Bass also suggested that there were four different components of transformational leadership, which can be referred to as 4i's:

- *Intellectual stimulation.* Transformational leaders not only challenge the status quo; they also encourage creativity among followers. The leader encourages followers to explore new ways of doing things and new opportunities to learn.

- *Individualized consideration.* Transformational leadership also involves offering support and encouragement to individual followers. In order to foster supportive relationships, transformational leaders keep lines of communication open so that followers feel free to share ideas and so that leaders can offer direct recognition of each follower's unique contributions.

- *Inspirational motivation.* Transformational leaders have a clear vision that they are able to articulate to followers. These leaders are also able to help followers experience the same passion and motivation to fulfil these goals.

- *Idealized influence.* The transformational leader serves as a role model for followers. Because followers trust and respect the leader, they emulate the leader and internalize the leader's ideals.

Benefits of transformational leadership

There is no doubt that being able to inspire people, stimulate them to think differently, and pay attention to their needs are commendable ways for a leader to behave. If leaders have good content and integrity and can present a case for change with enough enthusiasm to inspire people, they are more likely to win them over than if they had a communication style that lacks energy and passion. Being inspirational is most useful in situations where there is no evidence or the facts are unclear. Which in another way can be a weakness in the theory. It is up to the reader or practitioner to ultimately decide which side of the debate they support. However in this chapter and the case studies seen throughout the book, it does seem that the amount of evidence and examples support the stance that people will indeed take a 'leap of faith' if they feel inspired, motivated, and respect the leader. Which is a very powerful

Reflection point 5.7

- Look back at the Nando's case study in Chapter 1 and try to identify the transformational leadership characteristics of Robby Enthoven, the founder of the business organization. Can you identify some of the 4i's being demonstrated?

advantage if this can be truly harnessed within an organization. The vision of the Nando's founder in the opening case study is a good example of this.

Limitations of transformational leadership

There is a great deal of perfectly effective leadership that is not transformational. It is possible to lead by citing hard facts in a quiet, soft, or even assertive manner. Also, some might say that too much emphasis is placed on style over substance. In light of the 2009 corporate and political scandals, substance has become extremely important, including integrity, ethics, or character and content. There appears to be a growing demand for 'evidence-based' decision making where, to show leadership, managers and leaders need to cite hard evidence. Whether they can present a business case in an inspiring manner is not as important as having solid facts to back up the argument. Leaders can have great sales skills to get people on board but if they do so for unethical purposes, this style of leadership can be dangerous. Cult leaders, for example, are often transformational. Secondly, without good content, leaders have nothing worth saying so it doesn't matter how powerfully they say it.

Participative leadership means involving employees in making decisions. To be a participative leader, it isn't necessary to be an inspirational speaker. Transformational leaders make their mark primarily by promoting a vision in an inspiring manner. Generally we admire such leaders, but they aren't necessarily skilled at employee engagement. In essence they are like skilled sales people or promoters, so they want to sell you their vision. In today's knowledge-intensive world, the participative leadership style is likely to be more engaging and motivating for knowledge workers.

Another issue is the fact that transformational leadership has, for some people, become the very meaning of leadership while its transactional counterpart is identified with management. Some would say this is unfortunate. The beauty of a purely functional way of defining leadership and management (leadership promotes new directions; management executes them) is that you can leave the style question completely open.

So what are the implications for managers? Yukl (1994) draws some tips for transformational leadership:

■ Develop a challenging and attractive vision, together with the employees.

■ Tie the vision to a strategy for its achievement.

Reflection point 5.8

● Consider the transformational leadership model. Can you identify a leader who in your eyes portrays the attributes associated with this model of leadership?

- Develop the vision, specify and translate it to actions.
- Express confidence, decisiveness, and optimism about the vision and its implementation.
- Realize the vision through small planned steps and small successes in the path to its full implementation.

Summary of section

In this section we have seen a broad range of different approaches to leadership and management. We have explored some of the history of the research carried out and one of the purposes of this is to demonstrate how important the study of behavioural science has been in building our understanding of leadership and management over the last century.

Combining theories and concepts

To a great extent the study of leadership and management is an iterative process. That is, it has improved over time, with each major contribution from the research and theorists building up a firmer and wider understanding of the subject.

There appears to be no single correct way to define or go about developing leaders and managers in organizations. But there are firm commonalities when you compare what different organizations are saying about leadership in their organizations. In this respect the situation and contingency theory has much to offer in identifying that different situations require different types and styles of managers and leaders. Yet thinking back in the chapter to the CIS approach and the fact that senior managers or leaders can no longer rely on being able to provide solutions to all problems, then the transformational leadership theory has an important role to play. Moreover, in the process-orientated way that CIS advocates and which has found its way into many modern organizations, traces of Taylor's scientific approach can be identified.

Therefore in many ways the concepts and theories that have been researched and developed over time, particularly one hopes those reported on in this chapter, all have a contribution to make in gaining a deeper understanding of the nature of managerial work and the role and work of a leader. In this respect, combining concepts and theories is acceptable and a good way for organizations to derive their own unique approach to identifying and developing managerial and leadership competency in their organizations.

Applying leadership and management frameworks

In this section we try to aid the reader's appreciation as to how the frameworks relate to current examples within organizations and in different sectors, namely the public, private, and non-profit/voluntary sectors.

Box 5.3 A military view of leadership

Leadership is visionary; it is the projection of personality and character to inspire people to achieve the desired outcome. There is no prescription of leadership and no prescribed style of leader. Leadership is a combination of example, persuasion, and compulsion dependent on the situation. It should aim to transform and be underpinned by individual skills and an enabling philosophy. The successful leader is an individual who understands themselves, the organization, the environment in which they operate, and the people that they are privileged to lead.

The leader:

- persuades by giving direction and providing a vision that is communicated to followers
- sets an example by acting as a role model to influence others by actions, not just words
- demonstrates integrity
- inspires others by motivating, empowering, and encouraging them
- grows the organization by working for progress and development
- demonstrates leadership in times of turbulence.

Extract from the UK MoD *Leadership Handbook* 2010

Traditionally the military view of leadership has been associated with trait theory. However, in more modern times the influence of situational and contingency theories has come into play. Consider Box 5.3 and Reflection point 5.9.

Applying the leadership and managerial frameworks we've reviewed in this chapter to the public sector organizations and contrasting this with the private sector is a most interesting topic.

It appears from the weight of evidence and supported by a study completed by Dawson and Winstanley (1995) that it is the external component of leadership which differentiates the public sector manager from their private sector counterpart. There has been criticism from commentators in the recent past that the focus for leaders within the public sector has been that of looking inwards within the organization; that is, leading teams of managers who have responsibility for budgets, service efficiency, and managing the political issues that arise from conflicts and the overlap of strategies between government and other internal departments. Where the service includes the responsibility for managing professionals such as in the health services, a large percentage of leadership time is taken up by managing the issues related to this (Goodwin, 1998).

Reflection point 5.9

- Consider the above extract and try to identify where you think the main concepts and theories of leadership can be identified: trait, situational, contingency, transformational.

> ### Reflection point 5.10
>
> - Stop and think about why some of the models of leadership and management develop-
>   ment seen so far work to different levels of effect in public sector and private enterprises
>   and vice versa.

Given that external stakeholders in the form of public users, politicians, financial institutions, and the media, to name only a few, have a massive influence in how successful a public sector organization is, several commentators have identified how increasingly important it is to redefine public sector leadership and management capability.

A paradigm shift is required according to Goodwin (1998) if the leadership of health services in the future is to move away from operating within institutions and defined organizational boundaries, to leading across and between organizations and professional groups (who are in the main autonomous groups) in order to improve health and health services. This places an increasing importance too on the impact of developing the external leadership role of health service managers, particularly in management training schemes and in personal and organizational development. Which all require considerable thought and should not be underestimated.

In support of the above, Ring and Perry (1985) concluded in their review of strategic management by private and public sector managers that the key constraints on the behaviour and choices of the latter are around the ambiguity of policy directives, the relative openness of decision making, the greater number of influencing interest groups, the artificiality of time constraints, and the relative instability of policy coalitions. These views are further supported by a survey of public sector middle managers (Dopson and Stewart, 1989) which suggests the following reasons, among others, for differences in their attitude to change from private sector managers:

- a tendency in the public sector to criticize managerial mistakes
- a feeling of having an excessive number of constraints
- changes based on private sector practice seen as politically imposed
- a feeling of commercially orientated changes being at odds with public service values
- the devaluing of professional practice by having to become involved in administration and management
- the frequency of change initiatives.

An important conclusion from the study is that public sector managers tend to dwell on a job's constraints rather than recognizing its freedoms: something that leaders in the private sector treat as a norm and as essential in being an effective leader.

Reflection point 5.11

1. Pause and consider how leadership and management competency frameworks are deployed in your organization or one you are familiar with. Do they add competitive advantage and value? Or are they an effective HR tool for categorizing managers for appraisal and reward purposes?

Leadership and management competency frameworks

It would have been a temptation to write a whole chapter on the use of competency frameworks for leadership and management development. Apart from that being outside the terms and scope of this particular book, there are good reasons why this temptation has been avoided. First the author believes that the benefit and importance of competency frameworks in contemporary organizations are overstated and overvalued. Miller *et al.* (2001) identify two primary reasons why organizations use competencies: to try to measure performance of employees via appraisal, training, and other personnel practices; and as a means of articulating corporate values and objectives. In essence there is strong evidence that they can be used for purposes they are not intended for. Specifying and measuring against a set of competencies is a nice, neat, and systematic process which can clearly be an appealing approach for organizations. However, as Mintzberg (2004) points out, 'simply acquiring certain competencies does not make leaders and managers competent'. It is argued therefore that the primary focus for leadership and management development should be more about the application of a vision, attaining positive outcomes, inspiring others, and achieving organizational goals, rather than attaining a prescribed set of competencies.

Mini case study 5.1: Cellnet Mobile

This case study organization had embarked on its quality journey in the early part of 2008 under the direction of a new top management team.

Quality plans were developed early. Systems were reviewed and re-engineered. Natural work teams were formed throughout the organization. Performance measures were being put in place across the organization and at all levels to ensure alignment to corporate objectives. A new 360° performance review process had been implemented. An organizational downsizing had cut an average of three layers of management from each division of the organization and a 6 per cent general downsizing had reduced its workforce to about 8,000 employees.

By the early part of 2010, however, some serious organizational problems were beginning to emerge. Findings from the employee satisfaction survey showed that one of the most serious—and which was also shown to be the cause of many other organization problems—was widespread confusion about the roles and responsibility of the managers. Not only was the general workforce confused about the leadership responsibilities of the managers, but also the managers throughout the organization were uncertain as to their leadership role in the new order. In response to this situation, top management decided to assemble a cross-functional team. This team was chartered to assess the leadership role of organizational managers, and to identify the leadership development needs of their managers. The procedures used, whilst not 100 per cent perfect, provide other organizations with a model process for determining managerial needs:

- Step 1: Define what being a leader in this organization means.
- Step 2: Identify tailored leadership skills, knowledge and abilities.
- Step 3: Conduct management interviews for ownership.
- Step 4: Survey sample employees and managers (using behavioural competence definitions from Step 2 on where we are now).
- Step 5: Analyse survey results and findings.
- Step 6: Make specific recommendations for leadership development.
- Step 7: Design and implement a leadership programme for managers based on the outcomes that identified five specific areas of weakness: communication skills (first- and second-line managers); listening skills (first- and second-line managers); how to motivate others (first- and second-line managers); how to support others (first- and second-line managers); how to share information (second-line managers). In addition to these five specific areas:
- Step 8: Performance improvement. The following three leadership-related characteristics were also identified as weak amongst second-line managers; trusting of others; risk taking; inspiring others. There was no specific development programme proposed as a solution, but the HR director was given the task of improving this weakness within 12 months by working with fellow board directors.

Questions

1 In terms of importance to overall success of this business where do you think priority to invest in learning and management development should be placed: first-line manager, middle management, or senior management? Why do you think this?

2 What are the strengths of the approach taken?

3 Can you identify any flaws in this approach?

4 Try to split out and identify the management competencies from the leadership competencies which are trying to be developed.

Peter Emsell

This critical evaluation should be considered by students in reaching their own views on a competencies approach.

Current view of leadership and management

In some ways nothing has changed that much with respect to leadership and management since time began, insomuch as the impact of excellent leadership and

Reflection point 5.12

- Consider what differences one would expect to see between senior managers in leadership roles who operate in the private sector and public sector.
- Can these skills be learned, as advocated by Adair?
- Do you think that trait theory of leadership has a contribution to make in the selection and development of public sector leaders?

management makes a significant contribution to the successes of groups of people or organizations. History is littered with classical examples of this and no doubt this will continue into the future. In fact, it is arguable that the difference in impact that leaders can have in current and future times is and will become increasingly more important. This is as a result of the growth of global economies, technology, social changes, climate changes, numerous stakeholder interests, and diminishing global resources. All this will place increasing demands and have greater influence on the behaviour and performance of leaders and managers who seek to gain competitive advantage for those organizations they represent. Therefore it follows that developing the leaders of the future is an extremely high priority on any organization's agenda.

The challenge for current leaderships and practitioners is to use what past research and theory have taught us, and decipher this to apply what is a 'best fit' solution into a format that will be suitable for the challenges of the future. After all, a lot of the models of leadership and management originating from the past are rooted in human psychology and social structures that are related to groups' and individuals' interactions. It is the world around us that is changing and how we respond to that.

Mini case study 5.2: Global Servico, an Indian-based IT support company

At Global Servico we built our business model working with the global 2000 companies by servicing them out of their local market and India until a few years ago. We realized the need for expanding into emerging markets for couple of reasons: first, our global clients will need strong IT capability in these markets to support their expansion; and second, we saw strong companies from these markets emerge as global leaders. So we invested in building a global capability through a strong delivery presence in big emerging markets like China, Mexico, Brazil, and Eastern Europe.

Has this changed? I have spent significant time listening to customers across the globe during the last 18 months. Clearly, customers everywhere are looking for innovation both in operationally becoming more efficient and in the way they deliver their products and services. But I see a particularly strong appetite going forward for new technologies and business models in the emerging markets that we specialize in.

For instance, I've seen the new cloud-based computing models for applications and processes gaining currency in emerging markets. Rural cooperative banks and small and medium businesses in India are actually far ahead of their Western counterparts in adopting these models. In fact, companies from emerging markets, buoyed by strong domestic revenues and revival in growth, have been making adjustments to their global strategies and fine-tuning their investments in order to be part of the recovery process in the West and build on their global expansion plans.

Internally, the crisis and the resulting slowdown forced us to take a deep look at all our processes and bring in efficiencies. It has helped to create a firm-wide awareness on the need for continually optimizing our internal processes. Fortunately for us, our business model stays very relevant. While we are building new capabilities and constructing new business models based on what we hear from customers, we are continuing to expand our presence both in mature as well as emerging markets.

Vivek Patel is the CEO of Global Servico

Question

1 What best practices derived from the concepts and theories of leadership and management found in this chapter can be applied to this case of global growth and gaining competitive advantage?

Fictional case derived by Peter Emsell.

Summary of chapter

In this chapter we have looked at the definitions of the nature of work that is related to 'leadership' and 'management'. We have found that whilst there are differences there are also similarities that are difficult to separate out. In conclusion it is accepted that the two nouns 'leadership' and 'management' have come to be used synonymously with each other in the world of business and commerce, in all sectors, private, public, non-profit/voluntary, and in many respects also in a modern military setting.

We have had the opportunity in this chapter to look at some major concepts and theories of leadership and management that the authors feel are appropriate in order for the reader to gain a firm understanding of the subject. We have identified and explained several approaches: Taylorist, trait theory, situation and contingency models, action-centred leadership, and transformational and transactional leadership models. This mixture of concepts, theories, and models hopefully provides a good basis for understanding, and no apology is made for the time-aged references. They are solid and key to the principle of understanding. It was identified that the study of leadership and management and the nature of work that managers do is an iterative paradigm that is complemented by further research and application. One observation the reader may have noticed is that it is rare in any research into leadership and management to see contradiction in theories and concepts. Rather, it is more that the major research builds and enhances our understanding or identifies different insights. All of which qualifies the fact that leadership and management are more an art form

Reflection point 5.13

- Stop and think about what the future holds for leadership and management development. What will be the challenges? What will be the key skills and attributes required of managers in the future? How do they differ from the past?

than an exact science. Moreover, we can learn a lot about human psychology and social structures of the past and present that will serve organizations well in the future if adjusted to fit the challenges that the future will bring.

In terms of what the future holds, the changing world and the competition for wealth creation not only in the UK but across global markets leads one to believe that leadership and management development has a critical value and important part to play. All the theories and concepts seen in this chapter have at some point, particularly at their inception point and in the period following this, made a significant impact and percolated their way through into corporate development programmes, business school teachings, and reference books. It is likely that new research and studies will continue and best practices will come to the fore as organizations continue in the quest for greater competitive advantage, growth, and efficiencies in business performance.

It is also highly likely that many of the old theories of leadership and management will be repackaged into development initiatives that meet modern-day organizations and the challenges they face. After all, as we have seen in this chapter, many are based on human behavioural theory and social psychology. What will change, and which offers an exciting prospect, is the way development programmes are delivered and structured. Learning media and systems will change—podcasts, iPhone applications, video streaming, and virtual learning environments are with us now and will become more and more sophisticated in the future. Combined, they will have a key part to play in the development of leaders and managers of the future.

Questions

1 Make a list of five activities related to work that you feel would fit under the heading of managerial work and five that would fit under a heading of leadership work.

2 Compare the very early work of Taylor's scientific management to that of the concept of CIS (continuous improvement systems). What are the similarities and what are the differences?

3 Why was Fiedler's work on situational and contingency leadership considered so important at the time?

4 Trait theory has been around for a long time; why do you think it regained popularity in the 1970s and 1980s?

5 The concept of transformational and transactional leadership and management was made famous by which researcher/writer?

Discussion questions

1 There are benefits and limitations of the transformational and transactional theory. What are they?

2 Adair's model of action-centred leadership is explained by the use of a simple diagram. Can you draw, label the diagram, and describe its relevance?

3 What do you think are the major differences for leadership development in the public sector from those in the private sector?

Suggestions for further reading

Classical leadership: www.infed.org/leadership/traditional_leadership.htm
This website helps to bring a lot of the theories together. Michele Erina Doyle and Mark K. Smith explore some of the classical models of leadership. In particular they look at earlier approaches to studying the area via the notions of traits and behaviours, and at what has become known as contingency theory. From there they turn to more recent transformational theories and some issues of practice.

Finkelstein, S., Hambrick, D., and Cannella, A. (2008) *Strategic Leadership: Theory and Research on Executives, Top Management Teams, and Boards*, USA: OUP.
This book integrates and assesses the vast and rapidly growing literature on strategic leadership, which is the study of top executives and their effects on organizations. The basic premise is that in order to understand why organizations do the things they do, or perform the way they do, we need to deeply comprehend the people at the top: their experiences, abilities, values, social connections, aspirations, and other human features. The actions—or inactions—of a relatively small number of key people at the apex of an organization can dramatically affect organizational outcomes.

PART : 2

Understanding learning of leaders and managers

CHAPTER

6

How does learning occur in leadership and management development?

The aims of this chapter are to:

- define and examine the concept of learning.

- explore the distinction between formal and informal learning in management development.

- assess the contribution and complexities of informal and personal learning.

- discuss the reflexive nature of management development.

Introduction

This chapter aims to engage in the debates about the nature of learning—both in general and as applied to leadership and management development—and to discuss the key models of learning which are used in management development. It aims to distinguish formal and informal learning, examining their applicability, and in particular to examine the nature and importance of reflection in management development.

Reflection point 6.1: What is learning?

Before beginning the chapter take a few minutes to review each of the brief situations described below and then answer the questions that follow:

- Baby smiles whenever he sees his mother's face.
- Child who set off on a bicycle wobbles, turns round to check parent still supporting, gets faster and balances until finally realizes parent no longer holding her.
- A salesperson has to borrow a car for a day because his is off the road for maintenance. This borrowed car has many controls on the opposite side of the steering column from his own so he crunches the gears, turns on windscreen wipers when turning left or right. However, after a day driving the car he becomes familiar with it and decides he likes it. On returning to his normal car he has forgotten where the controls are and takes a day to gain confidence driving it again.
- Student sits with notes from lectures, reading and rereading until the small hours of the day of an exam—he passes.
- Working in a restaurant, a waiter rushes because the dining room is very busy, but slips and breaks a very expensive bottle of wine and glasses. He is shouted at in front of kitchen staff and warned about concentrating at work.
- A manager is promoted and attends the organization's Effective Middle Management course for two weeks. When she returns to work her previous colleagues think that she has changed. They find her distant, exacting and very autocratic. They are concerned that something is wrong and ask her about the course. She says it was the 'best thing ever' and is now sure that she can become the next operations director.

You may never have considered how people—children, adults, students, workers—learn. However, review the list of situations above and identify what learning may have occurred. You may wish to discuss your answers with a colleague.

Now summarize your thoughts in answering the questions below:

- What was similar about learning in the above situations?
- Does it occur in the same way for each situation?
- Do we all learn in the same way?
- Think of other situations—what have you learned from them and how did you learn?

This chapter reviews a wide range of ideas that contribute towards our ideas about learning.

The concept of learning

In order to further consider different approaches to management development in different settings, and to think about which ones might be most effective, there is a need first to discuss how adults (and specifically managers) learn. This is not straightforward, for a number of reasons. First, there are the difficulties of establishing what we mean when we talk about learning, since—as we shall see—it is quite a slippery concept. Second, because of the variety of settings in which we can imagine managers operating—at different organizational levels, in differing business sectors, in a range of organizational and national cultures, and so on. They will therefore be engaged in a variety of managerial tasks and processes and will be undertaking these in different ways. Third, because the managers as individuals will display an almost infinite variety of characteristics, some of which will be further explored in the next chapter: for example, personality type, management style, motivations, age, gender, and ethnicity. Finally, the nature of the learning may also be extremely variable: managers may be deliberately setting out to learn a new skill, they may be acquiring new knowledge and information, or they may be thinking about what went wrong with this morning's meeting.

Because learning in general is so complex and multifaceted, it is resistant to one or just a few explanations. Even attempting to define learning is not straightforward. There are many theories connected in one way or another to the learning process, and numerous attempts have been made to categorize the various theoretical approaches. In the context of learning within an organizational setting, we consider a number of these typologies below. First, however, we will turn our attention to definitions of learning.

Definitions of learning

Learning has been the subject of debate and study over many years and yet there is no one agreed definition. Most researchers who study learning have a preferred meaning, related to their area of study. Consideration of definitions of learning will also lead us to think about related terms of relevance in this discussion, such as training, development, and education.

A common definition used in training and development, and one that has survived for a number of years and is used by practitioners, is that of Bass and Vaughan (1966):

Learning is a relatively permanent change in behaviour as the result of practice or experience.

This definition carries a number of assumptions in it:

■ That learning is an active process on the part of the learner (*practice*) or it involves the learner in accessing previous *experience* to assess new information presented, through observing and understanding.

- That in order to be considered as learning, some long-term change in action is implied on the part of the learner (*permanent change in behaviour*).

- Therefore it involves something more than momentary mimicry, copying, or repetition. It suggests some change in the learner's understanding or *perceptual map*.

It does depend how subtly we choose to interpret behaviour, since we might learn a new piece of knowledge or a new skill but choose not to use it—arguably our behaviour will be subtly different, though, as we are changed by the acquisition of the new skill or knowledge.

Bass and Vaughan's definition works satisfactorily in a practical training example but it is more problematic in the case of management or leadership development, as can be seen from the examples in Mini case study 6.1.

Mini case study 6.1: How is a 'change in behaviour' confirmed?

Example 1: Skills and knowledge in practical work

A trainee manager learns to use a procedure to record absence of employees. The trainee is provided with instructions, observes a demonstration and then practises, following instructions as necessary. Finally, after a number of opportunities to practise, the trainee will reach the criterion set by the trainer, for example they are able to record different absences on an IT system on five occasions without reference to the instructions with 100 per cent accuracy. Having reached the criterion, they would probably be considered to have learned how to use this process.

In this example action and practice are required for the trainee to learn and if the trainer wants to confirm learning has taken place it is relatively easy to see the required change in behaviour or to check speed or assess accuracy of usage of the system. It is also possible to go into work and to check how the trainee manager is using the system some time later.

Example 2: Leadership and management styles

However, using the above definition, consider the learning of a manager who attends a workshop on leadership and management styles. On returning to work, there is little obvious change in behaviour. We can assume that the manager is equipped with a greater knowledge and awareness of a range of management styles, and perhaps the skills to apply them—but according to Bass and Vaughan learning requires a relatively permanent change in behaviour.

In this more complex example, the change in behaviour may be something that is difficult to detect—much of the range of management styles now available to our manager may not be appropriate to the context, any styles new to the manager may not need to be displayed for a period of time, and so on. Further, the outcome for the manager may be a heightened awareness of styles that they already possessed, and so changes in behaviour may not be visible to the observer.

Questions

1 What do you consider might count as a 'relatively permanent change in behaviour' in an example relating to your recent work?

2 Does it matter if the behaviour change isn't apparent—can we still say learning has occurred?

Anderson (1995) regards learning as:

The process by which relatively permanent change occurs in behavioural potential, as a result of experience.

This is a similar view to that of Bass and Vaughan, but significantly adjusts the definition in three ways that seem to address some of the difficulties identified in the former. First, by considering the notion of learning as a *process* rather than the change itself, Anderson suggests something more dynamic and complex than a straightforward move from practice or experience to change. Second, the change is considered to occur in behavioural *potential* rather than behaviour itself, which takes account of the situations where the learner is unable to, or chooses not to, alter their behaviour. Third, the change occurs as a result of *experience* that is unqualified and might therefore be defined more widely than in Bass and Vaughan's definition.

Marton and Ramsden (1988) also emphasize change, but focus not on behaviour so much as on the frames of reference through which people see and interpret the world. They offer the following definition:

A qualitative change in a person's way of seeing, experiencing, understanding, conceptualizing something in the real world.

This again suggests that observable behaviour doesn't need to change in order for us to consider that learning has taken place; rather that the change may remain within the individual and apparently hidden from view—although one assumes that behaviour *may* change as a result and certainly following a number of such changes in understanding.

To further widen our consideration of learning it is necessary to identify a more complex definition to encompass wider circumstances of learning, such as that of learning as part of an ongoing process of change in both individuals and organizations:

Learning is a dynamic process that manifests itself in the continuously changing nature of individuals and organizations exemplified by innovation, collaboration, culture shifts and personal development.

Bennet and Bennet, 2008, p 37

Learning can then be applied to individuals and organizations and seen as a complex process of ongoing change, having many influencing factors, individual, organizational, and contextual. Therefore, as a useful starting point, we will discuss learning and its links with related commonly used terms.

There are three related terms, commonly used in association with management development in organizations, each having a role in the development of managers—but seen to contribute in different ways and with different interpretations of learning. These are training, development, and education:

- Training is a term used, for example, in a course during which a trainee manager learns to achieve prescribed, predetermined specific outcomes as in Example 1 in Mini case study 6.1, and can be assessed against them. Trainers use a definition of learning linked closely to the first definition discussed (Bass and Vaughan), as a way to achieve required behaviours in people. There are numerous theories of learning that inform the many ways in which formal training is delivered, as will be discussed below. Training carries implications of having a trainer to deliver content, and of being related to a specific skill or topic area.

- Development is usually used to describe personal or management situations in which the outcomes are more individual and less formally prescribed. Development can also be used to mean maturation of an individual. It is often associated with specified stages through which each person passes on a journey toward adulthood and in which learning occurs. Lee (1994) talks of 'maturation' in describing an approach to management development which involves using a range of activities to aid the individual passage of managers to full competence, through formal and informal means. This is a more holistic concept and perhaps implies both a longer time frame and a greater range of methods, topics, and skills.

- Education can be seen cynically as helping students to learn sufficient to pass an assessment of specific outcomes, and is often associated with achievement of a qualification. Alternatively, it may be viewed as a way of engaging individuals in learning about their world, using as broad a range of concepts and ideas as possible whilst learning about themselves and 'learning to learn', to encourage ongoing development. Academic notions of learning usually focus on using others' knowledge to increase your own through cognitive processes, with assessments of knowledge gained. This has led to debates about the place of higher education in management development (Mintzberg, 2005) and the relationship of theory and practice (Reynolds, 1997). However, higher and further education are increasingly becoming involved in management development and even training, so that the boundaries are blurred and approaches are developed for learning.

Development of leaders and managers may use all three terms in various ways, depending on the situation. For example:

■ Management training may be used for occasions when managers are provided with knowledge and possibly skills related to a new procedure at work, such as in recruitment and selection. It might be the first time a manager is trained in certain techniques or due to changes required in how procedures are used.

■ Management education is used by organizations as a collective term to describe managers' learning linked to higher or further education institutes, for example completing an MBA.

■ Management development is often seen as the mix of numerous approaches used to aid learning of leaders and managers, often associated with their current and future roles in organizations. It is likely to have the aim of improving individual and organizational performance, probably in a long time frame, in a variety of ways.

All three are important elements in understanding how managers and leaders grow and are developed, or improve throughout their career. Training, development, and education may all provide useful learning for managers at different times and to meet different needs of managers, and each is therefore shaped by the many processes and factors that influence learning.

Mumford and Gold (2004, p 14) suggest that development includes all of the preceding approaches, seeing management development as:

An attempt to increase managerial effectiveness through a learning process.

It is then perhaps impossible to draw artificial distinctions between these three and probably more appropriate to look at the ways in which learning is used in all of them.

Typologies of learning theories

Harrison (2005) suggests four broad schools of thought on learning theory: learning as conditioning, learning as information processing, learning as social process, and learning as experience. A threefold typology—behaviourist, cognitive, and humanistic—is proposed by Mumford and Gold (2004) and also by Wiltsher (2005). Reid, Barrington, and Brown (2004) outline six groups of theory: reinforcement, cybernetic/information, cognitive, and experiential theories, plus self-development and mental processes. All these categorizations consider, in the main, the same approaches to learning theory—but choose to group them in different ways, using slightly differing terminology.

Reynolds, Caley, and Mason (2002) discuss learning theories in four clusters, but usefully present these in a matrix fashion by also analysing the clusters in terms of both their practical workplace-related application and the main issues arising out of their application. Each cluster is analysed in relation to its workplace-related application by using the three categories of 'for work' (learning outside the workplace that is intended to support the individual in the work role), 'at work' (employer-provided opportunities to learn) and 'through work' (learning arising directly from work experience). Their chosen clusters are ones which view learning in terms of behaviour, understanding, knowledge construction, and social practice, and they include theoretical approaches that have enjoyed some influence in the last 50 years or so. These include many of the same theoretical approaches as the typologies mentioned previously.

It is important to bear in mind that there are many overlaps and links between whatever categories we choose to employ and they should perhaps be viewed in this way rather than as discrete categories. One might consider each chosen category as successively building upon the others, adding more refinement in turn (although the theories involved haven't developed in such a neat, linear, chronological fashion). We have chosen to group approaches to learning theory into four main categories: behavioural, cognitive, social, and experiential as an attempt at some kind of synthesis of others' categorizations.

Our first category is the behavioural approaches of theorists such as Pavlov, Watson, Skinner, Thorndike, and Markle. This approach originated in the work of empirical psychologists working in the early years of the 20th century who were seeking scientific validation of their experimental work with animals and birds. This group of theories suggests that the behaviour of individuals changes as a result of responses made to applied stimuli, and the resulting outcomes. Given the definitions of learning discussed earlier, we can equate this change of behaviour with learning. These theories suggest that individuals can become conditioned to respond in a desired manner through some kind of reward which reinforces the 'appropriate' response to the stimulus provided. The reinforcement could be anything that strengthens the desired response to the stimulus—typically food with animals, but for humans we can apply the theory in relation to reinforcement such as praise, eye contact, positive feedback, or feelings of belonging to a group—all of which can be applied in a learning and development setting such as a training classroom. This approach can be applied to the gradual acquisition of skills by reinforcing (through praise and feedback, for example) incremental development of the contributing elements of the skill set.

Behavioural approaches undoubtedly have something to contribute to our understanding of how people learn, and can be applied in a range of situations that are of greater complexity than that of the original experimental work. There is much that they do not explain, however, and other approaches, as we will see, have built upon them successfully by addressing the wider cognitive, social, and experiential elements and, crucially, the issues of transferring learning from one situation to another.

Our second category is the cognitive theories of, for example, Kohler (1973), Festinger (1957), Bloom (1956), Gagné (1966), and Piaget (1963). These views of learning envisage much greater mental complexity than simple stimulus–response, and recognize the role of the individual in making sense of perceptions (stimuli) through existing mental frameworks, and indeed in changing the frameworks in the light of new data, in order to fully explain the world. This group of theories suggests a hierarchy of cognitive stages from straightforward behavioural responses to more complex problem-solving and conceptual thinking, making use of faculties such as perception, memory, and information processing. There is also an assumption that learning relates to the rational acquisition and interpretation of knowledge that is 'out there' in the world.

The third category in our typology includes the theories relating to learning as social practice, in which learners are actively involved as co-participants in a social setting with others in creating and applying knowledge and meaning, although a variety of different approaches are taken under the social learning umbrella. Within this category are approaches that emphasize the notion that knowledge and reality are in fact socially constructed rather than being objectively 'out there', and that learning comes from observation of others (which is necessarily in a social setting). Social theories of learning—such as those of Rotter (1954), Lave and Wenger (1991), Wenger (1998), Vygotsky (1978), Engestrom and Middleton (1996), and Bandura (1977)—are not set in opposition to notions of behavioural responses or of individual cognition, but build upon them.

Wenger (1998) describes the 'communities of practice' in which we are all necessarily engaged, suggesting that we learn as cooperative participants within them, and noting that we adopt different roles within each of them, perhaps as senior members in some and junior participants in others. Much of Lave and Wenger's work is based on considerations of apprenticeships in a variety of settings. Collison and Parcell (2001) identify three types of community (common interest in a topic or activity, common practice or understanding, and common commitment to specific goals).

Our final category is experiential learning, which encompasses theories relating to the ways in which we learn from, and make sense of, experience. We consider these approaches in more depth later in this chapter—partly because there is a growing recognition of the importance of learning through experience; indeed, most managers, when asked, say that they learned to do their job through doing it (Mumford, 1997). Most people can identify many tasks that they do as being learned through simply 'having a go' and yet it was not until 1984 that Kolb defined a theory of experiential learning which has since become very popular, that sees learning as 'the process whereby knowledge is created through the transformation of experience' (Kolb, 1984 cited in Mumford, p 93).

This theory describes four stages through which an individual is expected to go in order to learn effectively from an experience, which are:

- concrete experience
- observation and reflection
- developing abstract generalizations
- active experimentation.

Kolb's model of learning has been popularized by Honey and Mumford (1986) in the UK and developed into a model of learning styles.

There are a number of criticisms of experiential learning, including the lack of ability of experiential learning to explain ground-breaking discoveries not seen before (Miettinen, 2000), as well as the independence of the four learning styles proposed when they are seen as part of a cycle (Holman et al., 1997). Others point to the apparent lack of involvement of any social element in the cycle (Reynolds, 1997), and comment that it ignores the cultural, social, and individual differences in management (Holman et al., 1997; Hall and Moseley, 2005). Most of the criticisms suggest that the cycle does not take into account a number of the factors in a complex process. A development of the learning cycle is to see it as a learning spiral to account for the ongoing nature of development, for once having reflected and integrated learning from reflection into our personal understanding, we do not return to exactly the spot where we began but to a different starting point—so a spiral is probably a better representation of learning in this way.

We will return to issues of experiential learning later in this chapter, when discussing formal and informal learning.

Table 6.1 is a summary of our typology of approaches to learning theory.

Finally in this section, we wish to highlight three further approaches that are often discussed in the context of learning theories.

Adult learning

An additional theory to the initial categorization by Reynolds et al. is that relating to differences between ways of learning for adults and children. Knowles et al. (1998) suggested that adults learn in a different way from children or animals. Most of the theories of learning come from the study of children learning, known as pedagogy. However, Knowles (Knowles et al., 1998) used the word 'andragogy' to describe adult learning, which he believed was different due to the following factors:

- Adults have experience to contribute to learning and they are a good source of learning themselves.

Table 6.1 Outline of approaches to learning theory

	Behavioural	Cognitive	Social	Experiential
Outline	Behaviour changes through conditioned responses to stimuli	Mental frameworks used and developed to explain and make sense of the world	Learning requires a social setting to occur and be applied	Learning from experience through reflection, making sense and trying alternatives
Examples in application (but note that applications may relate to more than one category, dependent on context)	Induction programmes	Instruction manuals	Action learning	Mentoring
	Various forms of feedback	Case studies	Professional and personal networks	Diagnostic instruments
	Coaching	Books and magazines	Teams and committees	Learning logs and portfolios
	Vocational courses	CD-ROMs, DVDs, etc.	Project working	Secondments and projects
Potential problems	Learning transfer to new and different situations	Focus on theoretical rather than practical knowledge	Ignores power issues in groups; work pressures may get in the way	Managers may struggle with some elements—reflection, typically
	Lack of appreciation of contextual nuances			

- Adults use their current experience to assess new learning so that it has meaning in terms of its fit with what they already know.

- Adults already have experience of learning and so have developed habits of learning which may make them less open minded than children.

The main thrust of this theory is that adults require different treatment from children in a learning environment. They are likely to look immediately for relevance from learning and are likely to want to use and discuss their experience, so require a participative environment rather than being told. Involvement in learning, crediting experience, and establishing relevance are all key requirements for facilitating adults' learning, as many developers will know.

Although experience suggests to those involved in adult education that these issues are important, it is unclear exactly how an 'adult' should be defined. Age and physical attributes do not distinguish adults and children. However, for most leadership and management developers their trainees are likely to be adult, so being aware of this model of adult learning is helpful—although it must always be remembered that no group is completely homogeneous, so that variations within such groups will occur due to personal style and preferences; this will be further examined in Chapter 7.

Information processing/cybernetics

Research during the 1970s and 1980s into systems resulted in improved understanding about how people process and use information in learning. It also led to a focus on understanding of the operation of internal elements of systems, concerning the flow of information and importance of feedback in systems, much as a closed hot water system monitors and switches elements in the system to control water temperature. People were understood to operate in similar ways to control movements in learning through the use of cues about feedback.

These theories provided models of how people used information available to learn and to control actions to improve operations. For example, in learning to drive a car a learner driver has to first become aware of and then learn to use information about the sound of an engine and feel of the car to know when to depress the clutch to change gear. This information is easily available to an experienced driver but initially it is of little use to the learner. However, if the attention of the learner is drawn to the cues used by the experienced driver, then through practice and assistance from an instructor they learn what information to pay attention to so that they can make corrective changes to the gears. Information processing theory drew attention to such cues that are used by those who are experienced and can then be used by a learner, once they know what to attend to so that they can make the correct movements and learn more quickly than if left alone.

This theory provides a somewhat simplistic view of systems, reducing each system to an information-in, transformation, and information-out mechanistic system, with feedback then influencing operations. However, this simplistic approach emphasized the importance of awareness and use of minute and internal senses that can determine the difference between an experienced operator and a learner, as in the car driving example. It is of limited use as a theory of learning, more providing understanding of the processes involved and explaining the differences between a novice and expert and the importance of using feedback.

Competence model

This model extends that of information processing above into the training and development arena. It is widely used by trainers to help learners understand processes that they go through, and often quoted in books; yet its origins are somewhat less well known. It has been attributed variously to Dubin (1962), Robinson (1974), Straangard (1981), Howell (1982), May and Kruger (1988), and many others, and has been presented as a matrix (see Figure 6.1) or as a ladder. Nobody has been able to definitively confirm its origin. It builds on the ideas of cybernetics through our more recent understanding of the brain's ability to process multiple pieces of information at any time. The model provides a useful analogy in understanding learning, particularly of skills, and it uses the idea of information processing, awareness, and handling as well as the sources of tacit knowledge.

The model describes the move from novice to expert in four interlinked stages:

- *Unconscious incompetence stage*: in which a learner has had no experience and therefore has no comprehension of what is required to do a task, e.g. horse riding, and an expert may make it look very easy to such a learner.

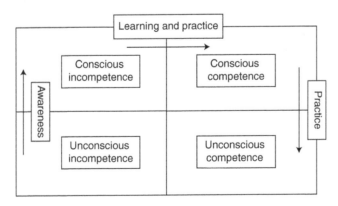

Figure 6.1 The competence model

- *Conscious incompetence stage*: during which the learner attempts the activity and begins to realize how much information there is to be aware of and the range of smaller skills involved in, for example, horse riding.

- *Conscious competence stage*: reached through practice and instruction so that a learner can do the basic tasks but needs to concentrate on each individual element and small skill to make sure the whole is achieved and they stay on the horse's back.

- *Unconscious competence stage*: only reached by some through continued practice to become an 'expert' in a particular field. In the riding example this would include being able to ride effectively over changing ground without having to focus on what to do—so the rider could think about where they were going, what feed the horse might need, and hold a conversation with other riders alongside. In this stage all of the skill routines are well established in the brain through practice and therefore information passes without effort on the part of the expert: it is 'hard-wired' in the brain.

The application of the competence model is used within training for psychomotor skills by providing an understanding of information usage in learning, particularly when combined with brain research, which, through brain imaging, provides evidence of neuron pathways developed in skilled performance. Brain research shows how skilled routines are hard-wired into our brain, to become automatic, so not requiring any conscious attention, as described in the model moving from conscious to unconscious competence. However, awareness can be re-engaged if necessary. To extend the driving analogy, above, an experienced driver has learned to drive a car without having to consciously consider the multiple routines being used or having any awareness of information being processed. However, should this driver suddenly be faced with unusual conditions, for example black ice, then they quickly become aware of the change and begin to monitor cues, the skidding wheels, the vehicles around them, and the way that the steering wheel must be turned in a skid, to avoid disaster. Therefore, in the competence model the driver returns momentarily to a former conscious competence stage in order to cope with the unexpected when usual information processing capacity is insufficient to cope with new requirements of the conditions. These additional processing requirements will subside once driving conditions return to normal and with them a return to the unconscious competence stage in driving—or with further practice over a long period of driving in such conditions, for example like a rally driver might require, then a phase of unconscious competence may be reached.

This model has intuitive appeal, and if we use ideas of brain processing it has some support—though it has not received serious critique due to its very individual nature. One might consider, for example, that since it is an approach focused on the internal assimilation of externally displayed skills and knowledge, it therefore necessarily has less to say about the important notions of the social nature of learning, or that it accepts as 'givens' the socially constructed nature of what it is to be 'competent' in a given sphere of activity. In management terms, for example, the nature and style of the competence displayed may be acceptable or desirable in one organizational or cultural setting but not in another. Consider, for example, the differing interpretations of managerial competence that might be found in organizations as diverse as the British Army or Google.

From a consideration of the variety of learning theories, it is apparent that all may have something to contribute to our understanding of managerial learning, whilst none can offer an explanation that is wholly satisfactory on its own. We can see the theoretical origins and underpinnings of many popular approaches to management development. It also follows that a good understanding of the theory will furnish us with our own views of what might be the most appropriate interventions in a given context, taking into account all the variations of the organization, the individuals concerned, and the nature of the desired learning and development. Arguably, if we are making decisions about management development interventions without any such theoretical understanding, then we are 'shooting in the dark' and operating on the basis of hunch or fashion.

We should also remember the importance of 'fitness for purpose' of any approach or intervention we might suggest or implement. No matter which approaches we use (bearing in mind the certainty that no single way will always be appropriate), we should ensure that they are suitable for the individual context in which we seek to apply them. Thus we should take account of the learners' characteristics, their motivations, the type of learning involved, the job role, the nature of the organization, and so on.

Summary of section

The main reason for considering how we might define and conceptualize learning is that this is a necessary prerequisite for making good decisions about developing managers and leaders. If we have not considered how managers learn, how can we establish what might be effective approaches to their development?

In this section we considered definitions of learning, beginning with the well-known and established definition provided by Bass and Vaughan (1966), but moving on to discussion of other approaches that look at learning in a slightly more complex and ultimately more satisfactory way. We also looked briefly at related terms such as training, education, and development—all of which are well used in management development.

From definitions, we approached the minefield that is learning theory, and suggested our own typology of learning theories as a framework to consider the range of theoretical approaches, and some of the practical implications flowing from them. Thus we have discussed our fourfold approach to learning theory as behavioural, cognitive, social, and experiential—recognizing the overlaps and links between these approaches. Table 6.1 gives a summary of our typology. Finally, we have briefly discussed three other approaches to learning theory.

Formal and informal learning

Up to this point most of the theories and models of learning discussed are found to be used in formal development initiatives, for example workshops, training, education, in which there are usually a stated aim and objectives to achieve. Formal

Reflection point 6.3

The following analogy has been used by Berg and Chyung (2008, p 230) to distinguish formal and informal learning:

> Formal learning can be likened to riding a bus, as the route is pre-planned and the same for everyone. Informal learning, then, is more like riding a bicycle in that the individual determines the route, pace, etc.

We extend this analogy in that even on the bus ride each passenger will see and recall parts of the journey that interest them and remain in their memory so that the same 'pre-planned route' does not necessarily result in the same outcome, even if, from a trainer's point of view, all passengers arrive at the same destination.

Try to identify occasions when you attend a formal presentation or training with a colleague. Immediately following the next event try to independently write down brief notes about the main information you heard and the key things you noticed during this event.

Compare your recollections and identify similarities and differences.

You have both been on the same bus ride and arrived at the same destination but did you have the same experience?

Why might this be?

learning forms the major part of an organization's training costs and is recognized by the organization and the individual. However, informal learning is less often recognized but it influences managers' learning and could provide a cost-effective approach to developing managers, if recognized and supported in organizations (Smith *et al.*, 2007).

Managers learn in a variety of ways, and few of them are formal, planned methods. Perversely, these minority pursuits over time became the only ones recognized as management development. It is suggested that an overemphasis on planned, formal management development excludes the real experiences of managers, which is on the one hand not logical, and on the other hand—and more importantly—reduces the credibility of developers when talking to managers about development. Pedler *et al.* (1994) refer to formal management development as unintentionally deskilling managers through the notion that there is an external expert for every type of problem. Conversely, they suggest that significant managerial learning comes from dealing with real problems rather than from being taught.

There is increasing awareness of the impact of informal learning, and Salaman and Butler (1994) identified it as one of the reasons that managers apparently did not learn from formal training. Mumford and Gold (2004, p 119) argue of informal learning that:

> Managers can be helped to recognize that these powerfully experienced managerial processes are also learning experiences, but that as learning experiences they could be improved, with significant benefit to themselves and to their organization.

They describe a model of management development which includes three types of learning, based on an initial model by Mumford (1987). The three types of learning are:

Type 1, informal managerial: which is not usually recognized as development but rather seen as part of a manager's tasks. Therefore it is 'real' but unstructured and has no clear objectives, so is unconscious and does not deliver effective learning and development.

Type 3, formal development: a term to describe planned, structured activities, often with clear objectives but usually completed away from work and so may be less 'real' than the manager's role and completed infrequently so seen as ineffective learning. The development is often seen as being owned by the facilitators or developers.

Type 2 is described as being between the two extremes of Types 1 and 3 and to take the advantages of both as far as possible. It is structured as part of the manager's work as far as possible but with the intention and objectives of developing the manager. It is owned and managed by the manager and is a 'real' part of their work.

By using this model, developers and managers can consider how best to move both Type 1 and Type 3 learning towards Type 2. Formal Type 3 development could be made more real and relevant to managers' job roles by including action planning, real cases, and plenty of group discussion by participants, for example. Informal Type 1 learning can be enhanced by attaching 'learning elements' to managerial job tasks, so that secondments (for example) are planned and debriefed not just to provide cover or achieve an outcome, but to extract the learning from them. Similarly, developing managers' reflective capacity in various ways will enable them to learn more effectively from informal, everyday experiences.

Other writers have used different terms to describe this informal Type 1 learning. For example, Marsick and Volpe (1999) talk of informal learning being unstructured learning, seeing it as reactive, incidental, part of normal work activity, and not recognized or encouraged. Others distinguish a different type of informal learning which is intentional and somewhat structured (Hodkinson *et al.*, 2003) and this type of informal learning is easier to see and describe, being involved in work activities but including mentoring or asking questions (Eraut, 2004). Berg and Chyung (2008, p 231) provide an analysis of different ideas of informal learning, including intentional and unintentional, and state that it is part of 'daily social interactions'. The conclusion of their research is that learning and development practitioners gain more knowledge through informal than through formal learning. Coffield (2000) talks of it being difficult to uncover, like the submerged part of an iceberg.

We will take a closer look at experiential learning theories and at notions of reflection in the remaining parts of this chapter. Ideas about experiential learning have become increasingly influential in leadership and management development, being widely used throughout organizations by managers, developers, and academics.

Experiential learning

We considered the theoretical underpinning briefly in the earlier section on learning theories.

Experiential learning is used in many different approaches to leadership and management development. It is seen as an inexpensive way of helping learning in any situation. The principles are used in outdoor development for executives, in personal development, and indeed many other approaches in training and development. It has the advantage over many other methods of being capable of being used in the workplace so that learners can learn in a 'real world' context as well as being used in off-job training.

Although many people intuitively agree that experiential learning is a model that probably underpins much of learning, it is not as simple as initially suggested.

Part of the model's strength is its simplicity, but the processes involved between experience and learning need further examination and explanation, as does the notion of 'experience' itself.

Schutz (1967) proposes the notion that discrete experiences are distinguished from the rest of our life experiences, and given meaning, through being given attention and reflected upon. The world is perceived as ordered naturally, consisting of a synthesis of past experiences and our knowledge of what we can expect in the future. Our experiences, he suggests, are mainly taken for granted, and only questioned (probably not very deeply) when particular problems arise. Dewey (1925) suggests that experience is a major element in learning and it has been argued that discussing learning without experience is meaningless (Boud, Cohen, and Walker, 1993). Beard and Wilson (2006) suggest that in fact the name experiential learning is a tautology, or at least the two words are 'almost inseparable' (p 19) because it is thought to be impossible to learn without having an experience.

Dewey used a chair to explain the importance of experience by identifying the numerous characteristics of a chair—colour, shape, feel, etc.—to examine the importance of clarity in understanding experience, and he suggested that experience had the quality of 'slipperiness' (Dewey, 1925, p 1). The meaning of this word is that even if a group of people have apparently the same experience of an 'event' (the chair) they are all likely to perceive different features; if they each wrote an account of the event they had experienced, these would probably be different in terms of the features of that event.

We all experience objects and events differently, since our previous experience and consequent interpretations of past events lead us to construct differing interpretations or understandings of current or recent events—so learning is subjective or unique to the individual. Memory also plays a major role in learning, beyond the scope of this book to consider in detail, but it also adds to the individual nature of learning. Each individual's reaction and response to a stimulus are interpreted through their own frame of reference and personal filters and motivations, and therefore are unique to each person. Consider, for example, two opposing groups of football fans describing a goal scored by one team. There will be differences in the perception, interpretation, and motivations of each fan within each group. If there are differences in perspective of such a relatively simple event, it is easy to understand how there might be criticisms from trainers who were asked to use experiential learning for managers who, due to its subjectivity, in effect require a personal programme and support.

Seibert's research (1999) identified other characteristics influencing learning, including social and environmental factors and emotions in learning.

It is worth briefly mentioning a more complex approach to understanding learning that is called the 'learning combination lock' by Beard and Wilson (2006), a

Mini case study 6.2: Role of perception in learning

We were working recently with a large national organization to support it as it moved from public sector into a competitive environment. Following a first round of downsizing, the spotlight fell on the learning and development department (L&D), as part of a total review of human resources. The human resources (HR) section had begun to implement the well-known 'three-legged stool' approach to service delivery (after Ulrich, 1997; Ulrich and Brockbank, 2005), to increase efficiencies through having contact centres for general enquiries; centres of expertise to develop strategy and policy, and advise on overall organizational initiatives; and business partners, who worked within business units providing support to managers who were expected to implement basic HR procedures. The model had been in operation for approximately 18 months and seemed to be delivering service improvements.

It was now that attention turned to L&D, at the annual training conference, to discuss how they could implement a similar model. It was interesting to note the different perspectives of stakeholders at this time:

- Learning and development professionals were unsettled by the idea and stated that they had provided good-quality training for many years across the businesses, informing managers about courses and events available regularly. They were busy and, from their experience, could not see the need to make the required changes or how these would deliver an improved service.

- HR professionals, having been through the process, thought that L&D needed to 'get into the real world and be brave enough to try a new experience', like they had been forced to do.

Managers and other stakeholders who were customers of L&D provided a variety of views:

- Some said that they had received a great service from L&D, who provided regular training, updating, and support to their staff, leaving these managers with little responsibility for training, and they wanted this support to continue. They were aware that L&D would be unlikely to be able to provide such a service in future.

- The experience of another group of managers had been of a distant L&D department which only provided limited, standardized training at times that did not always suit the business needs. This group hoped that the change would provide a responsive business-focused function that would no longer be a 'business cost'.

It is possible to see in this example that past experience and personal perspective provide the 'lens' through which all events are interpreted.

The organization is currently continuing the change process, which is being seen as personally painful, liberating, and challenging depending on whose perspective is taken as the outcome of restructuring is felt.

Jan Carmichael and Peter Emsell

metaphor that they use to describe learning from experience. The lock consists of six tumblers each representing a different element of the learning environment in which an individual exists and these include the internal personal and external environment and the senses used in learning to provide a systematic way of identifying factors to assess the many facets of learning. These writers (Beard and Wilson, 2006, p 19) provide a helpful definition of experiential learning as being:

> *the sense-making process of active engagement between the inner world of a person and the outer world of the environment.*

There appears to be increased interest in the processes involved in learning, along the same lines as the processes described above: for example, the model of learning developed by Bennet and Bennet (2008) through research on change; it also supports our contention (Routledge and Carmichael, 2007) that the learning cycle is useful but not sufficient to explain many features required in personal learning.

Reflection

Some commentators have argued that the learning cycle does not give sufficient significance to reflection (Boud *et al.*, 1985), which they see as a key element in learning and one that can be used at different stages and not just limited to one stage as in the Kolb model. Moon (2004) points out that reflection is often regarded as a difficult and unnatural process for managers. She sees reflection (2004, p 82) as:

> *a form of thinking—that we may use to fulfil a purpose or to achieve some anticipated outcome, or we may simply 'be reflective' and then the outcome can be unexpected. Reflection is applied to relatively complicated, ill-structured ideas for which there is no obvious solution and is largely based on further processing and understanding what we already possess.*

This explanation of reflection as sense-making, based often on what we already 'know', also emphasizes its personal nature. Reflection can focus on many different aspects of a situation, and in personal development it is important for a learner to consider numerous points of focus to get a full understanding of an event—for example, focusing on personal behaviour and that of involved others; reviewing outcomes, motivations, and learning (Routledge and Carmichael, 2007).

There has been debate about when reflection occurs and its characteristics. Seibert (1999) conducted extensive research to identify the key features of what he saw as two complementary modes of reflection:

■ Active reflection, or what Schön (1983) regards as reflection on action, is similar to the interpretation of reflection suggested above. It occurs following action, through stepping back from activity and—through a series of questions provided by a facilitator—a manager is helped to move in ever deeper reflection to address assumptions and beliefs and surface contradictions in their actions. This active reflection is seen as planned, taking place in conducive surroundings and supported by colleagues or a facilitator. Other writers use different terms for this type of reflection, while Beard and Wilson (2006) talk of retrospective reflection. Arguably, a key aspect of this reflection is the ability to challenge 'common sense'—those aspects of experience that are ingrained into individuals and groups without even being recognized. Without such challenge, managers will be using under-scrutinized patterns of thought, habits, procedures, and so on without realizing that is the case. These patterns of thought may be appropriate, but equally they may not be, and only this level of reflection can establish which is the case.

■ Proactive reflection, or what Schön (1987) calls reflection in action, is a momentary reflection when a manager works to achieve a task and is faced with trying to understand and respond effectively in the given situation. It occurs spontaneously, usually at work, taking a micro-perspective, and to respond to a change in current conditions as the manager attempts to correct a situation. This type of reflection is also known as concurrent reflection and has been suggested by Schön (1987) to be a feature of expertise that allows time to both interpret information and react appropriately in a scenario.

Mumford (1987) discussed a third type of learning, which he called prospective learning, in which a learner prepares for a given situation to plan actions and to consider options for a different events, for example going to meet a difficult client or calm nerves before an exam. A learner might try to visualize going into the situation and then control their emotions and reactions, and rehearse responses ready for the situation. Following the situation, retrospective reflection once again takes place to identify additional learning.

Schön is undoubtedly one of the most important writers in the area of reflection, and his work has influenced the subsequent development of 'reflective practice' amongst a range of professionals, including managers. He emphasizes the importance of reflection in surfacing tacit knowledge, and distinguishes between reflection in action and reflection on action, as mentioned above. It has been pointed out by critics that it is not always clear what is meant by these terms, although Eraut (1994) suggests that reflection in action (the more problematic of the two reflective forms identified by Schön) is at least to some extent conscious, that it has a critical function—questioning assumptions—and that it gives rise to on-the-spot experimentation. He considers that the term reflection has caused nothing but confusion and that it should be taken out of Schön's theory in order to rescue his original contribution.

Eraut goes on to discuss the importance of time, a variable which he suggests Schön largely ignores. When time is short, the manager must make rapid decisions and scope for reflection is limited—an example given is that of formulating questions in an unstructured interview in response to what an interviewee is saying. If the situation allows for a short time for reflection, it is beginning to be *out of* rather than *in* the action. Eraut prefers to think of reflection in these circumstances as a 'metacognitive process, in which the practitioner is alerted to a problem, rapidly reads the situation, decides what to do and proceeds in a state of continuing alertness' (p 145). He suggests that this rapid reflection in action is a different kind of process from the reflection on action that other writers from Dewey to Kolb have associated with learning from experience. One must also consider reflection relating to a series of related episodes of activity—is this to be counted as one subdivided action or as a series of several successive actions? The interpretation placed on them will determine whether one is regarding reflection here as in or on the action!

Eraut proposes the notion of a 'performance period' as a more helpful unit of analysis rather than a discrete task or activity—within this period, everything may be considered, thus making allowance for the real-life complexities, contextual differences, and unstructured nature of much professional work (Eraut's and Schön's context), including management. His model suggests limited time for deliberation unless built in by the practitioner—and so is dependent upon both motivation and time management on the part of the manager.

Reflection in the workplace

Many of the previous models of reflection have been developed in an educational context and with a focus on individual learning. However, as we have seen above, reflection always occurs in a context, it is always influenced by individuals' experience and the situation in which it occurs. Several writers argue that models of reflection must be adapted to fit into the workplace. Illeris (2004) drew attention to the importance of the interplay between the individual and organizational environment of a manager in developing a holistic model of learning at work which included an individual element, a social/cultural element, and takes place within a technological and organizational environment. These elements all contribute to the learning achieved. In support of this model, research by Rigg and Terhan (2008) found that introducing critical reflection was much more difficult within an organizational than in an educational setting, due to influences of politics, multiple stakeholders, and organizational pressures present within a workplace.

The influence of the knowledge economy and requirement for innovation within work was discussed with regard to its impact of learning at work (Verdonschot, 2006). Verdonschot proposed that personal emotional engagement and stories were of key importance, along with 'appreciative reflection' (p 3), in that reflection of positive experiences and successes had been found to be important in change and development situations, in contrast to the regularly used questions of 'improving what did not go well'. Emotion is an important, though only recently recognized, factor in learning that can have a profound influence on a learner's ability to learn. For example, if a learner experiences great excitement as part of learning, then the learning is likely to be anchored in this emotion. This influence can be both positive and negative, and practitioners talk about the importance of awareness of the 'whole person' in any learning or development intervention, in that it is not sufficient to teach skill or knowledge alone (Boud, Cohen, and Walker, 1993). If what is to be learned is at odds with an individual's feelings about it, learning is likely to be impaired (Callahan, 2002).

Reynolds and Vince (2004) have drawn attention to the impact of social and cultural aspects of learning, stating (2004, p 6) that:

> reflection is best understood as a socially situated, relational, political and collective process, and ... there are both theoretical and practical advantages to this perspective—especially in relation to management and organizational learning.

Recently Boud *et al.* (2006) have summarized many of the preceding ideas in discussing 'productive reflection' in work. Due to current organizational limitations on time and space for reflection and output requirements, productive reflection is focused toward performance outcomes rather than just learning. Boud *et al.* provide the following list of elements as indicating productive reflection (2006, p 22–3):

- An organizational rather than individual intent and a collective rather than individual orientation.
- Reflection is necessarily contextualized within work; it connects learning and work.
- It involves multiple stakeholders and connects players.
- It has a generative rather than just instrumental focus.

Mini case study 6.3: Local authority and reflection

A UK local authority in the north of England, responding to the many changing demands placed upon it—for example, by central government reducing funding whilst increasing responsibilities; by changing customer needs; and by frenzied media spotlight on issues such as child protection—sought to develop the capacity of leaders and managers to manage the required changes.

One set of approaches taken was to both develop a more reflective approach, and then to take steps to share the lessons of that reflection. A variety of approaches was used, with varying degrees of success in different departments of the organization. Ultimately, the initiatives were only sustained more than a year or two when particularly enthusiastic managers were involved. Successes were limited mainly to individual managers/teams, and there was limited organizational learning through sharing the outcomes of reflection.

Question

1 Which aspects of the theory presented above might account for the limited success of these initiatives?

Jon Haydon

- It has a developmental character.
- Reflection is an open, unpredictable process, it is dynamic and changes over time.

We see therefore that there are many different views of reflection, and this final examination draws together many strands from individual learning and yet contextualizes it and allows for ongoing change for both organizational aims and individual learning. Although this model encompasses many other ideas, it cannot be assumed that it is well developed or clearly articulated in organizations. Currently it is more aspirational that an everyday reality for many.

Reflexivity in management learning

Throughout this chapter we have presented a model of reflection that leads to questioning not just our personal behaviour but the underpinning assumptions and values that are part of our 'self'. We are encouraged to consciously evaluate ourselves and what we do and to look back, with this knowledge, to understand previous perspectives that change through re-evaluation.

Anyone involved in leadership and management development must be consciously aware of the need for reflexivity in all that they do and in personal values and beliefs. As we learn more about learning, it leads to questioning, reflection, and re-evaluation of ways in which we had previously learned and possibly beliefs we had about ourselves, our competence, and how we manage others. This leads to generative, developmental productive reflection that influences decisions made in future about the approach we take in future situations. It becomes, then, a continual learning spiral. Those responsible for developing others must be alert to ways in which learning about management learning and development can influence learners themselves and lead to re-evaluation of previous experiences and understanding future development opportunities.

Summary of section

In most organizations, formal learning and development, including management development, has the main focus of time and budget—in comparison to informal approaches. In reality, we might suggest that the majority of learning (managerial or otherwise) is informal—or at least that informal learning has the potential to be exploited to a much greater extent than at present.

In this section, we discussed Mumford and Gold's (2004) three-type model as an explanation of formal and informal learning and how both can be improved in practice. We considered Kolb's well-known experiential learning cycle (1984) and some of the criticisms levelled at it—largely based on the notion that it gives insufficient attention to the complexities of learning through experience. It is felt that the cycle offers a useful but insufficient explanation of the nature of personal learning in this way. This led on to a critical discussion of theories related to reflection, which is often seen as the most important yet least explained element of experiential learning. We considered the nature of reflection and discussed different types of reflection identified in the literature.

Summary of chapter

In this chapter we have explored the concept and definitions of learning, offering a typology of approaches to learning theory, whilst recognizing that learning is a complex topic that can never be satisfactorily explained by any single theory or approach. The notions of formal and informal learning and their particular application in terms of leadership and management development in organizations have also been considered, with the recognition that most organizations tend to focus on formal learning and could usefully pay greater attention to informal learning. A key aspect of informal learning is reflection, and the chapter has also discussed a number of aspects of reflection in various contexts.

Case study 6.4: Changing leadership development to capitalize on reflection and work-based learning

This case study is the second of three longer, integrative cases within the book that are specifically linked to the online resources. You will find supporting audio and text materials relating to these cases at the Online Resource Centre.

West Yorkshire Fire and Rescue Service (WYFRS) serves an area of approximately 800 square miles through 48 fire stations. It employs almost 1,700 uniformed staff, 340 fire and rescue staff and 60 mobilizing and communications staff working in various roles from firefighters to support staff. Each station has a station manager who is responsible for the overall operation and is supported by watch managers within each station. Each watch has a series of crews within it, with crew managers responsible for small staff groups within each watch. The principal aim or mission of this service is to:

> provide an excellent fire and rescue service working in partnership to reduce death, injury, and economic loss, and contribute to community well-being.

The strategic priorities or intent of this service are to:

- deliver a professional and resilient emergency response service
- deliver a proactive fire community safety and well-being programme
- provide a competent, skilled, safe, and diverse workforce
- provide effective ethical governance and efficient environmentally sustainable resource management.

Maintaining and developing 'strategic capability' is paramount in the WYFRS strategy. To achieve this it is essential that the operational leaders and managers are well trained and effective in their managerial and leadership roles. Some 18 months ago WYFRS decided to change the ways it developed leaders and managers.

This large fire and rescue service has, over the last 18 months, gone through a thorough review of its leadership and management development. The organization was keen to embed the language and behaviours of transformational leadership and management, and administration with the command role. This culture is one in which operational firefighters were expected to follow orders without question and managers made every decision.

The organization wanted to move to a culture in which in the everyday work environment staff were led through involvement and engagement. Leaders and managers, therefore, had to use a style day to day to encourage and explain so that staff were given opportunities to learn and show potential for leadership, which had previously been limited. However, in emergency situations there was still need for a hierarchy of command, with clear instructions followed to enable an efficient safe response. It is difficult for any manager to use this dichotomy of styles—autocratic command and transformational involvement—with equal ease and at appropriate times, just as it is important for firefighters to understand the need for these different styles.

Previously all of WYFRS's leadership development was completed through the National Fire Service College, which provided all training and development needs for managers from initial first-line training through to highest levels of leadership development. This training was specifically designed for all fire services, though it was not accredited training (did not provide a qualification in management) and did not always meet unique local needs.

WYFRS's senior team decided to take over leadership and management development at a local level, using in-house trainers and consultants, and to work with local colleges and universities to deliver accredited qualifications at levels matched to the needs of different groups of managers. An important part of the approach was to undertake an analysis of the organizational survey of transformational leadership behaviours, linked to a 360° feedback questionnaire of the specific competencies required in leadership. Every manager and leader received feedback from these analyses to help them to develop a personal plan to support the development of transformational leadership in the service. The key competencies for leaders to develop included providing direction, inspiration and encouraging high performance, showing concern for staff, and valuing their contributions, which required individual leaders who were assertive, persuasive, considerate, resilient, and self-confident to help them to exert influence without authority and offer coaching.

An additional initiative introduced was a series of development log books to support reflective learning. Managers and leaders who take a temporary promotion to the next hierarchical level, in preparation for a more permanent opportunity, were provided with a log book in which they reviewed and reflected on their learning against identified competencies, to encourage learning through work activities. This approach proved very popular. Then, once the individual is through the selection process for promotion, the temporary log book is used for accrediting prior learning against the role, which enables the individual to reduce their time in development for their new role.

All managers and leaders in the service use the log books, finding them a useful support mechanism to identify learning that takes place during their 'normal work', and to encourage self-critical review by managers that enables them to identify different ways to lead and manage others. It has been found to help the service to move from the typical command-and-control culture to one that encourages involvement and engages all in work activities.

The organization has found that development is more cost effective and takes less time, as well as helping to raise the academic levels and professionalism within the service. This learning has helped to benchmark practices with other organizations and to recognize the good practices already in place within the fire and rescue service.

Questions

1 Choose an organization you know and identify how it could use reflection in ways similar to this case study, to support the development of its leaders and managers.

2 Using the learning from the chapter, discuss with colleagues what you would do to introduce learning through work and reflection.

3 How would you persuade senior managers in the organization that it would be a good idea to try your approach? What would you expect the main benefits to be?

Copyright: Jan L. Carmichael and Peter Emsell, University of Huddersfield Business School

Questions

1 What is the well-known definition of learning proposed by Bass and Vaughan (1966)?

2 Can you identify the four clusters of learning theory identified by Reynolds *et al.* (2002)?

3 Outline Mumford and Gold's 'three type' theory.

4 What does Dewey mean by the 'slipperiness' of experience?

5 What do you think Wenger means by 'communities of practice'?

6 What did Schön call his two approaches to reflection?

7 Can you identify the four stages of Kolb's experiential learning cycle?

8 Can you suggest two criticisms of Schön's work on reflection?

Discussion questions

1 Identify a key group of managers in your organization—what would be the most appropriate approaches to develop their learning (formal or informal)?

2 Which aspect of theory would you take further in thinking about your own personal and professional development?

3 Why do managers report that they find it difficult to reflect? What advice would you give, based on what you have looked at, that would help?

4 Take each of the key ideas about how learning occurs and provide an example from your own experience of when you have learned in this way. Evaluate the different approaches from a personal perspective and discuss with others which one you favour, in what situations, and why.

Suggestions for further reading

Reynolds, J, Caley, L., and Mason, R. (2002) *How do people learn?* London: CIPD.
This research report, commissioned by the CIPD and referred to in this chapter, reviews much of what is currently known about learning. This chapter outlines the matrix approach taken by the authors in classifying approaches to learning theory, and which is worth exploring in greater depth in the original report. The report also considers the context for learning in organizations in the early 21st century, in which human capital is emerging as a key competitive element, and traditional training approaches are giving way to facilitation of learning. It considers aspects of learning in practice, as well as theory, and also takes a keen look at the debates around e-learning.

Schön, D. (1987) *Educating the Reflective Practitioner: Toward a new design for teaching and learning in the professions*, San Francisco: Jossey-Bass.
Schön is essential reading as a starter in considering aspects of reflection in professional (including managerial) work. He outlines different types of reflection, and discusses the notion of 'artistry' in professional work. Although he addresses professional work in contexts that are wider than management, there is much that is appropriate and of interest to those wishing to follow up an interest in notions of reflection in managerial learning and development. This source may be usefully supplemented by some of the critics of his approach to reflection.

Kolb, D.A. (1984) *Experiential Learning: experience as a source of learning and development*, Englewood Cliffs, NJ: Prentice Hall.
In the same way that Schön may be regarded as a gateway into consideration of reflection, Kolb is an obvious source with which to begin an exploration of experiential learning, and by extension a wider set of approaches to informal learning and development. His experiential learning cycle, although subject to some of the criticisms outlined in this chapter, is important not least because of its widespread use in organizations and in education. The subsequent development of approaches to learning styles based on the cycle has also been very influential, and students may wish to pursue further study of these aspects—but the original work by Kolb is a good place to start this particular journey.

www.google.co.uk or similar search engine. Input variations of 'competence model', 'conscious competence', etc., and explore a wealth of material relating to the model. This will lead you into a range of related areas related to leadership and management development including aspects of feedback, coaching, skills acquisition, self-development, and so on. You will generate a deeper and more personal understanding of the model—but be sure to treat web resources with care and consider their credibility!

CHAPTER 7

Individual differences in leadership and management development: why not clone managers?

The aims of this chapter are to:

- review factors that lead to differences in individual behaviour.

- identify the impact of individual differences on the work of managers and leaders.

- explore models of difference—personality, style, experience, etc.

- examine how the models of difference impact on leadership and management development.

Introduction

The chapter will explore models of personal difference and their influence in leadership and management. The models relate to personal characteristics and individual differences in personality (e.g. Myers and Briggs, 1980; Costa and McCrea, 1992) and emotional intelligence (Goleman, 1998) as well as a range of other factors which have been linked to differences in leadership or management. We attempt to develop a model to understand the factors that influence the work of leaders and managers.

Mini case study 7.1: Differences in managers and leaders?

For a number of years now I have worked with a team of colleagues running part-time management development programmes for managers who work in many different organizations. Some of these managers already lead large teams whilst others are early in their management career. The main features common to all are their willingness and desire to further develop knowledge, skills, and competencies in leadership and management.

At the beginning of the course, each group discusses the characteristics of a good manager and identify what, in their view, defines poor management. These questions form the basis for an ongoing discussion over the initial days of the programme and are used to encourage learners to think about management and discuss leadership styles they have experienced. This experience may come from managing others, being managed, or observing leaders in organizations.

An interesting finding from discussions is the similarity in participants' views, even when they come from a variety of different organizations and have varied experiences. It is also clear that, over the years of repeating this exercise, there are continuing similarities in the findings of groups.

When groups of managers are asked to select the four most important characteristics and skills, there is usually agreement among the group, with typical responses including:

- good listening and communication skills
- good interpersonal skills
- honesty and integrity
- knowledgeable about the organization and how to get things done
- ability to work with and motivate all staff
- being a role model
- coaching and influencing others in the organization
- ability to cope with ambiguity.

Throughout the programme, workshops provide opportunities for managers to discuss leadership and management and to explore the main academic models of management skills, comparing them with their own personal ideas. Usually there are many similarities, establishing good agreement about what makes a good manager, within research and personal experiences.

These managers complete work-related assignments for their personal development, addressing most of the key skills and knowledge discussed. At the end of the programme most participants have successfully developed a range of the relevant skills and recognized things to try to do differently.

Even when managers work on the same skill—for example, influencing or presentations—they do not become 'cloned'. They present and influence others effectively but not in an identical way to anyone else. It seems that, although groups identify common skills and characteristics and often work to personally develop these skills, they learn but retain their individuality and style.

Questions

1 What are the personal factors that maintain the individuality of managers on a development programme? (These are discussed within this chapter.)

2 What are the main organizational factors that might have influenced these managers, resulting in different outcomes from the programme?

Copyright Jan L. Carmichael

Factors that influence managers and leaders

Although organizations identify and use lists of skills and competencies to select and develop leaders and managers, no two managers are ever the same due to a range of personal, experiential, and cultural differences. These personal differences, along with those due to the environment, influence the behaviour of every individual at work, so understanding their impact is essential in management development.

How does knowledge of individual difference help?

Developers

Knowledge of the range of differences can help developers in preparing and facilitating programmes that are appropriate to managers' learning and personal style and in remembering that individual differences may also influence learning in all situations.

It can help developers to manage the development process and to understand if problems arise as well as the most appropriate ways to evaluate achievements.

Managers and leaders

Understanding individual differences can also help managers to examine their own behaviour and further enhance personal development of their leadership skills and abilities and to better understand those who work for them, to enhance teamwork, communication and organizational outcomes.

Factors that influence behaviour

At least four different categories of factors can be considered to explain individual differences in leadership and management development and these include:

- personal factors, including personality, learning, and our 'perceptual lens on the world', which has an overarching impact on how all experiences are interpreted

- cultural factors, due to an individual's culture and learning from their surrounding circumstances

- organizational factors are present due to the organization's culture and climate

- situational factors, which have a short-term influence, changing with the situation and very dependent on how we perceive a situation and various cues in it.

These categories influence managers at all times, in everything they do. Personal and cultural factors are present from birth and their effect on all individuals is present from early childhood, continuing to influence throughout their life, being relatively resistant to change. Organizational factors are present and learned with experience in an organization, being specific to that organization and may change over time. Finally, situational factors, as their name suggests, influence behaviour in individual situations, so depend on information available in every situation, though previous experience in similar situations can also influence behaviour. Of course the previous individual and cultural factors continue to influence us in all situations, so will also affect behaviour.

Each of the groups of factors identified in Figure 7.1 will be briefly discussed, to outline their influence on a manager or leader's behaviour; many are explored elsewhere in this book. To begin we look at long-lasting cultural factors, followed by shorter-term organizational factors, and finally situational factors, before concentrating on the personal factors that influence managers and leaders at work.

Cultural factors

Cultural factors are widely explored in Chapter 3, so this section will attempt to highlight the importance of understanding why they contribute to individuality. This group includes those factors that influence the heritage that each individual brings to their leadership or management role. They are what influences everyone from birth, related to the national and family culture and background, and are likely to increase possible diversity in behaviour among managers or leaders in organizations. The culture and environment in which children and young adults develop has a long-lasting influence on their life through the development of different cultural norms and life expectations, making it essential that organizations recognize the importance of diversity. For example, in assessment and development centres it is important

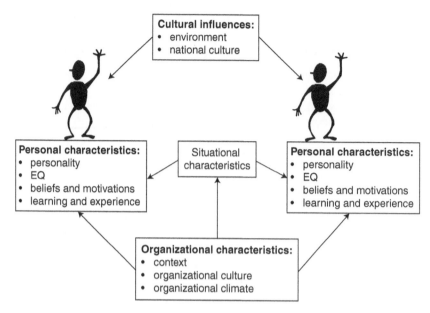

Figure 7.1 Characteristics that influence individual leaders and managers

that observers recognize that not all of the differences observed are due to the work-related skills being assessed and that they may be the result of cultural differences. Organizations must ensure that the skills and competencies assessed indicate potential for superior performance in the organization and are sensitive to differences within different cultures.

Some global organizations highlight their appreciation and understanding of different cultures within marketing campaigns; for example, HSBC Bank emphasizes its cultural sensitivity. However, all organizations, even those operating nationally, need to be aware of the impact of the global market for recruitment and to effectively manage differences within the workforce, as has been discussed in Chapter 3.

The importance of environment and family background in influencing career and life opportunities can be seen in the efforts by the UK government to open some professions to a wider range of people through encouraging all universities to take students from a wider variety of backgrounds. Cultural heritage has a lifelong, often unconscious, impact on individuals' perceptions, understanding, interpretation, and expectation of the world around them.

Organizational factors

Each organization has a distinctive history, culture, climate, strategy, and stakeholder groups that influence organizational objectives and leadership style. These factors are important in determining future strategies, and resource-based strategists recommend analysis of internal strengths and weaknesses as a first step to identifying

> ## Reflection point 7.1: Working in a different culture
>
> Think of an occasion when you have visited a foreign country, whether on holiday, business, or other purpose. Try to recall your initial impression of your new surroundings when you first arrived: the look of the town or city, buildings, people, ways of doing things. Even after some days we usually are unsure about cultural differences from our own, how to attract attention when needed, or mingle with crowds, how to cross roads, expectations of time.
>
> Think for a moment about how a new manager would feel arriving to work with a new team in an organization in a completely new environment. To manage effectively there are many additional elements to take into account to be able to manage and work effectively with employees from another country, due to cultural differences.
>
> Discuss with colleagues what differences may be apparent to this manager.

unique competencies that inform organizational strategies (Barney, 1995), as discussed in Chapter 2.

One key factor is organizational culture, described by Handy (1985) as 'the way we do things round here', which provides a simplistic but well-known explanation of culture, which includes many obvious features including policies, artefacts, history, 'stories' told about the organization, and also less obvious features to those who do not work within it, for example unwritten rules or norms. Organizational factors often operate to reduce national cultural differences as employees are assimilated into the organization.

These organizational factors affect the work of all managers and leaders. For example, a predominant 'management style' is developed to 'fit' with organizational culture. Organizational culture also influences the norms and behaviour of all employees, usually through the process of ongoing induction or orientation and throughout employment within different groups. Employees learn about organizational culture and climate through informal learning, rather than formal development and initiatives that may have limited impact if the informal organizational culture and group norms inhibit learners from using new behaviours (Salaman and Butler, 1994).

Situational factors

There are many situational factors that affect people's behaviour but are transitory to the extent that they must be understood for each specific situation and for every individual involved. They influence how we interpret others' behaviour and events in a situation which then impacts how we behave and because the process of perception, briefly described below, is very personal it explains how and why many aspects of leadership and management are unique to each individual.

The process by which we make sense of all of available information is perception, which involves paying attention to information in the environment; processing and interpreting it, in light of our previous experience, to make decisions about it and to therefore know how to respond. The information we perceive includes information about the environment, organization, our role, and others in the situation, including their body language and demeanour and many other facets of an encounter. The previous experience we have and our personal characteristics and cultural factors provide us with the 'perceptual lens' that is developed through life experience and influences how we interpret each new situation. Much of the process described occurs without conscious effort on our part and many aspects of our 'perceptual lens' are learned informally, by the manager through life experience. However, management development can provide further understanding and models to aid managers and leaders more effectively use important interpersonal skills.

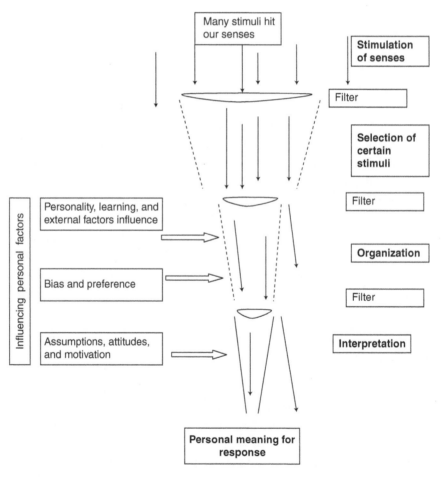

Figure 7.2 Filters of our perceptual lens: awareness, selection, organization, interpretation, and meaning. Copyright J.L. Carmichael

This is a simplified explanation of processes of identifying, processing, and using information about the outside world and because we can only ever experience the world through our personal frame of reference, which has developed over time, through personal experiences, we are all different. Each manager must be self-aware and understand their personal perceptual lens, including likes and dislikes, motivation, and personal biases which will shape the interpretation of situational cues in every encounter and therefore impact on behaviour.

All development initiatives are situations in which it is important that learners are prepared for what is to be presented and are also supported in working to implement learning; for example, if development is perceived as a threat to current ways of working, or of no relevance, then the development will have no impact. Motivation to implement new learning in an appropriate time scale is essential for development.

Summary of section

Managers and leaders are influenced by a range of different factors in their role at work. This section has attempted to provide a brief overview of the key factors that might be influential and how they work together, either emphasizing or moderating differences in resulting behaviour. The main categories of factors discussed in this section are situational, organizational, and cultural. There is greater discussion of the influences of these factors in Chapters 2 and 3.

Exploring differences in personal characteristics

This section will discuss the impact of personal characteristics on leadership and management and also on learning within management development.

It is easy to see how people differ from each other in terms of physical characteristics, for example hair colour, height, and many other characteristics. These differences are due to genetics as well as cultural factors and are obvious to all. Therefore it is probably not too difficult to accept that people are likely to be different in terms of mental processes and personality characteristics; indeed, working closely with other people helps us to recognize different personalities and thinking patterns.

Personal factors are wide ranging and varied and are thought to be relatively stable factors that influence many aspects of life and work. Although there are many personal factors, those selected for further discussion are considered most influential in management development and include:

- personality: for example, Five Factor Model, Myers-Briggs theory
- gender: suggested by some to influence leadership and management style
- emotional intelligence (EQ): many similar models of characteristics in leadership
- learning styles: see, for example, Honey and Mumford (1986).

Personality

For many years psychologists and psychiatrists have attempted to understand and develop models that help to explain personality differences. There is not space in this book to explore the history of personality and the many different models that have been developed. However, at the end of the chapter there are references to books that provide good analysis of work completed.

Personality is what makes each of us individual and is thought to underpin differences in behaviour between people, and results in differences in leadership and management. Within this chapter we will focus on two major personality theories that are frequently used in research and practice to understand and develop leadership and management. They are the Myers-Briggs Type Theory (Myers and Myers, 1980) and the Big Five Factor Personality Theory (Costa and McCrea, 1992).

Myers-Briggs Type Indicator

One model that is used extensively and is well known in leadership and management development is the Myers-Briggs Type Indicator® (Myers *et al.*, 2003; Myers and Kirby, 1994). It is commonly known as MBTI® and was developed by a mother and daughter team, Katherine Briggs and Isabel Briggs Myers, who took Carl Gustav Jung's (1923) ideas on personality typology and developed them through extensive research which continues today. It has a main research centre in the USA, known as the Center for Application of Psychological Type (CAPT), but the indicator is used throughout the world, being translated into at least 27 different languages (Kendall, 1998). Its use is closely controlled by its publisher and is only available to those trained and accredited to use the questionnaire.

The model is well researched and there is a rich resource of information about MBTI® and the influence of type on many aspects of life. It can be seen to be a very useful model to help individuals identify their own type, to identify and value differences that other types bring to any activity. The approach used to identify type is to complete a questionnaire which is scored to produce a 'reported type' which is checked through discussion with a trained facilitator, allowing a 'best fit' type to be identified for each individual. The descriptions of each type are written in a positive way and the model is believed to be developmental, allowing for changes through life and also encouraging personal development through greater understanding of the impact of the preferences. People are assessed on four dimensions, to identify their type in terms of one alternative in each dimension. A brief description of each dimension is provided below, in the order in which preferences are stated:

Extravert (E) or introvert (I)

These terms are commonly used today, though their interpretation here takes key elements from Jung's ideas (1923) that extraverts get their energy from the world around them, needing stimulation from their environment and to talk through decisions; they often speak first and think afterwards but are generally friendly and enjoy action.

Introverts get their energy from within themselves, tending to be more independent and spend time thinking about ideas rather than discussing them, and usually think through what they want to say before speaking.

Sensing (S) or intuiting (N)

This pair of preferences relates to our focus in gathering and dealing with information. Those with a preference for sensing focus on the 'here and now' and are good at handling detail and facts in information, trusting their senses. They prefer to have specific clear instructions to follow.

However, those who prefer intuition tend to look beyond immediate facts, preferring 'big picture' ideas, and focus on future happenings or making changes. They are less good with detail, preferring to deal with more abstract ideas or meaning.

Thinking (T) or feeling (F)

This dimension describes what an individual considers when making decisions. Thinkers prefer to make decisions based on logic and principles, and have a more objective, independent approach. They focus on fairness and impartiality in decision making.

Feeling types are people orientated, focusing on uniqueness and individuality. They prefer to make decisions by taking into account other people's and their own views and values and considering the impact of decisions on others.

Judging (J) or perceiving (P)

Because, like the first dimension, this is an overarching one and considers how someone prefers to live their life, it is reasonably easy to identify in others we know well. Those who are a judging type prefer to have an orderly, planned life and often do not like unexpected changes to their schedule. They like to work on one job at once and focus on completing a task so that, particularly when a deadline is given, they finish ahead of allowed time.

Perceiving types, however, focus on getting every piece of possible information and not completing a task in case more relevant information comes to light. They tend to start many projects but are less focused on completing until a deadline is fast approaching, and they often have many tasks ongoing at one time.

Table 7.1 provides a summary of the preferences in each dimension.

'Type' is seen as describing preferences people have for ways of doing things but it must be emphasized that everyone uses all preferences at different times. For example, we all have to both gather information (P) and make decisions (J) and even an intuitive person (I) cannot ignore facts (S) in making decisions. Each of these dimensions is obviously important to consider in its own right to understand how

Table 7.1 Showing orientation and related dimensions of MBTI®

MBTI® dimension	
Extravert (E) Outgoing, friendly, likes a lively work environment	Introvert (I) Quiet, focuses on thoughts and ideas
Sensing (S) Use and rely on information gathered through their senses; are focused on 'here and now', practical and good with facts, details	Intuiting (N) Use facts and details to form impressions, focusing on connections and concepts, forward thinking, and enjoy change
Thinking (T) Make decisions based on truth, principles, and logic; seen as businesslike and focus on impartial, fair decision making	Feeling (F) Prefer to take account of values and feelings in decision making, focus on harmony and treat people as unique individuals
Judging (J) Live life in a planful, organized way and do not like disruption to their schedule; focus on completing tasks, in time allowed	Perceiving (P) Live life in a spontaneous way, always prepared to search for more information before making decisions, so may begin projects and not complete all

people differ. However, when dimensions are considered together, providing a model of 16 different types, then interactions between dimensions add an important influence within each type. For further information about types, please see the reading list at the end of the chapter.

There has been some criticism of MBTI®, reviewed by Bayne (1995) in which he points to convincing evidence to counter each identified issue:

■ Descriptions of type are too vague and too positive, to which Bayne responds with research that most people consider the descriptions very accurate and that each type has identified development areas, so not all information is positive. However, presenting type in a constructive way ensures that individuals more readily accept and use them in self-development (Hautala, 2005).

Reflection point 7.2

● Review the MBTI® dimensions and try to identify what you believe your type is. You may wish to use references at the end of the chapter or research Myers-Briggs Types on the internet to determine your personal type.

● Think about the implications of your type for managing and leading others.

- A regular criticism of personality inventories, including MBTI®, is that people's behaviour is different in different situations and indeed this is true. However, knowing someone's MBTI® type can help to predict their probable preferences most of the time, whilst allowing for variation of behaviour due to specific circumstances.

- The use of words with common meaning to define each preference had initially caused Jung (1923) to think and discuss, at length, the names for preferences. However, as research on MBTI® continues more is discovered about these dichotomous dimensions and they become more accurately defined.

Generally, it seems that people can identify type using the personality characteristics described in MBTI®, which can provide guidance on strengths and areas for development, and Hautala (2005) states: 'Owing to [MBTI's] usefulness and comprehensible approach it has become a common method when studying leadership' (p 779).

Applications of type in leadership and management

There are many examples of use of MBTI® in organizations, for example in teamwork (Webster and Howard, 1989), in which findings suggest that although type-alike teams work together more quickly than diverse teams, the latter teams perform significantly in ambiguous tasks (Myers *et al.*, 2003). Fitzgerald (1997) discusses the use of MBTI® in leadership and management coaching, and many books provide guidance on understanding type in organizations, managing change, and communications (Hirsh and Kummerow, 1990), or dealing with conflict (Bayne, 2004).

MBTI® has been found to influence leadership and management style. Bayne (2000) discusses leadership in terms of four temperaments, based on work of Kiersey and Bates (1978). These temperaments are defined in terms of two of the dimensions and are often used in work on MBTI®. They are:

- SJ temperament: a stabilizer, traditionalist, who focuses on the organizational hierarchy and rules or policies and believes hard work is the route to success. This group are often good administrators.

- SP leader: a troubleshooter who is flexible and responds to immediate problems and will take risks to achieve outcomes.

- NF leader: a catalyst and energizer, who values harmony and cooperation. This leader believes in developing people and uses insight to help growth.

- NT leader: a visionary whose focus is on future strategy and who can cope with complexity, using models and concepts to facilitate organizational growth.

Therefore knowing an individual's type suggests their preferred approach to leadership, as Kiersey and Bates (1978, pp 152–3) explain:

Each style of leadership has its own unique contribution to make to the working situation. SJs lend stability and confidence. SPs make excellent problem solvers and lend excitement.

NTs provide vision and theoretical models for change. NFs lubricate the interpersonal fabric of an organization and can predict social consequences of the NT's theoretical models.

In 2000 it was found that 43 per cent of managers were ST temperament, compared with 36 per cent of the UK general population (Bayne, 2000), and transformational leadership has been linked to preferences for intuition, feeling and perceiving (Hautala, 2005), suggesting that it results in higher productivity and job satisfaction.

Use of type in career counselling is widespread, with lists of most and least preferred occupations widely available (Myers *et al.*, 2003). Research has shown that in Canada 57.8 per cent of a sample of nurses were SJ temperament (McPhail, 2002).

Bridges (2000) described organizational cultures in terms of type and used the 'Organizational Character Index' (Bridges, 2000, p 129) to understand different organizations and how they could be developed, or react to change.

As can be seen from some of the examples above, MBTI® has been used over a long time period to understand personality and value difference, and research is still ongoing.

MBTI® has also been used to identify learning styles and suggest teaching and learning preferences associated with different types (Lawrence, 1995). Myers and Briggs (1980) believed that the S–N dimension was important in learning, with intuitive types being able to deal with abstract meaning more quickly than sensing types, who prefer more practical step-by-step instruction. Therefore in management development it can be helpful to know MBTI® types to aid facilitation of learning.

It must, however, be emphasized that MBTI® cannot be seen as a single relationship in which all people of a type will behave in similar ways. As has been previously discussed, behaviour is far less consistent than this. There are many intervening factors, as already discussed, that influence situations and individuals. However, this model provides a good basis to understand other people in all situations and to facilitate managers' understanding of their own preferences, differences from others, and how to communicate, influence, and manage others effectively.

Mini case study 7.2: Using type to improve work relationships

Using type can help managers to understand their style more accurately and to see how it impacts on others. Working with a manager who had taken over a team some six months previously, I discussed his progress with him to find that he felt he was not getting the best from his team but did not know how to improve the relationship. He had heard of MBTI® and agreed to complete the questionnaire. He was an ISTJ manager, suggesting that he preferred a planned and structured work pattern, that he focused on 'here and now' practical issues, and made impartial decisions.

He managed a team of ten staff. The team had been together for approximately four years and had previously worked for a manager whose MBTI® preference was ENTP. The team worked effectively in the customer relations department of a retail supplier of electrical goods. Generally they dealt with customer queries, complaints, and after sales. Their work was varied and required conflict handling and sensitivity, with some ability to negotiate and agree limited discounts and upgrades for customers. Many of the group were SFP types, typical of a sales environment and good with customers, and dealing with practical issues and looking for options, without being too time focused.

Questions

Without stereotyping too much, try to decide:

1 What are the main differences that are likely to cause conflict between the new manager and the group?

2 What advice would you provide to the manager about the impact of his leadership style on the group?

3 What could he do to develop a better working relationship with the group?

Case study source: Jan L. Carmichael

The Big Five Factor Model

Unlike the MBTI®, the NEO-PI was developed through meta-analytical studies of many of the previous models of personality (Costa and McCrae, 1992) in which many previous studies of personality were re-analysed to attempt to find the main personality factors that underpin other models. The research produced a model of five independent factors and hence this model is also referred to as the Big Five Factor Model. The five factors include stable personality traits, briefly described in Table 7.2.

As can immediately be seen, there are links between the Big Five Model and the MBTI® scales, with strong correlations between the scales. Furnham *et al.* (2007) researched the links using correlational analyses and identified:

- MBTI® extraversion tended to be linked to openness and stability.

- MBTI® intuition tends to be linked with openness and introversion.

- MBTI® feeling types seemed to be agreeable and anxious.

- MBTI® perceiving types scored higher on openness and lower on agreeableness.

The Five Factor Model (Costa and McCrae, 1992) has been widely accepted and used in a range of organizations and it is assessed through a self-report questionnaire. It has been widely used to study management, leadership, and influence in organizations, as some examples below indicate. Manning *et al.* (2008) studied interpersonal influence links to leadership and management style. Agreeableness has been found, in research, to predict transformational management leadership style (Bono

Table 7.2 The traits and dimensions of NEO-PI (adapted from Manning *et al.*, 2008; Major *et al.*, 2006; Furnham *et al.*, 2007)

Trait	Brief description	Dimension extremes	
Agreeableness	Responsiveness and sensitivity to others; tendency to be cooperative and trusting	Introvert	Extravert
Extraversion	How comfortable a person is in social relationships; tendency to like people; likely to be talkative and assertive	Tough minded	Tender minded
Conscientiousness	The extent to which someone works in a structured and focused way; to be organized, reliable, and ambitious	Spontaneous	Conscientious
Openness	How open a person is to new experiences; having an active imagination and intellectual curiosity	Conventional	Inquiring
Stability	How well a person reacts to pressures of life; tendency to experience anger, anxiety, guilt, depression	Stable	Anxious

and Judge, 2004) and is also related to high scores in specific managerial skill assessments (Craik *et al.*, 2002). It has also been found to shape the tactics used by managers in different organizational roles (Cable and Judge, 2002), and is linked to strategies used by different team roles (Belbin, 1993). An interesting finding for development is that openness, extraversion, and conscientiousness, as assessed on the Big Five model, have recently been linked to assessments of motivation to learn (Major *et al.*, 2007), suggesting that individuals with these personality characteristics are more likely to be keen to learn and possibly to spend more time in training at work.

There is also more recent research (Belasen and Frank, 2008) which investigates the relevance of the first four stable personality traits with role behaviour identified in the quadrants of Quinn's competing values leadership framework (Quinn *et al.*, 2003). The factors are suggested to each relate one of the quadrants in Quinn's approach to leadership: agreeableness relating to the human relations quadrant; openness linked with open systems; assertiveness relating to the rational goal quadrant; and conscientiousness linking with the internal processes quadrant. For a further discussion of Quinn's model, please see the further reading at the end of the chapter.

Research findings suggest that there is a relationship between the behavioural role in Quinn's model and personality traits on the Big Five, even though not an exact match. Researchers (Belasen and Frank, 2008) suggest that openness is probably the most important trait in determining leadership behaviour, although other work experiences also have a major role to play. Although the research is more limited using the Five Factor Model (Costa and McCrae, 1992), it is a more recent inventory.

Although there are many other personality inventories that provide measures of individual personality, based on a model of similarities and differences against pre-determined population norms, the two models discussed are widely used to select and develop leaders and managers, providing explanations of difference and pre-ferred ways of working and leading that provide a better understanding of others who are similar or different. It must be emphasized that although traits underpin differences in behaviour, not all differences can be explained through personality; other features of the manager's abilities, skills, and life experience influence overall behaviour. It is the sum total of these differences that accounts for variations in lead-ership and management actions, though influence by other external factors must also be considered.

Learning styles

There are a number of different measures of learning style, with probably the best known being Honey and Mumford's model (1986) based on a model of experiential learning by Kolb (1984). Kolb's model identified four stages in an experiential learn-ing process: concrete experience; reflective observation; abstract conceptualization; and active experimentation, which were based on two dimensions of 'perceiving' and 'information processing'. In the model, thinking is either abstract or concrete and information processing is considered to be either active or reflective, so that four learning styles are identified (Kolb, 1984), namely: diverger, converger, assimilator, and accommodator.

Honey and Mumford (1986) popularized the model of four learning styles, based on the experiential learning cycle. These styles were:

- Activist: who prefers to be involved in the learning process, throwing themselves into new experiences. In management development these learners prefer to learn through doing a role play and discussion.

- Reflector: someone who prefers to reflect, observe, and make sense of learning around them; so in management development they will learn through watching others and feel uncomfortable if required to act without 'thinking time'.

- Theorist learner: who learns from using models and concepts, taken from theory, and often prefers to be provided with opportunities for reading or research to fully consider issues for development.

- Pragmatist: someone who prefers looking at the practical application of learning. In management development these learners prefer to learn what they think they will need at work and what they consider relevant to them.

Reflection point 7.3

- Using the information above and other reading, decide which your preferred learning style is and what the implications of this are for your current course.

Honey and Mumford (1986) developed a questionnaire, called the Learning Styles Questionnaire (LSQ), for use with managers to determine preferences for learning styles, scored against a 'normative sample'. Findings suggest that most people have at least one or two preferred learning styles and could learn to develop all four identified styles. Honey and Mumford identified activities that can be used to aid the development of each different style as part of a personal development programme, and through being encouraged to use different styles learners could develop less-preferred styles, so making more effective use of every available learning opportunity.

Another suggested use of LSQ is to identify a manager's learning style and to use this to help select a learning intervention that best fits with the learner's learning style (Honey and Mumford, 1992). For example, an activist would be expected to relish the opportunity to throw themselves into active learning such as role play, compared with a theorist, who is expected to prefer to listen, read, and review evidence from models and ideas for learning. Therefore in selecting a learning opportunity, it is useful to know and understand a participant's learning style so that the opportunity fits the learner's preferences for more effective learning.

Within management development, usually managers are encouraged to learn in a wide range of ways and from many different situations, for example through reading, discussion, and doing; and therefore managers are encouraged, even without conscious planning, to develop different styles.

The identification of learning styles based on experiential learning has been criticized for a lack of psychometric rigour, particularly in predictive validity (Allinson and Hayes, 1988; Furnham, 1995). However, Hayes and Allinson (1988) conducted a factor analysis of many learning styles questionnaires and found that the Learning Styles Questionnaire (Honey and Mumford, 1986) was the most reliable. They identified two main factors that underpinned the LSQ; these were factors of action and analysis. An additional criticism of all work on learning styles comes from Riding and Rayner (1998), who attempted to develop an overarching model of styles of learning from their research into cognitive style. These authors suggest that what are commonly called learning styles are in fact less stable learning strategies, developed through experience to enable learners to adapt in many different learning situations. These strategies (learning styles) are underpinned by a stable personal cognitive style, which is itself the resultant interaction of past experience, personality dimensions, and gender. This research suggests that learning styles, as defined by LSQ and other questionnaires, will change with the needs of a learning situation and as each learner develops more experience, so that these 'learning styles' might be expected to change over time.

Although there is debate amongst researchers about the changeability of learning styles or strategies, and while there appears to be a lack of scientific validity and reliability, the LSQ still remains a very popular tool in leadership and management development to help managers appreciate that there are different styles. This appreciation of different learning styles is helpful to developers and to managers in two main ways:

- It can be useful in determining a manager's preferences for different learning opportunities, to help make learning as effective as possible by the selection of appropriate interventions.

- When a manager or leader develops their staff it is helpful for them to appreciate that their staff have preferred learning styles that might influence how to make development as effective as possible. For example, an activist manager may believe that a member of staff will learn by being 'thrown into' new situations. However, for learning to be effective for staff that are reflectors or pragmatists, it would be important to provide additional support and experiences before this occurred.

It can then be useful personally and in developing others for managers to have a knowledge of learning style, even though learners' preferences may change with experience. A manager may also persuade others to stretch and build on current preferences by using learning styles.

Emotional intelligence

The definition and measurement of emotional intelligence has been debated since the 1990s when researchers suggested that 'rational' intelligence (IQ), assessed by traditional intelligence tests, contributed in only a small way toward a leader's effectiveness (Goleman, 1996). It was acknowledged that a minimum baseline intelligence (IQ) was required, but it did not predict leadership effectiveness (Bahn, 1979).

There have been many attempts to identify different forms of intelligence that explain differences in learning. Gardener (1993) and Bass (1990) reviewed the role of empathy and social skills in leadership. Since Goleman (1998) popularized the concept of emotional intelligence (EI), there has been continued research to identify what constitutes emotional intelligence; how it can be defined and measured; and to attempt to assess its impact in leadership and management. One of the difficulties with the research has been agreeing on exactly what constitutes EI, due to the number of different models put forward. Although relatively early in the research history of this topic, there seems to be an emerging consensus that this is a concept that is multifaceted, requiring many component skills and abilities, including social, emotional, and communication skills.

Riggio and Reichard (2008) summarize work on EI to provide a framework to investigate leadership effectiveness, based on emotional and social intelligence based on four main abilities that constitute emotional intelligence. These are shown in Box 7.1.

Riggio and Reichard's research has linked emotional intelligence to effective leadership and showed the importance of expressiveness, sensitivity, and emotional control and social skills in motivating and leading others.

There are ongoing debates about how EI can be assessed. Many researchers consider that self-assessments are inadequate and some other performance measures are required (Goleman, 1996). Rosete and Ciarrochi (2004) used additional measures of performance and 360° feedback by subordinates to confirm that leaders with higher EI were assessed as more effective. Hoffman and Frost (2006) found that social and emotional intelligences were linked with transformational leadership (Avolio *et al.*, 1999). EI has been found to have a positive impact on commitment of subordinates and effectiveness of work groups (Judge and Piccolo, 2004). Stein *et al.* (2008) showed that top executives differed significantly from the general population in terms of EI and those who ran high-profit businesses were found to possess higher levels of empathy, self-regard, and problem solving. It seems that possessing higher levels of EI has been linked with effective leadership and shown to improve organization effectiveness.

Others, though, point to the difficulties of developing emotional intelligence (McEnrue *et al.*, 2007) and therefore questions of how to develop emotional intelligence still remain.

This topic seems to have interesting potential in helping to identify effective leaders who can make improvements to organizational effectiveness, although further research is required to provide large-scale conclusive evidence.

Box 7.1 A framework of emotional intelligence in leadership

- *Identifying emotions*, which involves the ability to recognize in oneself and others, as well as the ability to express emotion
- *Using emotions to facilitate thinking*, which involves using emotions for improving thinking processes and harnessing the power of positive moods
- *Understanding emotions*, including the complexities and subtleties of emotions as well as their interrelationships
- *Managing emotions*, which involves skills in regulating and controlling felt emotions in a positive fashion.

Riggio and Reichard, 2008, p 170

Summary of section

Behaviour is underpinned, in all situations, by deep-seated dispositions and personal characteristics that influence how we perceive, interpret, and respond to circumstances. Personality factors and EI have been shown to influence leadership style and the effectiveness of leadership at work, so are used in assessment and development centres to identify future leaders. Whilst there is debate about the impact of gender on leadership and management, and care must be taken not to discriminate unfairly, learning style and learning strategies can be useful concepts in designing development interventions, though research shows that there is debate about exactly what will provide a reliable assessment of these.

Impact of difference at work

The model developed in this chapter attempts to bring together personal and other factors that help to explain how managers' behaviour may be influenced and make it individual to that manager. Behaviour is amenable to development, particularly when learning opportunities are appropriate to the individual's personal style. Although we have discussed how each can influence a manager's or leader's behaviour, there are many complex ways in which all factors interact, so that each individual situation has to be considered as unique.

A line of research that began in the 1980s in the USA, called person–environment psychology (Schneider *et al.*, 2000) has attempted to understand and investigate the interaction and influences of personal characteristics and environmental factors in organizations. The key findings were briefly discussed in the section on organizational factors, and suggest that organizational culture is determined, to a large extent, by senior managers, who also usually agree the mission and strategy in organizations. In particular, in smaller or start-up situations the owner or senior team has a major influence on the culture and business direction. People are attracted to an organization through their understanding of how it works and what it might be like to be an employee, often because they believe their values 'fit' with the organization. They may apply and will often be recruited because they are seen to 'fit' into the organization or team, as with, for example, recent notions of 'recruiting for attitude' in addition to skill (Callaghan and Thompson, 2002), and as can be seen in the use of assessment and development centres and talent management systems. If there is a good 'fit' between the individual's values and the organizational culture and climate, research has found that the individual reports higher levels of job satisfaction and is likely to stay with the organization. However, if not, then the individual is more likely to leave. This phenomenon was called attraction–selection–attrition (A–S–A) theory by Schneider (1987). Therefore similar people are attracted to and selected by an organization (Cable and Judge, 1997), over time reinforcing homogeneity among those who remain (Cable and Parsons, 2001). This approach can help to sustain an organization and reduce conflict, in stable environments. In addition, most orientation and development initiatives reinforce the dominant organizational culture.

Schneider *et al.* (1997) found this to be true among groups within organizations, particularly management teams, and longer term he suggested it could result in 'strategic myopia' and poor decision making, particularly in changing situations.

One issue raised for organizations by this research is that of individuality and diversity, in that there appears to be a tension between attracting employees who 'fit' and reinforcing a dominant culture through informal learning and attrition, whilst needing to maintain and develop leaders and managers who can think independently and maintain strategic competence.

It is interesting that more recent research has confirmed homogeneity in organizations in large-scale studies (Giberson *et al.*, 2005); and research into employee commitment (Pool and Pool, 2006) and into organizational identity and the impact of culture on engagement (Truss *et al.*, 2006) points to similar findings and also links these with improved organizational performance.

Organizations must ensure that all employees are treated fairly as individuals with a wide range of abilities that they bring to work that need to be harnessed by leaders and managed effectively. Decisions about recruitment, development, and treatment of all employees must comply with employment legislation and it is essential that organizations are sensitive to the differing needs and behaviours of different groups within the workplace, in order to maintain a diverse and motivated workforce.

In selecting and developing managers and leaders, attention should be given to all individual differences including personality and abilities and intelligences that are used in managing and leading others at work. As research shows, effective use of personal characteristics and abilities, in an appropriate organizational environment, can aid a manager or leader in working in ways that maximize benefit to the organization and allow personal development for the individual. Managers and leaders can also be developed to use skills and characteristics that they have in different ways as environments require to achieve desired outcomes. However, if there is mismatch between organizational or cultural requirements and the personal factors an individual brings, in the long term this individual may well choose to leave the organization to find one more aligned with their personal characteristics. Leadership

Reflection point 7.4

- Consider organizations that you have worked in. Would you agree that it is more comfortable to work in an organization with people similar to yourself?
- What are the positive and negative features of working in such an environment?

and management development then can be seen to be a way of maximizing organizational benefit from individual characteristics, abilities, and learning. It is essential in a turbulent, global world that organizations appreciate and manage difference of all kinds, not making negative evaluations of individuals on the basis of these differences.

Mini case study 7.3: Individual differences in Yourtown University

The university has a similar structure to most others. There are academics whose main roles are to teach and research, preferring to be free of procedures, and there are administrative staff who run systems, arranging rooms, meetings, clerical work, and the quality processes that ensure the effective running of the organization.

The university had been successful in bids for large amounts of additional external funding to research aspects of marketing, management, and environmental impacts of a planned worldwide sports and athletics event to be staged nationally in three years' time. In order to coordinate work and funding, a new Department was hurriedly put together, taking some academic staff from three existing schools in the university for their creativity in research and design of new courses within their current schools (Sports Sciences, Business, including Management, Marketing and Communications, and Environmental Science).

Administration staff were selected from across the university for their knowledge and accurate, structured, and timely operation of systems and procedures related to quality standards and finance.

Due to timing of the available funding and requirements to develop external contacts, there was no opportunity for a full induction for all staff. Small groups of academic staff were brought together for a short introduction, reminded of the importance of the success and expected outcomes of the venture, including research, conferences, and developing new courses for longer-term sustainability of this new department. They then began initial investigations, based on personal contacts, opportunities, and interests, to develop individual research agendas.

Administration staff were given an overview of the objectives, expectations, and structure and then asked to develop systems and processes for managing finance and information. This was achieved very successfully using the specialist experience of the administration staff to fit efficiently into current university procedures.

After two months, a new head of the department was appointed for her ability to develop and support research and ability to work with external organizations.

She found a somewhat chaotic situation in which there was little formal communication between administration and academic staff, or even among different groups of academics. Individual academics were at different stages of developing research, committing finance and resources as they went but without informing administration. Administrative staff were demotivated because no one used the newly developed systems, and frustrated in trying to get information from academics who saw them as meddling, bureaucratic, and stifling innovation.

The head of department has asked for your advice on how to improve the current situation so that all members of the department work together more effectively and appreciate different expertise and personal differences.

Questions

1 Identify some of the differences in individual staff that might account for the head of department's findings, taking account of what you have covered in this chapter.

2 How would you develop a team-building event to bring together academics and administrators?

Copyright J. L. Carmichael

Summary of chapter

The chapter has reviewed a wide range of different factors that have been found to influence learning of managers and leaders; in particular, the environment and the way it is perceived have an impact on how the world is interpreted . The personality and personal style of each leader or manager influences their learning and how learning is then applied in the work-place. Finally, ideas about homogeneity in organizations are explored.

Questions

1 What are the main categories identified in which people can be said to be different from one another?

2 Read the brief descriptions of each of the MBTI® dimensions and try to work out which is your preference on each one. How does this influence your approach to studying?

3 What are the factors in the Big Five Factor theory of personality?

4 Describe the main components of emotional intelligence.

5 What are the learning styles defined by Honey and Mumford?

6 What are the reasons that learning styles may change over time?

7 What is A–S–A and how does it influence organizations?

8 What are the main factors that influence how we perceive other people?

Discussion questions

1 Think of at least one manager you consider to be a good manager and one manager you consider not to be a good manager. List them as similar and different, in terms of what they are like personally, what they do, and how they do it.

2 You may wish to think of more than one manager in each category. When you have a list of similarities and differences, compare this with others' lists. Analyse your findings to try to develop a model from the lists, of what it takes to make a good or bad manager.

3 Are the items on the lists skills or personal characteristics?

4 Think about four or five of your friends or fellow students. Identify how they are different from you in terms of:

- their personality
- the way they make decisions
- the way they influence and communicate with others
- the way they learn.

5 Identify two organizations that you know. Discuss whether the requirements for being an effective manager are different in different organizations.

6 How would you devise a management training course on any well-known management skill, for example presentations or time management, for a group of managers who you knew represented all of the Honey and Mumford learning styles, to ensure that there was some element for each style?

Suggestions for further reading

Myers, I.B. and Myers, P.B. (1980) *Gifts Differing*, Palo Alto, CA: CPP.

Lawrence, G. (1995) *People types and tiger stripes*, Florida: Center for Application of Psychological Type.
These provide more information about MBTI.

Goleman, D., Boyatzis, R., and McKee, A. (2002) *The New Leaders: Transforming the art of leadership into the science of results*, London: Little Brown Books.
This provides more information about emotional intelligence.

Beard, C. and Wilson, J.P. (2006) *Experiential Learning*, London: Kogan Page.
This has a number of chapters dedicated to exploring individual differences and their impact on learning.

http://www.psychtesting.org.uk/about-psych-test/about-psych-test_home.cfm
This BPS psychometric guide provides guidance on all aspects of using psychometric tests and inventories for assessing individuals, along with good practice about their uses.

http://www.personneltoday.com/articles/2006/07/26/36574/psychometric-tests-how-to-choose.html
This provides further guidance on using psychometric tests.

Quinn, R.E., Faerman, S.R., Thompson, M.P., and McGrath, M.R. (2003) *Becoming a Master Manager: A Competency Framework*, USA: J. Wiley and Sons Ltd.
This both provides a comprehensive account of the model of management developed by the authors.

http://www.opp.eu.com/psychometric_instruments/mbti/Pages/default.aspx
This provides guidance on uses of and available training for MBTI, along with case studies from different organizations.

http://www.capt.org/
A wide range of books is available through the CAPT.

There are many websites that offer to explain learning styles and complete an assessment of your learning style. However, the best guidance is provided in the many books and leaflets written by Honey and Mumford, as in the references.

PART : 3

Learning processes, interventions and evaluation

CHAPTER 8

Leadership and management development processes to add value

The aims of this chapter are to:

- consider first the concept of management development (MD) adding value to organizations and second how planned processes (distinct from specific interventions considered in the next chapter) might contribute to it

- discuss how and why organizations need to consider these processes in an integrated, holistic, and appropriate, contingent manner.

Over the last few decades, there has been a growth in new ways of regarding some of the issues surrounding the recruitment, deployment, development, and reward of managers and other 'high value' employees. This chapter attempts to unpick some of these concepts, to identify overlaps between them, and to relate them to leadership and management development.

It aims, along the way, to highlight the key processes involved in effective development of the managerial resource within organizations—no matter what title is given to the attempt to do so.

The chapter aims to consider specifically a range of issues, including:

- the concept of added value

- management 'wrappers'

- talent management

- career management

- succession management

- competency frameworks

- identification of MD needs

- MD audit.

Introduction

The chapter considers a range of processes that organizations might use to assist their overall leadership and management development effort, supporting the delivery of specific interventions. These processes are discussed in the context of the need for all leadership and management development activity to add value to organizations, and in the context of wider concepts that have achieved some currency in discussions of leadership and management, such as talent management, succession management, and career management.

Processes to add value

All organizations—in addition to the specific interventions that are considered in the next chapter—will be likely to have in place processes to assist management development. These support the interventions, and taken as a whole may be said to comprise the total management development effort of the organization. We shall see that these processes will ideally be well integrated with one another and with the organization's strategic imperatives, but that this is often not the case.

Mini case study 8.1: Talent management within a housing association

The HR team in a housing association in the English/Scottish border regions was seeking to develop the organization's approach to attracting and developing talent. Effective leaders and managers at all levels were difficult to recruit and retain, and the organization had undergone much change arising from successive mergers with smaller housing associations.

There was no overall approach taken to the issue previously, with decisions on recruitment, recognition and reward, development, and promotion all taken in an ad hoc manner. They had recently been awarded Investors in People (IIP) accreditation.

There was a strong view from the board that the organization should try to become an employer of choice and seek recognition in one of the major 'Best Companies to Work For' lists.

Differing views were expressed within the team as to the way forward. Some thought they should embark on a 'talent management' initiative—a concept that was growing in popularity within the sector—whilst others took the view that they should just focus on getting each part of their current processes working consistently and effectively, building on the IIP success.

Questions

1 If you were the HR manager, what steps would you be taking? What would your chosen strategy be, and why?

2 What problems do you think you might encounter along the way?

Jon Haydon

By way of illustration, we can consider a basic model of learning and development activity such as the systematic training cycle. This model has been justifiably criticized as being unduly simplistic, and variations and developments have been proposed that show a more sophisticated understanding of the processes involved—but it will suffice for our current purpose. The cycle involves four stages, as illustrated in Figure 8.1:

- identification of training need
- design of training
- delivery of training
- evaluation of training.

The interventions described in the next chapter fall mainly into the delivery element of the cycle, but there are a range of processes that can and should support the delivery of a range of interventions—and it is these that we will now focus upon.

Organizations may characterize these purely as part of their MD activity, but they are at least equally likely to be seen as part of still wider efforts, which might be characterized as talent management, career development, or other concepts. Indeed, the wider one goes, the more difficult it is to separate MD from other aspects of HR such as reward, recruitment, or job design.

It is perhaps 'common sense' to suggest that all these processes, and indeed the interventions themselves should 'add value' or 'make a difference'—otherwise what is their point? The same argument, of course, would apply to any other activity within an organization such as recruitment, marketing, accounting, line management, and so on. The difficulty lies in establishing both what we mean by adding value, and whether any particular activity or process achieves it.

Figure 8.1 Systematic training cycle

Summary of section

In addition to the specific management development interventions that are discussed in some detail in the next chapter, a range of processes need also to be considered as part of the total management development effort of the organization. They are processes that support the interventions in a variety of ways. Depending how one interprets and conceptualizes these processes they may be regarded specifically as management development or as part of some other effort such as talent management. However one regards them, these supporting efforts need to be well integrated and need to add value to the organization.

The concept of added value

The concept of added value has a long tradition in different management disciplines, and in the context of this book it is an idea that will vary slightly, according to our notions of what constitutes management development. There are clear links to the evaluation of management development—a topic covered more extensively in Chapter 10. We might reasonably define management development as 'producing a management cohort in the organization that is more effective at achieving the organization's current and future goals than would otherwise be the case—and producing this outcome at a cost which is considerably less than the benefits of doing so'. The concept can be applied also to individual management development interventions—for example, 'Did our action learning programme improve our capacity to achieve our strategic objectives?'

Added value has roots in a number of disciplines including accounting, strategic and operational management, and marketing. Escover's (1994) views added value in the context of the growth and subsequent crisis experienced by large bureaucratic

Reflection point 8.1

Consider the tentative definition advanced above for a moment, and reflect on the following questions (and maybe some more of your own):

- How are we to know if—and to what extent—we have been able to produce a group of managers who are more effective?
- If we can say they are more effective, how are we to know that this has arisen from our MD activities?
- How can we know what would have been the outcome if we had done nothing?
- How can we establish the costs of the various processes/interventions?
- How can we quantify the benefits arising from this increased effectiveness in meeting current (and, even more difficult, future) goals?

organizations as they struggled in the face of more entrepreneurial and dynamic competitors in the 1980s and 1990s. He suggests that middle managers and functions which do not clearly and directly add value (including HR—and by extension MD) have come, and will continue to be, under extreme scrutiny in the battle to reduce costs and keep only those parts of the business that can be seen to 'add value'. He does not address issues of definition, however, or the difficulties of measurement—seeming to take at face value the notion that organizations needed to downsize and re-engineer themselves.

De Chernatony *et al.* (2000) discuss the meaning of the term, concluding that it is a 'multi-dimensional construct, interpreted differently by different people' (p 39). Their paper comes largely from a marketing perspective, and suggests that the notion of added value can be found variously in branches of the profession including pricing, consumer behaviour, and strategy.

Activity-based costing (ABC), overhead value analysis (OVA), and economic value added (EVA) are three financially based techniques that seek to both measure true value added but also to some extent (by integration with wider management processes) to change mindsets within an organization so that all management activity and decision making are focused on truly adding value to the business. OVA can be clearly related to Porter's value chain (see below) and seeks to examine closely all overhead activity. This is likely to involve both (internal) customer perceptions and ideas for service improvement, as well as scrutiny and analysis of costs. In relation to leadership and management development, the difficulties surround an assessment of value—both in terms of hard figures and customer perceptions, which may only take a short-term view or be based on limited understanding of the function's objectives and potential. There is a danger with this technique that, although results may be presented in numbers, they are derived largely from qualitative data—and this data ignores elements of power and politics within the organization.

Schneier (1997, p 14) discusses people value added (PVA) as 'an economic measure of productivity and organization effectiveness ... a ratio that measures value created relative to the capital investment in human resources'. He suggests that a high PVA results from an integrated approach to running the organization, embracing a strategy appropriate to the external competitive situation and the internal capability and processes that enable an effective implementation.

Value based management seeks to create an awareness of value in all management decisions, across all areas of the organization. It is designed to create a shift in the way all managers think about costs, profit, and budgets—going beyond traditional accounting methods.

Porter's value chain (1980) is a key contributor to notions of added value. The starting point is the idea that competitive advantage arises from both external factors and from the organization's internal resources (financial resources, physical assets, knowledge, human and social capital, etc.) and how they are managed.

The internal resources are especially useful as a competitive tool when they are unique, hard to copy, and difficult to poach. The value chain consists of linked primary activities of the organization, converting inputs to outputs, supported by underpinning activities including HR policies and practices (such as leadership and management development, amongst others). Other underpinning issues include technological development, infrastructure, and procurement activities.

Advantage or disadvantage (value added or subtracted) can occur at any point in the chain created by these activities, both within the activities and—crucially—in the links between them. The links are often characterized by intangible elements such as organizational culture, trust, tacit knowledge, and so on—these are elements that are particularly difficult to copy since they are unique to the organization concerned. They are also elements that would be impacted by leadership and management development activities and processes.

The model has a clear focus on the measurement of outputs and in our context this would require consideration of the contribution made by management development activities to the end results of the organization. The difficulty, though, is that much of leadership and management development's contribution relates to the intangibles involved in the links between activities—which are much less susceptible to measurement, certainly by hard measures.

Normann and Ramirez (1994) conceptualize some of the same components in a less sequential way than Porter, in describing a 'value constellation' where customers and suppliers jointly co-produce value. A number of other approaches to notions of added value have some relevance to this discussion. They are discussed briefly below, with the elements most pertinent to management development highlighted.

Treacy and Wiersema (1996) proposed a value disciplines model, which suggests that organizations should choose between three generic value disciplines—operational excellence, product leadership, or customer intimacy—as the strategic means to pursue competitive advantage. For management development, the implications relate to both the capacity of leaders and managers to engage successfully in the processes arising from each option, and the need for managers to align those processes in an effective way.

Goold *et al.* (1994) developed an approach which considers how parent companies operating a series of subsidiaries can best add value to their operations. They need to look at four possible means of creating value, each with its own potential downsides that would result in value destruction. These four options are stand-alone influence, linkage influence, central functions and services, and corporate development. These are largely choices relating to organizational structure, and each would have challenges and opportunities for adding value through management development. The nature of the parent company and the subsidiaries is of crucial importance in determining the most appropriate choice.

Green's model (1999) seeks to use three processes to assess added value, especially in relation to HR. These are to *align* people with the organization's purpose, to *engage* their commitment to its purpose, and to *measure* the resulting outcomes. Alignment might involve a variation of the balanced scorecard approach, originally developed by Kaplan and Norton (1996) as a measurement tool that focuses managers and others on key organizational objectives and processes. The measurement element leads into considerations of different approaches that will be discussed more fully in Chapter 10.

Cattell (2005) also identifies two elements to added value: adding value to the business and engaging employees so they are motivated to contribute accordingly. He identifies implications from this including identification of performance criteria aligned to business objectives, monitoring and measurement of performance, and the development of suitable skills. He regards it as a dimension of performance management.

Although different writers emphasize different elements when discussing added value, there is agreement on the notion of it being something that encompasses a wide range of organizational activity in pursuit of higher performance, including 'soft' elements—not just a straightforward accounting measure. The difficulty lies in translating these wider elements into a concept that—if it is to be meaningful—is based on hard measures.

Summary of section

The concept of added value is one that has a history in a number of different disciplines, and perhaps as a result is not always easy to pin down. In basic terms, it refers to the need for all activities to 'make a difference' and contribute positively to a successful organization. This implies the need to measure the value added, and there are a number of ways in which this can be attempted. As with all learning and development, measuring MD's contribution is fraught with difficulty, not least because quantitative measures do not necessarily work with some of the qualitative outcomes of successful development of managers. One of the main lessons from a consideration of added value is the need to ensure integration of all efforts in pursuit of the organization's goals. Management development is something which both contributes a crucial element of the organization's attempts to add value, but also needs to be seen to be adding value in its own right.

Management 'wrappers'

The related and overlapping notions of talent management, succession management, and career management can arguably be regarded as fashionable (to varying degrees at different times and places) wrappers for broad approaches to aspects of managing the human resource within organizations—all of which might encompass aspects of leadership and management development.

> ## Mini case study 8.2: Ensuring added value in a small manufacturing company
>
> A small company in a northern town, manufacturing soft furnishings, relies for its survival on keeping a tight rein on costs whilst constantly striving to improve quality and customer service.
>
> A major shortcoming over the years has been a lack of focus on internal management processes. There are few policies or consistent people management practices. A recently appointed general manager has responsibility to overhaul practices in this area, with a remit from the managing director to ensure any new activities are shown to 'add value'.
>
> He wishes to begin by looking at management development (there is very little of this at present for the half dozen managerial and supervisory staff) and asks you as a local MD consultant to make some suggestions—relating both to potential innovations in this area and how they can be shown to add value.
>
> ### Question
>
> 1 What kind of suggestions would you make in respect to both issues, and why?
>
> Jon Haydon

Talent management

Talent management is a concept, like many in management, which is difficult to pin down precisely, as it is interpreted differently by different writers and organizations. It has increasingly emerged in importance in the last decade or so, and has been consistently identified in surveys as a top challenge for organizations (Michaels *et al.*, 1998; Blass, 2007; PricewaterhouseCoopers, 2008). There may be a number of reasons for this including the rise of the knowledge economy (and knowledge workers can create more differential value than 'ordinary' production workers), changing demographics with an ageing population and fewer entrants to the labour market, and changing expectations of work amongst employees, which make them more likely to move on if their development aspirations are not met, or if they are not happy with their work–life balance or the ethical stance of the organization.

The original 'war for talent' research by McKinsey (Michaels *et al.*, 1998) focused not on the need for improved HR processes, but on the need for a changed mindset (a talent mindset) amongst leaders at all levels, as the means of gaining sustained high performance through strengthening the talent pool. The focus was strongly on managerial talent, whilst recognizing that similar issues applied to other employee cohorts. The authors identified five imperatives that organizations should act upon in order to 'win the war' for managerial talent:

■ Embrace a talent mindset—make talent the top priority, the area that no leader at any level should delegate (it is not the preserve of HR).

- Craft a winning employee value proposition—involving good financial rewards, but more importantly plenty of challenge and development in the job, with an open and trusting culture.

- Rebuild the recruitment strategy—from a passive choice strategy to a more aggressive and proactive search for talent at all levels at all times—a search that should embrace new sources of talent.

- Weave development throughout the organization—not just 'training' but by using stretching jobs, coaching, mentoring every day.

- Differentiate and affirm their people—reward high performers, help solid performers to raise their game and remove the weak performers (this presupposes rigorous and effective means of identifying who is in which category).

It is undoubtedly a concept that has become more fashionable in recent years—whether this is a passing fashion perhaps remains to be seen, but (as will become apparent below) the elements within it are not new—hence our notion of wrappers for a range of activities. Guest (2006) points out that, although there is an element of re-labelling involved in talent management, it enables organizations to review their practices, it integrates some old ideas, and gives them a freshness that is positive.

Watson (2008) identifies this relationship between the characteristics and approaches found within both management development and talent management. She considers MD to be an integral part of talent management, which needs to be integrated horizontally with other HR practices—and she points out that talent management also needs to take account of broader issues such as reward and culture. She presents a framework identifying key influences on, and the interface between, the two concepts. Although set in the context of the hospitality sector, it portrays well the issues that are found more generally. Influences highlighted include career management issues such as industry image, qualifications, mobility, and motivation; skills and competencies relating specifically to the industry and more generally in areas such as operations, leadership, and interpersonal skills; development practices, shared understandings, and the value of development and collaborative partnership approaches; and a range of internal (culture, values, HR systems) and external (structure and image of the industry, graduate expectations, and educational output) factors.

In relation to the imprecise conceptualization of talent management, the Chartered Institute of Personnel and Development's (CIPD's) *Learning and Development Survey* in 2006, for example, showed just over half of respondents were undertaking some talent management activities, whilst only 20 per cent of respondents had a specific definition of talent management. This suggests that organizations are recognizing the concept, without necessarily having a clear and shared understanding of what it is.

The CIPD (2009d, p 2) regard it as 'the systematic attraction, identification, development, engagement, retention and deployment of those individuals with high potential who are of particular value to an organization'. This definition clearly has a focus on high-value, high-potential employees (begging questions about who those might be and how they are identified) and is otherwise talking about all aspects of their management. In our context, leaders and managers are likely to be amongst those who are both identifying talent and identified as talent—and the development of these leaders and managers is a key part of talent management as defined in this way.

Others (for example Bones, 2006) are critical of the exclusive, elite-focused view of talent, and take a more inclusive notion of talent, as applying to a variety of roles and individuals across the organization.

Cunningham (2007) discusses alternative (though not mutually exclusive) approaches to talent management of either acquiring or developing talent, pointing out that organizations' desire for a 'quick fix' acquisition approach doesn't always bear fruit, since issues of 'cultural fit' come into play. He suggests the need for a more systemic approach, and discusses two strategic choices when considering talent management:

- aligning people with roles—with implications for recruitment and selection, learning and development, succession planning, and career management
- aligning roles with people—with implications for organization design, role design, reward practices, and working methods and environment.

He is keen to point out the interactions between these factors and suggests that issues of talent and performance are not resolved by focusing solely on one dimension.

Although there are differing views on what makes for talent management, there is agreement that it is a concept that embraces a range of managerial and organizational activity. The following processes would be included in most views of talent management: recruitment, reward, development, deployment, performance management, engagement, and retention. All these elements will have an impact on the development of managerial and leadership capacities in an organization, but many are not within the scope of this book. Some belong traditionally in discourses related to other areas of HR—but the talent management concept highlights the need to integrate all such

Reflection point 8.2: Alignment

- Which is the better approach to take in your organization—aligning people with roles or aligning roles with people?
- Why did you suggest that answer?

elements in pursuit of increased managerial and leadership contribution to the success of the organization. Although we focus on those processes more closely, and more traditionally, associated with leadership and management development, it is important to set them in this wider context. Without the appropriate culture surrounding distinct management development processes, they are clearly less likely to be effective.

Succession management

Hirsh (2000) regards succession planning as part of a wider concept—'succession management'—which also encompasses management development, human resource planning, recruitment and selection, and skills analysis. She considers succession planning to consist of identifying potential successors for key posts, either for the short term or for longer-term potential successors. Following this identification, a process of career planning and development activities is implemented for the individuals concerned.

The CIPD (2009c) identify a modern version of succession planning in opposition to the traditional highly structured, mechanistic, and top-down approach that was suitable for more stable environments with fixed organizational structures and long-term careers. The modern version, they suggest, has close links to wider talent management practices and seeks to balance the organization's needs with the individual's career management aspirations. Another feature of the updated approach results from the flatter organizational structures to be found in the early years of the 21st century, with career development moves to gain experience more likely now to involve lateral than upward movement. The CIPD also identify the need to integrate succession planning with competency frameworks, links to business planning, and a much greater degree of openness and fairness in the process.

Harrison (2009) regards succession planning as firmly part of the management development process, and highlights the need to develop managers and leaders particularly around the transition points in what she calls the 'leadership pipeline'. Its aim should be to 'secure the best leaders at every organizational level while offering motivating choices and appropriate development opportunities and resources at the key transition stages' (p 452). Managers and leaders will have a number of transition points in their career, but Harrison identifies three key transition stages as being the access to opportunities early in the manager's career in the organization, the plateau where further upward career advancement is unlikely, and finally the approach to exiting the organization.

Hills (2009) discusses differing approaches to succession planning—buying talent in or building it from within—and highlights the advantages and disadvantages of each approach. On the one hand, buying talent in enables the organization to bring in new ideas, acquire specialized skills, and keep pace with the market—but at a price, and with the risks of unproven talent and potential lack of cultural 'fit'. On the other hand, the less costly approach is to develop people to fit exactly what the organization needs, to enhance engagement of the existing workforce, and to have 'the devil you know'—but with less opportunity to inject new ideas and energy. There are similarities in approach to that taken by Cunningham (2007), as discussed above in the section on talent management. Woodall and Winstanley (1998) discuss succession planning firmly in the context of career management, from an organizational perspective. The boundaries between these concepts are not at all clear!

Career management

There are a number of different threads to be drawn together within notions of career management. There is a strong theme through much of the literature which highlights the two perspectives on career management owned respectively by the individual manager (or other employee) and by the organization. King (2004, p 47) brings this theme to the fore when articulating a definition of career management as:

> The design and implementation of organizational processes that enable the careers of individual employees to be managed in a way that encompasses organizational and individual career perspectives.

She discusses this dual approach as the search for an optimal rather than perfect fit between the perspectives of the two parties. The individual is likely to be seeking current career achievement and future success in meeting work and life goals, whereas the organization needs to develop people for both current and future needs. Woodall and Winstanley (1998) also identify the potential for conflict between individual and organizational goals in career management.

Another thread relates to the career paths followed by individuals and/or offered by organizations, many articulated through metaphors. For example, most of us can relate to the notion of a career 'ladder'. This is a concept used in common parlance and articulates a generally upward trajectory via a number of job or role rungs until an individual reaches their own particular height. Individual careers, of course, develop through the application of skills and abilities, but also partly from chance, and choices will be based on individual preferences, values, motives, and needs. Schein (1978; 1988) developed the notion of career anchors: eight motivations that guide career paths, which can be at least uncomfortable (and possibly psychologically harmful) if they are incompatible with the actual role or path chosen.

Schein's eight anchors are:

- *Technical/functional competence.* Career choice is based on technical, professional, or functional content of job role with value placed on recognition by peers and accomplishment of task.

- *General managerial competence*. Choice based on notions of organizational advancement, contribution to organizational success with value placed on pay, promotion, and status.

- *Autonomy/independence*. Value placed on autonomy and avoidance of close supervision and other irrationalities of organizational life, with motivation coming from public recognition rather than financial or status rewards.

- *Security/stability*. Choice based on need for security within an organizational career, and willing to trade this for loss of autonomy. Value placed on loyalty, steady performance, and promotion based on seniority—a good fit with a traditional bureaucracy.

- *Entrepreneurial creativity*. Choice dictated by need to create new products, services, or organizations that are closely associated with their own efforts. New challenges are important, as are power and freedom.

- *Sense of service/dedication to a cause*. Choice decided by personal values finding expression in area of work (e.g. environmental protection, world development, work with people), which is more important than financial reward.

- *Challenge*. Winning is all, and choice is based on need to continually overcome difficult obstacles or solve complex problems—this is of greater importance than financial reward, area of work, promotion, or recognition.

- *Lifestyle*. Flexibility is essential and choice is based on need to create an appropriate work–life balance (as we would know it today) so that the individual achieves integration with other important aspects of their life.

Alternative views and metaphors of career trajectories include stages (Schein, 1978; Super, 1984), spirals (Rapoport and Rapoport's triple helix, 1980; Driver, 1982), concepts (Driver, 1982), and three dimensional/climbing frame (Schein, 1978; Gunz, 1989). It is clear that the changing world of work (towards flatter organizations, end of 'job for life', etc.) suggests one or more of these approaches as being more appropriate than the traditional 'ladder', although some question the extent to which the 'old order' is dying and the extent to which a new psychological contract based on employability reflects reality.

Reflection point 8.3: Career anchors

- Do you recognize your career anchors in the typology above?
- If so, are you currently working in a broadly compatible area or are your immediate plans to do so?
- If your current career path isn't compatible with your anchors, reflect on what action you might take.

A third thread focuses on the various practices that might be employed within organizations as part of a concerted effort at career management. There are differing views as to what might be included, partly arising from differing notions of career management and the associated concepts discussed within this chapter.

Guest and King (2005) discuss the range of career management activities highlighted by the 2003 CIPD *Managing Employee Careers* survey, and point out that a number of these practices can be considered as part of 'management development'. The activities in the CIPD survey are broken down into five areas:

- basic career planning and support—developmental objectives, developmental reviews, informal career support

- internal job markets—open internal job market, online vacancy advertising

- developmental assignments—internal and external secondments, shadowing, career break schemes

- career information and advice—professional career counselling, career coaching, careers workshops and resources

- initiatives aimed at specific groups—e.g. graduate or 'high potential' development schemes, succession planning, development centres.

In recognizing the highly contextual nature of career management (from both perspectives), King (2004) proposes some general principles rather than a 'best practice' prescription. The general principles are consistency in presenting the organization's perspective, proactivity in matching to the organization's current and future strategies, collaboration and cooperation between employer and employee, and dynamism in remaining flexible in approach over time as circumstances change.

She suggests that many organizations might view career management as too complicated and with benefits far in the future, and therefore difficult to justify in relation to short-term financial payback. The same argument may be advanced in relation to investment in employee development generally, of course—and yet there is growing evidence of the importance of people as a source of sustained competitive advantage. It is also the case, as King points out, that when many organizations are facing recruitment difficulties and skills shortages, it is even more important for ongoing success to grow talent from within.

Guest and King's summary of the situation in the UK is that career management processes are used to identify and develop managers with potential for the highest contribution, and to retain talent, particularly within the larger private sector organizations. For most employees, including much of the current and future managerial population outside these larger organizations, career management is more about an individual responsibility to identify needs and pursue relevant opportunities.

The last thread—which has been touched upon earlier—relates to the conceptu- alization of career management and its relationship to other ideas of management development, succession planning, and talent management. Writers may not be overly concerned with these overlapping notions as such, but each tends to offer a view as to how they relate to one another. Guest and King (2005) examine career management in the context of possible solutions to the perceived problems of British management—problems which we have discussed earlier in the book and which have been the subject of many investigations over the years. They consider two widely recommended solutions—management development and career management—and discuss the extent to which either might improve managerial quality.

Career management is regarded as a highly future-oriented process and one that is of interest to both organizations and individuals, in general terms. The authors are clearly focused on career management processes within organizations aimed at their managerial cohorts. In relation to the question of these overlapping concepts, they regard career management as a concept wider than management development. The latter, they suggest, is 'one aspect of career management for an individual manager, but also a tool by which managers may be helped in the short term to oversee the careers of their subordinates' (p 254).

Summary of section

The related and overlapping concepts of talent management, career management, and suc- cession planning have been used by writers and by organizations to describe and delineate their practices in the areas of concern to us—how best to manage and develop the manager- ial resource for maximum organizational benefit. They have relationships to one another and to the idea of 'management development'. The difficulty is often to understand exactly what these relationships are, and where the boundaries lie between the various and some- times competing concepts. The notion of 'wrappers' is advanced as a means of explaining the shifting and unclear boundaries, and to suggest that in many cases a differing mix chosen from the same cluster of practices can be wrapped and labelled in a particular way, in a par- ticular setting.

There would be overlapping boundaries even if there were universal agreement on the meanings of the terms, which is not the case. The section discussed some of the main ideas within each 'wrapper' and it is suggested that context will dictate how an organization might choose to present similar clusters of practices.

Figure 8.2 represents our attempts to both make sense of the wrappers and to present them in a graphical form. It should be borne in mind, however, that any attempt to portray the concepts in such a way is doomed to fail because of the shifting, context-related bound- aries between them!

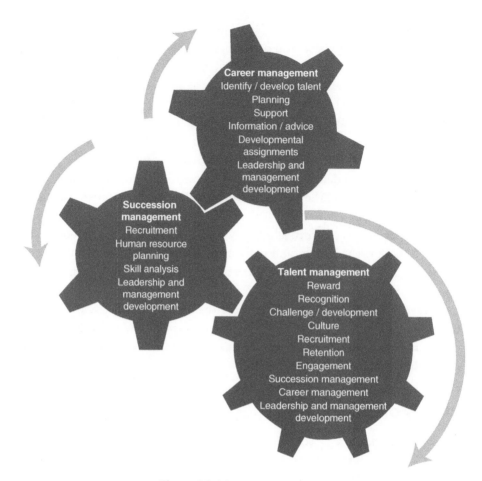

Figure 8.2 Management wrappers

Competency frameworks

Competency frameworks are widely used, particularly in larger organizations, and may variously be linked to other people management processes such as recruitment and selection, appraisal, identification of development needs, development activities, promotion, and reward. The concepts of competences and competencies has historical roots in the USA in the late 1970s, and in the UK between five and ten years later, and have been applied to both the organizational level and to wider developments such as the Management Charter Initiative (MCI) and S/NVQs (see, for example, discussion in Chapter 4). A key writer in the development of ideas about competencies was Boyatzis (1982), who defined them as 'the underlying characteristics of a person that lead to or cause effective and outstanding performance'.

There has been much written about the terms 'competences' and 'competencies', and it is not intended to rehearse the arguments here—the general notion (whatever term is used and whatever differences might be identified) is of an attempt to describe the skills, knowledge, behaviours, qualities, etc. that lead to effective (managerial in our context) performance.

Competency frameworks tend to group the competencies, subdivide them, and apply descriptors appropriate for differing levels of management, in order to make overall sense of them and provide a workable model for organizational use. Many organizations have developed their own specific frameworks, whilst others have used or adapted generic frameworks. They provide a template for whatever range of people-management practices the organization wishes to use.

Criticisms of the approach include the tendency to develop into highly structured and bureaucratic approaches in practice, and to focus too much on current notions of effective performance at the expense of flexible responses to changing circumstances. They have also been criticized for encouraging sameness at the expense of diversity, and can be expensive to design, implement, and monitor.

However, others suggest these drawbacks can be overcome—Sparrow (1992), for example, suggests a life-cycle element to competencies, which recognizes those of particular use for current, future, and transitional stages. Holbeche (2008), meanwhile, notes an increased tendency to include more elements in competency frameworks that encourage flexibility, innovation, learning, and cultural transformation. Boyatzis and Saatcioglu (2008) suggest that key competencies around emotional, social, and cognitive intelligence can be developed on a management education programme and that they can remain fresh for several years, but need continuous improvement and renewal to avoid being damaged by destructive organizational practices.

If competency frameworks are part of the management development processes (either within the organization or by use of an external framework of some kind), they are likely to be used in one or more of the following ways to support MD:

- as an attempt to align managerial (and other employee) skills and behaviour to organizational objectives and requirements

- to communicate desired behaviours to all managers

- in performance appraisal discussions, to identify development needs through discussion of strengths and weaknesses against the competencies

- as components in self-assessment or 360° approaches to performance management

- as a consistent vehicle for framing feedback to managers

- as a consistent thread linking all development activities

- to align management development activity to other aspects of HR practice in the organization (such as recruitment and reward)

- to drive all aspects of development centres.

Summary of section

Competency frameworks are common, in particular, in large organizations—and competency-based approaches are found in wider contexts such as national education and training frameworks and as the basis for management and professional qualification curricula.

They have faced some criticism for being overly cumbersome and inflexible, for describing current rather than future effectiveness, and for producing sameness rather than diversity. Design of the framework can to some extent lessen these drawbacks.

Competency frameworks are best utilized as part of a wider approach to managing the human (and in this case managerial) resource—in this way they can promote horizontal and vertical alignment within organizations.

Identification of management development needs

A number of techniques can be used to identify management development needs, and these may well be linked to aspects identified elsewhere in this chapter such as frameworks for competencies, career management, talent management, and so on.

The learning needs of managers will involve consideration of issues at a variety of levels, including the organization and the department (perhaps at an occupational level dependent upon the nature of the organization) as well as at individual manager level. Some efforts made to identify development needs will be part of a process at a particular time—a learning needs analysis relating to a proposed change initiative or major product launch, for example. Other ways of assessing development needs are more ongoing and are embedded within continuing organizational processes—identifying learning needs as part of an appraisal process, for example. These two approaches may well overlap—they are not mutually exclusive.

Analyses of development needs of the former kind might involve a range of techniques based around interviews, focus groups, questionnaires, diaries, or observations involving key stakeholders in the organization (relevant managerial cohorts, more senior managers, possibly team members, and so on). The organizational and/or departmental objectives will be reviewed, and relevant required skills/competencies arising from the review will be identified. These might be ongoing operationally focused objectives, or perhaps ones related to a specific initiative. There then needs to be a means of establishing the level of the required skills and competencies amongst the managers concerned.

Alternatively, a review might take place of required or desired managerial competencies within all or part of the organization—again leading to a consideration of the position of individual managers against the requirements thus identified. The review might be routinely conducted or arise from some form of critical incident analysis—where key problems are identified and analysed for (amongst other things) any learning needs.

There are overlaps between techniques used to identify task and skill requirements of particular job roles (e.g. those leading to the creation of job descriptions and person specifications) and those used in learning needs analysis at organizational, team, or job level. Many may be used to match an analysis of job with that of an individual to ensure a rounded view of the development needs of that individual in that particular role at that time. These techniques by themselves are less appropriate for managerial or leadership roles than lower-level or technical roles.

Each has advantages and disadvantages, and (as ever) the choice of method needs to take full account of the context in relation to issues of time, finance, culture, and so on. Diaries are subject to managers' omissions or falsifications and may be overly task focused, missing out other elements of motivation, approach, behaviour, and emotion. Observations run the risk of changing normal behaviour merely by the presence of the observer. Questionnaires, dependent upon design, may be too constraining of managers' responses, and interviews require skilled interviewers and a greater time investment than some other methods. Approaches using a mix of methods are likely to be more effective—questionnaires backed up by focus groups, for example (where questionnaires can help shape the agenda for discussion in a focus group) or diaries followed up by interview to explore some of the issues identified.

Critical incident techniques (CIT)—involving some of the techniques outlined above, most notably interviews—can be used to respond to problem areas, to explore the underlying reasons for repeated instances of poor performance by teams or the organization more generally. Less often, they may focus on particularly successful areas. Critical incidents are defined as events that contribute positively or negatively to variations from normal patterns of performance within the organization. By way of illustration, the same principle applies in the commonplace practice of looking at 'near misses' in health and safety management, so that lessons can be learnt and actions applied to avoid repetitions that may have more serious consequences on another occasion.

Alternatively, and in less of a 'crisis' approach, CIT can be used to establish from managers or others examples of particularly effective (or ineffective) actions or behaviour, or successful job performance generally—and these examples are then analysed to establish what contributory factors are involved and what can be learnt from them. It is slightly misleading to call it a technique—an approach would be a better word, since it can be applied in a variety of ways.

Another technique beloved of management development textbooks but apparently rarely used in organizations for this purpose is the repertory grid. It is a very systematic technique with roots in personal construct theory in psychology and can generate useful data quite quickly. It is, however, quite complex and requires highly trained interviewers. There is limited evidence to suggest the technique is much used in organizations to help identification of development needs.

These descriptions of approaches to analysing managerial development needs seem reasonably straightforward and uncontentious, and this may often be the case. It should be mentioned, however, that these analyses will be taking place in a context where power and organizational politics play an important role. Different stakeholder groups may have differing views on the causes of critical incidents or on the learning needs of particular groups of managers. Clarke (2003), for example, discusses a training needs analysis relating to care managers in a local authority Social Services department where issues of poor performance (and resulting training needs) are diagnosed differently by different groups within the organization—perceptions were 'significantly shaped by the much wider socio-political context' (p 149). The issue then arises as to whose analysis is taken as the 'correct' one in determining the most appropriate response. Clarke proposes a framework by which practitioners may make more informed judgements through consideration of the impact of organizational politics.

Identification of individual managers' development needs, then, may arise from a specific, wider review of some kind where individual implications are then considered. Alternatively, these development needs may be identified as part of a continuing process such as appraisal.

There are, as we know, a number of different approaches that can be taken to appraisal. The next chapter specifically considers 360° feedback as an approach used

Mini case study 8.3: Analysing management development needs in Alpha Wines

A new chief executive was appointed to a retail drinks chain with branches throughout the UK and Ireland. Management development had been highlighted in the recruitment process as an issue and she was asked to have an early focus on making improvements in this area of the business.

She asked the HR team to conduct a thorough review, and they looked at all aspects of current provision. They found that activity was ad hoc and inconsistent, relying on individual managers to identify their own needs and fight for resources to meet them. Although there was an existing appraisal process for all employees, including managers, it wasn't implemented effectively and so they recommended separate measures to address the problem of inadequate identification of needs.

The proposal was to develop a competency framework, use development centres to assess against it and help managers to develop their own plans, with a commitment to fund development interventions arising from the process. Although this worked quite well and was an improvement on previous practice, the weakness was in the lack of managerial support for development activities that were not off the job and/or qualification related.

Question

1 How could this weakness be addressed as the next stage in a process of improvement?

Jon Haydon

in management development—and this technique can be used as a one-off, as part of another intervention (a development centre, or linked to coaching, mentoring, action learning, etc.), or as the preferred method of routinely conducting managers' appraisals in the organization.

Managerial appraisals are likely to be linked to some mix of organizational and departmental objectives, personal targets, and desired competencies, with an attempt made to identify any learning needs to help the manager attain the objectives or reach the desired levels of competence. Discussion of appraisals generally (not specifically those of managers) in the literature tends to find broad agreement on the theoretical benefits, whilst acknowledging the many difficulties found in practice. The problems relate largely to issues of implementation (poorly defined objectives, inadequate training, lip service, and lack of follow through) and lack of cultural fit. Managerial appraisals that are designed to (amongst other things) identify development needs should ideally not be overtly linked to reward, as this will inhibit the open and honest discussions required to tease out any issues of performance improvement leading to required learning.

A means of addressing managers' development needs that is removed from the potentially contentious arena of the appraisal is the development centre. This is an adaptation of the techniques used in selection assessment centres designed to identify development needs against a given set of competencies or other criteria. Ballantyne and Povah (2004, p 142) define a development centre as:

the use of Assessment Centre technology for the identification of strengths and weaknesses to diagnose development needs that will facilitate more effective job performance/career advancement which in turn contributes to greater organization success.

A development centre is likely to run over two or three days and techniques used might typically include work simulations, psychometric tests, interviews, group discussions, self-administered inventories, and role plays. Feedback is provided throughout the process with the aim of encouraging both personal reflection and individual ownership of the development needs identified and agreed. The outcomes will include a development plan, and a centre will be ideally structured as part of a wider developmental process tied to organizationally agreed managerial competencies, strategic objectives, and an organized programme of interventions including support for self-development. There is some research to confirm, in fact, that their success depends upon the effectiveness of subsequent development and support (Neary and Lucks, 2005).

Although the development centre can be a thorough and effective means of identifying development needs, because of its cost and the investment of time involved it is more likely to be found in larger organizations. Because of the active involvement of the individual, the development centre approach also links well to career management processes.

Many organizations may also make use of self-assessment of needs by the manager—either on its own or linked to another process. This has obvious attractions for, in particular, smaller organizations. There are benefits in that the manager is well placed to understand the development needs in their particular context, and a more accurate perception may be encouraged by the use of support in the form of an individual (coach, mentor, or 'critical friend'), group (peer or upward appraisal), or analytical instrument of some kind (perhaps linked to identified skill sets).

Summary of section

Attempts to identify and analyse management development needs are likely to arise in one of two (not mutually exclusive) ways:

- as a discrete activity undertaken at a specific time, perhaps in response to a series of critical incidents or in planning for major change
- as part of an ongoing effort to keep abreast of changing development needs, and possibly allied to other organizational processes with overlapping aims.

Efforts at identifying needs may focus on organizational, departmental, occupational, or individual levels—although these may overlap in various ways, there is often likely to be an individual element since needs identified at the other levels will often need to be personalized prior to implementing interventions.

At levels above the individual, techniques are likely to be based around some form and mix of interview, observation, or questionnaire and to involve a range of appropriate stakeholders. The involvement of stakeholder groups suggests the need to take account of issues of power and organizational politics when drawing conclusions from the analysis.

At the level of the individual manager, identification of development needs is most likely to be based on an appraisal process of some kind, a self-assessment, or perhaps a development centre.

Management development audit

Finally, and briefly, in this chapter, we consider management development audits, which provide a link to Chapter 10 which discusses evaluation of MD processes and interventions.

An audit of management development processes and activity may form part of an evaluation process. It is a systematic process that might be undertaken as a one-off, or occasional, process—or it might be more ongoing. It is designed to establish a clear picture of what is going on, in relation to MD activity, and also to establish managers' views, feelings, and perceptions about both current and possibly future activity.

A key element is clarity as to its purpose—is it seeking to benchmark activity to some external framework or organization, for example, or is it designed to control costs or to identify improvements?

The audit should take a clear and rigorous look at all aspects of management development, including all aspects discussed in this chapter. This would include, for example, development centres, appraisal processes, assessment tools, competency framework, and so on.

Along with clarity of purpose, a well-planned audit will need to decide on issues of types of data to collect, whether to focus on inputs, outputs, processes, or some combination of these, and how to separate cause and effect.

This last point is crucial in all aspects of evaluation and will be picked up in Chapter 10.

Chapter summary

This chapter has considered a number of potential processes to be used by organizations in support of leadership and management development interventions, such as competency frameworks, methods of identifying development needs, and audits of activity. The

Mini case study 8.4: Integrating a value added competency framework

A travel company operating across the UK has a retail chain, airline staff, and overseas representatives, and wishes to introduce a competency framework into the retail stores to address some performance issues that have surfaced in some stores. The framework will apply to all staff but aims to address issues of reward, performance, and development of managers in particular. The three arms of the business operate independently, although the HR function, amongst others, is organized centrally.

The organization operates in a volatile, highly competitive market; it has expanded significantly in the last decade by both acquisition and organic growth; and it tends to operate in a reactive ad hoc rather than planned strategic manner. HR policies and practices are not consistent across the business, partly due to the historical growth pattern and partly arising from its approach to strategy.

The HR director can relatively easily put together a tailored competency framework for the business, but is determined to ensure that it will both add value and be seen to do so.

Questions

1 What advice would you give the HR director to help ensure that the competency framework genuinely adds some value to the business?

2 How might you then demonstrate this to key stakeholders within the business?

Jon Haydon

discussion has taken place in the context of the need to add value (and what that means has also been considered) and of a variety of 'management wrappers' that encompass broad approaches to aspects of managing the human resource within organizations—each of which might encompass aspects of leadership and management development. Thus we have considered the notions of, and overlaps between, talent, succession and career management, and their relationship to different interpretations of leadership and management development.

Questions

1 Identify the four stages of the systematic training cycle.

2 Porter's value chain (1980) is a key driver of the added value concept—can you identify the elements in his model?

3 Green's model (1999) identified three processes to add value—can you identify them all?

4 Why has the concept of talent management grown in importance in the last decade or so?

5 Identify three common components of a career management process.

6 What are the two basic options to consider in relation to succession planning, according to Hills (2009)?

7 How did Boyatzis (1982) define competencies?

8 Name three common elements of a development centre.

Discussion questions

1 What would be your personal interpretation of the overlapping concepts of talent management, career management, and succession management? Does it matter what they are called in a particular setting?

2 How could you ensure that management development processes in your organization are firmly aligned to both strategic objectives and any wider related processes?

3 What do you think are the most effective and appropriate methods to identify management development needs? How dependent is your answer upon consideration of the organization in which you work?

4 What do you think are the most relevant competencies for managers to possess in the early part of the 21st century—and how dependent is your answer on the culture of your organization?

5 Does management development 'add value' in an organization you are familiar with?

Suggestions for further reading

Either of Schein's works identified in the text and reference list will provide much food for thought about career management. How much do you think you will need to take responsibility for your own career—and to what extent will you need and/or expect support from your employer?

The Workplace Employment Relations Surveys (WERS), conducted every five years or so, highlight a range of issues of relevance to our discussions about career and talent management. Review the last few surveys and reflect upon any items that are of interest—particularly in areas such as work–life balance, psychological contract, training, and recruitment. What implications do the findings have for talent management? See list of references.

The chapter by Guest and King (2005) in *Managing Human Resources* provides a succinct treatment of some key issues highlighted in this chapter and the next, with a strong research underpinning. It is both thought provoking and accessible and will lead the reader to reflect upon many relevant questions.

Read the article by Boyatzis and Saatcioglu (2008) highlighted in the text and reference list, and consider the question: 'Can effective managers and leaders be developed?' This is clearly a key question for readers of this text, and the answer may lead you to reflect on other issues such as whether leaders are born, not made—or whether we should all just make the best of what we have in the circumstances in which we find ourselves.

Design and delivery of leadership and management development interventions

The aims of this chapter are to:

● consider the range of different management development interventions.

● discuss the overriding importance of context to these.

Interventions include planned formal events as well as attempts to capture more informal learning, and the chapter will encompass issues of definition and implementation. It focuses specifically on:

● action learning

● coaching

● management education

● management simulations

● mentoring

● organizational development

● outdoor development

● self-development

● 360° feedback

● other possible interventions.

Introduction

The chapter considers a range of potential leadership and management development interventions but discusses the importance of context as critical in making an appropriate choice of interventions for a given situation—there is most assuredly no 'one size fits all' solution. We acknowledge the ways in which such interventions might be categorized but suggest that these are ultimately not helpful, not least because of the complexities of defining and conceptualizing interventions and the artificiality of the distinctions implicit in the categories. Consequently, we opt for a presentation of interventions in alphabetical order.

We also acknowledge that somebody's favoured intervention might not be included or given sufficient weight—we do not claim this chapter to be entirely comprehensive in coverage of potential interventions. We seek rather to explore some that are both commonly used and/or effective, and to discuss the importance of careful consideration of contextual factors when making choices about an appropriate intervention.

Mini case study 9.1: Management development interventions

The learning and development team in a large local authority department was seeking to improve the effectiveness of its management development (MD). Historically, there had been little emphasis on MD, with the predominant approach being to encourage formal professional education and development. Managers at all levels were those emerging from individual professional groups, and were often poorly trained or equipped to manage (especially to manage people). Senior managers recognized some problems, but were unsure how to proceed. Wider changes were also taking place including the development of a new appraisal process, introduction of a new training policy, and an independent staff survey.

A range of initiatives was tried out, including:

- a more focused approach to management education provision
- a series of half-day MD workshops
- training for managers in coaching techniques
- introduction of a mentoring scheme
- action learning as part of the department's approach to quality enhancement
- promotion of informal learning through awards, intranet forum, special events
- improved evaluation of learning and development activities, including MD.

The majority of these initiatives were unsuccessful and were not sustained beyond the short term. The reasons were largely cultural—the only learning and development recognized as valid by many managers and employees was formal professional and management education, which in any case was insufficiently resourced. On the other hand, informal learning was regarded with some suspicion, especially when it challenged prevailing norms and assumptions. The relationships between senior managers and the learning and development (L&D) team were not always harmonious, and there were many external financial and political pressures on the department, which worked against innovation.

Questions

1 Which of the initiatives described above do you think would be most likely to have succeeded, and why?

2 Which would be least likely to succeed, and why?

3 What else might the L&D team have proposed in order to improve MD's effectiveness?

Your answers to these questions might suggest the importance of context—interventions that would be likely to succeed in one setting may struggle in a different situation.

In this chapter, we consider a variety of interventions and their strengths and weaknesses—but it is arguably impossible to escape the issue of context.

Jon Haydon

Management development interventions

Any textbook on leadership and management development is bound to discuss, sooner or later, some of the vast range of possible interventions that can be made in organizations. There are different approaches that can be taken to categorizing these interventions—formal/informal, planned/unplanned, classroom/experiential, face to face/distance, and so on. All attempts to do so will inevitably produce questions about particular interventions, which (depending on how they are defined, and how they are introduced) might be considered to be in one or other category, or more likely to straddle them. For example, should we regard action learning as being a formal or informal approach; or coaching as planned or unplanned—it all depends on the circumstances of their introduction and use, and indeed our specific notion of what we mean by them. And formal planned management training programmes may well contain elements of self-development and encouragement of reflection.

This chapter seeks to avoid such categories as being ultimately unhelpful, taking instead an approach to some of the major interventions on a case-by-case basis, trying always to recognize the subtleties of definition, use, and context.

We should also pause to consider the assumptions we are making, some of which have been considered in other chapters, about the nature of learning, the nature of leadership and management, and about the possibility and extent to which we can develop managers and leaders. In thinking about which interventions might be regarded as most effective, we encounter vast difficulties arising from the fact that evaluation of management development, as with much L&D activity, is notoriously poor. In any case, evaluation of effectiveness is by definition context specific—i.e. was it effective for us, here, now?

There are differing views about managerial learning and about which approaches to development are most effective, although there is a growing consensus amongst academics. This consensus recognizes first that most managerial learning occurs on the job—something that most managers might also recognize—and second that responses to this evidence should avoid oversimplified or 'one size fits all' responses.

Holman (2000) proposes four models of management education and suggests avoiding an over-reliance on either theory or action, preferring instead approaches that develop reflective or critical practitioners. He suggests, according to Bolden (2007), that these are more successful because they use experiential approaches building upon natural learning at work, and address the complexities of managerial work in practice. Van der Sluis-den Dikken and Hoeksema (2001) argue that the interaction between individual and organizational characteristics is the driver of management development outcomes, and that learning on the job depends upon work challenges being available. McCauley *et al.* (1994) identified four clusters of job characteristics contributing to development of successful managers: job transitions, task-related aspects such as high levels of responsibility or creation of change, obstacles of various kinds, and provision of support and advice. Managers' responses to developmental opportunities thrown up by work can be characterized as planned or emergent (Megginson, 1996), prospective or retrospective (Mumford, 1995), meaning or instruction oriented (Hoeksema *et al.*, 1997). All of these suggested approaches are similar, and indicate that managers may use both categories, whilst perhaps being more predisposed to one.

Formal management education has been criticized variously for being irrelevant through separation of theory and practice, through approaches that are scientific rather than professional (Bennis and O'Toole, 2005) and for lacking criticality or an emphasis on the subtleties of context (Grey and French, 1996).

Despite some of this evidence and criticism, practitioners often still hold on to preferences for more formal and sometimes qualification-based management development. For example, Mabey and Ramirez (2004) identify line manager and HR preferences for more formal development approaches—compared with informal approaches—in all European countries in their study. The trend towards formal management qualifications as an approach to development was more marked in the UK than elsewhere.

Reflection point 9.1

- Why do you think there is such a strong attachment to formal and qualification based development amongst managers and development practitioners?

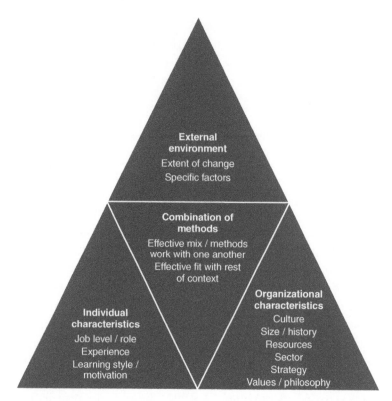

Figure 9.1 Range of contextual factors influencing choice of MD methods

Burgoyne *et al.* (2004) point out that we should avoid generic prescription:

The evidence on how leadership and management work is that they work in different ways in different situations. The practical implication of this is that to get the benefit of leadership and management development requires the design of appropriate approaches for specific situations rather than the adoption of a universal model of best practice.

In thinking about individual approaches, then, all of these issues, and others, need to be kept in mind—as well as the fact that any intervention is more likely to be successful when used in conjunction with others, and when it chimes with organizational strategies, manager preferences and motivations, and so on. Some of the relevant issues are highlighted in Figure 9.1.

The rest of the chapter considers, in turn, *some* of the variety of interventions that might be used. They are discussed in alphabetical order.

Summary of section

There is a huge range of management development interventions that could possibly be used in an organization, and also differing ways of categorizing them. We suggest that these categorizations are ultimately unhelpful, since different definitions, interpretations, and implementation may shift a given intervention from one category to another, or cause it to straddle more than one category.

Context is vital in considering management development interventions—when making choices about the most appropriate approach, it is important to consider a range of issues including organizational culture and strategy, the nature of the managerial cohort and how interventions might be combined to add extra value.

Action learning

Action learning is the creation of Reg Revans, and is, as the name suggests, a form of development that requires action to be taken, and that involves both learning from taking that action, and learning how to be more effective in future actions. Although a basically simple concept, it can be difficult to explain. Revans's writing on the subject can be quite dense and hard to follow, and action learning (as with many other forms of development) as defined and practised has generated a number of variations.

Essentially, action learning requires a number of (in this case) managers who meet regularly as a group (typically around six to eight people) in what is known as an action learning set. Each individual manager is committed to taking action on a significant problem or issue of their own choosing. There are differing options as to how action learning sets might be established. Depending on context, for example, it might be appropriate to have set members from different organizations, or from different parts of the same organization, rather than something more homogeneous. All other things being equal, it will be likely to be more effective to have as much diversity as possible within a set, as this will generate a greater number of perspectives to focus on each problem. However, context is all, and things that will be possible, or that will work, in one setting may not in another.

During set meetings, each manager in turns talks about their problem, and fellow set members question them about it—importantly, set members don't offer their own solutions to the problem. The aim is to provoke reflective thoughts on the part of the manager, who begins to see the problem from different angles and with new perspectives.

Having reflected, the manager will take action between set meetings and then come back to the next set meeting to outline how the situation has developed and

Reflection point 9.2

- 'Novice' set members sometimes find it hard to just ask questions and not offer their own solutions—why do you think this might be?

undertake the same process of questioning and reflection. The set meetings may be facilitated by a set adviser, or may in time become self-facilitating. There are general principles of confidentiality, and of equality—all set members have broadly equal 'airtime' for their problem, and all set members have equal status.

Over time, managers should develop successful approaches to their problems and may also have learnt about group processes, developed more confidence, built up a network of trusted colleagues, become more reflective, more responsible, and so on. Revans (1978, p 1) saw the aim of action learning as being 'to ensure that managers shall learn better to manage with and from each other in the course of tackling the very problems that it is their proper business to tackle; it has no truck with academic simulation of any kind'. This learning from one another is not just sharing what is known, but importantly is also about what managers do not know—airing doubts (Pedler and Boutall, 1992).

Mumford (1991) offers a summary of action learning that includes key ideas such as:

- Managerial learning should be about learning to take action, rather than merely analysing situations.

- This learning should involve taking action on the manager's own real and significant problems, not recommending action on someone else's problem.

- The learning process is a social process: managers are learning from and with other managers.

- Those providing support to the process do so as facilitators, not as traditional teachers or trainers—this is a distinct difference from many other forms of management development.

In Revans's view, learning came about from a combination of programmed knowledge (things that are already written down or otherwise capable of being passed on) and questioning insight (the crucial ingredient of critical reflection assisted by the questions of others involved in the process). He expressed this as the equation $L = P + Q$. There may be a role for theory within an action learning set, but largely in the context of planning or reflecting upon practical action.

Pedler (1997) considers action learning as having three interpretations: as being about changing the external world, about self-development, and about collaborative enquiry. At its most effective action learning will be about all three interpretations.

Action learning can be an exceptionally powerful form of development in different ways and on a variety of levels. It is also relatively cheap, requiring only the time of the set members and facilitator—and the paybacks can be immense in terms of increased profit, reduced costs, improved processes, and so on. It can be particularly effective in times of change, where new solutions and innovations are being sought, where managers have to work with the uncertainties of a turbulent environment (and when or where isn't there change these days?). For Newton and Wilkinson (1994) this notion of action learning as a tool for managing change is 'an indisputable fact'. Although it has gone in and out of fashion at different times and in different sectors, it has never really taken a central place in the management development activities of organizations generally. This may be for a number of reasons:

- To be really effective the organizational culture has to be right—it will not suit an authoritarian, command-and-control way of operating.

- It may be seen as too soft for the rigours of macho-oriented business managers.

- It may actually be too dangerous for organizations that don't really want managers to ask searching questions of the status quo and accepted ways of doing things.

- It is not always implemented in a form that is recognizably action learning, and is not as effective as it might be as a result.

Mini case study 9.2: Action learning for management development at Christian Aid

Christian Aid is a development charity working in 26 overseas locations, with a substantial staff presence in the UK. Their ethos is to support people to find their own solutions to the problems they face, and they have brought this principle to their MD programme as well. They are seeking to decentralize decision making in the organization, and this requires a strengthening of management capacity in all locations outside the UK.

Their management development programme links 360° feedback to action learning (AL). Their 360° feedback is based around four key areas: managing relationships, leading and managing a team, decision making and problem solving, and strategy and vision.

Each action learning set begins with participants sharing and discussing their 360° feedback, and choosing a project for the AL based on a workplace issue, but designed also to develop relevant skills.

Inevitably there have been one or two problems, but this is an interesting mix of two different MD approaches (see section on 360° feedback later in this chapter). It is worth noting, too, the clear 'fit' of action learning to the organization's management philosophy of self-directed problem solving, which applies equally to their goals for clients. It is also clear that the chosen approaches have a strategic fit to the objectives of decentralized decision making and empowering local managers.

Questions

1 What problems might you anticipate with this approach—especially the use of 360° feedback in this way? You might come back to this point after reading the section on 360° feedback later.

2 How might the organization go about an evaluation of this programme?

CIPD

Coaching

Coaching has enjoyed a remarkable growth as a management development intervention (indeed, as a wider learning and development approach) over the last ten to 15 years. It is, though, sometimes difficult to pin down as a practical tool because of the wide variety of ways in which it is conceptualized, and the range of settings in which it is employed.

It is sometimes regarded as a very specific, directive, skills-based, coach-led activity, and alternatively can be seen as a more wide-ranging, non-directive, learner-led activity. It can be considered as a discrete activity or as an integral part of management style; it may have a strictly limited short-term performance focus or be more expansive, looking at the whole person. It has been used to develop senior executives, new managers, women managers, and others; and it can be delivered by internal or external coaches or by line managers. It can be used in organizations to support individual development, to promote culture change, to help meet objectives—and it may be introduced formally and strategically, or in a more 'organic' or indeed ad hoc way.

It is clear, therefore, that any discussion of 'coaching' must take into account all these elements of the specific context. Equally, any introduction of coaching into an organization would need to take into account all these aspects in coming to decisions as to the most appropriate way forward for that context.

Parsloe (1999, p 8) defines coaching as being 'a process that enables learning and development to occur and thus performance to improve'. Whitmore (1996, p 8) regards it as 'unlocking a person's potential to maximize their own performance. It is helping them to learn rather than teaching them.' The CIPD (2008) regard it as 'developing a person's skills and knowledge so that their job performance improves' and suggest that it 'lasts for a short period and focuses on specific skills and goals'. Knights and Poppleton (2007) take a slightly wider view, suggesting coaching is 'an activity where an individual meets with a coach on a one-to-one basis to work on a range of work-related issues, some of which may also include personal factors'. Du Toit (2006) focuses on the sense-making aspect of coaching as an intervention, acting as a catalyst to help managers to deal with change effectively.

There are potentially overlaps with other 'helping' development strategies such as mentoring or counselling, and (depending on the approach taken) certainly a number of the skills required of the 'helpers' are similar. The growth of coaching may relate to its strength in helping managers to deal with change, its personal, one-to-one, tailored nature as a development tool, and the fact that it works well within the increasingly accepted paradigm of 'training to learning'—the move towards greater self-development, putting the learner rather than trainer at the heart of the learning process and the idea of lifelong learning.

There are many models of coaching available, and many different approaches taken by individual coaches and by organizations using this method. Barner and Higgins (2005) suggest that all coaches and their commissioners will, subconsciously or otherwise, subscribe to a particular overarching model—and they identify four theory models: a clinical model, a behavioural model, a systems model, and a social constructionist model. Each has its own notions as to the goals of coaching, the sources of change in the individual, the role of the coach, and the focus of the coaching.

The clinical model aims to help the individual to gain insights into themselves as a manager and as a person, and to effect changes based on these insights. They may use instruments such as Myers-Briggs Type Indicator (MBTI) to help this understanding of personality and behaviour, and the coach will be acting in a counselling or even therapeutic role—wherein lies a principal danger of this approach, if the coach is not equipped to deal with issues that may surface during coaching. Other drawbacks to this approach are the dangers of 'labelling' by the individual and others, or even the coach, all of which may impede change and development.

The behavioural model may have more modest goals relating to helping the individual to change problematic aspects of their behaviour. The coach will seek to promote change by assisting the individual to recognize the impact of their behaviour on themselves and on others, with an emphasis on improved performance through changed behaviours. The coach will act as guide or trainer, and will use feedback from a variety of sources to promote the desired changes. The drawbacks to this theory model are the possible tendency to miss wider personal or organizational issues that contribute to the issues under consideration; that the changes may be superficial as a result; or that perfectly acceptable behaviour can be seen as problematic in a given context.

The systems model suggests that the coach must fully understand the organizational context in which the manager is working, and that changes to these wider systems are required to support behavioural change on the part of the manager. The coach will need to engage the support of other organizational stakeholders to successfully effect change, and the difficulties of doing so are one major drawback to this model. Apart from the complications of effecting change across a variety of individuals and systems, key individuals such as the coachee's manager may resist the implication that they have a role to play in either the problem or the solution.

Finally, the social constructionist model focuses on the social identities of the individual and the importance of language in both describing and also shaping those identities. Issues might relate to how the individual sees themselves and how others in the organization see them—what individual narratives have been constructed, how have concepts (e.g. good performance, strong leadership, effective team) been constructed within the organization? The coach helps the individual to see how they (and others) frame their experiences and how new interpretations can be created to make changes to behaviour and perception. The goal of the coaching is still to improve performance, however, and this focus needs to be maintained. Other potential drawbacks are the failure to recognize the dynamic and subjective nature of the individual's story, and to dismiss something important as a result or to impose the coach's perspective and lose the individual's trust.

Reflection point 9.3

- We refer above to the shared skill set across coaching and other 'helping' development approaches—what do you think are the key skills required?

These four theory models explain the different approaches at a macro level, and it is possible to see within them some of the different definitions discussed earlier. The crossovers to other 'helping strategies' are also clear—counselling, for example.

The GROW model (Whitmore, 1996) is a well-known approach to coaching at a micro level. Although there are many other models and approaches used by coaches, the GROW model is a useful one to mention briefly because of its popularity and its apparent simplicity. It may be better named as the GROW sequence since it is suggested as a useful order for asking questions in a coaching session. Whitmore is clear that GROW sequencing without the context of awareness and responsibility is of little value. The key elements in coaching, he suggests, are the creation of awareness through questioning, and the development of responsibility, through choice, on the part of the person being coached.

The GROW sequence is a mnemonic:

- Goals—setting end and performance goals, and goals for the individual session
- Reality—clarifying the current situation
- Options—creating as many alternative courses of action as possible, and considering their pros and cons
- Will—decision time! Choosing the best option and making a plan of action.

Mini case study 9.3: Coaching in Bombardier Transportation

Bombardier is a world-leading manufacturer of transportation solutions, ranging from regional aircraft and business jets to rail equipment, systems, and services. With headquarters in Canada, it has a presence in 60 countries across five continents, employing around 30,000 people, 75 per cent of them in Europe. The majority of the leaders come from an engineering or other technical background, and a constant challenge is to develop the leadership and management capacity within this complex organization in addition to the technical competence.

Coaching has historically been used in different ways across the group's 11 operating divisions and has to a considerable extent become integrated into a management style. This has worked well, even given the manufacturing environment, and is seen as increasingly critical in a global and changing organization.

External coaching is offered at executive level and to high-potential managers, sometimes as part of a leadership development programme. It is seen as a high-cost intervention, however, and there is a resulting resistance to offering it more widely. There is also a lack of credible alternatives for this group, whereas there are alternatives lower down the hierarchy. Advantages perceived in using external coaches include their independence from the organization and consequent lack of preconceptions, their ability to offer fresh perspectives based on their experience working across other organizations; and confidentiality is also seen as more guaranteed with an external coach.

There is a pilot programme in Austria to develop internal coaches who would offer coaching to other departments as an alternative to external coaches. Coaching is seen as one intervention amongst many that contributes to a strategy of leadership development.

Prior to engaging external coaches, objectives are jointly agreed between managers, coachees, and HR. Coaching is, in the main, woven into other processes such as leadership and management development programmes, performance management or succession planning processes, and a previous 360° feedback process. Occasionally it was a stand-alone process.

Evaluation is mostly at an individual level and based on feedback from the coachee, their manager, and HR. There are plans to grow coaching further within the organization, including the development of internal quality standards to guide the sourcing of coaches and the management of coaching relationships in future.

Questions

1 Coaching is seen as important in responding to change in this case study. Why is it useful in this context?

2 If coaching is an integral part of management style across the organization, does it matter if external coaching remains the privilege of only the most senior levels in the business?

CIPD

Management education

Management education refers to the variety of qualification-based educational courses, at undergraduate or postgraduate levels, in business and management topics. There is some overlap into professional qualifications in business-related but more specific areas such as human resource management, marketing, and so on.

There has been a growth in management education in the last two or three decades—the MBA, for example, once the preserve of relatively few institutions and graduates, has become more commonplace, is offered in more institutions and countries, and in a growing variety of forms: full- and part-time, distance learning, in company, sector specific, and so on. But the MBA is not the sole element in management education, even though much of the criticism of the latter has been focused upon it. Management education is a growth area in rapidly developing nations (and those that were previously resistant to market capitalism) such as India, China, and Russia.

There is a wealth of management education provided in the form of postgraduate certificates and diplomas, undergraduate business degree courses, or (in the UK) HNC, HND, and foundation degree programmes. The management education market, in short, is nowadays much more diverse than it has ever been.

The debate about management education effectiveness has focused on perceived weaknesses of courses and providers, with suggestions that the products of business schools are strong on theory but not on practice. It has been argued by many (e.g. Margerison, 1991; Mumford, 1996; Willmott, 1994) that they are variously effective at policy or strategy development but not at implementation, that they are ill equipped for a changing world because of an overly technical view of management, that they show strong analytical and 'hard' skills, but not 'soft' people skills—the very areas that are becoming more important in 21st-century organizations. There is, in any case, the broader argument that management, by its nature, is not something that can be learned exclusively in a classroom since it involves subtle understandings of which actions to take in particular contexts. The debate about the purpose and effectiveness of management education and of business schools continues (McEnrue, 2002; Grey, 2002; Gosling and Mintzberg, 2004; Bennis and O'Toole, 2005; Quelch, 2005; Brotheridge and Long, 2007; Hay, 2008, for example), with the same broad themes about the relevance of teaching and research, the tension between theory and practice, and the nature of institutions and students. It is also possible that higher education institutions, that are at least one stage removed from business organizations, are likely to struggle to keep up to date with the changing realities of organizational life and to respond quickly and appropriately—the same would be true of professional bodies, for example.

Many of the criticisms of management education, however, whilst having some validity when initially made, may be focused on the wrong target, or one that increasingly does not exist. A management education programme that is entirely classroom based, that is full-time, that involves no elements of self-reflection, no engagement with organizational realities through placements, case studies, etc., that is focused on strategy and hard analytical skills to the exclusion of other curriculum areas is increasingly hard to find. Management education is increasingly likely to be part-time, post experience, taught using a variety of methods, focused across a wide curriculum, and with considerable emphasis on the practical alongside the theoretical.

Management education is still highly valued by practising managers as a 'developmental passport'—a means to both demonstrate competence and to assist in career progress and development both within and between organizations. It is also a familiar method for senior managers and developers, and it shows no sign of decline as part of the overall management development mix within the majority of (particularly) medium and large organizations.

Reflection point 9.4

- Do you think management education is inevitably flawed because of its classroom, not workplace orientation, or is there a cogent argument for managers to have access to a comprehensive toolkit of underpinning knowledge?

- What methods might be employed to make it more effective and relevant to 21st-century organizational life?

Management simulations

Management simulations and management games are an element in management development that can be deployed within a wider approach such as management education (Graham *et al.*, 1992) or formal in-house programmes (Bergin and Prusko, 1990).

Business/management games, often based on computer models, involve teams of managers working to resolve a given business scenario. Decisions made have consequences that result in a new set of circumstances to be worked with, and new information may also be introduced into the scenario periodically. The simulations may run for varying lengths of time, from hours to days, or possibly over a number of weeks with gaps between. These games assist with team working, as managers grapple with challenging and realistic (though not real) situations—and they can encourage managers to take a holistic view of a situation rather than one based purely on their own area of expertise. They may contain within them elements of role play or particular skills such as making presentations or negotiating.

Benefits of simulations of various kinds have been identified within the academic literature (summarized by Adobor and Daneshfar, 2006) as including the application of theory to practice (albeit simulated practice), the development of complex critical thinking skills as managers grapple with challenging problems, a growth in learner responsibility for learning as they become more actively involved in the process, improved motivation and self-belief amongst the learners, and improved team working or at least understanding of aspects of group dynamics.

One downside of management simulations is that they are just that—they are simulations of 'the real thing', although this is arguably better than methods that are completely divorced from managerial realities. It can be argued conversely, that simulations enable mistakes to be made and lessons learnt, in a safe environment. Some individuals will more willingly engage in this kind of activity than others, and their success depends on the facilitation skills of the developers as well as effective design of the simulation activities. Those based partially on real events are likely to be more effective since they are more reflective of reality.

Adobor and Daneshfar (2006) researched the factors that promoted the effective use of simulations in the context of management education. They found that the nature of the simulation and team dynamics affects outcome. The extent to which the simulation was perceived by learners as realistic was positively associated with learning, as was the ease with which the simulation could be used. Learners sought simulations that were reasonably complex, yet showed the link between their decisions and the outcomes—and simulations (the context here was of computer-based simulations) that were easy to use and provided suitable amounts of information. The extent of emotional conflict within teams led to a negative association with learning, whereas task conflict—in the sense of a variety of views that could be exchanged within the team—was positively associated with learning.

Mentoring

Mentoring is usually regarded as a longer-term development approach than coaching, with which it shares the characteristics of a one-to-one relationship and some of the skills required of mentor or coach. Clutterbuck (1998) points out that both coaching and mentoring are heavily dependent on providing sufficient personal reflective space for a learning dialogue to take place, and this is largely where the skills overlap between mentor and coach.

Whereas coaching can be carried out by defined coaches or by line managers, mentoring almost by definition will not involve the line manager. Clutterbuck and Megginson (1999, p 3), for example, regard mentoring as 'off-line help by one person to another in making significant transitions in knowledge, work or thinking'.

Whilst there are different emphases on the form of mentoring in different parts of the world, the shared elements of any approach to mentoring are likely to include the mentor being a more senior manager, possibly from a completely different function and certainly from a different team, and the relationship being long term, involving advice, provision of access to contacts and resources not normally available to the mentee, and a focus on the broad career development of the mentee.

As with coaching, different mentors and different organizations will approach mentoring from varying perspectives—they will be more or less directive, for example, and will work somewhere on a spectrum from challenging to nurturing. The best mentors and the most successful mentoring relationships will be able to adapt, and include just the right amount of direction, and the appropriate degree of challenge to suit the particular circumstances.

Mentoring is used for a variety of different purposes in management development, including the induction of new managers (it is common on graduate trainee schemes), the identification and nurturing of future potential, assisting managers with career development, enhanced learning transfer when used in conjunction with other development tools, promoting greater diversity (supporting managers from under-represented groups in their development and progression) and of course improved performance. Other benefits may include improved communication and networking through the business, greater understanding of organizational culture issues, and improved skills for both parties to the process.

There is considerable consensus from both the literature and from organizational examples regarding the characteristics of successful mentoring schemes. For example, Veale and Wachtel (1996), Forret *et al.* (1996) both refer to the need for voluntary participation, a format for matching those involved and contracting between them, clarity on length of process, a means of resolving mismatches, including ending the relationship, and the important role of the mentee's line manager (there needs to be a way of resolving any conflict with them, and they need to be broadly supportive). We might reasonably add the importance of support and training for those involved in the scheme, a clear purpose for the scheme endorsed by senior managers, integration with other management development activities, the importance of confidentiality, and the need for effective evaluation.

Organizational development

Organizational development (OD) has been influential in relation to management development and areas such as culture and change management, arising initially in the 1960s. There are competing concepts and definitions of OD, but general agreement that it is a process-oriented and strategic approach to improving organizations. It presupposes that change and development can be best grown from within the organization, rather than being facilitated by outside expert diagnosis and intervention. It grew out of, and developed through, a number of strands of thought, including wider societal notions such as a belief in economic and social progress, and increased openness and democracy. Humanistic psychology was a big influence on its development in the 1960s and 1970s, as was action research from the 1950s onwards, more participative forms of management, increasing interest in notions of the quality of working life, and the increasing pace of change from the 1970s onwards (Ten Dam, 1986). As with many aspects of management development, OD has to some extent been in and out of fashion at different times. It is currently becoming more popular again, notably in parts of the UK public sector.

Some would take the view that OD would include most efforts to improve internal organizational functioning, or any planned change programme. Others would be more limited, seeing OD as a change strategy based on a variety of specific techniques taken from behavioural science.

Reflection point 9.5

- Why are certain development approaches subject to the apparent vagaries of fashion—what influences them to become more or less popular at different times?

A well-known definition of organizational development is provided by Cummings and Worley (2005, p 1):

a system-wide application and transfer of behavioural science knowledge to the planned development, improvement and reinforcement of the strategies, structures and processes that lead to organizational effectiveness.

Earlier, Cahoon and Rowney (1986, p 15) suggest that OD:

encompasses a host of strategies, ideally reflecting a systematic approach aimed at more closely linking the human resources and potential of an organization to its technology, structure and management processes.

The approach is well summed up by Senior and Fleming (2006, p 343):

The OD approach to change is, above all, an approach which cares about people and which believes that people at all levels throughout an organization are, individually and collectively, both the drivers and the engines of change.

We might view management development as a subset of OD, where specific techniques or MD interventions can be seen to fit into a wider change process. Given some of the characteristics outlined above, it is easy to see methods such as action learning fitting particularly well with the idea of 'home grown' change and development and a suspicion of external expert solutions. Other MD approaches, not necessarily those with a clear and consistent fit to OD philosophy, might be taken with the aim of enabling managers to drive change in a humanistic fashion.

Woodall and Winstanley (1998, p 9) see management development ('has the twin aims of developing the individual for their own and the organization's requirements') as something of a bridge between organizational development on the one hand ('emphasizing the needs of an organization to grow and change') and self-development on the other ('focuses on ways in which an individual can help themselves to grow and change').

Some problems with the OD approach, according to Ten Dam (1986), include an emphasis on working with small groups that becomes more problematic the larger the organization, a tendency to ignore power and politics, and an assumption that these groups are stable, and perhaps most importantly, that OD has an internal focus, and that organizations need primarily to be outward facing. People can be, as the author points out, engaged in an OD process, 'learning to supply more effectively, efficiently and humanly, products or services that dissatisfy customers' (p 9).

As with other perspectives, if we wish to pursue aspects of an OD approach, it is important to be completely clear as to what our purpose is and what particular concept of OD we are going to work with. This will then suggest what more specific MD interventions we might introduce as part of our approach.

Outdoor development

Outdoor management development has been a popular component of organizations' approaches to developing managers, individually and as teams, for many years. Typically, outdoor development programmes mix physical activities which take participants well outside their comfort zones, with reflective activities to help the integration and transfer of learning. Programmes are likely to aim at the improvement of managerial skills in areas of leadership, team working, conflict resolution, problem solving, and so on—as well as making improvements in trust and cooperation in teams, and increased self-confidence and self-awareness in individuals. Despite its popularity, there remains little published empirical evidence of its usefulness as a development method—although it is by no means unique in this as far as management development is concerned.

Like many interventions, there is a range of provision that comes under the umbrella term. At one extreme is the 'survival training' approach where there is great emphasis on the physical activities which may be extremely rigorous and challenging. At the other are approaches which perhaps mix indoor and outdoor activities and which place a greater emphasis on experiential learning in different settings, without the more extreme elements of physical or mental challenge. More recently, Watson and Vasilieva (2007) describe a highly reflective approach in an outdoor setting which they call wilderness thinking. There are many approaches in between, all of which can be described as outdoor management development.

Irvine and Wilson (1994), in their critique of outdoor development, identify six components that should be present for it to be effective: a novel environment and/or activities, involving psychological though not actual risks; activities should match those taking part; and be capable of flexibility in application; there should be some match to an organizational environment; the focus should be on managerial rather than task-based skills; and review of activity with an emphasis on links to the workplace is essential. The authors go on to suggest that, actually, outdoor development is not the only way of achieving these six conditions, and that, therefore, claims of uniqueness for this approach are false.

The outdoor environment is seen as a potentially rich source of learning for a number of reasons: it is very different from the normal corporate environment, and encourages people to respond to one another as human beings to a greater extent as they are stripped of some of the trappings of power and status, for example. Dainty and Lucas (1992), Long (1984), and Galagan (1987) all refer to the impossibility of clinging to organizational norms that no longer exist in such a setting. Being far removed from normal routines in a completely new environment enables individuals and teams to focus more clearly on reflection, planning, and action (i.e. learning!) rather than anything else. The physical achievements of teams and individuals, probably far in advance of their initial perceptions, develop confidence and self-esteem more quickly and powerfully than by most other means—and the support and trust of colleagues in assisting those achievements is also a powerful motivating and team-building element of outdoor development.

The emotional aspect of development is one that is more applicable to outdoor development than most other types. Hamilton and Cooper (2001) regard the advantages of outdoor development programmes as including higher participation in learning, the opportunity to develop new patterns of thinking, the promotion of group awareness and trust, a more experimental approach to solving problems, and the opportunity to experience real emotions. Irvine and Wilson (1994), however, suggest that it is novelty (and other factors identified above) rather than the outdoors that provides these activities with their unique and potentially powerful contribution to management development.

In order to derive maximum benefit from outdoor development, it is important to ensure that sufficient emphasis is placed upon the reflective debrief of activities and that there is not undue emphasis on the action alone. Organizations also need to be very clear about the purpose of an outdoor development programme and what they hope to get out of it, for both individuals and teams. Although activities chosen may not apparently have any relevance to work, a good debrief will draw out the lessons and relate them to business situations. Activities are likely to have (albeit in a different context) aspects relating to organizational life (interpersonal skills, resource allocation, creative problem solving, etc.) that may need to be explored and consideration given to both individual and team approaches to these areas.

There may also be issues of diversity in outdoor development, and activities need to be designed that enable participation by those with a range of physical, mental, and emotional abilities. There are also health and safety considerations, relating to the physical activities undertaken, the environment in which they take place, and also the mental and emotional aspects where individuals may be placed under much greater pressure than normal. Hamilton and Cooper (2001) suggest that participants should be assessed for their levels of mental well-being prior to participation in certain types of outdoor development in order to ensure that they do not suffer an adverse effect.

In making use of outdoor management development, of whatever nature, it is important to take account of aspects of the context in which we plan to use it. It is imperative that we are clear what we are trying to achieve, and we should ask what this approach can bring that others might not? We might pay particular attention to

Reflection point 9.6

- The announcement of an outdoor development event is likely to engender great enthusiasm amongst some staff and considerable resistance amongst some of their colleagues. What factors might explain these two extreme responses to outdoor development?

the nature of our organizational culture, and perhaps the make-up of the managerial workforce in considering whether or not to use outdoor development.

Self-development

Self-development has in reality probably always been a significant element of management development practice, at least for some managers and some organizations. It is more and more important as part of a portfolio of continuing development, increasingly seen as an essential element in the moves towards lifelong learning, in which learners are seen as more central to their own development than learning and development professionals. This movement applies to a wide range of professions as well as to management practitioners.

Whilst there might be a danger that an organization espousing self-development might be seen to be abdicating its responsibilities towards its managers and staff, as long as this is done in the right spirit, and as part of a wider approach to management development, the outcomes should be beneficial. Indeed, the resource constraints of smaller organizations make this approach one that may be particularly useful to them. The control given to individuals to respond to their own unique context (organizational setting, career aspirations, strengths and weaknesses, learning style preferences, and so on) makes this approach one that is particularly important as a response to an increasingly turbulent work environment.

Pedler *et al.* (2006) suggest that a key part of any management development system must be an increase in managers' ability to take control and responsibility for, amongst other things, their own learning and development. They propose the notion that managerial action should always be thought of as experiment, since it is always possible to learn from the outcome, and to perhaps do things differently on other occasions. They also suggest that formal management development unintentionally deskills managers, because of messages that propose an expert solution to any management problem, including expert solutions to problems of managerial learning.

We might define management self-development as being personal and professional development for managers, with the individual taking responsibility for their own learning, and control of both the means and the objectives for that development. Although self-development emphasizes individual control and responsibility, it need not be a solitary pursuit, and probably should not be in many instances. The choice of method contained within the definition above means that self-development can involve any other form of management development, if the manager chooses to develop themselves in that way.

There are almost as many ways of approaching self-development as there are managers, but typically there will be some key stages that all will go through, even though particular tools and techniques will vary. Each manager needs to find their own way through the processes of self-development. The best models and self-development approaches recognize this diversity and seek to avoid too much prescription. Routledge and Carmichael (2007, p 16) recognize this in describing their ADAX model, noting that 'although the model appears to be a well-ordered neat garden, the reality may be nearer to a jungle'.

First, there needs to be an element of analysis and self-diagnosis on the part of the manager. This might include a wide range of diagnostic tools and instruments, it might involve existing organizational processes such as appraisal (or similar), it might involve feedback from managers, peers, or subordinates (formal and informal, sought and ad hoc), and it might involve personal reflection. The manager's situation should ideally be considered as widely as possible to take into account their characteristics, their strengths and weaknesses, the support available to them, their goals and aspirations, and so on. From an appropriate and tailored mix of these processes and activities, managers will be able to identify their own learning and development needs and priorities.

Second, as a result of the diagnosis, there will need to be a plan to address the perceived areas for development, the areas of interest, or whatever. This might involve a personal development plan (which might be part of a wider organizational approach to MD), a learning contract with a more senior manager or developer, or similar tool or process.

Third, action needs to be taken to achieve the identified goals or to implement the plan. This is where the full range of management development interventions could come into play. I might choose to achieve my goals, for example, by embarking on a management education programme, by seeking a coach or mentor, by reading, or by keeping learning logs of my day-to-day activities.

Finally, a process of review should be in place so that the manager can periodically reassess against their original objectives, against changed organizational context, against newly identified areas of interest, and so on. Hence we can see that this is a continuous process, as this fourth stage relates back to the first and then onto the second, and so on.

Megginson and Whitaker (2007) also suggest important additional stages of celebrating successes, acknowledging help, and building a network for future development.

All this sounds quite straightforward, and some managers may take this approach and learn effectively. Many others, however, will only be able to do so if the organization provides support to their self-development with the right culture, with feedback mechanisms, coaching or mentoring support, appropriate recognition and reward, and so on.

Individual managers—without support—may have difficulty in developing a broader range of learning styles. Typically, they may find reflection difficult without help and encouragement. A self-development approach may give greater weight to experiential learning (and there is nothing wrong with that per se) but if it doesn't also take into account more theoretical elements of learning, there is a danger that managers may miss a trick or two because they are stuck in old ways of looking at things.

Consequently, it is not sufficient to regard self-development as a stand-alone approach—it needs to be clearly part of the organization's response to developing managers, and the organization must make suitable provision to support managers in taking self-development forward.

360° feedback

360° feedback, sometimes called multi-rater or multi-source feedback, is a technique that can be used in management development as either a stand-alone method, or more effectively as part of a wider process. It can be seen as part of a self-development approach, for example, or may be a component part of development centres, coaching, or other management development processes. See Mini case study 9.2, for example, to see the use of 360° feedback with action learning. It provides managers with data about how they are seen by various stakeholders such as their peers, their direct reports, and their own manager, and to make comparisons with their own perceptions of themselves. Customers, clients, or suppliers may also be involved in a process of this nature.

Each of these stakeholders provides feedback on a range of managerial skills, competencies, behaviours, etc. The 'scores' are usually collated across a range of items and individual raters to provide ratings against more generic dimensions, such as managing people, responding to pressure, decision making, and so on. The combined feedback, if the manager is open to it and if the organization encourages a 'learning response' to it, can be a very powerful catalyst for development and improvement. Apart from management development, 360° feedback may also be useful in developing employee involvement, improved communication, and assistance in cultural change initiatives (Waldman *et al.*, 1998).

It can be powerful for a number of reasons. McCauley and Moxley (1996) highlight four key points in this respect. First, managerial work being relationship intensive means that others' perception of managers greatly influences how effectively they can work, and managers ignore this at their peril. Second, this kind of feedback often doesn't occur naturally in organizations, especially relating to direct reports, and particularly at higher organizational levels. Consequently, feedback on behaviour or management style through 360° may be the first a manager has ever received. Third, if feedback is constant across multiple raters, it is hard to ignore—if everyone perceives the same thing, there is bound to be truth in it. Finally, feedback becomes more important in times of change—previous strengths may not be needed (or may even now be a hindrance) whilst skills that are required may be untested. Feedback is an effective way of exploring both what is required in a new context and the extent to which the requirements are present.

Feedback is only the start of a developmental process, of course. As stated above, it can only be a catalyst for progress if the manager is open to it, and the organization is supportive—and the two factors are not unconnected. In order to encourage openness to feedback the organization probably should ensure that the 360° process is not linked to reward or promotion, since this may rather ensure defensiveness. Clarity of purpose (it is about development and improvement), confidentiality (the manager owns the feedback), and support (one-to-one discussions with coach, mentor, or other facilitator) are key components of attempts to promote the desired level of openness to the feedback.

Having discussed the feedback, the manager should be helped to identify some development objectives, and this may feed into existing processes such as personal development planning, perhaps as part of a self-development process. Organizational support also needs to be forthcoming to assist in meeting the objectives, and this could be in the form of time, money, provision of appropriate opportunities and managerial support. Without this support, the initial spur to development through the feedback will be lost—and it will be harder to engage the manager on future occasions. If the 360° process is part of a broader positive organizational approach to developing managers, it can undoubtedly be very successful.

As a specific example, Van Rensburg and Prideaux (2006) describe the application of a multi-source feedback programme in the context of professionals in a global professional services partnership, who needed to adopt management roles in addition to their professional roles. This professional/managerial interface is an increasingly common one in areas such as healthcare, education, legal and financial services. Van Rensburg and Prideaux suggest it is an effective method to achieve changes in behaviour and attitudes, and improved the leadership and management skills of the professionals in their study.

Other possible interventions

There are many other possible interventions that are used within organizations—no chapter could do full justice to them all. Projects, secondments, and deputizing are common managerial activities in any case, not necessarily in a development context. Given this, it seems a wasted opportunity not to make full use of them to extract development potential, by ensuring both prior briefings and reflections afterwards, possibly linked to other MD processes. They can also be used effectively as part of a planned process of development.

Development centres, again as part of wider processes, are an effective means of both identifying needs and encouraging managerial buy-in to development. Tools and techniques are likely to be similar to those employed in assessment centres for selection, including, for example, a range of interviews, psychometric instruments, tests, and observations. These were considered in greater detail in Chapter 8.

Summary of section

A selection of potential MD interventions has been discussed, and reference made to some other possibilities. These have been chosen as being amongst the most common approaches, and many of them are particularly appropriate to current conditions of change and turbulence in the environment in which managers and organizations are operating.

Chapter summary

A wide range of potential interventions to facilitate leadership and management development has been discussed, whilst recognizing that each might have contested conceptualizations amongst both academics and practitioners. The key element within the chapter, though, is the wider contextual discussion which suggests avoiding a 'one size fits all' approach—and that more successful approaches will be those that take full account of the external environment, organizational issues, individual characteristics, and the use of interventions in appropriate conjunction with others.

Reflection point 9.7

Have a look again at the case study with which we opened this chapter. Having read the chapter and thought about the range of possible interventions, and the importance of contextual factors highlighted in the chapter, consider the following:

● If you were leading the learning and development team, what steps would you take to move things forward? (This might be specific interventions, or might relate to the contextual factors including strategy.)

Questions

1 Can you identify two possible ways to categorize the many different management development interventions?

2 McCauley *et al.* (1994) identified four clusters of job characteristics contributing to development of successful managers—can you identify them?

3 Revans is particularly well known for 'inventing' which form of management development?

4 Barner and Higgins (2005) suggest four overarching models of coaching—can you identify them?

5 What are the factors in management simulations that might make them more effective as learning opportunities?

6 When using outdoor management development, which element is key to effectiveness in addition to the physical activities?

7 Describe the stages you would expect to find in any approach to self-development. McCauley and Moxley (1996) highlight four key reasons for the effectiveness of 360° feedback—can you identify them?

Discussion questions

1 Thinking about your own organization, or one that you are familiar with, what approaches to management development would work best, and why?

2 We have mentioned a few times in the chapter instances where one MD intervention has been combined with another—which of the interventions do you think work well together and why?

3 Thinking about your own development as a manager, which of the various approaches discussed are most appealing to you? What reasons lie behind your choice?

Suggestions for further reading

Follow up on the coaching GROW model—via Whitmore (1998) or elsewhere. What would be good questions for a coach to use at each stage of the GROW sequence?

Suutari and Viitala (2008) discuss their research showing the continuing dominance of traditional short-term MD activities, whilst longer-term experiential methods were considered more effective. You might wish to consider first the extent to which the findings can be generalized beyond the research context (Finnish senior managers). Second, it is interesting to consider what reasons might lie behind this apparent contradiction.

Pedler, M, Burgoyne, J., and Boydell, T. (2006) provide an interesting and useful guide to self-development for managers. The nature of the book is that one can dip in and out and use it flexibly. Try some of the many activities and reflect upon those that are most useful for your development at this time.

CHAPTER 10

Evaluation of leadership and management development

The aims of this chapter are to:

- critically evaluate traditional approaches to evaluation used in leadership and management development.

- analyse difficulties encountered in evaluating leadership and management development.

- examine the occurrence of evaluation in organizations and reasons for it.

- assess holistic evaluation strategies that can be used in leadership and management learning.

Introduction

The overall intent of this chapter is to critically review models of evaluation that can be applied in leadership and management development, and to examine organizational use of evaluation systems and processes, and identify appropriate paradigms used to assess the value of development of leaders and managers in organizations.

Many organizations seem to treat decisions about spending on employee training and development in different ways from spend on capital outlay projects even though often it involves substantial sums of money. Read through Mini case study 10.1 and try to answer the questions provided.

Mini case study 10.1: Training spend examined

A medium-sized company which imports, builds, and sells IT hardware and provides support on software applications and other equipment through the internet and telesales has recently grown through successful acquisition of its main rival.

The board has decided that it will invest in two related projects in the coming year:

- To introduce a new call handling and sales monitoring system
- To improve telesales through training and development of staff.

Both projects are seen as vital to the organization's further development, and the finance and HR directors, respectively, were put in charge of each project.

In order to purchase the system, the finance director set up a working party, involving the sales manager and two team leaders who were to operate the system. During a three-month period this small team identified technical and system requirements, developed a business case which outlined cost–benefit analysis, expected payback, and efficiency savings. This was carefully considered and eventually accepted by the board after numerous discussions. An implementation plan was agreed within the business to give estimated savings of ten full-time equivalent employees and time-to-process calls amounting to an hour per day for each call handler. Three potential systems were identified and the companies producing the systems were invited to tender for the work. Following presentations, one system was selected, based on its compatibility with the organizational set-up and expected efficiency savings. The total cost of the new system was £500,000 and arrangements were made for its instillation.

The second project, headed up by the HR director, was to provide an orientation to the new system, and in addition to provide coaching and development in sales techniques and customer service. Given difficulties of timing and other commitments, this director decided that a series of workshops on customer service skills sales techniques would be run for all call-handling operatives to encourage an increase in sales. The HR director contacted a consultant, who had worked with the organization previously, to help to develop managers' coaching techniques. This consultant recommended a series of workshops be arranged for all call handlers, including customer service, systems orientation, and sales sessions through three day-long sessions, in groups of 20 employees, over a four-month period. The cost of this training was to be £100,000. The cost to the business was, however, much greater, taking into account the time for each operative to be away from their workstation for training.

Although the money spent on learning and development activity in organizations amounts to a significant cost each year, still little research goes into systematically identifying the benefit gained from the spend. There are various reasons for this lack of interest in demonstrating value from training and development. Even organizations that do undertake an analysis of what needs are apparent might often be described as poorly prescribed. However, to be able to show that training and development demonstrate good investment for an organization, at the outset it needs to identify:

■ What is the nature of the problem thought to require some intervention?

■ Are learning and development appropriate responses?

■ What are the specific requirements of any development?

■ In what ways can achievement of the required outcomes be assessed?

Only having answered these questions will an organization have appropriate information to be able to measure the effectiveness, efficiency, or value of any training initiative. As discussed later in this chapter, evaluation of leadership and management development is even more complex.

Within this chapter we will focus on what is meant by evaluation in development, why it is frequently not completed in organizations, and how it can add to the decision-making process and strategic alignment in management development.

What is evaluation?

A common understanding of 'evaluation' is 'establish[ing] the worth of something' (Bramley, 1996, p 4), and in this chapter we explore the worth of learning and development for managers and leaders. Bramley explains that 'worth' is someone's view of value and that there are different perspectives that may be taken in evaluation, for example assessing training in terms of efficiency of use of resources for learning and development or in terms of learning of participants. Others link evaluation with assessment (Wilson, 2005) or focus on using a research approach (Millmore *et al.*, 2007), and an alternative approach to evaluation is to consider return on investment

(Phillips, 2003). There are then many different views that might be taken in evaluating a training intervention.

Training evaluation

Many current evaluation strategies used in management or leadership development emanate from approaches used to evaluate basic skills training which has traditionally formed key work for training and development professionals in organizations. Such training events use the well-known systematic training cycle (Reid *et al.*, 2004), in which training has clearly prescribed aims and objectives, usually devised through training needs analysis (TNA) that provides an assessment of the needs of trainees, against which programmes can be evaluated. Then, if a TNA identified a requirement for specific skills training it should be possible, following this training, to evaluate its worth by assessing trainees' new ability to demonstrate development of knowledge and skills that were initially identified in the TNA (Hamblin, 1974).

Evaluation and validation in training

Validation is at times confused with evaluation but may be distinguished from it, often forming the initial part of an evaluation strategy. Validation means ensuring that training and development achieve their stated objectives. Therefore part of the development of any training initiative would involve validating the content and approach of the course. This is often done by running through a new course with trainers or manager stakeholders so that they can confirm that the course delivers what is required (see Mini case study 10.2 for an example of training validation). Trainers need to validate training as a precondition to delivery to trainees and to evaluation of training.

Mini case study 10.2: Example of validating training

A large public sector organization has recently introduced a new performance management system. The training design team in the organization worked with the developers of the performance management process to design appropriate training to roll out to managers who would operate the system. Awareness training was also developed for staff that would be subject to the new process. In order to achieve this roll-out in the required four-month period, it would be necessary to train additional members of the delivery teams to deliver this programme.

A decision was taken that in order to validate the training it would be run with trainer deliverers as delegates in order to check that it achieved the aims that were required:

- an understanding of the overall performance management system
- how to complete and monitor performance reviews with staff
- how to complete paperwork for the system.

This approach also had a double purpose because as well as validating the training it allowed the new delivery team to learn what they would have to deliver to groups of up to 50 managers. In this way, by running the training with training deliverers who had been briefed about the new process, these people could both validate it and at the same time learn the training and check out delivery styles and timings.

Question

1 What methods could be used to validate the delivery team's achievement of the aims?

Jan L. Carmichael

The example in Mini case study 10.2 demonstrates how validation may be used to ensure that the aims and objectives can be achieved through the inputs and activities during the course. Once a course has been shown to be valid, to achieve the required aims it can be run with delegates and evaluated from their perspective.

Summary of section

There are different approaches to evaluating training, each requiring the collection and analysis of information relating to the training under review. Validation is a prerequisite of evaluation, and indeed of training design, though it is not necessarily sufficient for positive evaluation. In the next section the common methods of evaluation will be assessed for their application to leadership and management development.

Models of evaluation in training

Traditional models for evaluating training were those that originated with the systematic training cycle and still can be found in use today. Kirkpatrick (1998) developed a model of four levels of evaluation, in which each level was causally related to those below it. The levels are briefly described in Box 10.1, beginning with the lowest level of evaluation.

Hamblin (1974) suggested a similar model to Kirkpatrick's, but with the final level four split into:

- Departmental impact—has training affected performance?
- Ultimate level evaluation which assesses the overall organization's profitability and survival.

Hamblin's split of the final evaluation level distinguishes between changes due to training in a department and an organization as a whole. The distinction may be

Box 10.1 Kirkpatrick's levels of evaluation

- Reactions of learners to the content and overall training experience, often assessed by reaction sheets or 'happy sheets', completed at the end of training. Assessment focuses on how learners felt about the training, trainer, and environment and is a personal, subjective assessment.

- Learning achieved through training—usually assessed through questioning during training and testing, throughout, and at the end of training. This level is sometimes known as external validation. Tests can provide an objective measure of the retention of learners or may assess simulated use of skills.

- Application of training at work—for development to achieve the required outcomes in work it should have an impact on the behaviour of learners when they return to work. This can be assessed through observations, review with learner's manager, and performance reviews.

- Organizational results of training are the final level of evaluation in this model and they are also the most difficult level to specify measurable outcomes, so are usually the most difficult to assess. Ideally they require a pre-training assessment or TNA to have been undertaken that can be used as a baseline to assess learning so that organizational impact may be assessed in financial terms or by assessing improved effectiveness.

useful in situations where a manager's learning can be applied to result in differences in the manager's department but this does not impact on the overall performance of a global organization due to other complicating factors. It becomes increasingly difficult to assess value at the higher levels, related to individual application, departmental, and organizational results, in both models.

Evaluation of training and development can be completed using the models described above either wholly or partially. However, this requires the collection of a wide range of data from those involved using:

- at lower levels: reaction to the inputs and learning from the intervention, using reaction sheets, tests of knowledge, and questioning participants

- at higher levels: the extent to which learners have been able to use learning to change behaviour at work, assessing workplace changes through observation or measurement or performance management processes which may, long term, lead to changes in the organization.

Mini case study 10.3 provides an example of how the models have been used to evaluate a major diversity training initiative across numerous organizations.

Mini case study 10.3 is included to provide an overview of how evaluation can be attempted using the Kirkpatrick model for a cultural change programme in a number of different organizations. It was undertaken independently of the design and delivery of the training, using a research project methodology, and supports the view of Millmore *et al.* (2007) describing evaluation as research. Following the research

Mini case study 10.3: Evaluation of a diversity training initiative

I worked as part of a team to evaluate an innovative diversity training programme, developed by a partnership of public sector and charitable organizations in South Yorkshire. These organizations required an external evaluation of the initiative that had been running at the time for approximately 18 months. All had previously run diversity awareness programmes, based on legislation and organizational procedure. However, they agreed on a more radical approach to address attitudinal dimensions and to build on a positive understanding of diversity. The evaluation was to take stock of what had been achieved and to decide on the best way forward.

This diversity training had been devised and was run by the Garnett Foundation. This charitable organization had researched diversity within the major employers, conducted interviews with staff and other stakeholders to develop a play that was taken from incidents that had been identified as typical within the organizations, made suitably anonymous.

The play ran for approximately 60 minutes, using professional actors. It was followed by an innovative technique, 'forum theatre', during which small groups of the audience each 'owned and directed' one of the play's characters as they replayed small segments of the play or related vignettes. It allowed groups and individuals in the audience to try out behaviours and to see the effect on other characters. Each group could stop the action to redirect their character, and often partway through a scene the characters would move groups, to hear from the character how they felt and what they wanted to achieved. The whole experience lasted half a day and included groups from within the audience having the opportunity to discuss issues raised by the event in allocated groups so as to gain experience and perspectives from people in different organizations.

The training ran in small theatres and at each session the audience was mixed from all organizations. All attended in casual dress, identified by their first name only, so that neither their organization nor position was known to most of the audience. It was felt that this would leave people free to say what they felt, so that hierarchy would not influence discussions.

On being asked to evaluate this initiative we spent time with the key stakeholders to understand the initial drivers and subsequent objectives set. Discussions took place with the Garnett Foundation to include some of the findings from their research as baseline information and to confirm the rationale behind the approach taken.

A research project was developed over a six-month period to gather and analyse data for the evaluation. Research included:

- interviews with key stakeholders from each of the organizations represented to establish their reasons for becoming involved; objectives for their organization, and additional supplementary activities planned
- collecting data from each organization about the incidents of discrimination or issues related to diversity
- questionnaire to a large random sample of those who had attended the training from each organization and where possible from across all levels of the organizational hierarchy, to assess previous experience of diversity training, retention of knowledge presented, changes that they had personally made, or had heard others had made

- analysis of initial reaction data (happy sheets), gathered from each participant before they left each event

- a random sample of interviews with participants, across all organizations and levels to gather additional qualitative information about the training and to gauge views about personal, departmental, and organizational changes, following the training

- finally, at the end of the period when most of the training had been completed, discussions with stakeholders to gauge their views about achievement of objectives and success stories; and follow-up activities that they were aware of.

Question

1 Taking each level of Kirkpatrick's model in turn, identify which data has been gathered for evaluation, then identify any additional information that could have been collected:

- participants' reactions

- participants' learning

- application at work

- departmental changes

- organizational changes.

Jan L. Carmichael

project a report was produced which confirmed positive reactions (Level 1) almost unanimously. However, it is important to consider the circumstances in which this information is usually gathered from learners. Many trainers will be aware that if reaction sheets are used at the end of an event many participants are keen to leave and give only limited thought to completing the forms. The responses may therefore be neutral or more positive and with little explanation to aid the trainers' improvement of the course. Occasionally they may have very strong positive or negative feelings about an event to record, so reaction data can be extreme, but again with limited explanation. Both of these are assessing participants' reaction to the 'inputs' of an event, not to the important aspects of its use and organizational worth. Reaction data is influenced by the perceptions of the trainer, so if they have developed a positive relationship with trainees or provided a relaxed break away from work, they may receive very positive evaluations. The reverse is also true; however, actual learning may be the same in both cases. A trainer may be seen as having an influential role in the learner's organization—for example, having a presentation from senior executives in training may influence what trainees feel able to say in evaluation. Therefore there are a number of cautions in using reaction data.

In the above example of research to evaluate the diversity initiative, we were also able to provide evidence of personal learning and changed behaviour (Levels 2 and 3) based on questionnaires from a random sample of staff and the follow-up

> ## Reflection point 10.1
>
> - Think about the last time you were asked to complete a reaction or feedback sheet. It may have been at the end of a training course, lecture series, or other event. Many of these sheets require only tick or cross responses to multiple-choice or rating scales. Others may additionally provide space for qualitative feedback. Did you honestly take time to consider your responses or did you complete the form as quickly as possible, based on how you felt in the final session of the event? Many people agree that this approach to reaction level evaluation is not helpful in assessing the worth or added value from training.

interviews. However, in terms of organizational change (Level 4), though we were able to find some initial indications of changes—for example, the development of diversity champions and support groups in some organizations—the evidence was more limited. These findings are in line with many (e.g. Yorks *et al.*, 1999) who have criticized this model of evaluation for its increasing difficulty in gathering evidence for evaluation at higher levels. There are difficulties of identification of appropriate organizational baseline measures to compare before- and after-training behaviours that would provide measures of improvements made due to training. In the above case there were few quantitative organizational performance measures available, across all organizations, prior to the initiative. Those that were available—for example disputes and grievances connected to diversity—were limited in number and in the relatively short time of the evaluation, although there were some indicative changes, it was not possible to ascertain evidence of major cultural organizational changes.

Difficulties in evaluating at different levels

Often developmental interventions for organizational culture change take a long time to have an impact. For example, a talent development initiative to increase numbers of candidates suitable for senior management posts might involve providing coaching and support to all employees identified as having suitable potential. Even assuming there was capability to provide the required coaching and mentoring within the organization, it would take time to be able to demonstrate a positive outcome from the initiative. Therefore evaluation data for higher levels of evaluation should be gathered when sufficient time has lapsed to allow for application and any added value to be apparent, even when initial reaction data and learning suggest positive evaluation. Even if there is a delay in collecting this data, allowing time for the individuals to apply learning that might influence departmental evaluation and organizational impact, there are many different variables that intervene to limit expected influence in the organization. For example, Kolb *et al.* stated that 'the organization's ability to survive and thrive in a complex dynamic environment is constrained by the capabilities of managers who must learn to manage both this greater environmental complexity and the complex organizational forms developed to cope with the environment' (Kolb *et al.*, 1994, p 146–7).

Holton (1996) provided a comprehensive account of all factors that impact on learning and development and identified only three levels to evaluate:

- learning
- individual performance
- organizational results.

He argued that trainees' reactions (Level 1) were not causally related to the three levels above. Kirkpatrick's model assumes causality between levels (Yorks, 2005) in that a positive reaction is expected to result in learning which in turn will affect behaviour and will then impact on organizational results. This causal link has not been supported by research. For example, Dixon (1990) attempted to correlate trainees' reactions with test scores following learning and found that positive reactions did not relate to learning, and Latham and Saari (1979) attempted to remove intervening variables but could not prove the effect of training.

Reviewing the links between levels, there appears to be an assumption that learning results from a positive reaction. However, some negative experiences lead to learning. For example, some unpleasant experiences in childhood, such as touching a hot kitchen stove or the impact of bullying at school, can result in strong learning for the sufferer. This can also be true in the case of management and personal development where learners are challenged about their personal views or behaviour and powerful learning can result from such events. Most people can think about times when they learn from negative experiences, which demonstrates learning without a positive reaction, as in Mumford and Gold's (2004) examples of managers learning from mistakes.

The numerous criticisms of Kirkpatrick's approach to evaluation include those already discussed and the criticism that evaluation is seen as separate from the design of an intervention, but in fact the two are inextricably mixed. Evaluation measures should be specified as an essential element of the needs identification, during which measures of prior knowledge, competence, and skills of learners are assessed in order that required outcomes are specified.

Kearns (2005) suggests that these models define the final level of evaluation in a loose way so that it is not possible to specify and measure, in quantitative terms, organizational benefits to be achieved from training. It appears to be the link between learning and work application, which leads to organizational outcomes, that has been most problematic in evaluation. This specific issue is known as 'transfer of training', and will be further discussed later in the chapter, with reference to leadership and management development.

CIRO Model

CIRO (Warr *et al.*, 1970) is a different model of evaluation more widely used in Europe, to evaluate four different aspects of development:

- context: any environmental influences within the organization, understanding the reasons and issues associated with the initiative

- input: what is included and how delivered

- reaction: impact on learners, though not necessarily behavioural changes

- output: impact on learner's behaviour, work and the organization.

The first letter of each level of evaluation gives the name of this model. It provides yet another perspective in evaluation, though it is infrequently used in the UK compared with Kirkpatrick's. It considers a broader range of elements of training than Kirkpatrick's model, taking account of the context in which training occurs, and it recommends ongoing evaluation, during training, so that the context and inputs are considered and improved as training progresses. This has been found to be useful for understanding the possible impact of training. It also distinguishes between the inputs and outcomes of training so that it considers the trainer's perspective and relates this to the outcomes achieved, from the learner's point of view. CIRO provides different and wider perspective than Kirkpatrick's model and is more applicable for leadership and management development, though there are still difficulties in measuring output and gathering and collating sufficient data for full analysis due to the relatively loose definitions of the four aspects.

Tennant *et al.* (2002) produced a model of evaluation that brought together the Kirkpatrick and CIRO models. It involved taking measures from the company's, trainees', and trainers' viewpoints at various stages prior to, throughout, immediately after, and a longer time after training. They also took account of process, context, and outcomes to apply the new model in manufacturing training:

- Initial assessments were made prior to training, including skills, reactions, and the organization's objectives. These were repeated during the training, also taking account of trainers' feedback to improve training, and were repeated immediately after training, to assess new skills and attitudes (Levels 1 and 2).

- Once trainees were back in work further assessments were made 'to identify whether [the trainees] can apply what they learned in their workplace environment' (Level 3) (p 237).

- For level 4 evaluation, assessments of performance were made on an ongoing basis.

This example demonstrates the range of measurement necessary for effective evaluation. In their research, Tennant *et al.* confirmed that many organizations studied did not have sufficiently effective systems of measurement to evaluate training. An interesting question raised was 'whether the depth of training is sufficient to realize benefits in behavioural change and skills development which lead to realization of business benefits' (p 235), citing evidence from Japan where much greater time is given to training employees relative to UK organizations. If their contention is correct and more time is required to add value through training, perhaps an argument can be made for not taking additional time to evaluate, trying to demonstrate worth that cannot be demonstrated? However, it is true that until training is seen as contributing to strategic organizational objectives it is unlikely that training time will be increased to possibly allow evaluation to demonstrate its true value. As we will see below, other means of holistic evaluation are suggested to provide this required link to business strategy.

Summary of section

Models of evaluation presented so far provide a number of different ideas about what to assess in evaluation and were mainly developed to evaluate specific training interventions. Kirkpatrick's model of levels of evaluation excludes external considerations, focusing on measures required by trainers to validate, assess learning and its impact. The CIRO model provides a broader perspective, taking account also of context and making an assessment of the inputs in training which are often implied or informally reviewed by trainers, within the former model. These traditional models of evaluation can be used to evaluate certain more formal elements of leadership and management development but do not provide a comprehensive account of benefits and learning in it. More holistic models of evaluation are required to fully assess the worth of initiatives and process for developing leaders and managers and will be discussed below.

Evaluating leadership and management development

As we have seen, many of the traditional models of evaluation have limitations when applied in practice, even when used to review a single training event. There are examples of initiatives where these models have been applied. For example, Adams and Waddle (2002) provided practical examples of evaluation of management development initiatives using blended learning in the hospitality industry through the use of individual questionnaires about learning styles, transfer of learning, and using interviews along with organizational measures of long-term changes in satisfaction. Gilligan and Boddington (1995) used these methods to evaluate self-managed learning in healthcare in the UK whilst Williams *et al.* (2003) used similar techniques to demonstrate that return on investment can be calculated for outdoor experiential learning.

However, examples are limited and apart from measures of inputs to specific development events assessing the impact of leadership and development are difficult.

Reflection point 10.2

From what you know about leadership and management development programmes so far, try to identify what additional problems there may be in evaluation. To aid your identification it might help to list these difficulties under the following headings, thinking about learning from other chapters:

- understanding about leadership and management
- nature of leadership and management development
- learning theory in development
- context and environment.

Difficulties in evaluating leadership and management development

There are a number of difficulties in attempting to evaluate leadership and management development using the models discussed so far. These are included in Box 10.2. These difficulties lead to a range of specific issues which influence leader and manager development in different organizations and make evaluation difficult and potentially ineffective. Even if specific defined elements of delivery are evaluated, during a programme, seldom is a thorough and systematic evaluation of all completed.

Box 10.2 Common difficulties in evaluating leadership and management development

1 Lack of understanding about leadership and management:

　a Lack of clarity of definition about leadership and management.

　b Variety of roles that are included in leadership and management.

　c Individual influence of each leader or manager on their role.

　d Constantly changing nature of what leadership and management are and their organizational contribution.

2 Nature of leadership and management development:

　a Leadership and management development programmes are often long term and varied.

　b The time from completing a development programme to being 'fully competent' can be up to five years and so be influenced by many factors.

　c Reflexivity within development can lead to questioning of the status quo and current initiatives themselves.

　d Consumerism in leadership and management development or buying from the many off-the-shelf solutions to poorly identified problems.

3 Our current understanding about learning:

a Many individuals are already operating in management roles when they undertake. development and so outcomes are influenced by role expectations and previous learning.

b Informal learning has been found to exert a strong influence on management learning (Marsick and Watkins, 1997).

c The individual nature of preferences in learning.

4 The context and environment in which learning occurs for leadership and management development:

a Organizational factors may encourage or limit application from development for any manager or leader, depending on surrounding culture and expectations. These issues often influence transfer of learning into work.

b Organizational politics can influence what it is appropriate to say in evaluation. Beard and Irvine (2005) noted that if leadership and management programmes were used by senior management as a way of controlling more junior managers, it was difficult to get an objective evaluation because comments may be seen to challenge the accepted orthodoxy.

Evaluation, like many other tasks in organizations, is usually not a neutral activity. Most development activities result from a belief, even poorly specified, that it will improve outcomes or actions of managers and leaders, to achieve a desired organizational aim and it may be unpalatable for a person to hear that objectives have not been achieved, or achieved only to a limited extent. Many factors, identified above, can influence outcomes of evaluation. Transfer of learning is an important issue that requires further consideration.

Transfer of learning

Problems of transferring learning into a new environment can result in measures of evaluation of application to department and organization being low. The problem encountered is when training that occurs in a training environment is not subsequently transferred to a work environment. Training away from work has benefits of lack of interference and interruption, allowing learners to focus on learning new knowledge and skills. However, to get benefit from training, it must be used once an employee returns to their work environment, with many other distractions. Transfer to enable application of learning is, therefore, important in all development including that of leaders and managers who have more freedom and therefore choice in what they do as a result of learning and to what extent they use development within their work environment.

Transfer of learning has many facets and has been extensively studied by Holton *et al.* (2000), who explained flaws in Kirkpatrick's (1998) evaluation model. Holton identified a model of factors influencing transfer (see Box 10.3).

Box 10.3 Factors that influence transfer of learning (Holton 1996)

- secondary elements, including personal characteristics, job attitudes, learner readiness
- motivational elements, including expected utility of training, personal motivation, and effort
- environmental elements, including supervisor and peer support, feedback, sanctions, and external events
- outcomes of learning and performance
- enabling elements, for example ability, transfer design and linkage to organizational goals.

It has been suggested that making learning more abstract and providing generalized principles in training aid transfer to different contexts (Schunk, 2004). However, recent research in Denmark (Nielsen, 2009) suggests that transfer from an educational setting is aided by 'horizontal learning' through situated learning (Lave and Wenger, 1991) methods and support from more experienced learners as well as group activities. Many other researchers have cited contextual issues in the workplace that may lead to lack of transfer of new skills for a manager. For example, Salaman and Butler (1994) studied managers' apparent lack of learning from development, identifying key issues of the peers' influence to do things as they have always done them; loss of political power within the workplace through following new work procedures; lack of personal motivation to use new behaviours when previous ones have served the manager well to that time. There are elements of tacit

Box 10.4 Mechanisms to support transfer of leaning

- Ensure the alignment of learning with organizational strategy.
- Make learning relevant and explain its significance to learners.
- Identify key transferable principles with learners.
- Ensure relevant excellent training is followed up with action-oriented planning.
- Make learning as much a part of work as possible, with practice.
- Manage the performance of learners to apply learning.
- Reward those who apply learning.
- Design work, following learning, to aid transfer.
- Try to minimize other factors through ongoing review and follow-up.
- Provide peer support mechanisms, for example group meetings, for applying learning.
- Continue support for learning over a long period.
- Encourage a learning climate.

Jan L. Carmichael, adapted from various sources

knowledge, specific contextual and cultural issues that are learned while a manager or leader works, through experience and informal learning, and that influence the application of any new learning at work.

Research to overcome some of these issues (Holton *et al.*, 2000; Longnecker and Ariss, 2002; Kirwin and Burchall, 2006; Bramley, 1999; Leimbach, 2010) has suggested a range of actions, often used in management development, as in Box 10.4.

Transfer of learning is a developing research area and key to understanding apparent shortcomings in evaluation, particularly at higher levels. Other researchers (Yeo, 2003; Senge, 1990) pointed to the importance of developing a culture of learning as a strategic imperative in which organizations recognize the importance of informal social and work-based learning for their contribution to intellectual capital and individual competence that are intangibles in evaluation.

Summary of section

Difficulties in evaluating leadership and management development are similar to other development interventions but also have additional problems due to the nature of leadership and management and the individualized, organizational context which constitutes the work environment for these groups. Therefore methodologies more able to take account of multiple perspectives in a changing environment are required.

Holistic approaches to evaluation

More recently approaches to evaluation have taken a more overarching view, assessing outputs from organizational learning and development generally, rather than independently assessing inputs of specific interventions. Leadership and management development is strategic activity, key to organizations' future, and has a reciprocal relationship with organizational development. It is 'reflexive' in that it leads to reinterpretations of management or leadership roles and increased self-awareness and understanding so that often a final end point is not what was envisaged at the beginning of a leadership initiative. Those holding leadership and management positions usually 'shape' (Lee, 1994) their role to fit their individual skills, style, and personal characteristics, all contributing to organizational strategic capability but which is impossible to measure through traditional evaluation methodologies. More holistic means are required in which outputs are measured to take account of added value and support provided for achievement of organizational objectives. A useful typology of such approaches, developed by Portsmouth University (Anderson, 2007) is based on a partnership model of Learning to ensure that:

- Learning processes deliver value to the organization.
- Learning resources are deployed in a cost-effective way.

Box 10.5 Four perspectives on evaluation (Anderson, 2007)

- *Learning function measures*: provide an assessment of the value of learning and development to an organization, taking account of all formal learning interventions. It requires assessment of 'training days' and spend on training; how effectively organizational capability is developed and supports critical activities in terms of efficiency and effectiveness, taking views of various stakeholders.

- *Benchmarking and capacity measures*: continually evaluating learning and development initiatives from the perspective of key performance measures and 'good practice' standards, both external and internal, as part of ongoing improvement.

- *Return on investment*: a different approach assessing the benefits of all development activity relative to its costs and considering its contribution to organizational objectives and will be discussed further below.

- *Return on expectation measures*: assess the extent to which stakeholders' expectations of development activities are accomplished and if other changes are apparent from learning. It takes into account informal gains from learning and relies heavily on organizational survey data.

Adapted from V. Anderson (2007) 'The value of learning – A new model of value and evaluation', Change Agenda, London: CIPD.

However, 'value is defined by the receivers of learning and training contribution and not by the trainers' (CIPD, 2007, p 3). Anderson's (2007) typology suggested four different approaches to evaluation in organizations, each requiring different measures of training and development. Within the report, each perspective is fully examined to provide details of different measures essential and the data to be collected. However, time, effort, and expertise are essential to gather all of the information required and these are not always available in every organization.

Anderson's typology emphasizes different approaches taken in evaluating learning and development, each approach giving a broader perspective than previous models—although learning function and capacity measures are probably closest to the measures in Kirkpatrick's evaluation model, but look at overall training and development within an organization, not specific interventions. These measures help to provide data to assess cost effectiveness, ensuring that money is spent wisely. However, they require comparator data and provide limited assessment of informal learning. Benchmarking, internally or against other organizations, has become a popular measure, using for example the quality scorecard, developed originally by the European Foundation for Quality Management and recently adopted to assess different elements of HR in organizations.

Two approaches that have not yet been widely discussed in this chapter include return on expectation, which is a relatively new and forward-looking means to assess future-focused capabilities, or pay-forward (Harrison, 2009) and preparedness for developing talent and learning of staff, through development work completed to date. It relies on survey data, taken over time, to show trends and assessments against other organizations.

Finally, return on investment (ROI) is a more business-focused approach to evaluation, treating spending on learning and development as any other major investment, to calculate a payback. Phillips (1991) added an additional level to Kirkpatrick's (1998) model in which the fifth level was used to calculate, in monetary terms, the cost of an intervention and its implementation against the monetary impact it had, to estimate cost to benefit achieved. This approach requires a careful specification and calculation of the benefits expected from an initiative, preferably in monetary terms, along with a calculation of the costs of running the course, which most organizations find difficult to assess. There is an argument about whether it is necessary to include an additional level for this step if a clear business need for development is established initially.

Kearns (2005) took the approach further by presenting an evaluation and learning system to be applied to all training and development in an organization, consisting of eight stages, beginning with a thorough analysis with all stakeholders, to identify business needs and benefits expected to be accomplished through the development, carefully distinguishing what cannot be achieved from training. He emphasizes that every business need must be prioritized and stated in quantifiable terms. This potentially difficult and time-consuming stage then provides all measures necessary to evaluate any intervention. All development interventions are considered and split into the categories shown in Box 10.6, linked to the appropriate evaluation strategy

This model requires a constant quest for bottom-line impact which can only be identified through a series of questions relating to how performance improvement or cost reduction is demonstrated. Although easier with certain types of development, for

---

Box 10.6 Kearns's learning system model

- *'Must have' training*, without which the organization could not function. This is the basic and mandatory training for all staff and therefore essential so that there is no benefit in evaluating it; all that is to be done is validate it. However, Kearns cautions that this category must be carefully selected.

- *Added value training*, designed to improve the bottom line and should be evaluated for its ROI. Therefore initial needs analyses should identify cost reduction, process, or expected performance improvements.

- *'Nice to have' training*, for which clear monetary evaluation measures cannot be devised, Kearns argues, should be postponed until such values can be assessed.

The consistent argument throughout his approach is that a quantifiable monetary improvement linked to the business objectives should be identified, otherwise development is not sufficiently focused.

example sales training, it is apparent that much of leadership and management development would fall into the final box in the model and so would be unlikely to get support because immediate bottom-line value is difficult to identify and measure.

Although a strong case may be made for attempting to assess immediate monetary value derived from development, discussions in the book so far have indicated the difficulties in evaluating leadership and management development and isolating the impact of any training (Yorks, 2005). However problematic it is to assess immediate return on investment, leadership and management development makes an important contribution to organizational capability and performance (Swanson and Arnold, 1997) and managers' capability to meet demands for organizational growth and change (Akuratiyagamage, 2007). Work on experiential learning and 'learning to learn', resulting from management development programmes, cannot usually be shown to have immediate bottom-line impact, but Reynolds and Vince (2007) make a strong case for its benefits to an organization, and the strategic nature of developing leaders and managers suggests that ways must be found to demonstrate its real worth.

Evaluation as a process

An approach proposed by Yorks (2005) is evaluative enquiry, focusing on value added through collaborative continual improvement methodology. Evidence is gathered at regular periods: prior to, during, and following any development, gathered from all stakeholders affected by the initiative throughout its life, with an intention of improving and developing the initiative and the organization. Preskill and Torres (1999) suggest that this approach to evaluation can be a catalyst for individual, group, and organizational learning, through a process of participation in discussion, reflection, and continual improvement. Seppänen-Järvelä (2004) used internal process-orientated evaluation in a similar way to promote a management development initiative in a Finnish public sector organization as shown in Figure 10.1.

The approach is more focused on wide-ranging aspects of the organizational system that supports effective performance, including development in its context, and requires input from all parties. Brinkenhoff (2006, p 304) provided an analysis of the impact of development among different successful organizations suggesting that:

Best estimates are that 80 per cent or more of eventual impact of training is determined by performance system factors, while the remaining 20 per cent or so is driven by variations in the quality of the training intervention itself and the characteristics of the learner, such as inherent ability and motivational values.

Therefore it is vital to have alignment between organizational strategy and direction and all development, particularly that of leaders and managers. Brinkenhoff (2006) recommends evaluation through appreciative enquiry, taking account of all stakeholders' views of 'the entire learning-to-performance process' (p 306) so that

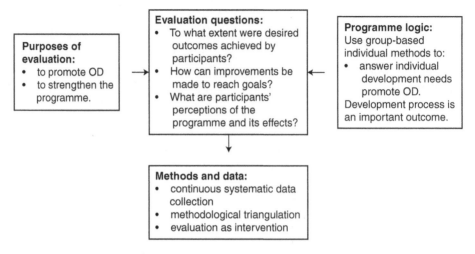

Figure 10.1 Process-orientated evaluation

each element of the systems involved in producing alignment, encouraging, and supporting learning as well as elements to sustain performance becomes the subject of data gathering to evaluate learning for enhanced performance.

These holistic approaches could be seen as a method of organization development in itself having far wider implications and impact than evaluation alone. It is a holistic approach to leadership development, including training, informal, and unconscious learning, and reviews the systems that support use of learning for strategic organizational gains, taking views from all stakeholders.

Summary of section

A developing view of evaluation is presented, not focused on evaluating input 'training', but focused on learning and impact of learning, for participants and other stakeholders, which contains a wide range of formal and informal experiences not previously included. The approaches require involvement of an organization in processes of continual review and improvement of all organizational systems that support high-level performance and specification of variables to understand the true value of leadership and management development.

Evaluation in organizations

In a recent survey of human resource development (HRD) practitioners (CIPD, 2009) some 70 per cent had specific budgets for learning and development, with the median spend being £220 per employee. Therefore many organizations spend well in excess of this amount. However, although large sums of money are spent on development initiatives, Tamkin *et al.* (2003) found that few organizations did little more than

Level 1 evaluation of learning and development, leading Russ-Eft and Preskill (2005) to state that evaluation was 'stuck in a quagmire' (p 71), with new holistic approaches only beginning to develop. In leadership and management development the situation is replicated, with 63 per cent of organizations 'never' evaluating leadership development in terms of return on investment (Osbaldeston, 2005), and more recently Mabey and Terry (2007) reported a lack of anything other than lower levels of evaluation in management development.

Reasons for this lack of evaluation are varied and surveys of HRD professionals indicate that time, resource, and lack of appropriate metrics contribute. Harrison (2009) argues that in some instances HRD professionals lack the necessary skills and knowledge to complete an effective evaluation, for example the skills of consultancy, investigation, and research. Evaluation takes a large amount of time and effort and substantially adds to spending on development interventions and, in many cases, learning and development teams are so stretched that it is impossible to give this time due to moving onto the next development event. A recent CIPD survey (2009) found that learning and development professionals spend only half as much time on evaluation and monitoring as they do on the overall planning of the function or delivering courses. This suggests that HRD professionals are not taking a strategic view of the benefits of learning and development which requires them to be able to measure and demonstrate value. Anderson (2007) confirmed the importance of demonstrating the value of learning in organizations in times of economic difficulty and the CIPD *Learning and Development Survey* (2009) found that 60 per cent of learning and development professionals questioned believed that there would be a greater focus on training evaluation during the next year, with many indicating that there was also a marked rise in leadership development initiatives, at least partly due to the economic situation of organizations.

Therefore it is vital that HRD practitioners in organizations develop effective evaluation strategies, including leadership and management development initiatives. These will require putting emphasis on the learner's viewpoint of the value taken and application of learning from development and acknowledging different perspectives to consider, for example the politics in providing evaluation for a sponsor and addressing long-term value added by such initiatives with equal vigour, within organizational culture and changing environments. It is probable that different approaches will be required to assess each element, whilst also reviewing learning strategically for the whole organization.

Summary of section

Organizations have, until recent times, paid limited attention to evaluation of leadership and management development, although methodologies have developed and have been used. More holistic measures, including all learning and performance systems, seem to offer opportunities for HRD professionals to demonstrate organizational value from development with the identification and continual assessment appropriate measures which will help demonstrate value for these practitioners.

Chapter summary

This chapter has discussed meanings and models of evaluation, including the classical models of Kirkpatrick (1998) and ideas about evaluation as a holistic process. We found that evaluation has only limited utility in organizations, although models recently introduced attempt to take a broad view and integrate different facets of it, including approaches to added value through evaluation and ways of evaluating informal approaches to learning. Evaluation starts early in a formal learning process, with clear specification of need which can assist HRD professionals in demonstrating the value of interventions and linking all learning to effective capability and performance management systems allows even informal, unintended learning to be recognized in terms of creating value for an organization.

Mini case study 10.4: Evaluating first-line management development

In national charities, first-line managers of local shops are selected from within the staff in each shop so that they are very familiar with their requirements, run almost entirely by volunteers. The new managers have been employed in one shop for some time and understand the unique culture of the organization.

Once selected for the role of first-line managers each learner is given a store to manage and put on a nine-month development programme that has a number of different facets. The development programme features include: formal sessions, action learning, mentoring, and contact details of a an experienced manager, working in a nearby town, and are described in more detail below.

Learners are provided with a development file to record learning from all of the training and development interventions they attend, which include formal sessions, action learning groups, and work shadowing opportunities. The file is also used to record 'critical incidents' that occur during their nine-month development period, that are discussed during meetings with mentors and regional development specialists who visit the trainee regularly during the period. This 'mixed' approach of learning on the job includes:

- access to online learning materials that they complete prior to attending day-long workshops
- workshops organized by a central training department, which cover the main people, resource, and financial systems and procedures in the organization
- action learning meetings, usually once per month, to support learners in applying learning from workshops
- a mentor, identified from among the senior management team, to support their development
- development file to record personal learning and development.

These activities have been found, informally, to be effective over the three years since the programme was developed.

However, there has not been a full evaluation of this initiative during the time, although reaction sheets are collected following each formal session and trainee-managers are finally 'signed-off' during months 9 to 11 following the course (i.e. immediately at the end of the training period or in the two months that follow).

Questions

1 You have been brought into the organization to advise on what approach could be taken to evaluate the first-line managers' development programme. Identify what approach might be taken and what information should be collected.

2 You should also provide guidance on how information could be used to provide ongoing measures of the success of the initiative.

Questions

1 Name and describe each of Kirkpatrick's four levels of evaluation.

2 How is the CIRO model of evaluation different from Hamblin's?

3 How is return on investment calculated?

4 What are the main criticisms of Kirkpatrick's model?

5 Why is experiential learning difficult to evaluate?

6 Explain what is meant by 'return on expectation' evaluation of learning.

7 Identify suitable benchmarks that could be used by organizations to externally assess leadership development.

8 What is the difference between a process approach to evaluation and Kirkpatrick's model?

Discussion questions

1 If asked to evaluate your course, what criteria would be relevant?

2 Think of a course you have been on; it may be for anything. How was it evaluated?

3 Using the Kirkpatrick model, take an example of training in interview skills, decide what information you would collect, and how you would do this, completing the boxes below for each level.

Levels	When?	What info?	How?
Reaction			
Learning			
Application			
Results			

4 What are the main issues in evaluating leadership and management learning in an organization?

Suggestions for further reading

Bramley, P. (1996) *Evaluating Training*, London: CIPD.
Provides a good and practical account of many different approaches that can be used in evaluating training and development, with examples.

Kearns, P. (2005) *Evaluating the ROI from Learning*, London: CIPD.
Reviews a wide range of models of evaluation and presents a thorough model based on his own work, including examples, that provides an approach which could be used.

Tamkin, P., Yarnall, J., and Kerrin, M. (2003) *Kirkpatrick and Beyond: A review of models of training evaluation*. IES Report 392. Brighton: IES available online at www.employment-studies.co.uk/pdflibrary/rw39.pdf.
Provides research into different models of evaluation used in organizations.

Anderson, V. (2007) *The Value of Learning: from Return on Investment to Return on Expectation. Research into Practice*, London: CIPD.
This research is part of a major initiative by CIPD to examine how organizations assess training and development and to provide a framework that can be used by organizations. Additional material is available on the CIPD website that considers the impact of the current recession on HRD and how it raises the importance of having in place appropriate measures to evaluate all learning and development.

PART : 4

Contemporary issues in leadership and management development

Developing leaders and managers for a diverse workforce

The aims of this chapter are to:

- assess what diversity means in organizations and the occurrence of diversity in the workforce.

- discuss evidence for and against increasing diversity at work.

- consider the implications for managers of managing a diverse workforce.

- discuss issues of developing disadvantaged groups to increase their participation in management—particularly women, ethnic minorities, older workers, and religious groups.

- draw conclusions about the future constitution of managers in organizations and how changing workforces will impact on managerial requirements.

Introduction

In this chapter we aim to critically review a range of evidence of the changing nature of employees in organizations, with the working population becoming more diverse. Managers are expected to manage an increasingly diverse workforce with changed expectations that leaders and managers have to be aware of and work with to achieve required organizational objectives. Therefore, there are development implications for current managers.

An additional implication of the increasingly diverse workforce is the changing population from which leaders and managers are selected; organizations have to find ways of involving a diverse group and encouraging under-represented groups to apply for senior roles. The consequent development implications are discussed.

Equality and diversity

As can be seen from the figures in Box 11.1, there remains a good deal of discrimination and inequality even after 30 years of legislation to support minorities and although there have been some advances in terms of numbers in employment and pay gap overall, statistics indicate that there remains inequality for women, ethnic minorities, and other minority groups in organizations and leadership and management.

Diversity and equality have a range of different meanings as used in psychological, sociological, and employment literature. One simple definition of diversity in employment is:

Valuing everyone as individuals—as employees, customers and clients.

CIPD, 2004

It is linked to notions of 'equality' in all spheres of life and work, and valuing the individual differences that people bring to whatever they do. In Chapter 7 we investigated some individual differences that impact on management development. However, they are due to individual preferences and do not usually lead to discrimination or adverse impact for groups in employment. Kandola and Fullerton (1998) distinguish diversity and equal opportunities in a number of ways, with equal opportunities being closely linked with human resource management and legislation to protect specific identified groups in employment and society more broadly. Although specific groups are identified for protection, in legislation, this does not suggest that these are the only differences that exist, some of which cause 'inequality' around the world. There are many other obvious individual characteristics that can distinguish them from other people, including language and dialect, physical features, and abilities, as well as many less overt features. Loden (1996) identified primary characteristics, which are mainly inherited characteristics, while secondary characteristics are those by which individuals are listed in Box 11.2.

Box 11.1 Diversity facts and figures

The population of Great Britain is approximately 58 million and is estimated to include:

- 10 million disabled people (who have a limiting long-term illness or disability that restricts daily activity). Employment rates for men with disability are 52 per cent, compared with 85 per cent for men who are not disabled.
- 4.6 million people from ethnic minorities. Unemployment rates for ethnic minority women are 9.1 per cent compared with 3.7 per cent for white women and 10.7 per cent unemployment for ethnic minority men compared with 4.6 per cent of white men.
- 2.3–3.2 million gay, lesbian, or bisexual adults.

Source: EOC 2006 Facts about Men and Women in Great Britain

Statistics show that employment rates for ethnic minorities stand at approximately 60 per cent, compared with the working-age figure of approximately 74 per cent (UK Commission for Employment, 2009; Spilsbury and Campbell, 2009).

9.4 million people are over the age of 65 now—there will be 12.4 million by 2021 (Phillips, 2009).

Girls outperform boys in GCSE and A levels, and in further and higher education, but there is subject segregation at A levels and in apprenticeships with 90 per cent hairdressing apprentices being female and 98 per cent apprentices in construction, motor industry, and plumbing are male.

Similar segregation occurs in employment, with women constituting the majority of the workforce in health and social care (79 per cent), education (73 per cent), hotels and restaurants (56 per cent): and the minority of the workforce in manufacturing (25 per cent), transport, storage, and communication (24 per cent), construction (10 per cent).

Women receive approximately 17 per cent less pay than men, the biggest gap in the EU (Eurostat data), with the gap being greatest at senior management level. Statistics from the Institute of Directors (2008) suggest that the pay gap for directors widened from 19 per cent in 2007 to 22 per cent in 2008 (*Management Today*, 29 February 2008).

White women and ethnic minority women and men are concentrated in low-paid jobs. In major organizations, 35 per cent of managers and senior officials are female but only 17 per cent of directors and CEOs.

Statistics taken from a variety of sources, as indicated above

What do these figures suggest to you about the successes of 30 years of equality legislation?

The basis of unequal treatment

This is usually based in 'in-groups and out-groups' in a society and if the 'in-group' choose to use their power in negative ways against other minority groups then discrimination and prejudice can grow. The development of in- and out-groups was demonstrated by Jane Elliott in the now famous experiment which has been widely repeated since her initial findings in the 1980s. In this experiment a group of children was split into two, depending on their eye colour, either blue or

> ## Box 11.2 Loden's dimensions of diversity
>
> Primary dimensions:
>
> - gender
> - ethnic heritage
> - race
> - mental/physical abilities
> - sexual orientation.
>
> Secondary dimensions:
>
> - religion
> - work experience
> - geographical location
> - organizational role and level
> - family status
> - communication style
> - work style
> - education.

brown. They were first told that blue-eyed people were better, more creative, and intelligent, and gradually those in this group became the 'in-group' and were found to discriminate against those in the other group. The following day the group was told that information from the previous day was incorrect and that the brown-eyed students were the better group. Following this information the groups were found to have changed beliefs and the brown-eyed group were now the in-group with all of the consequent feelings of associated preference and superiority whilst the other group changed to become the discriminated-against out-group.

There have been many other experiments which demonstrated and observed the influence of a dominant group on other out-groups, both in laboratory and field experiments (Tajfel and Turner, 2004; Allport, 1954). The main outcomes suggest that once someone associates with a particular group they notice differences from other groups, even if these are trivial and the group identification is purely cognitive. Then their behaviour is directed toward self-interest and that of their in-group, as the quote below explains:

> [A]d hoc intergroup categorization leads to in-group favoritism and discrimination against the out-group.
>
> *Tajfel and Turner, 2004, p 57*

If this theory of intergroup comparison is applied to groups in the workplace it provides an explanation of why there may be potential for intergroup conflict or

Reflection point 11.1

- Consider a time when you have felt different from others. How did it feel? How did it influence your behaviour and confidence?
- To what extent did you accommodate others' views and to what extent were you alienated?

discrimination against minority groups identified as out-groups, due to differences from the majority in-group becoming over-emphasized. Within the workplace, where differences are obvious from the majority in-group they may be magnified, making discrimination against those seen as members of out-groups more likely, through both conscious actions and unconscious attitudes.

Of course, just because a group can be identified as different from the majority does not excuse prejudice or discrimination against this group, and legislation has been developed in most countries to avoid discrimination against specific groups. Within the UK and Europe there is legislation to eradicate discrimination on the grounds of sex, gender, religion, race and ethnicity, disability, sexual orientation, and age.

Cultural diversity, as discussed in Chapter 3, can influence the ability of an individual employee to 'fit' within a group in organizations, and the above discussion explains how misunderstanding and feelings of not belonging within the dominant culture can occur.

Benefits of diversity

Diversity is about valuing and celebrating differences. It has been found (Kandola and Fullerton, 1998; Ross and Schneider, 1992) to bring benefits to organizations in terms of:

- better representation of the local community amongst staff
- avoiding bias and possible claims of unfair treatment
- greater understanding of customers' and clients' needs
- greater creativity and wider perspectives considered

Reflection point 11.2

- Think of out-groups that you can identify from your own experience.
- Usually it is one major characteristic that distinguishes such groups from the in-group. Identify these characteristics for the out-groups you have chosen.
- Now consider how many characteristics members of the out-group have in common with most other people in the in-group.

- improved decision making
- better talent management and use of available human resources
- avoiding losing available talent, so reduces recruitment costs
- maintaining workforce motivation and commitment
- encouraging greater numbers of application in recruitment
- being ethical and fair
- making the organization better informed, more adaptable, and able to understand different global cultures.

A number of advantages relate to adding value through diversity, and improved management of talent and human resources have become key drivers for many organizations. However, to gain benefit from such advantages organizations must put time and resource into developing and managing diversity, and managers are key within this effort. We suggest later that this requires both a more diverse managerial group and a greater understanding of diversity amongst all managers. Goss (1994) identified two main drivers of diversity, which were entitled:

- The human capital perspective. An organization cannot gain the full advantage of all employees, in terms of abilities, experience, skills, and motivation if there is discrimination and employment is limited to certain groups.
- The social justice perspective. It is both ethical and principled to encourage social equality through promoting processes which do not allow bias or discrimination. This moral argument is also thought to attract a wider group of potential employees who bring in a wider range of skills and experiences.

The composition and changes in the labour force that we have identified mean that it will be essential to recruit a broader range of employees in coming years. For example, the greatest increase in numbers in the workforce in coming years will be amongst women, minorities, and those over 60 years of age. Therefore the composition of the workforce in the UK is likely to continue to become more diverse. As organizations trade and employ workers around the world it is essential to have an understanding of people in different cultures and to encourage sharing of knowledge gathered globally.

Summary of section

This section considers some of the evidence relating to existing and historical inequalities and resulting problems of creating more diverse managerial cohorts. There is discussion of the notion of in-groups and out-groups as the basis for a lack of diversity in organizations, as well as consideration of the benefits of more diverse and inclusive organizations.

Diversity in organizations

Although much is understood about the factors that explain inequality and there are notable examples of successful initiatives to increase diversity at work, there are still major inequalities that can be identified. The figures at the beginning of this chapter provide an overview of the different employment experiences and opportunities of different groups. Findings suggest that generally women, ethnic minorities, those with disabilities, and older workers are disadvantaged, and segregated in occupations that are usually low paid and remain at the lower levels of many organizations, subject to the 'glass ceiling' (Davidson and Cooper, 1992).

There have been many initiatives to attempt to overcome prejudice and encourage greater fairness but Kanter (1997) explained three difficulties faced by minorities at work:

- The behaviours of minorities are noticed, particularly when linked to poor performance.
- There is a tendency to exaggerate difference between the minority and the majority group.
- There may be misinterpretation of the actions of people in the minority to maintain stereotypical views.

Models of managing diversity

There have been different policy approaches in organizations' management of diversity which have developed over time (Thomas and Ely, 1996; Kandola and Fullerton, 1998; Harvey and Allard, 2002; Kirton and Greene, 2000). Organizations respond to different pressures, resulting in different responses to diversity over time, with the most recent being to manage diversity in an organization to add value. All of these approaches can be seen at different stages in organizations today. The approaches are briefly described in Table 11.1.

As can be seen, there are difficulties using each approach to diversity and some have argued (Thomas and Ely, 1996; Gormley, 1996) that the implied control of 'managing' diversity runs contrary to what is required in the action. Moore (1999, p 212) highlights some of the organizational and development implications flowing from different perspectives on diversity. She suggests, for example, that diversity naïveté (a similar construction to differentiation in the model in Table 11.1) may lead to 'one-sided "romantic" training interventions focusing on "celebrating ... diversity"', [that] may heighten awareness ... but [are] unlikely to help tackle the potential problems associated with diversity'. She goes on to outline the implications of a perspective of integration, where supportive organizational policies and structures enable successful skills development for the management of diversity.

Table 11.1 Approaches to managing diversity and their associated problems

Approach	Description	Problems
Reactive	Organization denies that there are any issues in diversity for it to address. It fails to see potential for discrimination or opportunities through actively encouraging diversity.	Potential for discrimination to occur due to lack of understanding and risk of failing to comply with legislation. Most organizations have moved beyond this stage now.
Assimilation	Everyone is treated in the same way to limit any differences. Often linked with affirmative or positive action. Assumes a homogeneous workforce but bases culture and values on those of the majority.	An organization is heterogeneous and the minority's views and perspective may be inhibited or hidden in an effort to fit in with the predominant culture.
Differentiation	Emphasizes differences between groups, often based on identified equality groups, e.g. race, gender, etc., so that an organization benefits from using different knowledge and views.	Identifies and puts minorities into 'pigeonholes', which can be limiting for individuals and does not encourage employees to see similarities.
Radical perspective	Taking the idea of equality to introduce positive discrimination. Based on ideas that if there is not a fair distribution of all groups in employment, then discrimination is unfair. Intended to lead to equality of outcome.	Currently positive discrimination is illegal in UK, though being debated and used in USA. It can lead to questions of true ability and competence for those selected in this way.
Integration	Recognizing and appreciating differences in individuals to develop policies to cater for all and to maximize individual potential, through monitoring, communication, and culture change, and making diversity a strategic objective.	It is difficult to provide for the needs of all employees within a business environment and it may produce different out-groups who believe their needs are not catered for within organizational policies.

Although there are different approaches to diversity and models of how organizations should implement diversity management, there is still no one successful way of achieving equality in organizations. Evidence of this can be seen in the cases that are taken to equalities bodies and the continued work of the Equality and Human Rights Commission within the UK, and explained in terms of difficulties of changing an organizational culture and dealing with difference in fair ways that allow businesses to operate efficiently.

Whatever the overall approach chosen by an organization it is the managers within that business environment who are expected to deal with different groups at work

Reflection point 11.3

- Research some well-known organizations, from private, public, and not-for-profit sectors, and try to identify the approach they take to diversity:
  - What is their policy?
  - Which areas or groups are identified within the policy?
  - What information is provided about procedures and practices for members of the public?
- Try to identify which of the approaches identified in Table 11.1 they seem to have taken toward managing diversity.

that are critical to its success, and therefore diversity is important in two major ways within management development:

- to find ways to encourage disadvantaged groups in an organization to become managers to enhance and build diversity in the organization (developing minorities for management)

- to develop and support all managers to be able to encourage and effectively manage diversity within their role (developing management for minorities).

It is these two priorities for managers that will be the focus of the remainder of the chapter.

Perceptions of management

Much of the early research into leadership and management used available leaders and managers, most of whom were male and often white middle class; therefore the predominant 'model' of management was the one identified within these studies and it has dominated the writings about these topics for many years.

Gender

Management has traditionally been seen in most countries as a mainly male occupation (Collinson and Hearn, 1996). Schein (1976) suggested that management was more closely linked to a range of masculine characteristics, for example being independent and career orientated, decisive, assertive, and confident, and it was against these that anyone entering a management role was assessed. Research confirmed that attitudes to social roles and stereotypes of men and women influenced decisions made about management (Carmichael, 1995; Davidson and Burke, 1994). Even though there has been legislation and a range of initiatives to support diversity in organizations, there often remains the dominant model of masculine management within organizational cultures. Consequently, although women constitute half of the workforce, men are still more likely to be in managerial jobs (*Labour Force Survey*, 2008). Many women, particularly those with caring responsibilities, are either unwilling or unable to fit the stereotypical role expected in management and make choices about whether they remain in large organizations where there are stereotypical expectations of managers. Even those who make such a choice often find their behaviour misinterpreted when compared with male colleagues. For example, research on speaking over others in discussions has shown that this is acceptable for a male and yet a similar behaviour from a woman is interpreted by males as being persistent and annoying (Spender, 1980). Statistics in the opening box of this chapter show that women often find themselves in segregated occupations or subject to glass ceilings (Davidson and Cooper, 1992).

As more women move into leadership positions in larger numbers, more research on women as leaders becomes possible. There are two distinct groups of researchers into sex differences in leaders:

- One group says that there are no differences between males and females in terms of leadership (Powell, 1990; Powell *et al.*, 2002) or emotional intelligence (Hopkins and Bilimoria, 2007).

- Other researchers identify clear differences in behaviour, with women being seen to be have a more democratic leadership style (Eagley and Johnson, 1990), to have better people management skills (Rutherford, 2001), and a more transformational style linked to interpersonal skills and consideration for others (Bass and Avolio, 1997; Alimo-Metcalfe, 1995).

Whether there are gender differences that impact on effectiveness of leaders and managers will continue to be widely debated. The difficulties for research are in isolating the actual influences of gender from those of informal social and cultural learning of individual managers and the gendered expectations within organizations, all of which influence how an individual's behaviour is interpreted.

Race and ethnicity

As can be seen from the initial statistics in this chapter, those from minority ethnic groups suffer higher unemployment generally and, like women, are less likely to become managers or leaders in large organizations. Various reasons for this finding have been suggested, for example that ethnic minorities work predominantly in manufacturing and transport, sectors that have been in decline (Daniels and Macdonald, 2005). Lower educational achievement of ethnic minorities has also been suggested to account for employment differences, though Modood *et al.* (1997) showed that although there were differences in education it did not explain employment differences. Research to explain the employment patterns of ethnic minorities suggests that there are factors that disadvantage this group, including early patterns of geographical settlement in more deprived areas and suffering from more poor health, but there is still evidence of discrimination (Parekh, 2000).

The pattern of employment of ethnic minorities, like females, is low relative to white males in the UK, though for different reasons and segregated into different sectors. Smaller numbers in leadership and management may also be explained in the same way as for females in that 'models' of management taken from the predominant group in those roles (white males) may not provide the most appropriate way of assessing the contribution of ethnic minorities. It must also be remembered that this is not a homogeneous group, for it includes many different cultures and backgrounds.

Individuals from any of the minority groups who are seen as different from the 'norm' of an organization's management population may be considered not appropriate. However, it then becomes difficult to increase diversity without challenging predominant attitudes and characteristics, possibly though a radical approach. Writers have identified a need to change, suggesting that there are business benefits to be gained from a diverse workforce generally (Kandola and Fullerton, 1998) and that diversity in leadership and management is essential in a global world so that one country's characteristics do not dominate global organizations to the detriment of other groups (Daniels and Macdonald, 2005), as well as being required from an ethical standpoint.

Although discrimination against identified minority groups (gender, race, ethnicity, age, disability) is illegal, as we have seen above there are many overt individual characteristics that are used to distinguish between people and even more hidden values and beliefs that can lead to inequality. A recent and much quoted example is that of a young man who was discriminated against for his beliefs about the need to be 'green' and protect the planet. An employment tribunal has confirmed that these beliefs are similar to a religion, for which there is protection against discrimination in legislation.

Age and generations

There are also issues of age or generational difference in the way leadership and management are perceived. Among the various aspects of diversity recognized as arising from changing demographic factors in many countries, the impact of age and generations has been less extensively considered than many other factors. Arsenault (2004) points out that this issue is becoming more acute as generations are working together to a greater extent as traditional bureaucratic organizational structures make way for those with a more horizontal style, supported by new technologies.

The broad notion of generational differences, based on collective experiences and memories and leading to inter-generational diversity of attitudes and values, is supported by a number of writers (for example, Schuman and Scott, 1989; Rentz and Reynolds, 1991; Schewe and Meredith, 1994; Conger, 2001; Lyons *et al.*, 2005). The concept when applied to work and organizational life is often discussed in relation to work values including security, personal and professional growth, and work environment (Super, 1970; Smola and Sutton, 2002; Lancaster and Stillman, 2002) or leadership style (Zemke *et al.*, 2000; Conger, 2001).

There are differing views as to the categorization of different generations, in terms of both the labels applied to them and the dates that are considered to define their limits. It is also recognized in much of the literature that there are also those born on the cusps between generations, who will share some of the collective memory and experience of both, and some of the generational cultural characteristics of both. Broadly, the literature considers the generations to be those born between the 1920s and the end of the Second World War (known variously as the Veterans, GI Generation, or Matures), those born between 1945 and the mid 1960s (fairly universally known as the Baby Boomers), those born between the mid 1960s and 1980 (Generation X is a common label), and those born since 1980 (Millennials, Internet Generation, or Nexters)—although there is obviously a need to keep delineating and labelling the generations as time goes on.

Each generation is likely to have both particular attitudes to work and preferred leadership styles (as both leader and follower), and this clearly has implications for leadership and management development. For example, it is suggested by Arsenault (2004) that Veterans tend towards a directive leadership style of great clarity, based on respect for formal authority. Baby Boomers, by contrast, prefer a collegial and consensual leadership style, with a greater degree of participation, whilst Generation X looks for egalitarian relationships based on honesty, fairness, and competence, with a high tolerance for change. Finally, Arsenault suggests, Nexters like leaders with the ability to bring people together, having a belief in collective action and a polite relationship with authority. Others have tracked generational changes in work values, and noted a trend which shows a lessening emphasis on personal growth, a growth in importance attributed to work environment (including colleagues and surroundings), and a decline in the general importance attached to work as a part of life.

Later in the chapter, we consider how we should be developing our managers to deal successfully with the impact of these generational differences.

Summary of section

This section begins by looking at models of managing diversity, describing distinct approaches to diversity. Each has its problems, being (respectively) related to hiding differences, pigeon-holing groups, or creating new out-groups, whilst valuing differences.

The section considered perceptions of management in relation to gender, ethnicity, and generational differences. Traditional male, white, middle class notions of management mean that women and minority groups find it more difficult to be taken seriously and to be regarded as effective. Succeeding generations have developed preferences for both their own leadership style and for what they seek in their own leaders—thus creating further issues to be considered within the mosaic of diversity management.

Developing minorities for management

Background and current situation

As has been discussed above, there have been efforts to improve work opportunities for minority groups and increase diversity in most organizations. These attempts have been successful to varying degrees for the different minority groups in the UK. For example, women now constitute approximately 50 per cent of the UK workforce compared with 44 per cent in 1989, and whilst the numbers of ethnic minorities in work have increased there are still minority groups whose chances of employment are limited, for example those with a disability.

There are also situations in which if minorities are employed in a culture that does not recognize and embrace diversity, time, money, and effort can be wasted in trying to increase the diversity of the workforce. This was characterized as a 'cycle of disillusionment' (Noe, 2008, p 376) because as an organization attempts to increase numbers of minorities by recruiting greater numbers from minority groups, other employees believe that the new recruits have been given special treatment and managers make no attempt to develop or provide appropriate support for these employees. Eventually such employees do not feel able to contribute and become disillusioned, so leave the company.

Therefore there is a range of issues associated with encouraging greater numbers of minorities into management:

- The 'models' of leadership and management are those developed predominantly from white males because it is this group who traditionally held such roles and the required characteristics are often not challenged.

- Selection and development into management roles often take place through more informal routes, like the 'old boy' network (Davidson and Cooper, 1992) than traditional recruitment and so exclude those who are not seen as the same as the majority group.

- As we have seen elsewhere in the book, assimilation to the predominant organizational culture can be a major determinant of success or otherwise in a role, particularly as one moves to the top of the hierarchy (Schneider *et al.*, 2000).

- Expectations about behaviour and 'norms' of behaviour in a role may not match the preferred ways of working of those in minority groups.

As can be seen from the issues outlined above, many are not obvious because they are simply part of an organization's culture, and managers or decision makers may not even be conscious that such decisions perpetuate stereotypes and may not be fair to minorities of all groups.

Those who did not conform to this masculine stereotype were seen as not appropriate for managerial work, so that they had a choice to make: 'that of whether to learn to fit the dominant paradigm of management or to play another game, do management differently' (Bryans and Marvin, 2003, p 112).

These issues relate to organizational culture and appreciation of difference and changing the workplace to encourage employment of all minorities to add value. Such changes can only be addressed slowly, over many years, in a supportive organization culture and climate, using appropriate legislation and selling the benefits of equality to organizations and individuals to build a diverse workforce.

Current initiatives

There have been numerous initiatives and interventions employed to help to increase diversity in management. Many of these initiatives are examples of good practice and often use current development technologies and techniques to support specific groups.

In this section we will review a number of initiatives used with specific groups to establish the principles used and evaluate their potential for wider application.

Mentoring

Mentoring has received wide application to aid the movement of different minority groups into management and is used in management development generally, as discussed in Chapter 9. This chapter will consider evidence of its application in developing minorities in management.

Mentoring usually involves a manager working closely with someone from a lower hierarchical level and out of a direct line management relationship to help them to understand their organization and develop their career toward more senior roles. As we have already seen, even today senior managers in many organizations are white males and therefore this group supplies most mentors. Although research is not conclusive on the impact of gender and ethnicity in mentoring relationships, some themes emerge.

A recent review of race and gender in mentoring (O'Neil, 2002) found no differences between males and females in terms of their ability to form mentoring relationships. However, difficulties experienced in developing diverse mentoring relationships stem from findings that it is easier to socialize with those who are seen as similar to ourselves, having similar experiences and views, and that are identified as being in a similar social grouping (Clutterbuck and Ragins, 2002). Therefore mentors and mentees are more likely to choose and more easily develop relationships with those who have similar backgrounds and perceptions.

Heinrich (1995) suggested that stereotypes are more likely to influence behaviour in cross-sex mentor relationships, reinforcing the differential power relationships traditionally found in organizations between males and females. Concerns have been identified about the possible actual or perceived sexual relationship that can occur in a close mentoring dyad (Ragins and Cotton, 1991), so potentially limiting the informal and social access that a woman may have to a male mentor (Ragins and McFarlin, 1990). Similarly, although fewer in number, same-race mentoring relationships provide more psychosocial support than found in cross-race mentoring, possibly due to limited understanding of experience and perceptions and social taboos limiting mentor relationships (Thomas, 1989).

With support and the right types of organizational culture supporting diversity, over time it is likely that gender, ethnicity, race, and other differences can be addressed through mentoring. However, researchers report that:

Existing research supports the idea that diversity represents an initial barrier to the development of mentoring relationships.

Clutterbuck and Ragins, 2002, p 32

Such findings confirm the difficulties of using mentoring in organizations to improve workforce diversity in leadership and management or wherever in a business. These issues are similar for both the legally identified groups and less visual differences at work, for example sexual orientation or religious beliefs.

One difficulty identified in research is the relative scarcity of female and non-white mentors in organizations who could provide role models and mentors and avoid the problems of cross-race and cross-gender mentoring. One approach recently tried to overcome difficulties of finding mentors in the same organization is an e-mentoring project in the UK that provides mentors from across the country (Headlam-Wells, 2004). This programme provides support for professional women moving into higher management and for those on career breaks wanting to get back into management. The main benefits of mentoring for career development include (Headlam-Wells, 2004):

- reflected power from their mentor
- feedback
- access to resources and senior managers
- insights into politics within an organization.

Mentors are also found to benefit from the relationship in terms of gaining information, promotion, and renewed interest in work.

Positive action

Although positive discrimination is illegal within the UK and most European countries, positive action is legal, provided there is a demonstrated need to encourage greater participation for certain minority groups in the workplace, for example women or ethnic minorities. Positive action involves encouraging such identified groups to apply for roles, providing support, possibly in terms of training, for the individuals from the disadvantaged group and then selecting them alongside other candidates from all groups, majority and minority. Research (Liff and Dale, 1994) identified problems with positive action in recruitment of minorities because it left questions about their merit for the role and caused some negative behaviour from the majority group towards individuals recruited through positive action.

Support networks

A major impetus for developing networks for minority groups is the finding, through research, that managers in many organizations benefit from being associated with a support network. In many organizations this was known as the 'old boys' network' that has in the past supported mainly white male managers through association with other similar managers. These networks often operated in informal ways (Kanter, 1977), allowing members of such networks to advance within an organization so that it was 'more about who one knew than what one knew'. In order to try to equalize the use of informal networks, there have been a number of initiatives in organizations, particularly within the public sector, that encouraged the development of groups designed specifically to support minority groups, for example Women's Network and Black Workers' Network that provided opportunities for employees from minority groups to meet together for activities, discussion, and support. These groups could provide a 'voice' for the minorities and sometimes provide support and development for those within them, overcoming isolation and breaking down barriers (Linehan, 2001) for minority managers.

Ibarra (1992) found that men benefit more than women from networks because women are often torn between socializing and using it more instrumentally, for personal gain. Women often are excluded from male networks due to having dependents or other responsibilities and so the thinking behind women's networks was to provide the same support that males enjoyed. However, minorities' and women's networks often do not provide the same support as the old boys' network because they do not provide access to the same influential senior managers, so that although they support their participants they can be seen negatively as further separating these groups from the majority of the management population.

Women-only and minorities-only training

Women-only and minorities-only training was popular within certain organizations, being seen as a way of providing support to help people in those groups

Reflection point 11.4

- How might/does it feel to be from a minority group in an organization, for example ethnic minority, women or older workers and to be selected for special training, with others in that group, to get into management?
- What has been your experience, or what might your thoughts/feelings be?
- Would you/did you feel 'special' or 'different'?

adapt and learn to cope within the business. Part of the rationale for such groups relates to difficulties experienced in mixed gender and race groups in training. Research suggests that traditional stereotypes can interfere in training in mixed groups (Hite and MacDonald, 1995), and women are less accepting of inappropriate behaviour towards them than in the past, so that training experiences may become a 'battleground' for the sexes or different minority groups (Reynolds and Trehan, 2003).

Many of the same arguments about mentoring apply in minorities-only training, so that individuals feel part of the group due to similarities with other participants and being members of a specific group, e.g. women's, ethnic, racial, or disabled groups. However, it can also be seen to further alienate a minority group from other groups, occurring in an artificial situation whereas in reality minorities need to work alongside the majority of the workforce, using accepted behaviours and strategies to aid coping in future.

The difficulties with minorities-only training is that often minorities are still expected to conform to majority expectations and become 'assimilated' into the majority culture, accepting its norms and developing behaviours and styles that may not fit their personal or cultural style. Therefore, although development for specific minority groups might provide support networks and allow discussion of experiences and strategies, these groups must learn to work within the status quo which advantages the majority.

The identified minority groups involved may be separated even further from the majority and their differences in behaviour, style, and ways of managing perceived as a problem, requiring change. It also leaves the predominant existing culture unchallenged. A more integrated approach would perhaps consider whether the styles and difference epitomized by such groups can be used to add advantage, providing alternative perspectives to the norm.

Diversity is about appreciating difference and encouraging understanding to add value to an organization, so there is a difficult balance to be achieved, providing appropriate support to encourage minority groups into management whilst retaining individuality of a manager.

Summary of section

The section explores some of the difficulties of encouraging greater numbers of minority populations into management positions. There are some structural issues relating to the historical 'white male' models of management, the informal selection routes into management, and assimilation of minorities into prevailing cultural norms in order to succeed.

A range of current initiatives is discussed, including mentoring (where consideration is given to the barriers found by female and minority ethnic mentees), positive action, support networks, and minorities-only training.

Developing management for minorities

Apart from the development and encouragement of those from minority or under-represented groups to become managers, and to progress through the management ranks of organizations, the logic of diversity and the changing demographics of workforces around the world also imply a need to develop the ability of managers of all backgrounds to manage those workforces as effectively as possible.

Two approaches

There are basically two approaches that organizations and developers of managerial talent might take to this issue. In terms of method, any and every development technique (see Chapter 9) might be utilized, although we will highlight some examples below—but the overall approach will be either to develop greater awareness of diversity amongst the managerial cohort or to develop managers' skills and competencies to be able to manage diversity more effectively. These two approaches are not mutually exclusive, however—there is an argument that a raised level of awareness (depending on managers' starting point) might be a necessary prerequisite for skill development, or at least will provide a contextual basis for it, and skill development is likely in itself to also lead to greater awareness. Wiley (1996) discusses the approaches taken, and lessons learnt, by some large US corporations in developing some of the earliest diversity programmes. A number of them identified the need for awareness training to be followed by skills training and ultimately a wider cultural change programme.

Developing the managerial cohort to be able to more effectively manage a diverse workforce is not just a question of approach or technique, but also requires an appropriate organizational culture—one where there is scope and opportunity for discussion of diversity issues in an open way, and perhaps where there is an agreed theoretical framework for their consideration. The right policy framework will also need to be in place, and our development interventions will need to fit coherently with other HR processes. Effectively, we are talking about continuous change for the organization—and its ability to respond sensitively to new situations will require a rethinking of many aspects of organizational life, including management style, communications, motivation, reward, and so on—but we must remain focused here on the issues specifically related to 'developing management for minorities'. Successful development interventions, though, are most likely to occur as part of a more holistic and comprehensive approach to diversity.

There are many writers who point out the different approaches that may be taken to diversity training, and also some of the problems associated with them. Grant and Kleiner (1997) discuss awareness-based training, a largely cognitive approach aiming to provide information, heighten awareness, critique stereotypes, and consider attitudes and values. In contrast, they identify skill-based training as largely behavioural and aimed at providing tools for managers to interact successfully in a diverse work setting by developing new skills and reinforcing existing ones.

Awareness based development

In relation to the awareness-based approach, there is much still to be learnt about the various influences in terms of their degree of effectiveness. Wiethoff (2004) identifies the lack of theory and models exploring their relative success or failure. Badhesha *et al.* (2008) discuss the relative merits of focusing awareness training on specific groups (e.g. awareness relating to women, ethnic minorities, etc.) or more widely on several groups or on diversity per se. There are arguments to be made on both sides of this debate—that narrowly focused awareness training may be divisive and yet may also have a positive effect on broader attitudes relating to diversity; and that broader awareness training may dilute the effectiveness of impacts relating to specific groups. The authors suggest that organizations should certainly decide what their objectives are for awareness training, and that it may not be possible to simultaneously achieve both changed attitudes to a particular group and improved attitudes to diversity generally.

Thomas and Ely (1996), Nemetz and Christensen (1996), and Moore (1999) suggest that awareness-based interventions may be ultimately unsuccessful, particularly as they can create negative reactions from participants. They also have potentially a much less powerful impact on attitude and behaviour than group norms or other sources of influence, and so they need to avoid merely paying lip service to diversity, but should form part of the wider approach mentioned above. Loden (1996) suggests that many awareness-based programmes generate more heat than light—the heat coming in the form of backlash from majority populations (e.g. white males).

Mini case study 11.1: ING—awareness of diversity benefits

ING Group—the multinational banking, insurance, and asset management company—regards diversity management as a contributor to long-term profitability. This is based on a recognition that a diverse and inclusive culture will better enable it to anticipate and respond to customer needs, that customers in any case place more emphasis upon diversity and corporate social responsibility as part of their decision making, and that a diverse workforce will be better equipped to generate innovative and challenging solutions to business problems.

They instituted an awareness-raising programme based on showing the business benefits, but wanted to do so in a lively and memorable way. They chose a drama-based training approach, using actors to deliver a range of role plays, supported by employment law specialists to reinforce the legal aspects. This three-hour workshop examining the moral, business, and legal case for diversity was initially delivered to around 1,000 UK managers, receiving positive feedback, and is now used in ING's induction programme. It highlighted a range of inappropriate behaviours, including sexism, racism, and bullying.

Questions

1 Whilst a more participative approach might be more memorable, do you think it will have a greater impact on people's level of awareness?

2 To what extent do you think awareness raising of this kind will tackle the complex issues of diversity in organizations?

3 Do you think managers will respond more positively to one or more of the moral, business, and legal cases for diversity?

Based on Dawson (2005) 'Raising awareness of the benefits of diversity at ING', *Human Resource Management International Digest* Vol (13)2: 20–21.

Skills or competency-based development

The skills or competency-based approach to diversity is generally held to be more likely to yield sustained results. Attempts to identify the skills required are varied, although there is consensus around some areas.

Higgs (1996) focuses on developing successful managerial team working in the context of cross-cultural, multinational organizations. He considers the need for an effective framework to analyse and understand national or other cultural differences, suggesting that those developed by Hofstede (1983) and Trompenaars (1993) are particularly useful. These are discussed in more detail earlier in this book, in Chapter 3. Higgs suggests (p 38) that there is a need to create an environment that both 'acknowledges and values cultural diversity and develops individuals' cultural awareness and sensitivity'—echoing the two dimensions of awareness and skills approaches that have been mentioned already. He suggests that much of what is known, in general, about effective team working can be applied successfully in the context of diversity management.

Hofstede (1983) proposes a framework to build cross-cultural competencies involving the building of awareness, developing knowledge, and building skills for adaptive behaviours for success in differing contexts. Kakabadse and Myers (1994) also propose team-based development to achieve cohesive team working, shared vision, effective dialogue, and review mechanisms based on feedback.

The team-building and communication elements are also reflected by Whiteley (2004), who identified five key competencies for diversity leadership:

- strategic diversity focus

- role modelling and championing

- managing difference in teams

- managing flexibility

- communication and implementation.

He discusses approaches to the development of these competencies, including the use of a development centre (with actors involved in role playing), coaching, feedback, and personal action planning. All these methods are aimed at developing the desired behaviours amongst leaders and managers, so that they can in turn model the appropriate inclusive behaviours throughout the organization. In this way, it is intended that diversity takes its place in the mainstream of the organization, rather than at the margins.

Grant and Kleiner (1997) identify six skill or competency areas, as shown in Box 11.3.

Although the language is different, there are overlaps with Whiteley's suggested skills in areas such as communication, championing, and flexibility. Swanson (2002, p 267) also picks up the notion of dialogue as a key element in improved diversity management—'the ability to effectively talk through the dimensions of difference in the organization'. Most proposed skill or competency sets emphasize open

---

Box 11.3 Six diversity competencies (Grant and Kleiner 1997)

- self-awareness: recognizing one's own assumptions about those who are 'different'
- clear-headedness: using valid evidence rather than stereotypes in decision making
- openness: support for those who are 'different', sharing the rules of the game and providing access to mentor support
- candour: engagement in constructive dialogue about differences
- adaptability: willingness to change old ways of doing things that stand in the way of diversity
- egalitarianism: commitment to encourage all employees to develop and to participate fully in the organization

communication, adaptability and flexibility, active championing and implementation, as well as team-working skills. Some also emphasize the strategic, visioning element.

Interventions

There are examples from the literature of all kinds of development intervention being used in pursuit of either awareness or skills-based approaches to diversity. Given the need to address some deeply held values and embedded behaviours, it seems clear that relatively short-lived and one-off interventions are unlikely to succeed. Tools and techniques chosen should reinforce one another in pursuit of the organization's particular diversity objectives, and will of necessity be context specific, but those approaches involving elements of reflection, feedback, and planning in a real or realistic setting seem most likely to succeed. Hence, we find examples of the use of mentoring, coaching, action learning, role plays involving professional actors, action planning, and so on—all of which are better equipped to effect real attitudinal and behavioural change than many other interventions we might use. They are likely to be most effective when used in a holistic way and employed over the long term. They also need to be integrated into wider organizational processes such as performance management, reward, communication, recruitment and selection, etc.

Mini case study 11.2: Encouraging minorities into management in retail

Statistics indicated that a large private sector retail chain had above-average numbers of ethnic minority employees working at lower levels in stores. The company was keen to encourage some of these minority staff to develop and work toward management roles. There were a number of organizational initiatives to support minorities into management, including a black workers group, an Asian network, mentoring opportunities available, identified career structures and succession planning process, a policy for developing staff, and support from human resources managers.

However, although there were initiatives, when research was conducted it was found that few ethnic minority staff took up the opportunities.

Further research was undertaken in stores that had a particularly high population of ethnic minorities, to ascertain what the inhibiting issues might be, how staff felt about the organizational initiatives, and what might be done to improve the situation.

Questions

1 What might be the main reasons for the lack of current success of the initiatives?

2 Identify, from reading in the chapter, what might be done to improve the current situation.

Taken from an unpublished MA dissertation by C. Berry

Interventions such as presentations, standard training courses, or e-learning (lacking the interactive, feedback, reflective elements) may be helpful in support of other methods but are unlikely to succeed in their own right.

Chapter summary

Essentially, there are two approaches that can be taken to developing managers so that they can more effectively manage an increasingly diverse workforce. These are based on awareness raising or on skill or competency development, and both approaches have advantages. Whatever approach is taken, there is also the need to consider wider questions of cultural change, policy, and process development, and the crucial need to integrate these various efforts.

Awareness-based diversity development has had something of a chequered history, and has been criticized for being too simplistic, ineffective, and for provoking a majority backlash. Consideration of competency-based approaches, however, suggests that awareness raising is an important precursor for successful implementation—or indeed as part of a skills-based programme.

Questions

1 How would you define diversity?

2 What are the main groups identified in diversity initiatives and in what other ways can organizations be diverse?

3 How would you describe the difference between assimilation, differentiation, and integration?

4 What are the different leadership styles preferred by different generations, as discussed in some of the literature?

5 What kind of managerial styles are generally associated with women and with men?

6 Can you identify some of the advantages and disadvantages of mentoring as an approach to developing managers from under-represented groups?

7 What other approaches to the development of 'minorities for management' can you identify?

8 What are the two main approaches taken to developing managers to be more effective managers of diverse organizations?

Discussion questions

1 Discuss the pros and cons of providing management development for minorities-only groups in isolation.

2 How might organizations be persuaded to embrace the opportunities of developing managers from minority groups?

3 Why do you think it is so difficult to achieve success in managing diversity?

4 What would be the most appropriate approach for your organization to take in trying to improve its ability to manage diversity?

Suggestions for further reading

Harvey, C. and Allard, J. (2002) *Understanding and Managing Diversity: Readings, Cases and Exercises*, New Jersey: Prentice Hall.
This book provides a wide range of perspectives on diversity. Although predominantly American, it describes a wide range of activities as well as cases that can be used to explore diversity issues.

Trompenaars, F. (1997) *Riding the Waves of Culture: Understanding Cultural Diversity in Business*, 2nd edition, New York: McGraw-Hill.
A seminal text on issues of cultural difference in management, exploring the problems that can arise when working across cultures either within the same organization or with customers, suppliers, etc. The book considers the issues involved in trying to achieve consistency across the organization whilst taking the best from each culture in which it operates, and remaining sensitive to the differences between them.

Kandola, B. (2009) *The Value of Difference: Eliminating Bias in Organizations*, Oxford: Pearn Kandola.
Kandola suggests that we need to acknowledge our own bias before our organizations can make progress in successfully managing diversity. Having done so, he then suggests ways in which we and our organizations can reduce and eliminate bias. The book draws heavily on research into human behaviour, and also has an emphasis on the social justice arguments to support diversity as well as the business case.

Daniels, K. and Macdonald, L. (2005) *Equality, Diversity and Discrimination: A Student Text*, London: CIPD.
Provides a clear and practical overview of what equality and diversity mean and where they impact individuals and organizations. The book provides clear guidelines and examples for anyone requiring an understanding of what the issues are in employment.

CHAPTER 2

Developing ethical leaders and managers

The aims of this chapter are to:

- understand the underpinning theory of ethics and principles of business ethics.

- understand the importance of leadership and trust in public and private sector organizations.

- appreciate the ethical dimension to the leadership and management of human resources.

- understand the meaning of corporate social responsibility, the concept of sustainable ethical business, and the growing role of leaders and managers.

- understand the ethical dilemmas that leaders and managers face when working in an international context.

- consider effective ways of developing ethical managers.

- understand the additional and associated framework that needs to be in place with organizations to support ethics in management.

- gain an understanding of international culture and ethics.

- understand the role of business schools in teaching and educating managers in business ethics in a leadership context.

Introduction

There are no universally agreed rules of ethics, no absolute standards or controls, and no fixed and firm reference points. This is fascinating given how important ethics have become in modern life and society, with the shift over the last few years by both public sector and private sector organizations towards environmentally friendly and ethical policies, particularly in relation to the continued debates about global warming, the exponential increase in consumption of the planet's finite resources, the 2008–9 property and banking crisis, topped by the many other political and social challenges being faced internationally and here in the UK. With this backdrop in mind, the need for organizations to adopt an ethical standpoint that is rooted in their core values will be paramount for the sheer existence of many of them. Customers, governments, employees, shareholders, and society as a whole have far higher expectation levels than ever before on ethical matters related to the strategies, leadership, and management of organizations. More than ever before it has become a key responsibility of leaders and managers within organizations to set the ethical standards, to walk the talk, and ultimately take responsibility for adopting an ethical standpoint on a whole broad range of issues. Societal and environmental pressures have pushed ethics to a central position in the modern world of business and commerce.

Mini case study 12.1: Business ethics challenges

Everyone knows right from wrong. Don't they? Wrong. People disagree about the definition of right and wrong all the time. That is why the topic of business ethics is currently front and centre in the media and in canteens and around the water cooler and coffee machines in most organizations.

Daily we await the next Enron, WorldCom, Northern Rock, Royal Bank of Scotland, or political scandal—to name only a few. Whatever such story hits the press, it is difficult to ignore business ethics as an issue. And as our world becomes more complex, sometimes the right answer, the one that meets the needs of the most stakeholders—employees, customers, potential employees, shareholders, and board members—lies somewhere in the middle.

Think about these business ethics scenarios that happen in organizations every day:

- An employee surfs the internet, shopping for personal items on company time.
- A factory manager decides to ship products to a customer even though he knows the parts have a quality problem and the customer probably won't notice.
- An employee spends several hours a week on her company mobile phone sorting out domestic issues and talking with her children and friends.
- A manager shares important company information with a competitor for their potential gain.

- A store misrepresents the quality or functionality of an advertised sale item.

- An employee takes office supplies home to stock his home office.

- The organization has a recycling policy as part of its corporate social responsibility programme. It takes more time to recycle many items, so employees simply throw them away in the rubbish bins.

- A finance officer accounts questionably for purchases and expenditures in order to balance the books.

- A customer tells a supplier that their cheque is in the post when he knows he hasn't written the cheque.

- A business expense claim is made for an item when the item is going to be used for personal benefit and nothing to do with business activity.

Do any of these situations sound familiar? Of course they do. You encounter these and others like them regularly if you spend any time in organizations.

Do the individuals involved even consider whether the choices they are making are ethical? After all, the factory manager may think that the most important issue is to get the parts to the customer on time. Or the employee rationalizes in their own mind, 'I give this organization lots of overtime and thinking time outside work hours, so I deserve the time at work to surf the web.'

Question

1 Consider your organization or one where you have previously worked or that you know of. Think of some example of work practices like the ones above that you came across, the people involved, and their motives for the actions they took. Were the actions right or wrong? Were they bad people or good people making questionable ethical choices?

Character Counts www.charactercounts.org

Before we commence on the pathway of what needs to be done and how we go about developing ethical leaders and managers, it is worth spending some time to review our understanding of what we define by ethical management and looking at some of the behavioural theory that is key to gaining a deeper grasp of the subject. In this chapter we will also go on to take a look at the importance of taking into account international culture when developing ethical practices and competency, which in today's global business environment cannot be overlooked. Towards the end of the chapter we look at the associated support framework that needs to be put in place in order to supplement ethical leadership and management development. This includes a short review of the roles and responsibilities of business schools in the educational process, which is considered by many to be very important in the formative stages of development of many high-level and influential leaders and managers operating in the sectors of public administration, private sector businesses, and also those operating in the voluntary or non-profit-making sectors.

Definition of ethical management

Here is just a sample of the definitions that can be found by a few minutes' research of dictionaries found on the internet:

- relates to moral principles or the branch of knowledge dealing with these
- the rules of conduct recognized in respect to a particular class of human actions or a particular group, culture, etc.: *medical ethics*; *Christian ethics*; *business ethics*
- moral principles, as of an individual: *His ethics forbade betrayal of a confidence*
- that branch of philosophy dealing with values relating to human conduct, with respect to the rightness and wrongness of certain actions and to the goodness and badness of the motives and ends of such actions.

The modern Oxford Dictionary says:

> *ethical: being in accordance with the accepted principles of right and wrong that govern the conduct of a profession.*

Interestingly this definition goes on to say by way of an example of usage: 'morally correct: Can business ever be ethical?' By this it is getting to the point that in some schools of thought, predominantly the free market capitalism era of 1970–80, it was held that the prime purpose of business is to exploit opportunities to increase wealth for its stakeholders. The suggestion is that being 'ethical' can at times and in some circumstances be a barrier to the prime purpose of a business.

With this underpinning paradigm in mind we should not be surprised that in the teaching of leaders and managers from that era, business ethics took a back seat. The prevalent view was that of free markets and 'profit maximization', which was supported by economists such as Friedman (1970), Williamson (1975), Jenson (1976), and Richardson (1972). This approach was the basis for the development and education of leaders and managers not only in that era but well into the 1980s and 1990s—Goodwin (RBS), Hornby (Halifax), and others from the banking sector being prime examples.

It is only since the turn of the century (2000) that business ethics and awareness of multiple stakeholder interests aside from the traditional shareholder started to come more centre stage in terms of commercial and political importance, and in turn the corresponding development and formative education of leaders and managers who grew up in this era.

Concepts emerged such as 'triple bottom line', developed by Elkington (2004), which advocates that modern organizations have multiple stakeholder interests and that organizational performance should not only be measured in financial terms but also in terms of human capital and the planet's resources in order to calculate its performance as a long-term sustainable business. Further developments in ethical business reporting have been seen over the last decade with the introduction in the USA in 2002 of the Sarbanes-Oxley Act (SOX), also known as the Public Company Accounting Reform and Investor Protection Act. Similar protection acts have since been introduced in Canada, Japan, Germany, France, and many more countries. SOX was introduced as a reaction to a number of major corporate and accounting scandals, including those affecting US companies such as Enron, Tyco, and WorldCom. These scandals, which cost investors billions of dollars when the share prices of affected companies collapsed, shook public confidence in the nation's securities markets. For the average person in the street (small stakeholder) it resulted in mass unemployment in the communities these companies were located in, and affected personal wealth through pension schemes and small shareholdings. The scope of this book does not stretch as far as a full review of the SOX regulations. The point of raising it is to strengthen the viewpoint that since the turn of the century more transparency and an ethical standpoint have become central to the leadership and management of organizations. The transformation to multiple-stakeholder organizations and ethical business models are with us to stay and as such leaders and managers need to understand and buy into the underlying ethical principles as well as being able to comply on a day-to-day basis with auditable management requirements that extend beyond traditional accounting practices.

Ethical management theory: deontological and virtue ethics

Although there is no firm set of answers about ethics, we can try to define what 'ethical' and 'unethical' mean and therefore increase our understanding and make it a little easier to get to grips with and hopefully provide a framework that will allow for the development of leaders and managers.

One useful way to conceptualize the subject of ethics for the purpose of this book and particularly this chapter is to consider business ethics as 'values in action'. By this we mean that business decisions are made by applying judgement that is closely related to underlying principles and values of that particular organization and the leaders within organizations. For a deeper understanding it is useful that we turn to the study of philosophy.

In deontological philosophy an act is morally right if it can be judged by all reasoning persons to be appropriate as a universal principle of conduct, irrespective of the person's situation or role in the action. This is in contrast to consequentialist theory (where the ends justify the means). In an organizational setting the means are particularly important as the means are often the policies and procedures (rules) that guide people within the organization towards making the right decision or outcome. This approach to ethics determines goodness or rightness from examining the acts, rather than third-party consequences of the act or of the person doing the act (Robert, 1967). 'Objectivity' is the critical point, as opposed to 'subjectivity', which is the case with virtue ethics.

Virtue ethics seek to describe what characteristics a virtuous person would have. They argue that people should act in accordance with these characteristics. This is the principle behind the school of moral philosophy known as virtue ethics and has developed from as far back as the ancient Greek philosophers Plato and Aristotle, but is brought up to date in more modern times by the likes of MacIntyre (1988).

Deontological ethics seem a more appropriate foundation and offers more in gaining an understanding about ethics in a business sense, as the paradigm is based on rules, obligations, and duties. For example, the act may be considered the right thing to do even if it produces a bad consequence, if it follows the *rule* that 'one should do unto others as they would have done unto them', and even if the person who does the act lacks virtue and had a bad intention in doing the act. We have a *duty* to act in a way that does those things that are inherently good as acts ('truth telling', for example), or follow an objectively obligatory rule.

It is sometimes described as 'duty' or 'obligation' or 'rule' based ethics, because rules 'bind you to your duty'. The term 'deontological' was first used in this way in 1930, in *Five Types of Ethical Theory*, by C.D. Broads. Eighty years on and the theory is just as useful in understanding the dilemmas of ethical leadership.

Summary of section

So far we have seen how the study of ethics goes back many, many years and although this book is neither a history nor psychology book, it is useful to go this far back to gain a firm understanding of how ethics are built into basic human behaviours. Equipped with this basic understanding will help in applying these theories to modern organizations.

Addressing ethics in leadership

Leadership has a moral dimension because leaders have influence over the lives of others. Because of this, leaders have a huge ethical responsibility in the decisions they make and how they exercise the power and control their position affords them.

We saw an example of how important the meaning of this is in the UK Parliament in early 2009 regarding the scandal over MPs' expenses claims. The MPs caught up in the scandal—including the Prime Minister, Gordon Brown, and Opposition Leader, David Cameron, not to mention most of their senior cabinet and shadow cabinet—had fallen into the trap of simply believing it was ethical to operate within a set of written rules that referred to what can be claimed and what cannot be claimed, conveniently disregarding any exercising of judgement or application of public values, for the benefit of their personal gain. Note that in the early stages of this scandal the House of Commons Speaker at that time, Michael Martin, was in pursuit of personal victory of the decision to defend the rules of the House rather than seeing the objectivity and the ethics underpinning the situation. Leaders who make decisions subjectively and personally for reasons of building power, reputation, and wealth seem to entirely miss the point about ethics, and this fundamental blind spot prevents any real ethical objectivity. In this case the strength of public opinion was underestimated regarding the unnecessary waste or consumption of public money. Moreover, MPs' neglected the 'moral duty' that the public believed MPs in such a position of power should hold. The shock of it all and the corresponding public outcry were more about the collective lack of objective awareness and the apparent blind spot so many had shown in the defence of their personal actions. As we all now know, this resulted in a massive lack of trust by the public and several MPs losing their positions.

The business world is also littered with examples of where a moral and ethical dimension to leadership has been missing. WorldCom and Enron in the USA are well-reported examples and will be referred to later in the chapter. In the UK in the period 2000–5 we saw MG Rover broken up and sold after the Phoenix consortium ceased trading in 2005, and Primark's unethical practices in clothing manufacturing. There are many more examples, making business ethics one of the most debated topics of our times.

The main lessons to be learnt for future improvement are that skills training on how to adopt an ethical, honest, and 'objective' viewpoint are required. Secondly that a supportive framework is put in place within organizations to ensure the critical 'checks and balances' are there in order that ethical leadership and the application of positional power is not abused.

Personal traits and character

A person's traits and character have influence over their leadership style and ethical standpoint (Northouse, 2009). Remember that there are many traits related to effective leadership. By becoming aware of your own traits and how to develop them, you will be well on your way to becoming a successful ethical leader.

Identifying one's own traits and gaining an understanding and awareness of them can be a great benefit for leaders and managers. Then in turn, this skill and methodology can spin round and be used to gain an insight into others' characters and traits. Both approaches are important parts of the subject of leadership and management development—particularly in matching traits of character found within an individual's personality to those that are aligned to the ethical values of the organization and the leadership and/or managerial role the person is being appointed to. Later in this chapter we will look at techniques that assist in making this alignment.

Table 12.1 The six pillars of character

Trustworthiness

Trustworthiness is the most important element, and involves being sure to do what you say you'll do.

- Be honest.
- Be reliable.
- Have courage to do the right thing.
- Don't deceive, cheat or steal.
- Build a good reputation.

Respect

While we have no ethical duty to hold all people in high esteem, we should treat everyone with respect.

- Be tolerant of differences.
- Use good manners.
- Be considerate of others.
- Work out disagreements.

Responsibility

Ethical people show responsibility by being accountable, pursuing excellence, and exercising self-restraint. They exhibit the ability to respond to expectations.

- Do your job.
- Persevere.
- Think before you act.
- Consider the consequences.
- Be accountable for your choices.

Fairness

Fairness implies adherence to a balanced standard of justice without relevance to one's own feelings or indications.

- Play by the rules.
- Be open minded.
- Don't take advantage of others.
- Don't blame others.

Caring

Caring is the heart of ethics and ethical decision making. It is scarcely possible to be truly ethical and yet unconcerned with the welfare of others. This is because ethics are ultimately about good relations with other people.

- Be kind.
- Be compassionate.
- Forgive others.
- Help people in need.

Citizenship

The good citizen gives more than they take, doing more than a fair share to make society work, now and for future generations. Citizenship includes civic virtues and duties that prescribe how we ought to behave as part of a community.

- Share with your community.
- Get involved.
- Stay informed: vote.
- Respect authority.
- Protect the environment.

Character Counts www.charactercounts.org

In addition to being about a leader's character, ethical leadership is also about the actions of a leader. Actions refer to the ways a leader goes about accomplishing goals. Ethical leaders use moral means to achieve their goals and this is critical to determining if they are an ethical leader.

Power is an important factor that can be used in a positive way to benefit others or in a destructive way to hurt others. A leader needs to be aware of and sensitive to

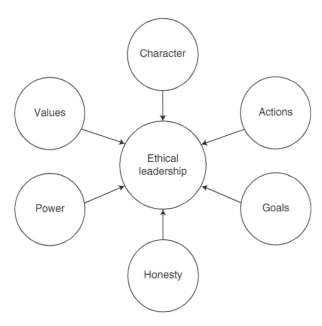

Figure 12.1 Factors relating to ethical leadership

how they use power. How this is achieved says a lot about that leader's ethics. Honesty is about speaking the truth and creating trust in the minds of others. It includes all varieties of communication, both verbal and non-verbal. Clearly honesty also plays an important part in ethical leadership.

Figure 12.1 summarizes the main factors that contribute to ethical leadership.

Approaches to business ethics

At the minimal end of the spectrum, Friedman (1970) proposes that since business managers are employed by shareholders to manage their property (shares in this case) the overriding responsibility is to do what shareholders wish them to do with their property. According to Friedman, shareholders generally wish to make as much money as possible from their shares. Therefore the overriding responsibility is to maximize profit. If property rights are paramount in a business, then it is morally legitimate for employees to do what is required to meet that end within the confines of the legal system that governs corporate organizations. In this school of thought it must be pointed out that this is not being unethical but focused on what is actually required.

An alternative approach which avoids the overriding duty to shareholder which Friedman puts forward is offered by Rawls (1971), a Harvard professor; in his work entitled *A Theory of Justice*. Rawls offers an approach of deriving a notion of fairness which can in turn be used to ascertain fairness in a particular situation. In this paradigm it is suggested that we should project ourselves to the original position in which we are ignorant of our actual status and position regarding the current

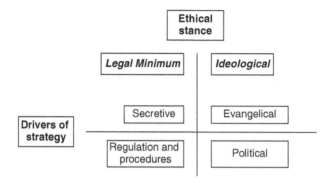

Figure 12.2 Strategic formulation and ethical stances

situation we are faced with. We should then ask ourselves from this hypothetical position of impartiality, 'What would be the fair resolution in this current situation?' Followers of neuro-linguistic programming would term this 'reframing' (Grinder and Bandler, 1983). Rawls suggests that a reasonable citizen when adopting such a stance would opt for a resolution that would favour the less advantaged groups—thus adopting a more welfare-humanistic approach rather than the managerial-performance school of thought that Friedman proposes.

The leader or group of leaders in an organization clearly have a critically important part to play as the formulators of strategy and how the strategy is communicated. Their ethical stance and ideology are often articulated to other stakeholders and the public at large in mission, vision, and values statements. A useful way of illustrating this was put forward by Johnson and Scholes (1998). The matrix in Figure 12.2 shows how an organization's ethical stance can be seen in relation to the business drivers. The diagram helps an understanding of how ethical leadership manifests itself across a range of large organizations in the public or private sector.

Secretive

If strategy is driven by managers who see other stakeholders and the corporate governance requirements largely as constraints, they may be secretive about the organizational purposes and see little value in a mission or vision statement that reflects an ethical position. When these do exist they are simply paid lip service and are not powerful influences on the strategic development of the organization.

Evangelical

In contrast to the above, managers who have a missionary zeal for the organization are likely to use the mission statement in an evangelical way to sell purposes and ethical stances to other stakeholders as well as members of the organization.

Regulation and procedures

Where strategy is dominated by powerful external stakeholders, whose main concern is that the organization complies with the corporate governance arrangements, complying with regulations and procedures becomes the purpose and any sense of a mission may be lost. This is classic faceless bureaucracy found in the central planned economies of Eastern Europe prior to 1990.

Political

In contrast, if strategy is dominated by external stakeholders with a missionary zeal, the purposes of the organization may become highly politicized. So the ability to produce a mission statement acceptable to all stakeholders can be difficult. It will most likely include reference to the topical political issues of the times, such as carbon reduction, ethical trade, social responsibility, and so on, in a desire to win good public relations.

Ethics apply in all sizes of businesses

Even at the level of small and medium-sized businesses there is a role for ethical management. In every new business launched, whether a one-man band or a fully fledged corporate enterprise, the owners must adopt a code of ethics for the business. For small businesses this may be unwritten or contained within the underlying assumptions found in the policies and procedures in the staff handbook. Yet still the code exists. Larger organizations have specific written codes of ethics and employees are trained in them and are required to adhere to their code.

Business owners who toss ethics aside by promising to do one thing and delivering another thing entirely usually do not last too long in the marketplace. A code of ethics is as important as a marketing plan, a solid financial strategy, and a strategic business plan. Consider a small business that enters into unethical practices, be they exploitation of workers, use of substandard raw materials in the production process, not being truthful about business or financial reporting matters, or in marketing of their products or services. Once customers become aware that the business does not have high ethical ideals that are aligned to their own, they will take business elsewhere. It therefore follows that having a code of ethics alone is not the answer. It is the leaders of businesses large or small that is the critical factor in maintaining an ethical stance within a business.

Owners of businesses or directors of those businesses who fulfil the leadership role have a crucial part to play insomuch as constantly examining their own values and principles. If they routinely engage in unethical practices they cannot help but pass those values and principles on to other people working in the business that they hold a position of power over. Smaller businesses suffer more because unethical practices and behaviours are easier for customers to take notice of. So leadership and managerial behaviour is essential in every size and type of organization for it to be successful and sustainable over the long term. Today more than ever before consumers are paying more attention to corporate governance and proper behaviour of businesses, and their owners or leaders. In a marketplace that has many businesses with similar products it is safe to say that ethics can be an important market differentiator—besides which, the people connected will be able to sleep soundly at night.

Summary of section

In this section the reader should now be aware of how the basic principles of ethics have been brought into the world of commerce and business. We have seen some examples and tried some activities in order to reaffirm and broaden this understanding. In this next section we will introduce the reader to how ethics can also apply at a macro level in the form of corporate social responsibility and how a theoretical framework can help in shaping training programmes.

Business ethics and corporate social responsibility

Over the last 30 years the subjects of business ethics and corporate social responsibility (CSR) have increasingly been discussed in both academic and business forums. The rise in prominence of these terms is considered by many to be due to public scandal and mismanagement of firms (Croft, 2003; Porter and Kramer, 2006). A number of high-profile cases have arisen, in particular with organizations such as Enron and more recently the issues with the sub-prime lending market in the USA, and revelations regarding working conditions in producing clothing for organizations such as Gap, Nike, and Primark. In addition to these well-publicized cases, people are becoming increasingly aware of environmental issues such as global warming, sustainability, and the increasing gap between rich and poor countries.

The UK government is also raising the profile of CSR and ethics; in 2004 the government, through the then DTI, and with the Association of Business Schools, the British Chambers of Commerce, and Business in the Community, launched the CSR Academy. As part of this combined initiative, the DTI (since dissolved) created a competency framework, designed to help HR managers integrate CSR and ethics into their organizations.

As far back as the 1950s the discussion regarding CSR picked up pace, beginning with the notion of 'companies doing the right thing' and growing government legislation relating to the environment and health and safety. During the 1970s and 1980s there was a shift in thinking which gave rise to the notion of 'corporate social responsiveness', where organizations took an offensive position towards CSR by

> ## Box 12.1 Competency framework for managers
>
> - understanding society: roles of governments, businesses, trade unions, civil society
> - building capacity: develop networks, alliances
> - questioning 'business as usual': challenge others' 'usual' attitudes, adopt new ways of thinking
> - stakeholder relations: build internal and external stakeholder relationships
> - strategic view: take a strategic view of the business environment
> - harnessing diversity: respect diversity and adjust approach to different situations
> - whistle blowing: use a system of communicating internally without fear of retribution
>
> Institute of Business Ethics

developing strategic frameworks to rationalize and operationalize social responsibilities. However, during this period the UK government introduced a plethora of legislation in areas such as equality, employment law, and health and safety, therefore it could be argued that organizations were forced to develop strategies to cope with increasing and changing legislation. During this period the concept of 'corporate social performance' also became popular, which discussed the link between CSR and organizational performance. This notion continues to appear in recent CSR literature, most notably in Elkington's 'triple bottom line'.

> ## Reflection point 12.1
>
> - Discuss why the UK government has seen the need to become involved in CSR and business ethics.
> - How can the above competency framework help in this respect?

The triple bottom line

The triple bottom line (TBL) is also known as 'people, planet, profit' or 'sustainable business accounting'. 'Triple bottom line' was coined by John Elkington in 1994. TBL captures an expanded spectrum of values and criteria for measuring organizational (and societal) success. In practical terms, triple bottom line accounting means expanding the traditional reporting framework to take into account ecological and social performance in addition to financial performance.

The concept of TBL demands that a company's responsibility be to stakeholders rather than shareholders. In this case, 'stakeholders' refers to anyone who is influenced, either directly or indirectly, by the actions of the firm. According to the stakeholder theory, the business entity should be used as a vehicle for coordinating stakeholder interests, instead of maximizing shareholder (owner) profit.

Taking the alternative phrase 'people, planet, profit', 'people' (human capital) pertains to fair and beneficial business practices toward labour and the community and region in which a corporation conducts its business. A TBL company conceives a reciprocal social structure in which the well-being of corporate, labour, and other stakeholder interests are interdependent.

A triple bottom line enterprise seeks to benefit many constituencies, not exploit or endanger any group of them. The 'upstreaming' of a portion of profit from the marketing of finished goods back to the original producer of raw materials, e.g. a farmer engaged in Fair Trade agricultural practice, is a not unusual feature. In concrete terms, a TBL business would not use child labour and would monitor all contracted companies for child labour exploitation; it would pay fair salaries to its workers, would maintain a safe work environment and tolerable working hours, and would not otherwise exploit a community or its labour force. A TBL business also typically seeks to 'give back' by contributing to the strength and growth of its community with such things as health care and education. Quantifying this bottom line is relatively new, problematic, and often subjective. The Global Reporting Initiative (GRI) has developed guidelines to enable corporations and NGOs (non-governmental organizations) alike to comparably report on the social impact of a business.

'Planet' (natural capital) refers to sustainable environmental practices. A TBL company endeavours to benefit the natural order as much as possible or at the least do no harm and curtail environmental impact. A TBL endeavour reduces its ecological footprint by, among other things, carefully managing its consumption of energy and non-renewables and reducing manufacturing waste as well as rendering waste less toxic before disposing of it in a safe and legal manner. 'Cradle to grave' is uppermost in the thoughts of TBL manufacturing businesses, which typically conduct a life cycle of products to determine what the true environmental cost is from the growth and harvesting of raw materials to manufacture to distribution to eventual disposal by the end user. A triple bottom line company does not produce harmful or destructive products such as weapons, toxic chemicals, or batteries containing dangerous heavy metals, for example.

Currently, the cost of disposing of non-degradable or toxic products is borne financially by governments and environmentally by the residents near the disposal site and elsewhere. In TBL thinking, an enterprise which produces and markets a product which will create a waste problem should not be given a free ride by society. It would be more equitable for the business which manufactures and sells a problematic product to bear part of the cost of its ultimate disposal.

Ecologically destructive practices, such as overfishing or other endangering depletions of resources, are avoided by TBL companies. Often environmental sustainability is the more profitable course for a business in the long run. Arguments that it

> **Reflection point 12.2**
>
> ● In small groups discuss the pros and cons of the TBL approach to business accounting.
>
> ● Make lists and compare your findings between groups.

costs more to be environmentally sound are often specious when the course of the business is analysed over a period of time. Generally, sustainability reporting metrics are better quantified and standardized for environmental issues than for social ones. A number of respected reporting institutes and registries exist including the Global Reporting Initiative, CERES, Institute 4 Sustainability, and others.

'Profit' is the economic value created by the organization after deducting the cost of all inputs, including the cost of the capital tied up. It therefore differs from traditional accounting definitions of profit. In the original concept, within a sustainability framework, the 'profit' aspect needs to be seen as the real economic benefit enjoyed by the host society. It is the real economic impact the organization has on its economic environment. This is often confused to be limited to the internal profit made by a company or organization (which nevertheless remains an essential starting point for the computation). Therefore, an original TBL approach cannot be interpreted as simply traditional corporate accounting profit *plus* social and environmental impacts unless the 'profits' of other entities are included as social benefits.

This highlights the important and central part that CSR has to play in today's global marketplace; this ethical approach to international business is something that business leaders and managers need to understand and be familiar with. Hence the need for this competency to be included in any leadership and management development programme. Good leaders strive to create a better and more ethical organization. Restoring an ethical climate in an organization is critical, as it is a key component in solving the many other organizational development and ethical behaviour issues facing the organization.

International culture and ethics

One of the dilemmas that managers encounter when working internationally involves what they should do when work practices that are illegal or viewed as wrong in the home country are legal and acceptable in the host country. An example in a HR management capacity might include discrimination on the grounds of gender, race, age, sexual orientation, when recruiting or compensating. The use of child labour is taboo in Western countries but remains common and woven into the cultural fabric of life in many Eastern European and Asian societies. Similarly, health and safety standards and working conditions are considered to be much worse in Eastern

European and Asian countries through the eyes of the Western societies. A further example of cultural and ethical dilemma is in the way contracts for work are awarded and won in different international settings. In the UK and particularly where public sector finances are involved, there are strict codes of practice and rules around tendering and the awarding of work contracts. The ethical stance is based on fairness, transparency in the decision-making processes, and objectivity of the individuals involved. Unfortunately this framework is rarely found. Donaldson (1999) tried to provide a framework for decision making in a multinational business environment that could help in understanding these dilemmas. He states that to resolve these dilemmas the task is to tolerate cultural diversity while drawing a line under moral recklessness. His approach involves 30 fundamental international rights recognized by the United Nations, such as the right to non-discriminatory treatment, freedom of speech, freedom to work in fair and safe conditions, the right to earn a decent standard of living, and so forth. Whilst this approach helps, it does not provide a practical set of guidelines for the behaviour of businesses and managers operating in an international environment. In the end the ethical behaviour and conduct of businesses and managers at home or/and abroad depend on a general set of guidelines established by the leaders of these business organizations.

Developing ethical managers

There has been some resistance to the inclusion of ethics in leadership and management training and development in the past but there is absolutely no resistance now. In recent years there has been a high level of concern with regards to ethics in organizations. This has prompted organizations to provide a range of initiatives to improve their approach and standing with regards to developing ethical managers. Having a code of ethics that provides guidance on how business is done, and linking this to performance and appraisal systems normally via a competency framework have become more prevalent. Introducing training programmes for managers is also a growing trend. Training is seen by many as the means to reduce wrongdoing and increase desirable behaviours and attitudes. But what can organizations realistically expect from this type of training? Ethics and ethical behaviour are very difficult to shape and control. Organizations can use training to some extent to ensure compliance to a code of practice or to institute standards, thereby reducing exposure to legal requirements and practices—such as taking gifts, conflict of interest, harassment, or fraud. Compliance can be made mandatory. Training in the policy and procedures can help remove any misinterpretation and be a way of invoking compliance. The threat of disciplinary action hangs over managers and leaders if they knowingly break these rules, having had the awareness and procedural training.

It is in the grey areas where ethical behaviour is a matter of judgement and values where training becomes less effective. Consider the MPs' expenses abuse already referred to. Several MPs insisted they had done nothing wrong in terms of breaking the rules and saw nothing wrong in making so-called bona fide claims for personal items and services related to their second homes.

Yet it was seen by the public that this was not warranted and not an ethical use of taxpayers' money, just because they were operating within the rules. It was still wrong to take money for such claims. Values and ethics are difficult to define and apply right and wrong judgement to.

In the next few sections we look at some basic techniques that can be used as a foundation to develop leaders and managers in ethical decision making. There is a chance to try these techniques by completing the activity questions.

Objectivity and fairness

From what we have seen so far, we can conclude that rules and law alone are not a basis for ethical decision making. So what is the basis for ethical decision making? It is suggested by the Institute of Business Ethics that objectivity and fairness come strongly into play. They recommend a simple ethical test or, taking it a step further, having a code of ethics for business decisions. It is important to understand, however, that developing a code of business ethics will not stop unethical behaviour; but it will give people something to think about, a measurement against which to assess their own behaviour.

It might appear to be stating the obvious but the above simple exercise is not often practised in everyday life and in business decision making. It is often the case that managers who are involved in the decision-making process can become attached to the build-up and background to a decision that invariably influences the outcome. True objectivity is hard to achieve, especially for leaders under pressure. Similarly, fairness is difficult to define let alone apply. Detachment is a huge part of the process because objectivity is almost impossible without personal detachment. So how do we

---

Box 12.2 A simple ethical test for managers making business decisions

Transparency

- Do I mind others knowing what I have decided?

Effect

- Who does my decision affect or hurt?

Fairness

- Would my decision be considered fair by those affected?

Institute of Business Ethics

develop managers to flip their attention from one where they are engaged and committed to a frame of mind where they can become detached and objective in order to make better-quality and ethical decisions?

Neuro-linguistic programming techniques

One possible solution is to introduce, develop, and coach managers in some of the techniques that are found in the subject area of neuro-linguistic programming (NLP). In simple terms objectivity in this context of 'ethical leadership and management' means the leader or manager must be able to see the other people's viewpoint. In NLP there are techniques and skills such as 'different perspectives' that can be

Box 12.3 How to use 'different perspectives'

Use it to review an interaction with another person—or to prepare for a forthcoming one.

Do two rounds. The first round provides insights into the current situation. The second round enables you to benefit from the insights gained in the first round—while mentally 'wiring in' the learning.

First perspective

See the situation through your own eyes. You are primarily aware of your own thoughts and feelings. Enables you to consider your own needs.

Second perspective

Imagine what it is like to be the other person. Put yourself in their shoes—as if you are looking back at yourself, seeing, hearing, and feeling as the other person.

Third perspective

Take a detached viewpoint. Imagine you are looking at yourself and the other person 'over there'—seeing the two of them speaking, gesturing, etc. Pay particular attention to non-verbal behaviour such as the body language and the sound of their voices. Then consider, as a result of taking this view, what advice you wish to give 'yourself' about how you are handling the situation.

Adapted from Routledge and Carmichael, *Personal Development and Managerial Skills.*

Reflection point 12.4

● Consider where you think this technique could be of value in a workplace situation.

---

learnt and honed through practice and experience to improve awareness and effectiveness. In this NLP mental technique you mentally review (or preview) a situation from a number of different standpoints in order to enrich your appreciation of what is involved. For leaders and managers this can be a very useful approach to developing their own objectivity, as well as being a role model of behaviour for those around them.

Personality assessment tools

The more interest is shown in making the correct decision about recruiting and internally promoting leaders and managers who have an ethical standpoint, the more sophisticated the systems are becoming. Time and money are being invested in identifying methods and techniques that can aid the measurement of the inherent traits that can be associated with ethics. Accordingly it has become commercially viable for occupational psychologists and the organizations they work for to further develop these.

Research has proved that personalities are distinctive and each individual behaves according to certain distinctive patterns throughout a variety of situations. The 'Big Five Factors' of personality (see Chapter 7) are five broad domains or dimensions of personality which have been scientifically discovered to define human personality. Following this line of reasoning, anyone's personality can be measured along these five dimensions using a variety of questionnaires. Personality traits are intrinsic differences that remain stable throughout most of our life. They are the constant aspects of our individuality and this is the value they can bring to organizations when they are fully understood.

There are many personality assessment tools that are derived from the Big Five Factors (Costa and McCrae, 1992) and that can be used to gain an insight to a person's character, traits, and underpinning ethical values. The 16PF® personality questionnaire is just one example that can be useful in a leadership and management context (see Figure 12.3).

Based on behavioural psychology research, personality assessments like the example above can be valuable predictors of behaviours and provide an insight into a person's character and traits. When used in a leadership development capacity it is normal to use the outcomes from such assessments in a development plan that addresses any gaps or shortcoming. To get the best from such assessment tools they must be well

Measures a set of 16 traits that describe and predict a person's behaviour in a variety of contexts. Interpreted by a qualified practitioner, it aims to provide comprehensive information about an individual's whole personality, ethical standpoint, revealing potential, confirming capacity to sustain performance in a larger role and helping identify development needs.

The 16PF can be used in a wide variety of contexts, and at many different levels; specifically:

Development	Selection
• executive coaching	• graduate recruitment
• line manager coaching	• executive selection
• leadership development	• assessment for potential
• development planning	
• succession planning	
• outplacement	
• career transition and planning	
• career guidance	

Figure 12.3 The 16PF® personality questionnaire

This is OPP Limited copyrighted material. 16PF® is a registered trade mark of the Institute of Personality and Ability Testing, Inc. (IPAT) in the USA, the European Community and other countries, and IPAT is a wholly owned subsidiary of OPP Limited.

designed, validated, ethical, and non-discriminatory, appropriate to what is being assessed, and administered by trained professionals. It is normal practice in a recruitment context and indeed a development context to combine personality assessments with a competency interview where questions can be asked in relation to specific ethical behaviours and experience that are appropriate to the leadership and managerial behaviours required in the organizational setting.

Summary of section

In this section we have seen the importance of the work of Elkington in developing the 'triple bottom line' concept and how organizations are using this as a benchmark for ethical leadership. The writer of this section also believes that self-awareness and personality profiling have a role to play in developing ethical competence in leaders and managers within

Reflection point 12.5

• Consider where and how you think the 16PF® personality questionnaire could be used in organizations.

organizations. Therefore in this section we have seen some techniques that can be used as a development tool for improving capability in ethics.

Developing leaders and managers who operate in a global context

Briscoe, Randell, Schuler, and Claus (2009) suggest three steps be considered by business leaders to help ensure their employees behave in an 'absolute' fashion both appropriately and ethically:

- Develop a clearly articulated set of core values as the basis for global policies and decision making.

- Train international employees to ask questions that will help them make business decisions that are both culturally sensitive and flexible within the context of those core values.

- Balance the need for policy with the need for flexibility or imagination.

A fourth step could be added to this: Provide awareness training or practical exposure to cultural differences. Many companies who operate internationally have identified the benefit of providing potential leaders and managers with an awareness of the cultural differences and business practices of other countries. A well-used method for this is through CSR programmes. The company in the example below is one such organization that commits millions of dollars a year to CSR programmes and encourages employees to become involved in a personal development capacity.

Consider the following extract from an interview with John Crawford, a former HR director of Johnson & Johnson, the international healthcare company, who now works as vice president human resources for Biomet Orthopedics, a China-based company.

There is an important need within the development of leaders and managers for a solid level of competence to be attained before an international assignment. The need for language and cultural empathy and adaptability, also the need for 'virtual skills' and 'matrix management' skills. They need to manage across many time zones, often with little time and less resources and less direct reporting structures than previous generations of managers. Influencing ability also becomes key, at home in the First World and comfortable in the Third World, they need to have a more 'work–life–work' balance than the solo work ethic of earlier generations, they need to be inclusive and supportive to local culture, ethnic and diverse groups of people, sometimes to the detriment of the company. CSR programmes and particularly overseas projects provide fantastic learning opportunities in this respect.

Support frameworks to facilitate ethical leadership and management

Whates (2006) suggests that four elements are necessary to quantify an organization's ethics:

- written codes of ethical conduct
- ethics training for executives, managers, and employees
- availability of advice on ethical situations (i.e. advice lines or intranets)
- systems for confidential reporting (whistle blowing).

Putting these four elements into a supportive framework within an organization gives it more chance of becoming truly more ethical. The Institute of Business Ethics website provides an extremely useful source of information for this. It provides advice and examples of how these can be developed in a 'best fit' approach to meet an organization's needs.

Written codes of ethical conduct

To ensure unethical behaviour does not occur or is minimized, organizations need to develop self-regulatory practices that are based on clearly defined ethical guidelines (Dowling and Welch, 2004). These are typically referred to as codes of conduct which in the globalized economy can be used to ensure that all members in a supply chain understand how they are expected to behave and act. Many organizations with sizeable procurement departments will be familiar with such internal codes of conduct and the managers and professionals who make up these departments may well be associated to a professional trade association or institute who similarly apply codes of conduct. However, it must be pointed out (Crane and Matten, 2007) that what is legally right or wrong can be different from what is morally right or wrong.

Ethics training for executives, managers, and employees

At the very outset and well before any time and money are invested in training, it is critical to the level of success that an investment in ethics training can bring to ensure people joining the organization, particularly in leadership roles, are aligned with the organization's core values. In this context the importance of sophisticated selection methods at the recruitment stage comes into play. There is an old saying amongst seasoned HR professionals that you 'recruit for attitude and train for skills', which has a ring of truth when individuals are being assessed for suitability for not just a job but in joining an organization. We saw earlier in the chapter how personality assessment techniques can facilitate the identification of this, typically combining a personality assessment exercise and a competency-based interview as part of the selection

Mini case study 12.2: Making ethics real: objective ethical codes of practice

A well-known major manufacturer of equipment used in construction and farming takes ethics training seriously. The company provides annual ethics training for its over 90,000 employees. A central part of the training is realistic job scenarios that each employee must respond to. The scenarios are written in house and different scenarios are given to employees depending on their job role and duties and including all levels, managerial and non managerial. The employees are encouraged to consult the organization's code of ethics as they consider their responses. The scenarios provide realistic work-related situations that prompt employees to consider how they choose to behave. Here is an example of a scenario that might be given to plant floor maintenance manager.

A team manager is approached by a team member: 'I've noticed that another member of my team is using a cleaning agent that seems to work well. I started adding it to my cleaning solution too and it seemed to help with cleaning. Can I continue to use it?'

Question

1 What would you do?

- Say, 'No, this is not part of your remit and work practices.' Stop it immediately and discipline both employees.

- Do whatever it takes to get the job done.

- Check with the environment and safety group to make sure the cleaning agent being used is a safe combination and change the work practices.

This organization's scenario-based ethics training approach makes the content relevant to the worker's duty area and forces employees to apply the 'objective ethical code' to their everyday work.

Adapted from Character Counts www.charactercounts.org

process. Ensuring the alignment between an organization's mission and values and the personality type and ethical values of an individual can be a very important aspect of an organization's hiring practices. Once in the organization, assuming the attitudes and 'moral compass' are aligned, it becomes relatively easy to train people in how to apply the 'checks and balances' and work to the rules of the organization when making decisions. The moral compass in this setting refers to personal characteristics like those we saw earlier in the chapter which identified the six pillars of character: trustworthiness, respect, responsibility, fairness, caring, and citizenship.

Having selected leaders who have alignment in terms of values and attitude to those required by the organization, investment in ethical training and the development of the skills of executives and managers in this respect should clearly be more effective.

Availability of advice on ethical situations

Many organizations, in fact most these days, have an intranet system that contains guidance and advice for employees on a wide range of issues related to working within organizations. It becomes fairly easy with this facility in place to include guidance policy documents on how the organization views ethical matters and what to do or where to go in order to escalate a decision or gain a greater insight in ethical matters. External websites of professional institutes offer guidance in professional areas such as procurement, human resources, international trade, legal and regulatory affairs, and financial accounting practices. Leaders and managers should be made aware of where to locate further information and guidance from advice lines, intranet, and internet sources. This can be done within induction programmes, ongoing individual performance reviews, regular employee communication briefings.

Systems for confidential reporting

Confidential reporting systems, often referred to as whistle blowing, are becoming common in many organizations and particularly those who sign up to the Sarbanes-Oxley audit systems. The strength and effectiveness of such systems are determined to a large extent by the leaders of the organization and the commitment they put into reports received through such channels.

Mini case study 12.3: Ethics at WorldCom

When *Time* magazine editors named WorldCom's Cynthia Cooper and Enron's Sherron Watkins two of their People of the Year for 2002, they were acknowledging the importance of internal whistleblowers—employees who bring wrongdoing at their own organizations to the attention of superiors.

At WorldCom, Cooper pushed forward with an internal audit, alerting the board of directors' auditing committee to problems, despite being asked by the company's CFO to postpone her investigation. According to *Fortune* magazine, 'If Cooper had been a good soldier; the whole incredible mess might have been concealed forever.' At Enron, accountant Sherron Watkins outlined the company's problems in a memo to then CEO Kenneth Lay.

But by the time Watkins and Cooper blew the whistle, much damage had already been done, and the shareholders and employees were the ultimate losers.

Questions

1 How does an organization create a culture that encourages employees to ask questions early—to point out issues and show courage in confronting unethical or illegal practices?

2 And then how can a company ensure that timely action is taken?

3 In other words, how does an organization encourage internal whistle blowing?

Markkula Center for Applied Ethics

The responsibility of business school teachings

Sumantra Ghoshal (2005), a professor of strategy, wrote an article entitled 'Bad management theories are destroying good management practices', in which, to coin a phrase, he 'turned on his own' regarding the cynical theories used in mainstream modern businesses, and criticized business schools and the curricula they adopt and teach which manifests these. He made the following observation:

> Business schools do not need to do a great deal more to help prevent future Enrons: they need only to stop doing a lot they currently do … business school faculties need to own up to being part of the problem in creating Enrons. It is our theories and ideas that have done much to strengthen the management practices that we are all now so loudly condemning.

Commentators are advocating that many of the academic models and theories-based concepts which are derived from the past should be reviewed and evaluated for their value in the post-2008 credit-crunch world. Blame has been laid at the doors of some very well-known business schools who played a key part in the education of business leaders, particularly in the banking and financial industry, who took high-level—some would say reckless—risks in areas such as packaging and selling on debt and in the use of complex financial derivatives instruments that whilst being legal are ethically suspect. Many of these techniques and the underpinning knowledge were learnt in major business school MBA programmes.

Consequently business schools have been heavily criticized and cited as being a principal cause that resulted in almost bringing down the world's financial markets. This maverick approach to teaching of business finance and free market practices as well as advocating a 'win at all costs' leadership style has been seen as widely unethical in the aftermath review of the collapse of the world banking systems.

For business schools, bringing CSR and business ethics into the mainstream means that the teaching of these subjects does not any longer sit on the periphery as isolated courses with such titles as 'CSR and Environmental Management Studies'. Instead the teaching of CSR and business ethics now sits at the core of all the main group of educational subjects such as Law, Accounting, and Leadership and Management. Clearly the intensity of the teaching will vary but signs are that it is becoming an increasingly popular subject area for dissertations and case studies. All of which indicates a recognition that business schools have started to wake up to the collective responsibility to teach and increase understanding in the area of ethical business in order to avoid repeat outcomes.

Chapter summary

In this chapter we have seen how ethics have become a central issue in the way leaders and managers go about running organizations: how they make decisions, conduct themselves

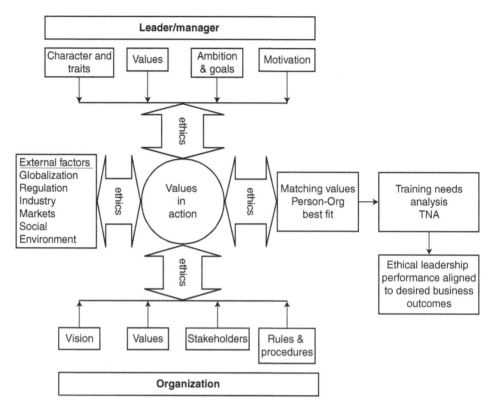

Figure 12.4 Model of ethical leadership

with other stakeholders, contribute to business performance and use their positional and personal power to influence other members of the organization to take ethics seriously and adopt responsible values. Figure 12.4 summarizes to a large extent the forces in play and offers a framework for how ethical leaders and managers can be developed.

There is a need to revisit ethical leadership and trust. The public's trust in business leaders has never been weaker. According to recent research (Edelman Trust Barometer) which measures perception of public trust in the US and European businesses, this dropped from 58 per cent to 38 per cent from the start of 2010. Scandals like bankers' bonus systems and the UK public's loss of trust in Parliament and the well-documented MPs' expenses claims scandal have brought public trust in its leaders, from all walks of life, to an all-time low.

If organizations from all sectors, public, private or the third sector, cannot address this problem, an economic turnaround may be delayed indefinitely. Banks will not lend money, innovation will slow down, trade across borders will fall even more rapidly, and governments will suffer from a lack of confidence and subsequent over-regulation. Unemployment numbers will continue to rise and consumers will not spend on anything considered non-essential. A complex modern economy simply cannot function unless people believe that its institutions are fundamentally sound.

Regaining trust simply will not happen on its own. Moreover, trust is not something that can rightfully be asked for on the basis of 'blind faith' from organizations' stakeholders and the public.

In a *Harvard Business Review* article, two highly respected academics who have studied organizational behaviour for decades, James O'Toole and Warren Bennis, argue passionately that all senior managers must build a culture of transparency and ethical business practices to repair this problem. Without strong leadership from the top, managers hoard information and flatter their bosses instead of questioning tired assumptions and speaking the truth. What is needed next, claim O'Toole and Bennis, is 'a culture of candour' (2008).

The overarching principle is that we should be rethinking trust. The argument put forward is that most of us trust people too easily. As social animals we are hardwired to do that. In recent years the public and consumers have been hoodwinked into trusting people and institutions that were behaving badly. So while pundits believe that organizations need to rebuild consumers' trust as soon as possible, in fact the exact opposite applies: we should remain sceptical and demand that our institutions become more worthy of trust. In support of this view, this chapter has highlighted that a robust system of ethical management is required in order to make the step change.

Whates (2006) said that the four elements necessary to credibly quantify and govern an organization's ethics are:

- written code of ethical conduct
- ethics training for executives, managers, and employees
- availability of advice on ethical situations
- systems for confidential reporting.

Good leaders strive to create a better and more ethical organization. Restoring an ethical climate in an organization is critical, as it is a key component in solving the many other organizational development and ethical behaviour issues facing the organization.

Mini case study 12.4: Ethical business—recipe for sustainable success at Johnson & Johnson

Johnson & Johnson are just one well-reported organization that have developed a successful global organization with a strong ethical stance that provides a useful example of clearly articulated values that are 'absolute' in how they are applied in the day-to-day working practices of the organization.

J&J is the largest broadly based healthcare company in the world; it operates in a decentralized model made up of many different operating companies. Famous for its Johnson's Baby brand, J&J is a globally respected organization with a local feel to its companies operating in the pharmaceutical, medical device, and consumer healthcare markets. It has been successfully returning double-digit growth for the 70 years it has been trading. Many commentators wonder how J&J continues to adapt to these changes and consistently deliver results and stay ahead of its competitors.

At the core of what all J&J companies stand for is the company credo, which apart from a few edits over the years has remained largely unchanged. The values that guide decision making are spelt out in J&J's credo. Put simply, J&J's credo challenges all employees to put the needs and well-being of the people they serve first.

Robert Wood Johnson, chairman from 1932 to 1963 and a member of the company's founding family, crafted 'Our credo' himself—long before anyone ever heard the term 'corporate social responsibility'. 'Our credo' is more than just a moral compass. J&J believe it is a recipe for business success. The fact that J&J is one of only a handful of companies that have flourished through more than a century of change is proof of that.

The credo focuses on four key constituents, ranked in order of importance to the company:

- First is the customer and the duty the company has to patients, doctors, nurses, and surgeons.
- Second is the employee and how fairness and respect are key to ensuring employee satisfaction (a very early nod to today's 'engagement agenda').
- Third is the responsibility J&J has to the environment and the community, to take care of them and those less fortunate than themselves. It also talks of the need to bear its fair share of taxes and that its suppliers are entitled to earn a profit, a clear commitment to long-term sustainable and ethical relationships.
- Fourth and last is the return on investment for the stockholders. This is listed last as the philosophy goes that if J&J get the top three right, the last one will take care of itself. History shows so far that to be quite an accurate philosophy.

This credo is the foundational guiding principle for all decision making at J&J.

J&J has the credo embedded in all of its human resource processes, so it recruits employees using situational questions around attitudes and behaviours listed in the credo.

It is in all learning and development too, with credo awareness training and ethical business conduct for new employees, and is incorporated in and/or referred to in all other types of training. Managers and existing employees get involved in 'credo challenge' sessions often run by senior executives to stimulate discussion and sound, ethical decision making.

All employees have objectives in the form of 'what' they need to achieve and all have objectives on the 'how' they do things; this links to the credo in the form of global leadership competencies.

The employee satisfaction survey has the credo in the fabric of the questions, and organizations and managers are held accountable for the results.

Question

1 How does J&J ensure its managers operate fairly and ethically?

Extract from an interview between Peter Emsell (author) and John Crawford (former De Puey International Ltd).

Questions

1 What is the difference between deontological ethics and virtual ethics?

2 Which of the above approaches is more appropriate to business ethics?

3 Why do you think objectivity is important in business ethics?

4 Little was taught to leaders and managers about business ethics and social responsibility until after the turn of the century. Why do you think it has become a much more central topic?

5 List the types of recruitment assessment methods you are aware of that purport to assess attitudes and behaviours at the selection/recruitment stage when individuals are joining an organization.

6 Do you think psychometric assessment methods work as a predictor of ethical fit in an organization?

7 Are there any shortcomings of such assessment methods, and if so, what do you think they are?

8 How important do you think it is to have formal written codes of ethical conduct and a whistle-blowing policy within an organization in order to support ethical business?

9 What do you understand by the term 'triple bottom line'?

10 Do you think it is fair that business schools should shoulder some blame following the 2008 credit crunch and subsequent economic recession, and why?

Discussion questions

1 Traits and characteristics
Think about an organization in which you work or are familiar with. Go back in time and think about a leader in that organization and some of the key decisions that they have made. Try to identify examples of the six pillars of character that were evident in their decision making.

2 An organization's core values drive ethical practices
Reflect on what other examples you have come across where a company's core values incorporate global working and drive ethical practices in a similar way to the J&J example. Discuss these in small groups.

3 Objectivity: using neuro-linguistic programming techniques
Consider an ethical decision that you have been involved in making that involved others and in which you tried to apply fairness. Now work through the 'different perspectives' technique used in NLP. Would your decision have changed?

4 Leadership and trust: rethink trust as a cultural value

In small groups, consider your organization and its stakeholders (suppliers, customers, employees, shareholders, *et al.*), and the internal and external challenges it faces. Try addressing the following questions:

- How do leaders embark on such a mission of rethinking trust as a cultural value?
- What are the pitfalls along the way?
- How do the leaders in an organization overcome these?

Suggestions for further reading

Elkington, J. (1987) *The Green Capitalists, Industry's Search for Environmental Excellence*, London: Gollancz.
This is a very useful read for those learning and management development professionals who are involved in CSR projects or work for organizations who have build environmental initiatives into their overall business strategies.

Strong, K. *NLP in Business*, www.whitedovebooks.com

Whates, P. (2006) *Business Ethics and the 21st Century Organization*, London: BSI.
NLP provides a very useful set of tools for use by learning and management development professionals, who in turn can introduce these into leadership and management development programmes. This book provides practical examples which may be useful in this respect.

CHAPTER

13

Developing leaders and managers with a global competence

The aims of this chapter are to:

- provide an understanding and appreciation of the context for international management development.

- focus on the context within a framework of international economics, structures of markets and supply chains, governmental regulations, and cultural issues.

- define global leadership and the need to develop leaders who can manage the increasing complexity of running global organizations.

- consider the creation of a set of international leader competencies that define the key behaviours required to provide effective leadership of global organizations.

- review the future of international management development.

Introduction

The global economic crisis has created new challenges for management development and leadership as well as highlighting the need for a deeper understanding of international economics, structures of markets and supply chains, governmental regulations, and culture issues. In this chapter international management is explored considering both the present and emergent trends.

Mini case study 13.1: The growth of China as an economic power

China is one of the fastest growing economies in the world. The National Bureau of Statistics of China (2009) indicates that there are over 3.25 million Chinese corporations employing 774.8 million people. In the context of the rapidly expanding business economy in China, there have been many changes in its business environment.

Wilson (2008) cites consultants McKinsey and Company: 'given the global aspirations of many Chinese companies, over the next 10–15 years they will need 75,000 leaders who can work effectively in global environments; today they have only 3,000–5,000'. Indeed, neither the multinationals nor local Chinese companies have progressed much in this area. The need is for leaders who can be successful in complex, matrixed organizations where English is the lingua franca.

The current Chinese leaders were mostly born in the 1950s and 1960s and experienced the Cultural Revolution. At that time education was sporadic and centralized planning was the norm. Today's leaders achieved their positions through hard work, tenacity, and perseverance, and experienced significant adversity.

Not all of these leaders are strong strategists, innovators, or problem solvers, and are comfortable with an authoritarian management style. Their strengths lie in building relationships and big-picture thinking rather than details and execution.

Commitment and loyalty are developed from those who work with these leaders. They are fairly stable and with a low turnover but there is a distinct shortage of management talent suited to entrepreneurial enterprise in this generation.

The future leaders, born in the 1970s, experienced uninterrupted economic growth and prosperity and so like the generation before them lack business acumen, entrepreneurship, creativity, and the capacity for execution as well as people management skills.

This then gives a cause for concern amongst the multinationals given their need for staff development and engagement.

The current Chinese middle managers have core strengths in team leadership, teamwork, organization agility, and relationship management.

They are a well-educated group which has received little formal management training but are keen to succeed.

Promoting them before they are ready or losing them to a competitor is a risk such that the members of this group aged 30–34 years have a high turnover rate at 25 per cent of the workforce in a given year. This contributes to a lack of stability in the leadership pipeline.

Many economists see China as central to the emergence from the global recession with their heightened purchasing power and opening marketplace.

With so much dependent on China delivering results, many organizations struggle with the question of whether to use expatriates for key leadership positions or to develop leaders from within, which can take significant time and money.

Managers from Hong Kong, Taiwan, Singapore, and Malaysia are often transferred or poached to fill key posts in China. Foreign-born Chinese people are a further possible solution to the problem given their education, Western business style and language capability.

However, this strategy, whilst solving a short-term problem by filling the talent gap, creates issues through a lack of localization, the process of transitioning a position from expatriate to local status. A further problem is the perceived glass ceiling for locally born Chinese.

Expensive expatriate packages to attract talent from outside the country has resulted in significant internal inequity.

Wilson (2008) indicates that the median cost for these packages can soar to over 200 per cent more than for a locally hired Chinese person in the same position at executive or function-head level.

A further complexity is introduced when considering the challenges associated with attracting, motivating, and retaining employees, specifically including managers.

An appreciation is then needed of the factors that influence employee behaviour in China. Much of the existing research in this area has been based on Western theoretical models that do not always consider differences in culture and values (Triandis, Dunnette, and Hough, 1994). As a result, some of the existing research may not be relevant for understanding employee behaviour in Chinese organizations because individuals in the Chinese culture may endorse a very different set of cultural values than their counterparts in Western cultures. This is exemplified by Hofstede (2003; 2005), who showed that those in the Chinese culture are more likely to value collectivism, high power distance, and a long-term time orientation than those in the West.

Additional understanding would seem to be required of the theoretical development and research on employee behaviour in China. A special issue of the *Journal of Managerial Psychology* is anticipated in 2010, focused on employee behaviour in China.

Questions

1 In small groups consider the complex issues raised above. In reality the use of expatriates and a development programme for leaders and managers may be a winning combination.

2 Which development interventions do you consider work best? Your choice may include some of the following:

- defined career paths for grooming leaders

- mentoring

- individualized development plans
- leadership coaching delivered by internal coaches
- overseas assignments
- challenging development opportunities
- rational experiences
- classroom training.

Provide a rationale for your responses.

Reflection point 13.1: Fundamentals in building a leadership programme

- Using your own organization or one of your choice as the basis of this exercise, in small groups consider the following:
  - Define your leadership strategy and alignment with the business requirements. Now identify and build your agreed definition of leadership requirements.
  - Define your unique leadership success profile. What would be your agreed definition of leadership requirements?
  - Assess the current and future pipeline of leadership talent. How would you conduct a leadership assessment exercise to determine the strengths and gaps of current and future leaders?
  - Build and implement a systematic development process. What key interventions should be included?
  - Measure progress towards achievement of the programme. What key metrics would you consider?

Contextualization of the tasks

The perception of China as operating an authoritarian, sweatshop economy with little regard to the environment or concepts such as corporate social responsibility has changed.

In reality a more sophisticated picture of Chinese managers emerges. There is high regard for rules, customer focus, and impact on the environment. Learning and development are valued and there is a willingness to learn from mistakes (www.i-l-m.com/research-and-comment/2515.aspx).

In the same way as the UK has a growing statute book of employment laws, Chinese growth is rapid, although enforcement might still remain patchy. Employees work a maximum of 40 hours a week, eight hours a day, with two rest days a week. However, in practice employees often put in a 12-hour day and can be required to do unpaid overtime and in busy periods work seven days a week.

All trade unions belong to the All-China Federation of Trade Unions (ACFTU), which has a statutory duty to protect employees' rights and supervise employer compliance with labour contracts. The ACFTU website describes the organization as 'the voluntary choice of hundreds of millions of workers', and is the only workers' federation allowed to operate in China, representing 135 million workers in 31 provincial autonomous regional and municipal federations and ten national individual trade unions. Any union established must be registered with the ACFTU. The ACFTU is a quasi-governmental body and is designed to support and facilitate governmental policies with entrepreneurs and to ensure the continued control of the working population.

In January 2008 the People's Republic of China Labour Contract Law 2007 came into force. All workers are now required to have written contracts, giving unions new power to negotiate at industry level and introduce new rules on fixed-term contracts. This is a move to force employees into more long-term arrangements. Probationary periods are reduced and the period before which an employee can work for a competitor is now reduced from three to two years.

The above points highlight the need for careful human resource planning in the new environment that is China.

Trends and challenges of corporate learning programmes

The economic crisis combined with the increase in the number of corporate procurement and supply chain universities and the perceived lack of in-house programmes that cover operational responsibilities such as conducting negotiations and process management as well as strategic management tasks such as supply chain risk management had revealed a competitive gap.

Nestlé, Swisscom, and Airbus have all established corporate procurement or supply chain management universities.

Distance learning has replaced e-learning in popularity and is building on familiar internet tools that are now being used effectively in corporate education, such as podcasts, webcasts, forums, and chat rooms.

Numerous human resource managers have identified self-coaching as a future skill and have incorporated it into their curricula. Managers experiencing growing pressures welcome a coach on the sidelines.

Many participants of MBA programmes have used the economic downturn to sharpen their professional profile. This has been particularly the case in America.

Distance learning can reinforce and maintain the learning process and offer the opportunity for flexibility. Networking and interaction between fellow students and teachers alike can be maximized by this approach.

The media have often stated in headlines that MBA programme graduates caused the economic crisis. It is to be remembered that the quality of MBA programmes had often been called into question previously. It may be that business schools need to consider whether their programmes sufficiently address the ethical dimension.

Business schools will need to address the lessening dominance of America in the world markets and the rise of China and India as new global hubs for economic development and networks.

Personal communication, personal development, and people skills are now seen as vital to prepare students for leadership and management, to ensure that they have the necessary intercultural competencies and communication skills.

Educational programmes aimed at professionals have to undergo permanent adaptation to maintain credibility in meeting current requirements. Financial economics programmes must be different from those courses offered 12 months ago.

There is a growing trend towards shorter programmes and this is possible due to the modular structure of many programmes which are spread over several years.

Programmes will need to take specific client and target group requirements into consideration whilst maintaining quality standards.

Supply that meets demand will define success.

Identifying and developing leaders for a global context

The globalization of human resource management and its impact on leadership identification and development in response to corporate globalization have been reinforced by the economic crisis which has clearly shown the connected and interdependent nature of our world.

Globalization ranges from moving more aggressively into emerging markets, especially the BRICs. This term was first used by US investment bank Goldman Sachs to refer to Brazil, Russia, India, and China as a bloc, highlighting the emergence of these continent-sized countries. These markets are integrating international acquisitions, moving from a regionalized organization to one globally aligned along core business processes, and evolving from a headquarters-centric to a globally integrated organization.

Although the industrialized countries continue to dominate world trade and investment, there has been a rise in the proportion of international business conducted by the developing world and specifically the BRICs.

These four countries are not a single unit and they have considerable differences. Russia and Brazil have large amounts of natural resources, Russia as an ex-communist

European country has a different cultural heritage from Brazil's, a former Portuguese colony. China and India lack many natural resources but both have a population of more than one billion citizens, whereas Brazil and Russia have 185 million and 143 million respectively.

China and India are currently both low-wage economies. They manage this in different ways, China using its labour-cost advantage to gain competitive advantage as a global manufacturing centre, whilst India focuses on services.

Multinational enterprises need to take a different view of each of the BRICs in their business conditions, production locations, target markets, and as players on the world stage.

Economic emergence and political recognition will combine with a strengthening of their currencies and responsibility for a larger proportion of the world's total stock market capitalization to ensure a growing global importance.

The political philosophies of these countries mean that political elites have to be considered as much as business leaders.

International managers will need to learn how to build non-market-related considerations into their relationships with these countries as the geographic centre of international business shifts; Sitkin and Bowen (2010) provide further elaboration and case studies in relation to the BRICs.

Sparrow, Brewster, and Harris (2004) have identified six key success factors to meet the globalization challenge:

- *Strategic alignment.* Alignment with corporate strategy and local business strategies furthers leadership behaviour in the interest of the overall organization. A targeted balance can be achieved through a governance framework that directs strategic decision making and control.

- *Executive engagement.* Engaging senior and top executives in leadership identification and development along the whole value chain to build buy-in and strategic alignment is a further key success factor. Companies are increasingly engaging management in leadership development and argue that many CEOs at leading companies such as GE, 3M, and Nokia have adopted the executive-led model of developing leaders.

- *Integrated talent management.* Identification and development of global leaders and their successors require an integrated framework ensuring that this population

Reflection point 13.2

- What are the implications of the BRICs' rise in importance in world trade for international leadership and management?

is comprehensively managed. Human Resources is key to the alignment of corporate learning and development with local learning and development.

■ *Standardization versus centralization.* Global guidelines and standards supported through an integrated human resource IT system ensure that focus and resources are allocated to the right activities and that global consistency and the required quality are attained.

■ *Business partnering.* Business partnering and planning support sustainable implementation of global leader identification and development. This incorporates strategic human resource and learning and development objectives, measures, and resources as well as evaluation through performance indicators validated by top management.

■ *Global competency development.* Development of global leadership competencies that apply across a company and are capable of dealing with diversity in its different forms is vital to the development of global leadership.

In contrast to the advantages of global consistency referred to above, organizations that are moving towards universal leadership competency models may fail to recognize that leadership requirements vary by level, culture, and situation.

This may be overcome by linking leadership competency requirements to a future-driven approach of the company's strategic and organizational capabilities.

The success factors might assist one company to rethink its current practices whilst confirming another company's journey.

Defining global leadership and global careers

Finding consensus on a definition of global leadership is not easy. Harris, Brewster, and Sparrow (2003) discuss this problem, reporting Bass (1985) and his findings across 3,500 studies of leadership in the USA. These included many classical theories in shaping managerial behaviour and development: trait theory, Theories X and Y, the Ohio State and University of Michigan behavioural theories, the Managerial Grid theory, situational, contingency, and path–goal theories.

Yuki (1994) found little empirical evidence supporting these theories in their country of origin and so bringing into question their applicability in other countries.

Cross-cultural studies indicate strong connection between culture and leadership styles.

Cross-cultural frameworks like Hofstede's (1980), Trompenaars's (1993), and Laurent's (1986) suggest significant differences in managerial values across nations.

The Global Leadership and Organization Behaviour Effectiveness (GLOBE) Project (House *et al.*, 2002) was a multi-phase, multi-method project with researchers across the world examining interrelationships between societal culture, organizational culture, and organizational leadership. The project involved 150 social scientists and management students from 61 cultures.

The GLOBE project findings on leadership reveal variations in scores around leadership dimensions. However, three styles were universally regarded as most effective:

- charismatic: visionary, inspirational, self-sacrificial, integrity, decisiveness, and performance-orientation attributes
- team-oriented: attributes interpreted differently by individualistic cultures as opposed to family or group cultures.

Overall, the GLOBE research findings support the view that leadership is culturally contingent, although the key dimensions of effective leadership are consistent across societal clusters.

The importance of developing leaders who can manage the complexity of effectively running global organizations remains a top HR priority as well as that of CEOs and organizational leaders.

Nestlé, voted Best International Company for Leadership Development by *Chief Executive Magazine*, said the continuing success of the company rested on the talent the company nurtures. They want to make sure that employees at regional companies maintain their original cultures but follow the same Nestlé principles.

In order for a global organization to effectively develop its senior managers it has to align its career development systems to the needs of key individuals.

However, individuals increasingly focus on developing their individual career capital as they no longer believe in a job for life or have the same loyalty to their organizations.

Organizations wish to retain their high-potential employees through human capital development.

It is changes to the psychological contract and the lack of job security that have led individuals to focus on self-development to increase their chances of success in internal and external job markets.

Traditionally in multinational organizations, international assignments were seen as part of individual career development as well as the development of the organization's human capital.

There is an increasing reluctance to have high-potential employees take up such assignments due to dual-career and family issues as well as evidence that during the assignment or on their return many move to other organizations (Suutari and Brewster, 2003).

This component of international management development needs review by organizations.

Creating an international management development strategy

International management development (IMD) and the responsibility for it will depend on:

- the involvement of the CEO and the senior team
- the global strategy
- human resource and line capabilities
- senior management involvement.

There has been renewed interest in nurturing internal talent within organizations after it became appreciated that understanding an organization does not come quickly.

Developing the next generation of global leaders and the development of an IMD strategy are key tasks for the senior management team given its critical nature to ensure success.

Alignment with global strategy

A number of global strategic orientations can influence the structure of IMD. These include:

- *Headquarters oriented.* This is appropriate for organizations with a strong control system from head office. Such organizations have a centralized business strategy.
- *Separate operating units worldwide.* In these organizations IMD is rarely practised; rather they manage potential within individual country operations.
- *Regionally oriented.* In such organizations the senior regional managers will liaise with the country-level management teams to identify high-potential employees who will then be moved around regions and promoted.
- *Globally oriented.* In an integrated global organization the responsibility for identifying and nurturing high potentials is usually a joint task for senior managers from all parts of the organization's global operations, who will then oversee succession for the next tiers of global management.

HR and line capabilities

HR capability is required to take the lead on the design and development of leadership competencies, IMD learning interventions, mentoring and coaching schemes, and the management of mobility in the development of assignments.

There would be close involvement of line managers to ensure a successful partnership approach.

Summary of section

This section has explored the notion of global leadership and the difficulties of having consensus on a definition of this concept both nationally and internationally. The interrelationship between societal and organizational culture is considered through the GLOBE project. The image of variations of leadership dimensions is created amidst the increasing complexity of running global organizations.

Managing the IMD process

Following the establishment of an overall strategy within the organization, a set of international leader competencies can be formulated which define the key behaviours that are required to be effective at the most senior levels in the organization. These competencies will aid the selection of external candidates as well as assessing potential and development needs within the organization.

Competencies can be viewed as a signal from the organization to the individual of the expected areas and levels of performance.

Competencies provide a map or indication of the behaviours that will be valued, recognized, and perhaps rewarded by the organization.

Competencies can be understood to represent the language of performance in an organization, articulating both the expected outcomes of an individual's efforts and the manner in which these activities are carried out.

In order to ensure both diversity and credibility, it is key that the global leader competency frameworks established are representative. Country and regional views need building into the framework.

The framework must also include detached guidelines on how the framework will be embedded in the core HR activities of the global organization. These include:

- recruitment and selection.
- performance management.
- development.

Auditing for diversity in the high-potential pool for organizations to ensure they will have both gender and geographical diversity on their senior management teams, close attention must be paid to the way diversity is built into all the organizational factors that influence the talent pipeline. Checking that the organization is meeting its diversity objectives, both present and future, is a priority for top managers.

The diversity audit includes:

- checking entry-level selection systems, promotion systems, international assignment selection techniques

- checking promotion rates, turnover, international experience by gender, ethnicity, and geographical representation

- interviews with a representative sample of employees from different cohorts of high-potential individuals to explore their perceptions of career enablers and blockers

- developing internal talent pools around the world.

It is important that there is a balance between home-grown and acquired talent in order to create a senior management team in international organizations.

The ratio between home-grown and acquired talent should allow organizations to maintain their corporate culture whilst gaining talent from other leading-edge organizations.

A wide variety of techniques might be used to identify talent within the organization to ensure that there is in place a rigorous process of leadership development.

Methods used might include:

- local general managers submitting names of high-potential individuals annually to the corporate centre

- the corporate centre monitoring performance review data

- 360° feedback

- use of assessment and development centres

- collating evaluations from leadership development courses.

Obstacles that will need to be overcome are the local operations that might be too small or cost conscious to want to spend time developing individuals who then might be moved elsewhere in the organization. Similarly, some managers in local or regional operations might be reluctant to let outstanding performers progress to roles outside their area.

Approaches to succession planning

International organizations used to plan careers for their high potentials and this would include a series of international assignments on the way to the most senior positions in the organization. The unpredictability of global business during the 1990s led many organizations to expect employees to self-develop and to find their own development opportunities and assignments with little intervention from the corporate centre.

Whilst today the uncertainties surrounding the retention of high-potential employees is greater than previously, most global organizations consider IMD as being valuable in ensuring a succession for top jobs as well as enabling them to be perceived as an attractive employer in a competitive global market. The planning perspective has moved from one of position planning to that of people planning.

This approach might include:

- management development review boards which regularly consider development decisions for people in key positions and those who might occupy those positions in the future; a corporate management development function coordinating these activities

- competency frameworks used to identify performance and potential ratings; this then feeding into systematic review procedures whereby people and position dimensions are integrated; those employees who rate high on both may then be given an assignment that stretches, rotated to another function, country, or work on cross-border projects

- annual management development discussions forming part of a corporate review which would include finance and strategy

- use of assessment centres based on organizational international leader competency frameworks to identify development needs and so entry to executive-level openings.

Management development and succession planning often have to acknowledge potential issues. The key issues include:

- the exploitation of existing skills versus development of new skills
- job-based logic replacing people-based logic
- a focus on high potentials rather than a wider focus on all talent
- the organization's priorities, which may conflict with those of the individual employee.

Designing IMD programmes

Traditionally, high potentials were sent to prestigious teaching institutions with little planning of application or transferability of the learning experience.

The current IMD programmes take an integrated approach. The focus is on performance, innovation, and change, and is less dependent on a culture of rules, hierarchy, and tradition.

Live business issues or projects are used to develop high potentials, such as:

- the future of advisory services
- making 6 Sigma global

- offshoring options for key services
- new industry model
- advisory quality framework.

PricewaterhouseCoopers use such methods, noting an increase in participants' intercultural sensitivity, self-confidence, and gender respect for more junior people.

The level of developmental investment on such programmes is substantial.

Evaluation of IMD programmes

HR professionals and line managers face the challenge of evaluating the effectiveness of IMD programmes (CIPD, 2005).

The IMD programme's aim is to increase the potential of international managers. By focusing on changes in the following areas, evaluation can occur:

- increase in intercultural skills
- greater flexibility and adaptability
- broader understanding of global business
- expanding social networks.

There should also be clear indications of improvements at the organizational levels specifically:

- strategic and operational outcomes from projects
- higher retention rates of high potentials
- developing strong global networks to foster organizational learning and capability.

The effectiveness can be measured by a variety of measures including:

- self-reports
- post-course feedback
- 360° evaluation before and after programmes
- strategic and operational results
- cohort analyses of promotion and retention rates.

International mobility

The traditional pattern of IMD was a two- or three-year assignment to an overseas operation. Currently rotational assignments tend to be shorter and involve working in more than one country. Living and working in a different culture, with an immersion experience, remains the key factor.

Expatriate postings still remain the form of mobility most often used (Organization Resources Counsellors, 2004).

Organizations will consider a number of factors when making decisions as to whether someone should be sent on an international assignment. These factors will include:

- the cost of the package
- the acceptability by local operation and government
- dual-career and family constraints
- the individual's level of readiness
- measuring the effectiveness of the development experience using the experience for future career progression within the organization.

Organizations need to take a strategic approach to the filling of international vacancies and whether or not this will support their global strategy.

Mini case study 13.2: International Bank Corporation's resourcing philosophy

International Bank Corporation (IBC) recognizes the centrality of international assignments for developing a diverse global management team. Both permanently international managers and international assignees are used. IBC relies predominantly on international assignees and its approach is outlined in its international resourcing philosophy. This can be summarized as follows:

- The bank is committed to developing its talent and strengthening the diversity of its people in senior management.
- International experience is seen as necessary for talent development in the group.
- Selected local talent should be encouraged to work abroad and across businesses/functions as part of their development.
- Group businesses have a collective responsibility to provide opportunities in developing the group's talent.

Questions

1 Why are people so important to organizations?

2 How far are the terms 'human' and 'resource' incompatible in the context of managing people effectively and efficiently?

3 Identify the internal resourcing philosophy of other organizations. In what ways are they similar/different?

Expatriate pre-departure

Organizations will make decisions as to whether or not an international assignment is desirable for management development purposes after considering:

- the cost of the package
- dual-career and family issues
- the level of preparedness of the individual
- effectiveness of the development experience
- the acceptability of the assignment by the local operation and government
- potential use of the experience for future career progression within the organization.

Organizations will take a strategic approach to consider how the filling of international vacancies can support their global strategy. HSBC distinguishes between local/global short-term business needs and the long-term development of its future leaders.

Your responses to Reflection point 13.3 might have included technical and managerial ability, stress tolerance and resilience to manage cultural adaptation and individual anxieties, emotional ability, communication skills for both social and business relations, cultural empathy with the local culture.

Training and support for an expatriate assignment significantly increases the chances of success of the assignment. Mead (2005) reports that for Americans failures of international assignments are within the 15–40 per cent range.

Failures incur heavy costs to the organization as well as intangible losses such as goodwill from those involved at a local level with the assignment and loss of self-esteem, loss of career, and domestic disruption experienced by the expatriate.

Following a training needs analysis, training and support may be identified in the areas of technical training, management training, cross-cultural training, and language training.

The extent to which the manager's partner and other dependants adjust to living in the new culture is also a major influence on the success or failure of the assignment. Many organizations accordingly extend training and support to partners and dependants.

Reflection point 13.3

- What are the key factors that would influence you when identifying selection criteria for managers to work internationally?

Reflection point 13.4

- Your company has asked you to design a training package for a manager and his wife who will shortly be posted abroad. Outline the content of the training intervention, specifying and justifying the reasons for your choice of approach and the methods you will adopt.

Pre-departure preparation may include training and briefings as well as visits and shadowing.

A home business sponsor can offer a further level of support to the expatriate, thus ensuring that they are a member of the talent pool and are valued by the business and are suitable for the investment of an international secondment, as well as ensuring a suitable role utilizing the newly acquired international skills when the expatriate returns to the home country.

Mini case study 13.3: The Thai secretary

This mini case study asks how cross-cultural training can be made more appropriate.

A few years ago, Bill represented his American multinational as regional manager in Asia. He made regular visits to his firm's subsidiary in Bangkok. The local manager, Charnvit, came from an old-established Thai family.

Bill enjoyed the visits but had never grown used to the behaviour of Charnvit's secretary, Malinee. When she asked if he would like coffee and then served it, she approached on her knees. Charnvit explained that in traditional culture, this was the style by which a subordinate showed respect for a superior. But Bill mocked him as an 'oriental potentate', and Charnvit was growing tired of his good-natured chaffing. When a franchised self-assertiveness course was advertised, he arranged that Malinee should enrol.

On his next visit, Bill was astonished at the change when Malinee appeared round the door and asked casually, 'Coffee, Bill?' He was congratulating Charnvit on his decision to provide Malinee with the sort of training that better equipped her for the modern business world, when she returned to serve the coffee—on her knees!

Questions

1 What had Malinee learned? What had she not learned?

2 What implications does this have for cross-cultural training?

3 Could either Bill or Charnvit have also benefited from cross-cultural training? Why?

Performance management

Performance in expatriate assignments can be measured by different criteria. Common benchmarks identified by Mead (2005) include:

■ Success is measured relative to the expatriate's performance back home. The expatriate is performing at least as successfully and possibly more so.

■ Success is measured relative to the job description. The expatriate is at least fulfilling the specifications of the post, and possibly exceeding them.

■ Success is measured relative to the circumstances. In very difficult circumstances the expatriate is performing better than could be expected.

Repatriation

A survey of 100 multinational companies (Cendont International Assignment Services, 1999) indicated that nearly 70 per cent of organizations had a formal repatriation policy; more than half did not measure or track what happened to repatriates on their return home.

Further figures from other surveys (GMAC Global Relocation Services/Windham International, 2000) show that over 25 per cent of repatriates leave their organizations within two years of an international posting.

The effective management of all stages of an international assignment—pre-departure; whilst overseas; pre-repatriation; post-repatriation—are key to ensuring the success of the assignment and full development and retention of the manager sent on the assignment.

Long-term assignments remain the most common form of IMD. However, increasing issues with dual-career couples and increased costs of an expatriate package have raised the profile of alternative forms of international working. These mainly include short-term assignments of less than one year and international commuting, where an employee travels from the home country to work in the host country on a weekly or

Reflection point 13.5

● How would you as a home business sponsor (HR manager) within the expatriate's organization conduct pre-return planning six months before the expected return?

● Your responses could include obtaining copies of performance appraisals together with an updated assessment of current capabilities, agreeing preferred roles and in what business areas, manage expectations regarding promotion, find out about any mobility issues, obtain an updated curriculum vitae.

bi-weekly basis. Frequent flying, where frequent international business trips are made without relocation, is a further method. These methods are more difficult to manage, as are the setting and evaluation of IMD objectives.

The advantages of international assignments are linked to the goals of international work and key links are identified by CIPD (2005b):

- cost and risk management
- business development
- knowledge and skills transfer
- filling skills gaps
- developing future leaders
- diversity goals
- control
- coordination.

Many different people have interests in the expatriate's performance and these could include:

- managers to whom the individual reports at headquarters
- managers to whom the individual reports in a joint venture or subsidiary
- colleagues
- subordinates
- the expatriate themselves.

They may all make evaluations which could be formal or informal and apply different criteria.

Summary of section

This section has focused on international management development initiatives and the need for them to form part of an integrated talent management strategy. Global employer branding for recruitment and selection and reward packages as well as the IMD process are seen as being important to success in managing organizations internationally.

International leader competencies

The competencies model

The traditional psychometric approach argues that there is an identifiable set of competencies that is linked with success and failure of the international manager. There is often a tension between what skills and competencies organizations think they should be looking at when they recruit and the skills that are actually needed to make a success of working overseas.

Openness to experience, tolerance of ambiguity, introversion, the ability to generate and inspire trust in others, and proactive information seeking are often neglected when recruiting managers in the home market but need actively seeking when internalizing the organization.

The second approach, a clinical risk assessment approach, is preferred by those HR professionals who consider that there are limits to the use of personal competencies as a selection criterion for international employees. The reasons for the failure of an international manager often go beyond issues of the manager's cultural adaptability; maturity, stability, and adaptability of the partner, dual-career difficulties, national attitudes to mobility, and pay arrangements also play a role in the success of the assignment. The supporting structures around the assignment with regard to localization policies, management structures, reporting relationships, accountabilities, and responsibilities as well as technical difficulties also play a part (Brewster, Sparrow, and Vernon, 2007).

Cost control over international managers and the growth of international joint ventures often mean that there is a limited pool of willing and mobile candidates.

In the early 1990s the expansion of the European common market led to debate of what makes an effective Euro manager. The language used came from the management competencies approaches and models set out by Argyle (1967) and Boyatzis (1982).

American Express set the following competencies for their international managers:

- leadership skills: an ability to create vision, direction, and values which motivate others

- the intellect, flexibility, courage, and imagination to recognize and respond to the rapid pace of change

- the cultivation of a broad knowledge of the history, culture, law, and languages of Europe, and the ability to set aside nationalism and its prejudices and stereotypes

- willingness to be a team member who can work in multinational project groups and be prepared to move to different countries and cultures.

Ford (Jackson, 2004) characterized their international managers by:

- accelerating change

- increasing technical complexity of decision making

- a need to exert influence and leadership in a participative manner rather than through the traditional command structure

- learning from experience, implementing continuous improvement, and the need to take a systems view of the business rather than a narrow specialist or functional view.

The Ashridge Management College surveyed 50 American, British, and Japanese international companies to ascertain which characteristics of international management they most valued (Barnham and Oates, 1991). In order of perceived importance the broad competencies covered:

- strategic awareness
- adaptability in new situations
- sensitivity to different cultures
- ability to work in international teams
- language skills
- understanding international marketing
- relationship skills
- international negotiating skills
- self-reliance
- high task orientation
- open, non-judgemental personality
- understanding of international finance
- awareness of own culture.

The issues in accepting the above as relevant international competencies when selecting, rewarding, and developing key international managers are the differences in the ways managers are perceived in different countries, the different degrees of internationalization of countries, and the problems inherent within the competencies model itself, both methodological and cultural.

The idea of competencies of international managers may not be sufficient to gain an understanding of the requirements for managing across cultures. An ability to cope with frustrations, isolation, failure, to network successfully, gain support, and anticipate differences is also needed, Shell's famous 'helicopter view' competence may be difficult to teach and acquire.

It could be argued that the qualities needed of international managers are untrainable traits.

Interpersonal skills can, however, be learned and an understanding of oneself and the other person's culture can be developed.

The competencies approach is focused on the construction of typologies from empirical work. The Management Charter Initiative in the UK and American Association Competences Model as well as the competencies approach for assessment centres and training further reinforce the practical, pragmatic, and empirical orientation.

Reflection point 13.6

- What is the relationship between national culture and the use of the competencies approach?
- How do management competencies required for managers by companies vary across different countries?

The concept of competencies can be argued to be based on analysing complex human action by taking it apart. This then ignores the holistic whole in favour of the parts.

There are issues with the cross-cultural transfer of the competence approach itself. For example, American management theory is built on the basis of scientific management, Japanese management emphasizes equality as the basis for competition and cooperation, basing its practice on collective responsibility. All members feel responsible for the organization.

These contextual differences have implications for management behaviour and so it is difficult to speak of individual management competences in the Japanese collectivist context.

The use of competencies in management selection and learning and development should not be rejected outright. There are practical uses in conceptualizing aspects of management that can be selected and developed.

Summary of section

Creating a set of international leader competencies that define the key behaviours required in order to be effective at senior management levels in the global organization is a key first step in developing leaders.

The competency framework must then be integrated into recruitment and selection, reward, and learning and development processes through a culturally sensitive process.

The future of international management development

The traditional approaches to international management development have become less effective for organizations. The changing nature of the psychological contract has led to individuals focusing on developing their own career capital and so becoming more marketable to ensure security as the job for life has disappeared.

unpredictable global economic and political context has made succession ng difficult for organizations.

se two trends have affected the nature of international management development from the organizational and individual perspective.

Box 13.1 Psychological contract

Argyris (1960) first applied the psychological contract to the workplace. This reflected the belief that employees and employers created psychological contracts that allowed the expression and gratification of each other's needs. If management respects employees' rights to develop and grow and use their own initiative, then employees will in return respect the right of the organization to evolve.

Levinson *et al.* (1962) and Schein (1965) furthered work on the psychological contract but it was not until Rousseau (1989) that growing interest in the concept was supported by the interception of the psychological contract as consisting of implicit and explicit promises. This has led to contemporary research in this area being concerned with the contents of psychological contracts and their structure, and the effects of violations on employee attitudes and behaviour.

Quoted from Conway, N. and Briner, R.B. (2005) *Psychological Contracts at Work: A Critical Evaluation of Theory and Research*, Oxford

Evidence of a large proportion of managers leaving their employers after returning from an international assignment highlights the issue of retaining the human capital they are seeking to develop.

A further problem is the difficulties experienced by organizations looking ahead to identify the competencies needed from leaders in the future.

Evans *et al.* (2002) identified dualities or tensions between the opposite poles involved in global leadership in the 21st century. These included global–local, change–continuity and accountability–teamwork. The argument that Evans *et al.* present is that there are deeper challenges to the current ways of thinking. There are no solutions to the tensions, so for managers trained to think in terms of solutions this is difficult. Evans *et al.* see managers as having one foot on either side of the fulcrum of a see-saw which is in constant motion. Good leadership can then be a fluid movement or a bitter struggle. This global mindset is one of the critical roles of HR management.

Increasingly international management development will be driven by a balance between high-performing and motivated individuals and their employers to agree ways that both sides of the psychological contract can be met.

It will be increasingly important to understand and take account of people's busy lives and build in time for family and leisure. This will need to be seen in the context

Reflection point 13.7

* Consider a situation when you joined an organization, college or any other organized group. Were you aware of both the written and the unwritten contract that was at the centre of the relationship? Were they the same or what were the differences?

of how different cultures view career development and family obligations to ensure that the best global talent becomes part of the succession planning process.

Summary of section

The challenges facing organizations in developing their future leaders have been considered. The focus has been on nurturing key talent across the world, embracing diversity, and using learning and development creatively in the management process.

Chapter summary

This chapter has considered the current and emergent trends within international management development.

An understanding and appreciation of the context of IMD have been provided, considering the structures of the markets and the BRICs.

A definition of global leadership has been identified to draw a picture of the leaders required to operate efficiently and effectively in increasingly complex global organizations.

The creation of a set of international leader competencies has been considered which would enable behaviours of effective leadership of global organizations to be identified and developed.

The future of international management development has been considered.

Questions

1 How would you prepare an expatriate going on a long-term international assignment to (a) work in the local culture and (b) live in the local culture?

2 Evaluate the training and support provided by your organization to the following groups when they are expatriated:
  - the chief executive officer
  - staff on long-term assignments
  - staff on short-term assignments
  - dependants of the above.

3 How is each group supported before, during and after expatriation?

4 How is each group debriefed after expatriation?

5 How might support for each group be improved?

6 Identify which BRICs companies are likely to become global leaders and household names by the mid 2010s. Consider the primary (energy, mining, agriculture), secondary (industrial, manufacturing), tertiary (hi-tech manufacturing), and tertiary (banks) sectors.

7 What are the advantages and disadvantages of expatriate staffing?

8 What are the advantages and disadvantages of local staffing?

Discussion questions

1 Executives of international companies need to be able to adapt to the corporate and national cultures in which they work, without losing sight of their individualism. Discuss Maitland's (2006) comment:

The danger for any leader is only being able to operate within one of these styles. If you take an autocratic style into a culture that expects more democratic or meritocratic style, the chances are that you will trip up.

2 What do you consider to be the key challenges facing organizations in developing their future leaders? Discuss.

3 How would you integrate an international leader competency framework into recruitment and selection, reward, and development processes across all global business units through a culturally sensitive process?

4 Review the arguments for adopting a formalized development planning system for international managers utilizing a people as opposed to a position planning perspective.

Reflection point 13.8

- Using your multinational company or one with which you are familiar, compare the type and extent of corporate leadership exercised across the international subsidiary network.

- Think of four subsidiary organizations and rank them in terms of cultural distance (Hofstede). Using your four examples, consider the following:

  - How is each type of subsidiary managed differently in terms of staffing (i.e. expatriates versus local managers)?

  - How have the preferred methods and extent of control changed during the life of the subsidiary operation?

- The multinational you have selected decides to post one of its staff to manage your subsidiary for a two-year assignment. Assume that the manager is 35 years old and male and will be accompanied by his spouse and their daughter, aged 10, and their son aged 8. Do the following:

  - Decide on the country of headquarters. Choose from USA, China, Norway, New Zealand.

  - Decide the manager's rank and functional specialism.

  - Decide the relationship between headquarters and the subsidiary. (How far is the subsidiary empowered to design and implement its own strategy?)

  - Write the manager's job description, considering:

    - the need for management and technical expertise

    - headquarters' need to control the subsidiary.

Suggestions for further reading

Ambler, T. *et al.* (2009) *Doing Business in China*, 3rd edition, Abingdon: Routledge.
A case study approach combined with a theoretical framework for understanding Chinese business culture.

Schein, E.H. (2004) *Organizational Culture and Leadership*, 3rd edition, San Francisco: Jossey-Bass.
This text shows how to transform the abstract concept of culture into a practical tool that managers and students can use in organizations.

Liu, H. (2008) *Chinese Business Landscapes and Strategies*, Abingdon: Routledge.
This book provides fascinating insights into one of the fastest growing economies in the world, and one that will influence the global future. Theoretical, academic, and practical views relating to Chinese business and management are provided.

Luo, Y. (2007) *Global Dimensions of Corporate Governance*, Oxford: Blackwell Publishing.
This text provides insights into how multinational corporations should deal with global shareholders and other stakeholders.

CHAPTER 1

Summary and thoughts for the future

The aims of this chapter are to:

- summarize the key issues that have been identified as important in developing leaders and managers

- discuss how these might influence managers and leaders of the future

- endeavour to identify some upcoming themes that are likely to emerge, and to pose some ideas for topics for research in the area of leadership and management development

- identify how these current issues might continue to influence leadership and management development

- provide some thoughts about possible 'hot topics' in the areas of leadership and management development as potential areas for further research.

Introduction

This book has taken a critical view of the current state of leadership and management development; its links and integration with organization strategy; and the importance of different internal and external business contexts in understanding leadership and management, and how to develop them effectively.

We have outlined historical perspectives in defining leadership and management, and in identifying models and approaches to our understanding of the role and contribution of managers and leaders. They lead us to question some of the proposed differences between leadership and management and to identify the key role that both play in different organizations, depending on their current state of organizational development and environmental context.

We discussed at some length the importance of a reciprocal relationship between organizational strategy, organizational development, and the development of managers and leaders; and considered different processes and interventions used in developing leaders and managers. Finally we looked at a number of contemporary issues in developing leaders and managers.

The main section below will summarize the key findings from each chapter and attempt to identify current issues that will require further research and practical work as organizations continue to develop a wider range of leaders and managers, equipped to deal effectively with the future. We conclude with a final case that is linked to the book's related internet resources (for details see first chapter).

Key issues in chapters and looking forward

The first theme within the book reviewed the organizational and contextual issues to be addressed in leadership and management development and critiqued definitions of leadership and management, along with approaches to development.

The second chapter reviewed a range of different approaches to organization strategy, and tools and techniques to analyse it, but yet still identified many organizations in which understanding and integration of strategy with HR processes and development of leaders and managers are more rhetoric than reality as organizations maintain outdated views about what they need from managers and how to support the development of leaders and managers.

We explained the critical role of a leader in enabling the creation of strategy and the various levels of influence the leader can exert in terms of the power afforded to them by the stakeholders, core values, and structure of the organization. They play a key role in facilitating the delivery of the chosen strategy and releasing the potential of the workforce. From what has been learnt in the first few chapters it should now be becoming quite clear that creation or formulation of an organization's strategy depends foremost on the leaders who are involved simply but decidedly choosing what to do and how things are to be done.

We explored several models of leadership and one of the most important that has emerged and become popular in modern organizations is the transformational leadership paradigm of Bass (1990). A key concept of the transformational paradigm and other related behavioural models is that leadership capability can be learnt and applied. It is not something that people are born with or have developed in their young formative years of education. Along with action-centred leadership as prescribed by Adair (1973), they are commonly referred to as 'nurture' models, as opposed to the 'nature' models from the school of thought that believes leaders are born with the traits associated with leadership.

In essence the behavioural competence school of thought that broadly includes transformational leadership, action-centred leadership, and situational and contingency models confirms that it is highly feasible that people can be developed, new skills taught and learnt in an effort to create effective leaders. Examples of these are explained in Chapter 2 and it is a critically important point for all students of the subject and practitioners of leadership and management development to understand.

In support of this we have seen that the need for competent and committed people that are managed and led effectively comes high on the list of the critical success factors that contribute to success of an organization. This is borne out more recently by the human capital models of Pfeffer, Huselid, Guest, and others. All agree that people management practices and the way people are led and managed make a substantial contribution to organizational performance outputs. This is not to play other functions down at all; indeed, the IT, financial systems, and marketing functions play a key part in the make-up of a successful organization. Yet in simple terms, everything that an organization does, in the end, depends on its people and how they are managed and led.

In order to provide a balanced approach, in Chapter 2 we also looked at a fairly recent and contrarian perspective to the behavioural competency school of thought. That is the 'strengths-based approach' and the work done around the turn of the century by researchers and writers such as Marcus Buckingham and his former colleagues from the Gallup organization. They focus attention for organizational performance around the harnessing of 'talent' and 'strengths'. Moreover, they highlight the importance of the first-line manager in organizations. Managers play a significant role in creating an environment within which individuals can thrive, discover their talents, and use their best selves daily. In essence, great managers help people to identify and leverage their unique strengths. The manager thereby takes on a facilitative, enabling role that was not identified as significant in earlier schools of thought.

In conclusion of what was learnt in Chapter 2, it makes the point that the challenge for an organization is first to understand its own influences, culture, values, internal processes, strengths, and weaknesses through some of the concepts and approaches we have identified. Only when it has developed a competence in doing this will it be able to move to the point where an appropriate and value-adding human resource development strategy and courses of actions can be put in place that recruit, develop, retain, and motivate top-class leaders and managers.

The use of resource-based strategy is relatively new and requires a major change in the thinking of leaders to ensure competitive advantage and it has yet to have a noticeable impact on public sector and not-for-profit organizations, requiring further adaptation in its language and application.

Chapter 3 provided a brief overview of organizational context that has an impact on leadership and management development and then took a deeper view of international contexts, the influence of emerging economies, and impact on management development. The international dimension was continued in Chapter 13.

As these new economies continue to develop, the more traditional models of leadership and management development (often based in US and UK cultural assumptions) are increasingly being challenged. This is an inevitable outcome from the development of globalization and the differential growth patterns experienced by different nations and regions. Particular approaches will inevitably be more applicable and successful in one national context than others, in the same way that applies to different organizational settings. Successful international organizations will need to manage these issues sensitively, and academics and leadership and management development practitioners will need to examine emerging approaches to see what might usefully 'transplant' to other settings as well as being appropriate in its home context.

Chapters 4 and 5 reviewed approaches to management development, from a historical perspective and then moving forward to introduce models of management development in organizations today, into which particular processes and interventions may fit.

It is plain that there is a wide range of approaches to leadership and management development, which have grown from a developing understanding about what organizations need from managers and leaders—and also what motivates leaders and managers in organizational roles. Historical approaches were often for management development because leaders were often considered to be born rather than developed. A key tension that has emerged over time has been that between organizational and individual needs (Woodall and Winstanley, 1998) and the appreciation that different leaders and managers may require and respond to different means of learning.

Current ideas about integrating learning with work have grown from our needs to provide cost-effective means of developing managers, as well as from an increased appreciation of the effectiveness of such approaches. They therefore have both a practical and a theoretical backing.

In Chapter 5 we looked in some detail first at the definitions and the nature of work that is related to 'leadership' and 'management'. We found that whilst there are differences, there are also similarities that are difficult to separate out. The chapter concluded that it is accepted that the two nouns of 'leadership' and 'management' have come to be used synonymously with each other in the world of business and commerce, in all sectors—private, public, non-profit/voluntary, and in many respects also in a modern military setting.

We took the opportunity in this chapter to look at some major concepts and theories of leadership and management. There are multitudes of these in the academic domain but the ones used are those that the authors feel are appropriate for the reader to gain a firm understanding of the subject. The ones used are the early Taylorist viewpoint of management, trait theory, situational and contingency models, action-centred leadership, and transformational and transactional leadership models. This mixture of concepts, theories, and models hopefully provides a good basis for understanding and gives an insight into how the contributions of writers and researchers from the early 1900s to the present day have unfolded. It was identified that the study of leadership and management and the nature of work that managers do are an iterative paradigm that is complemented by further research and application. It is without doubt that in the future there will be new angles and perspectives that become popular. However, it must be remembered with a small dose of cynicism that fundamentally despite whatever angle or approach comes to the fore, what is being talked about is the psychology of human behaviour and the social interaction between people that is at the heart of the subject and has been since time began.

One observation the reader may have is that it is rare in any research into leadership and management to see contradiction in theories and concepts. Rather more that the major research builds and enhances our understanding or identifies different insights. All of which qualifies the fact that leadership and management are more an art form than an exact science; moreover, that we can learn a lot about the human psychology and social structures of the past and present that will serve organizations well in the future if adjusted to fit the challenges that the future will bring.

Chapter 5 provides an overview of how leadership and management are defined, the difference between the concepts and ways in which these are understood in different organization cultures. Definitions of leadership and management arose from ideas of those involved at the outset of industrialization when rigid organization structures limited leadership authority in the hands of owners and a few decision makers. However, with the advent of observational research into management in different organizations, ideas about managerial roles and responsibilities began to provide a different perspective, which has continued to develop as different models have been introduced to understand management and differentiate it from leadership. These models have included looking at skills of managers, roles, functions, and competencies of management, to name but a few. Whichever models are employed, they must be appropriate for each organization's structure and culture and are likely to change as the organization develops.

As the rate of change in organizations increases, so too does the need to evaluate the relevance of leadership and management models used and the ways of identifying, selecting, and developing managers. It seems from our research that the important factors for organizations is to have frameworks of management and models of leadership that 'fit' current contingent organizational needs and are capable of development themselves, rather than employing 'best practice' models that do not fit with organizational culture and values.

The next key theme in the book is that of understanding how managers and leaders learn, linking to theories about adult learning and workplace learning. The basic concepts covered are, of course, important to all people developers, though focused in this book on the realities of learning for leaders and managers and about topics that are so closely linked to an organization's development and survival, and influenced strongly by culture in organizations.

Increasingly leaders and managers are expected to share their knowledge and experience through coaching and mentoring, thus also supporting the development of others. Skills and knowledge associated with these activities have become an important part of the leader's own development, and this is likely to continue, especially given the wider context in which the focus of learning and development professionals is shifting from training inputs to the effective support of individual learning.

We identify and discuss a range of key factors that influence individuality in development because of its increasing importance to our understanding of how all development processes or interventions might impact on participants. It is important to understand how each individual learns effectively and what effect this learning may have in order to efficiently support individual managers and leaders.

As we learn more about mental processes, brain functioning, and individual difference, the work of developers, and of managers or leaders who develop others, can be made more effective. From the viewpoint of those responsible for development in organizations, we can recognize how to add value through personalized interventions rather than assume that all learners need to learn the same things in the same ways. This is already happening in many cases, but is likely to become more important in the future—impacting on learning processes, technologies, and interventions.

Based on the above section, the book's next theme evaluates a range of processes and interventions used in developing leaders and managers today. We include a number of approaches that can be integrated into work, using Mumford and Gold's (2004) model as Type 2 interventions, taking the best from both more planned and purposeful development, which is still seen by managers as relevant and adds value to their work.

We examined in Chapter 8 the range of labels attached by organizations to processes related to leadership and management development—talent management, career management, and succession management, for example. We outlined the contested nature of the definitions and also of the component parts applied in different settings—but there is undoubtedly some commonality in the processes used in support of leadership and management development, and an increased need to be seen to be 'adding value' through these processes. In the financial circumstances at the end of the 21st century's first decade, it seems unlikely that this focus will lessen!

The major changes in leadership and management development seem to have been a move away from focusing exclusively on formal education or major training initiatives for all managers, often run by management development practitioners in big organizations, to something more customized to individual needs and in 'good practice organizations' taking account of individuals' preferred learning, and utilizing opportunities that are provided through normal work practice.

There is a continuing tension, for some leaders and managers, between the needs of their organization and personal needs that individuals believe they have, and in some cases between organizational preferences for organizing development and individuals' preferred approaches to learning. There are also tensions between leaders' and managers' traditional preferences for 'action' and the undoubted benefits of reflective practices in questioning established ways of doing things.

Future developments in using groups of managers to self-facilitate learning which is relevant to their needs and in using techniques that focus on integrating work with learning may intensify the above-mentioned tensions or may in fact help to bring together organizational and individual needs by recognizing the importance of informal learning and workplace learning and their role in cementing organizational culture, values, and managerial behaviour.

Approaches such as action learning have come in and out of vogue over a number of years, and they undoubtedly have much to offer an organization that genuinely wishes to challenge accepted ways of doing things, that seeks to continuously transform itself in pursuit of competitive advantage. However, we must also recognize that many organizations are not like this—that they seek survival or modest growth rather than global advantage. Organizational cultures may well be resistant to action learning or similar approaches because they can pose a threat to established norms and to dominant managerial and leadership groups.

The key lesson from a consideration of both processes and specific interventions within leadership and management development is the need to avoid 'off-the-shelf' solutions and instead to create responses that are in tune with the organization's (and individual's as much as possible) aims, values, culture, and specific competitive setting. This holds true as much now as it ever did—and organizations are perhaps beginning to get it more than ever before. This trend also seems likely to continue, especially as such approaches are likely to be more cost effective in the long run.

Evaluation processes and techniques are critiqued within this theme—with the findings that there has been an increased focus on the value that any intervention or process adds, rather than the simple financial-cost model used in appraisal of other capital spending. It has also been recognized that few organizations evaluate at any level higher than two (learning) for any development activity, with most using only 'reactionnaire' sheets. Although the methodologies are available, it is usually found to be too difficult to gather sufficient good-quality data and adds substantially to the cost of development to gather necessary information. However, without such information it is impossible to demonstrate real added value for any development.

In the future, as organizations adopt development methods that fit within normal work activity and involve less formally recognized training or development, the current methods of measurement become less appropriate for evaluation—and newer ways of assessing development, focusing on individualized learning, are required. Perhaps more personalized assessment of worth of development will arise but until time and resource are put into evaluation there is little impetus or opportunity for such methods to be developed. Recent research by CIPD (2009) takes a holistic approach to evaluation and may help to stimulate research in this area.

The final theme in the book takes a look at some more contemporary issues in developing leaders and managers and one of the first of these was the issue of diversity. There are a number of ways in which diversity impacts on leadership and management development and within the chapter we evaluate two:

- With increasing workforce diversity, there is a more diverse group from which leaders and managers emerge. However, statistics show that in many organizations leaders and managers tend to come from the majority groups in organizations. Therefore we ask: 'How can we encourage and develop more individuals from minority groups into these important roles?'

- An additional issue of having a more diverse workforce is that development initiatives for managers and leaders should include knowledge and skills necessary to manage an increasingly diverse workforce and to recognize different needs of at least the main minority groups.

Many organizations are found to be quite conservative when selecting managers and leaders and often encourage assimilation of individuals into the predominant organizational culture, thereby perpetuating models of leadership and management that have been previously been successful.

However, in changing times where the workforce is different and has been found to have different expectations (Generation Y and on), it is important that organizational leaders and managers reflect such groups in society and enable organizations to adapt to future needs. It is, then, vital that diversity is nurtured in organizations and new ways are found to identify and encourage leaders and managers from across the whole spectrum of available human resources. Once effectively developed to enable movement into leadership and management positions, these individuals can then act as role models within organizations to enable them to most effectively use available resources and knowledge.

In Chapter 12 we saw how ethics have become a central issue in the way leaders and managers go about running organizations. Ethics are at the foundation of how they make decisions, conduct themselves with other stakeholders, contribute to business performance, and use their positional and personal power to influence other members of the organization. Organizational leaders also have a major responsibility in ensuring others take ethics seriously and adopt responsible values.

In order to gain a deeper understanding of ethics it was essential in Chapter 12 to go back in time and review some fundamental issues about the origins of ethics, what they are and how they manifest themselves in different international, cultural, and organizational settings.

It was pointed out how important the teaching of ethics within business schools has become, to the point where most courses in the prospectus have ethics and ethical management woven into the core subjects.

Corporate social responsibility (CSR) and the popularisation of the triple bottom line (TBL) concept of corporate accounting have become important subject areas for students to understand—both from a theoretical sense and also from a practical application point of view for when students eventually move into roles in private, public, and third sector organizations.

Building on the work of Whates (2006), it was prescribed that four elements are necessary to quantify an organization's ethics:

- written code of ethics and standards
- ethics training for executives, managers, and employees
- availability of advice on ethical situations (e.g. advice lines or intranets)
- systems for confidential reporting.

Good leaders who strive to create a better and more ethical organization could do worse than adopt this best practice as a way to restoring an ethical climate in organizations.

The global economic crisis of 2008 onwards has created new challenges for management development and leadership. In Chapter 13 ideas introduced in Chapter 3 are extended to examine global leadership and the creation of a set of international competencies that define the key behaviours required of effective global organizations. It seems clear that an increased ethical element, combined with a response to the likely need for greater transparency, will be key elements in the toolkit for leaders and managers in the future.

What is clear within this book is that there is no one best way to develop managers or leaders. There are many different strategies and methodologies used, at least partly due to:

- organizational culture and values
- organizational type and stage of development
- national culture in which the organization is operating
- the changing nature of global careers
- diverse views of career development and work–life balance
- individual differences in personality, learning style preferences, and so on.

Therefore diversity of approach is important for effective and efficient development of leaders and managers in an organization, to address the issues identified above and the individual nature of those in such organizational positions. Individual, cultural, and organizational diversity are key issues and their importance is likely to grow as current models are challenged by those developed in different cultural settings. In addition, the variety of organizational types, sizes, and cultures involved in having to develop leaders and managers from an increasingly diverse pool is likely to lead to new methods being adopted.

Assessing and demonstrating the effectiveness of all approaches and interventions is key for developers in maintaining organizational support. Although current methodologies exist, they have limited application in organizations; so new thinking must be adopted which allows easier evaluation of added value to the organization. There also needs to be greater appreciation of the value of informal and integrated learning, and over longer time periods than traditional training programmes.

As budgets for development of all staff have to compete with other organizational priorities for scarce resources, many organizations respond by outsourcing development of staff. However, the reciprocal relationship of leadership and management development with organizational and cultural development results in risk to the organization of outsourcing these important activities, without very careful monitoring.

Concluding case study

As pointed out in the introduction chapter, as well as the mini case studies found within chapters, the book provides three major case studies that can be used as the basis for class discussion or summative and formative assessments.

Case study 14.1 is the last of these three longer, integrative cases that are specifically linked to the online resources. You will find supporting audio and text materials relating to these cases on the Online Resource Centre.

Case study 14.1: The ABC strategic health authority

Leadership and management development in the NHS

A case study based on a forward-thinking strategic health authority

In 2005 the NHS knowledge and skills framework (KSF) was introduced into all UK NHS trusts. The KSF defined and described the knowledge and skills which NHS staff need to apply in their work in order to deliver quality services. It provides a single, consistent, comprehensive, and explicit framework on which to base the review and development of staff. It was designed to support the development of individuals, teams, and services, promoting equality for and diversity of all staff, with everyone using the same framework for career development and progression.

The aspirations of all stakeholders involved—political, professional, management, and trade unions—are to:

- ensure improved patient care
- assist new ways of working to deliver the range and quality of services required
- improve the recruitment, retention and morale of all staff
- improve access to career and training opportunities through KSF
- meet equal pay for work of equal value criteria.

KSF is a nationally enforced strategy, and as such was a priority for each strategic health authority (SHA) and trust to ensure its implementation. Within this mandatory framework SHAs were given the scope to meet the requirements through localized and best-fit solutions, applying the priority and investment according to the needs of each part of the NHS organization.

The CIPD (2009) Learning and Development Annual Survey Report highlighted that the development of leadership and management skills was rated by 81 per cent of respondents as being most important in meeting business objectives in the next two to five years in the NHS. The introduction of new programmes to develop the role of line managers (61 per cent) and efforts to develop a learning culture across organizations (50 per cent) were also highlighted as the greatest changes in learning and training methods.

In 2007 this along with other influences led the Department of Health to issue a statement saying:

> *A key priority for the NHS in England is to build sustainable leadership capability amongst key staff across the NHS, in order to help managers of all disciplines, starting with Executive Directors and senior staff, to deliver the best health and best care for patients.*

Local response

The local response of the SHA was the creation of a local NHS working party, comprising staff from the local university business school and school of human health sciences, the aforementioned strategic health authority, and primary care trusts to decide upon local action following these national mandates and initiatives. Key stakeholders were asked to indicate what they thought were their local leadership development imperatives working with the NHS key skills framework. The working party established an overall view of the key leadership development imperatives which they felt were aligned to the key strategic issues faced locally. To determine these issues the group conducted a training needs analysis with key stakeholders from across the SHA, including foundation trusts, mental health trusts, and other NHS providers.

Meeting the needs for leadership development in the NHS

The business school over a number of years had already developed an understanding of the complexities of management within healthcare settings. This has been achieved in two ways:

- First, it had previously delivered the Certificate in Management Studies (CMS) in partnership with other NHS trusts and as such believed it could build upon the success of these relationships to produce a fit-for-purpose leadership and management programme aimed at first-line and professional/technical managers.

- Second, the business school continues to manage and deliver the MSc in Professional Leadership by Action Learning, working with a variety of senior and executive NHS staff. Again, based on the success and experience gained in this area of executive development it was thought that a bespoke and tailored solution could be found to meet the needs of the SHA. Moreover the MSc in Healthcare Management was seen as a progression to the CMS programme.

Both the business school and the SHA believed in the fundamental principle that leadership can be taught to junior and senior managers through a blend of practical and theoretical learning and development initiatives. Therefore the transformational and transactional leadership models, a cluster of behavioural theories of leadership and best-practice leadership of change concepts were identified as fundamental building blocks for the programmes—as was developing a wider understanding of the importance within public sector management of being able to effectively manage the transactional and interpersonal complex relationship with stakeholders. A further important consideration in finding appropriate solutions was to ensure the internal and external pressures of managing the ethical and diversity issues found in the NHS was a key factor.

It was an essential prerequisite for these development programmes to ensure that mapping of modules against the NHS knowledge skills framework was in place. After all, it was a national framework used in healthcare and a government investment. It was of similar importance to ensure that evaluation and assessment methods were put in place so that progress and value for money could be measured and reported on.

Course structures

The courses have been designed to give students a thorough understanding of the complexities of managing within a healthcare setting. They draw upon some existing management modules where appropriate, with new modules reflecting the specialist nature of the course, which we defined through a training needs analysis, assuring achievement of the requirements of the stakeholders in the NHS working party.

Integrating the leadership and management development programmes to other aspects of strategy

In addition to these more formal learning programmes, there was a lot more going on in the organization that needed to be considered in an integrative approach. Continuing professional development was an important aspect for both the individual and service development. Staff appraisal was identified as central to the identification of training needs. Recent and associated health service reforms in the UK in the form of the 'Agenda for Change' project had linked some key HR components—appraisal, training, pay, and career progression.

Additional benefits of the programmes

Across the SHA and the various NHS organizations included in the working party, it was identified that there were further aspects of their respective HR strategies that would benefit from this learning intervention. Their frameworks for managing and developing people were based on the four pillars within HR in the NHS plan (2005), which were:

- making the NHS a model employer
- providing a model career through the 'skills escalator'
- improving staff morale
- building people management skills.

As many members of the working party represented learning organizations in their own right, these areas were considered core to services and service development.

The two programmes were introduced in 2010 and the early feedback is encouragingly positive. However, with the recent political pressures to reduce spending in the NHS and with the arrival of a new government, these are uncertain times and a test of the resolve in the perceived importance of leadership and management development—not just in the NHS but in the public sector as a whole.

Questions

1 In the light of all the material presented within the book (and, of course, your own experience), which aspects of the case do you think are the most important indicators that this approach will succeed?

2 Conversely, are there aspects of the case that you feel might have been addressed differently (or perhaps additional work undertaken) in order to improve the chances of success?

3 How important do you feel leadership and management development might be in a situation of severe resource constraint and demands from the government for more effective use of existing resources?

Glossary

BRIC's The term first used by US investment bank Goldman Sachs, referring to Brazil, Russia, India, and China to highlight the emergence of these continent-sized countries. The economies of these countries have been growing rapidly in the first years of the 21st century and are expected to become major economic powers in the future.

'Best fit' approach describes a situation where the best course of action or strategy is the one best suited to a particular organization.

Contingency theory This style is dependent on the interaction of internal and external factors with the organization. For example, the ability to lead is dependent upon the perception of subordinates of and by the leader, the leader's relationship with them, and the degree of consensus on the scope of a given task.

Command and control style describes a management and leadership style that is top-down and traditional in its origin. The manager issues commands to subordinates and maintains a tight control over all the tasks allocated to them.

Competencies The sum effects of many personal, environmental and situational factors, and training that influence a person in the way that they achieve what is expected of them in a particular work role. There is a debate about the difference between competences and competencies, with the former being defined in terms of activities required of a role, whereas competencies take into account how an activity is achieved and what input characteristics influence it.

Equality and inequality refers to the treatment of different groups of individuals in the workplace. Within the values of most organizations there is the notion of equal treatment for all and this has come to be associated particularly with discrimination against specific minority groups.

Ethnocentric A management approach in which few foreign countries have any autonomy; strategic decisions are made at headquarters. Key positions in the domestic and foreign operations are held by headquarters' management personnel.

Expatriate One living in a foreign country; a corporate manager assigned to a location abroad.

'Glass ceiling' is a commonly used term to describe the limitations put on the movement of women into management. It refers to the finding that many minority groups are unable to progress up an organizational hierarchy above a certain level, for example are not able to get into senior management.

Globalization The trend away from distinct national economic units and toward one huge global market.

GLOBE Project The Global Leadership and Organizational Behaviour Effectiveness Project examining inter-relationships between societal culture, organizational culture, and organizational leadership.

Guanxi Informal relationships which are a major social dynamic in China, Taiwan, Singapore, and Chinese societies elsewhere. It is the set of personal connections which an individual can draw upon to secure resources or advantages when doing business or in the course of social life in the Chinese world.

Hierarchical organizations A term used to describe an organization that has multiple levels of reporting lines and with narrow spans of control.

In-groups and out-groups refers to the different perceptions of members of a group being more or less privileged within a society. Some groups are seen to be different from the majority group on certain personal or social characteristics and these differences from the majority, though relatively minor, may become magnified to distinguish them further from the majority. This can lead to discrimination or differential treatment of groups. In-groups are those that are associated with a majority and privileged.

Multicultural A diversity -orientated organization where people from non-traditional backgrounds can contribute and achieve to their fullest potential.

Multinational corporations (MNCs) Companies that invest in countries around the world and who own and control operations in more than one country.

Normative sample A large data set (usually called 'norms'), taken from an identified sample, for example senior managers and leaders in large organizations, against which similar data from any individual can be checked, to ascertain where within the norm group their data indicates they fit. The outcomes might be 'much as others in the norm group' or 'at the lower end of the data set'. This concept is widely used in psychometric testing to establish how individuals compare and contrast with larger groups similar to themselves.

Psychological contract Argyris (1960) first applied this term to the workplace and refers to employers' and employees' beliefs in the employment relationship, the individual and the organization regarding the implicit understanding as to what their mutual obligations are.

Reaction sheets A short paper questionnaire usually completed at the end of a training event to assess the participants' experience of the event. These tend to focus on assessing reactions to: the food and facilities, trainers, topics covered, and overall outcome of training, often using multiple response questions. They are commonly known as 'happy sheets' because they are often completed as participants leave an event and have little time to provide a measured or reasoned response and are to assess a 'general' level of content with the event.

Reflexive is a term used to indicate that a development activity leads those going through development to evaluate their own beliefs, knowledge, and behaviour as part of the development. It often leads to double-loop learning, in which the very assumptions on which the development is based are questioned, along with ideas about the role and behaviours of leaders and managers.

Situational theory This style agreed with Contingency theories on the basic idea of there being no single correct solution to organization. Determining the best person to lead in a certain situation is influenced by the situation and the environment in that point in time.

Taylorist approach describes the scientific approach to management that was derived by Frederick Taylor in the early 1900's. The approach breaks work down into component parts and attempts to gain maximum efficiencies and outputs from the detailed study of work-related tasks. Sometimes referred and related to time and motion studies.

Transformational Leadership Theory Transformational leadership is a style of leadership that leads to positive changes in those who follow. It is said that Transformational leaders are generally energetic, enthusiastic, and passionate. Not only are these leaders concerned and involved in the process, they are also focused on helping every member of the group succeed.

Training Needs Analysis (TNA) Part of the systematic training cycle, used in training staff in practical, operational skills. The cycle begins with a TNA to establish what skills, activities, and knowledge are required to complete a task. The employees to undergo training are assessed as to their current levels of knowledge, skills, and ability to establish the 'gap' to be filled through training. A systematic analysis then provides a trainer with information to develop training to meet identified needs and it also provides measures against which to evaluate the training provided.

Transfer of learning is when a learner has to learn to use their 'new learning', possibly from off-the-job training programmes, in a work environment with the disruption and disturbance which is avoided by off-the job training. However, transfer is important for managers and leaders following all development in terms of their opportunity and ability to use new ideas in the work environment.

Transfer of training occurs when what is learned in one context is used, or interferes with learning in another context. Employees who are trained away from their normal work environment have to transfer learning into the workplace and may require support to do this.

References

Adair, J. (1973), *Action Centred Leadership*, London, McGraw-Hill.

Adams, D., and Waddle, C. (2002), 'Evaluating the return on management development programmes: individual versus organizational benefits', *International Journal of Contemporary Hospitality Management*, 14(1): 14–20.

Adobor, H., and Daneshfar, A. (2006), 'Management simulations: determining their effectiveness', *Journal of Management Development*, 25(2): 151–68.

Akuratiyagamage, V. M. (2007), 'An integrated approach to management development: A framework for practice and research', *VISION— The Journal of Business Perspective*, (11)4, Oct–Dec: 1–11.

Aldridge, M. E., and Nolan, K. J. (2000), '3M's leadership competency model: an internally developed solution', *Human Resource Management*, 39(2–3): 133–45.

Alimo-Metcalfe, B. (1995), 'An investigation of female and male constructs of leadership and empowerment', *Women in Management Review*, (10): 3–8.

Allard, J. M. (2002), 'Theoretical underpinnings of diversity', in C. Harvey and J. M. Allard, (2002), *Understanding and Managing Diversity: Readings, Cases and Exercises*, New Jersey: Prentice Hall.

Alliger, G. M., and Janak, E. A. (1989), 'Kirkpatrick's levels of training criteria: thirty years later', *Personnel Psychology*, (42): 331–42.

Allimo-Metcalfe, B. (1995), 'An investigation of female and male constructs of leadership and empowerment', *Women in Management Review*, (10)2.

Allinson, J., and Hayes, C. (1988), 'The Learning Styles Questionnaire: an alternative to Kolb's inventory?', *British Journal of Management*, (25): 269–81.

Allport, G. W. (1954), *The Nature of Prejudice*, Reading, MA: Addison-Wesley.

Anderson, J. R. (1995),–*Learning and memory: an integrated approach*, Chichester: John Wiley.

Anderson, V. (2007), 'The value of learning—a new model of value and evaluation', Change Agenda, London: CIPD. Online version available at www.cipd.co.uk/subjects/lrnaddev/evaluation (accessed 18 August 2009).

Argyle, M. (1967), *The Psychology of Interpersonal Behaviour*, London, Penguin.

Argyris, C. (1960), *Understanding Organisational Behaviour*, Homewood, IL: Dorsey Press.

Argyris, C., and Schoön, D. (1974), *Theory in Practice: Increasing professional effectiveness*, San Francisco, CA: Jossey-Bass.

Arnold, J., Silverster, J., Patterson, F., Robertson, I. T., Cooper, C. L., and Burnes, B. (2005), *Work Psychology*, 5th edition, Harlow: Financial Times Prentice Hall.

Arsenault, P. M. (2004), 'Validating generational differences: a legitimate diversity and leadership issue', *The Leadership and Organization Development Journal*, (25)2: 124–41.

Atkinson, J. (1984), 'Manpower strategies for flexible organizations', *Personnel Management*, August.

Badhesha, R. S., Schmidtke, J. M., Cummings, A., and Moore, S. D. (2008), 'The effects of diversity training on specific and general attitudes toward diversity', *Multicultural Education and Technology Journal*, (2)2: 87–106.

Ballantyne, I., and Povah, N. (2004), *Assessment and Development Centres*, 2nd edition, Farnham: Gower.

Bandura, A. (1977), *Social learning theory*, Englewood Cliffs, NJ: Prentice Hall.

Barham, K., and Devine, M. (1991), *The Quest for the International Manager: A Survey of Global Human Resource Strategies*, London: Economist Intelligence Unit.

Barner, R., and Higgins, J. (2005), 'Understanding implicit models that guide the coaching process', *Journal of Management Development*, (26)2: 148–58.

Barney, J. (1995), 'Looking Inside for Competitive Advantage', *Academy of Management Executive*, (9)4: 49–65.

Barney, J. B. (1991), 'Firm resources and sustained competitive advantage', *Journal of Management*, (17)1: 99–120.

Barnham, K., and Oates, D. (1991), *The International Manager*, London: Business Books/ The Economist Books.

Bass, B. M. (1985), *Leadership and Performance beyond Expectations*, New York: Free Press.

Bass, B. M. (1985), *Leadership and Performance beyond Expectation*, New York: The Free Press.

Bass, B. M. (1990a), *Leadership and Performance beyond Expectations*, New York: The Free Press.

Bass, B. M. (1990b), 'From transactional to transformational leadership: learning to share the vision', *Organizational Dynamics*, Winter: 19–31.

Bass, B. M., and Avolio, B. J. (1997), 'Shatter the glass ceiling: women may make better managers', in K. Grint (ed.), *Leadership: Classical, Contemporary and critical approaches*, New York: Oxford University Press.

Bass, B. M., and Vaughan, J. A. (1966), *Training in Industry—The management of learning*, London: Tavistock Publications.

Bass, B. M. (1985), *Leadership and Performance*. New York: Free Press.

Bayne, R. (1995), *The Myers-Briggs Type Indicator: A critical review and practical guide*. London: Chapman and Hall.

Bayne, R. (2004), *Psychological Types at Work: An MBTI Perspective*, London: Thomson Learning.

Beard, C., and Irvine, D. (2005), 'Management training and development: problems, paradoxes and perspectives', in J. P. Wilson (ed.), *Human Resource Development: Learning and Training for individuals and organisations*. London: Kogan Page.

Beard, C., and Wilson, J. P. (2006), *Experiential Learning: A Best Practice Handbook for Educators and Trainers*, 2nd edition, London: Kogan Page.

Beardwell, J., and Clayton, T. (2007), *Human Resource Management: A Contemporary Approach*, 5th edition, Harlow: FT Prentice Hall.

Beer, R. (1990), *Intelligence as Adaptive Behavior*. New York: Academic Press.

Belasen, A., and Frank, N. (2008), 'Competing values leadership: quadrant roles and personality traits', *Leadership and Organization Development Journal*, (29)2: 127–43.

Bennet, A., and Bennet, D. (2008), 'A new change model: factors for initiating and implementing personal action learning', *The Journal of Information and Knowledge Management Systems*, (38)4: 378–87.

Bennis, W. G., and O'Toole, J. (2005), 'How business schools lost their way', *Harvard Business Review*, (83)5: 96–104.

Bennis, W. G., O'Toole, J., and Goleman, D. (2008), *Transparency: How Leaders Create a Culture of Candor*, San Francisco, CA: Jossey-Bass.

Berg, S. A., and Chyung, S. Y. (2008), 'Factors that influence informal learning in the workplace', *Journal of Workplace Learning*, (20)4: 229–44.

Bergin, R. S., and Prusko, G. F. (1990), 'Systems thinking: the learning laboratory', *Healthcare Forum Journal*, (1): 32–6.

Berry, C. (2010), *The Career Progression of Non-whites in a Retail Environment*, Unpublished MA dissertation, University of Huddersfield.

Blass, A. (2007), *Talent management: maximising talent for business performance*, London: Chartered Management Institute.

Bloisi, W., Cook, C., and Hunsaker, P. (2003), *Management and Organizational Behaviour*, London: McGraw-Hill.

Bloom, B. S. (ed.) (1956), *Taxonomy of educational objectives: the classification of educational goals. Handbook 1: cognitive domain*, London: Longmans, Green and Company.

Boddy, D., and Buchanan, D. (1992), *Take the Lead: Interpersonal Skills for Change Agents*, Prentice Hall, London.

Bolden, R. (2007), 'Trends and perspectives in management and leadership development', *Business Leadership Review*, (4)2: 1–13.

Bones, C. (2006), quoted in Warren, C. (2006), 'Curtain call', *People Management*, 23 March: 24.

Bono, J. E., and Judge, T. A. (2004), 'Personality and transformational and transactional leadership: a meta-analysis', *Journal of Applied Psychology*, (89)5: 901–10.

Boud, D., Keogh, R., and Walker, D. (1985), *Reflection: Turning Experience in to Learning*, London: Kogan Page.

Boud, D., Cohen, R., and Walker, D. (eds) (1993), *Using Experience for Learning*, Buckingham: The Society for Research into Higher Education and The Open University Press.

Boud, D. (1993), 'Experience as the base for learning', *Higher Education Research and Development*, (12)1: 33–44.

Boud, D., Cressey, P., and Docherty, P. (eds) (2006), *Productive Reflection at Work*, London: Routledge.

Boyatzis, R. E. (1982), *The Competent Manager: a model for effective performance*, New York: John Wiley.

Boyatzis, R. E., and Saatcioglu, A. (2008), 'A 20-year view of trying to develop emotional, social and cognitive intelligence competencies in graduate management education', *Journal of Management Development*, (27)1: 92–108.

Bramley, P. (1996), *Evaluating Training*, London: CIPD.

Brewster, C., Sparrow, P., and Vernon, G. (2007), *International Human Resource Management*, London: CIPD.

Bridges, W. (2000), *The Character of Organizations: Using Personality Type in Organization Development*, David-Black Publishing.

Brinkenhoff, R. O. (2006), 'Increasing impact of training investments: an evaluation strategy for building organizational learning capability', *Industrial and Commercial Training*, (38)6: 302–7.

Briscoe, D., and Schuler, R. (2004), *International Human Resource Management*, London: Routledge.

Brotheridge, C. M., and Long, S. (2007), 'The "real-world" challenges of managers: implications for management education', *Journal of Management Development*, (26)9: 832–42.

Bryans, P., and Marvin, S. (2003), 'Women learning to become managers: learning to fit in or to play a different game?', *Management Learning*, (34)1: 111–34.

Buckingham, M., and Clifton, D. O. (2001), *Now, Discover Your Strengths*, New York: The Free Press.

Buckingham, M., and Coffman, C. (2005), *First, Break All the Rules: What the World's Greatest Managers Do Differently*, 2nd edition, New York: Simon and Schuster.

Burgoyne, J. (1988), 'Management development for the individual and organization', *Personnel Management*, June, 40–4.

Burgoyne, J., Hirsh, W., and Williams, S. (2004), *The Development of Management and Leadership Capability and its Contribution to Performance: the evidence, the prospects and the research need*, London: Department for Education and Skills: 49 (www.dfes.gov.uk/research/data/uploadfiles/RR560.pdf).

Burnes, B. (2009), *Managing Change*, FT Prentice Hall.

Burns, J. M. (1978), *Leadership*, New York: Harper and Row.

Cable, D. M., and Judge, T. A. (2002), 'Managers' upward influence tactic strategies: the role of manager personality and supervisor leadership style', *Journal of Organizational Behaviour*, (24)2: 197–214.

Cahoon, A. R., and Rowney, J. I. A. (1986), 'OD for managers: some fall-out from empirical results', *Leadership and Organization Development Journal*, (7)1: 15–16.

Callahan, J. L. (ed.) (2002), *Perspectives of Emotion and Organizational Change, Advances in Developing Human Resources*, Sage and Academy of Human Resource Development.

Cameron, R., and Neal, L. (2003), *A Concise Economic History of the World*, Oxford: Oxford University Press.

Carmichael, J. L. (1995), 'What do we believe makes a good manager?', *Management Development Review*, (8)2: 7–10.

Carnall, C. A. (2003), *Managing Change in Organizations*, 4th edition, Harlow: Financial Times Prentice Hall.

Carr-Ruffino, N. (1996), *Managing Diversity: People Skills for a Multicultural Workplace*, Cincinnati, OH: International Thompson.

Cattell, A. (2005), 'Performance management and human resource development', in Wilson, J. (ed), *Human Resource Development: learning and training for individuals and organizations*, 2nd edition, London: Kogan Page.

CEML (2002), 'The contribution of UK business schools to the development of managers and leaders', London: Council for Excellence in Management and Leadership.

Cendant International Assignment Services (1999), 'Policies and Practices Survey 1999', London: Cendant International Assignment Services.

Character Counts: www.charactercounts.org.

Chatzel, J. L. (2004), 'Human capital: the rules of engagement are changing', *Lifelong Learning in Europe*, (9)3: 139–45.

Chen, M. (2004), *Asian Management Systems*, London: Thomson.

Chen, P.-J., and Choi, Y. (2008), 'Generational differences in work values: a study of hospitality management', *International Journal of Contemporary Hospitality Management*, (20)6: 595–615.

Child, J. (2002), 'Theorizing about organisation cross nationally, Part 1, An Introduction', in M. Warner and P. Joynt (eds), *Managing Across Cultures: Issues and Perspectives*, 2nd edition, London: Thompson.

CIPD (2002), 'Developing managers for business performance: what your board needs to know today', London: CIPD.

CIPD (2003), 'Managing employee careers', London: CIPD.

CIPD (2005a), 'International management development', London: CIPD.

CIPD (2005b), 'Learning and development: annual survey report 2005', London: CIPD.

CIPD (2005c), 'Training to learning, change agenda', London: CIPD.

CIPD (2006), 'Learning and development: annual survey report 2006', London: CIPD.

CIPD (2006), 'Talent management: understanding the dimensions', London: CIPD.

CIPD (2007), 'Learning and development: annual survey report 2007', London: CIPD.

CIPD (2008), Coaching fact sheet: www.cipd.co.uk/subjetcs/lrnanddev/coachmntor/coaching (accessed 10 July 2009).

CIPD (2009a), 'Latest trends in training and development survey': online survey available at www.cipd.co.uk/onlineinfodocuments/surveys/ (accessed 19 August 2009).

CIPD (2009b), 'Promoting the value of learning in adversity', Guide ref. 4846, London: CIPD. Available online at www.cipd.co.uk/ (accessed 18 August 2009).

CIPD (2009c), 'Succession planning', Fact sheet, London: CIPD (http://www.cipd.co.uk/subjects/hrpract/general/successplan.htm (accessed 2 October 2009).

CIPD (2009d), 'The war on talent? Talent management under threat in uncertain times', London: CIPD.

Clarke, N. (2003), 'The politics of training needs analysis', *Journal of Workplace Learning*, (15)4: 141–53.

Clegg, S., Kornberger, M., and Pitsis, T. (2005), *Managing and Organizations: An Introduction to Theory and Practice*, London: Sage.

Clifford, J., and Thorpe, S. (2007) *Workplace Learning and Development: Delivering Competitive Advantage For Your Organization*. London: Kogan Page.

Clutterbuck, D. (1998), *Learning alliances—tapping into talent*, London: CIPD.

Clutterbuck, D., and Megginson, D. (1999), *Mentoring executives and directors*, Oxford: Butterworth-Heinemann.

Clutterbuck, D., and Ragins, B. R. (2002), *Mentoring and Diversity: An international Perspective*, Oxford: Butterworth-Heinemann.

Coffield, F. (ed.) (2000), *The Necessity of Informal Learning*, Bristol: The Policy Press.

Collins, D. L., and Hearn, J. (eds) (1996), *Men as Managers: Critical Perspectives on Men, Masculinities and Managements*, London: Sage.

Collison, C., and Parcell, G. (2001), *Learning to fly: practical lessons from one of the world's leading knowledge companies*, Oxford: Capstone.

Conger, J. (2001), 'How Gen X manage', in Osland, J., Kolb, D., and Rubin, I. W. (eds), *Organizational Behavior Reader*, Uer Saddle River, NJ: Prentice Hall.

Connerley, M. L., and Pedersen, P. B. (2005), *Leadership in a Diverse and Multicultural Environment Developing Awareness, Knowledge and Skills*, London: Sage.

Connor, J. (2000), 'Developing the global leaders of tomorrow', *Human Resource Management*, (39)2–3: 147–57.

Constable, J., and McCormick, R. (1987), *The Making of British Managers*, London: British Institute of Management and Confederation of British Industry.

Conway, N., and Briner, R. B. (2005), *Understanding Psychological Contracts at Work: A Critical Evaluation of Theory and Research*, Oxford.

Costa, P., Jr, and McCrea, R. (1992), *NEO-PR-R Professional Manual*, Lutz, FL: Psychological Assessment Resources, Inc.

Craik, K. K., Ware, A. P., Kamp, J., O'Reilly, C., Straw, B., and Zedeck, S. (2002), 'Explorations of construct validity in a combined managerial and psychological assessment programme', *Journal of Occupational and Organizational Psychology*, (75)2: 171–93.

Crane, A. and Matten, D. (2007), *Introduction to Business Ethics*, Oxford, Oxford.

Cummings, T. G., and Worley, C. G. (2005), *Organization Development and Change*, 8th edition, Ohio: Thomson South Western.

Cunningham, I. (2007), 'Talent management: making it real', *Development and Learning in Organizations*, (21)4: 4–6.

Daft, R. L. (2006), *The New Era of Management*, Thomson South-Western.

Dainty, P., and Lucas, D. (1992), 'Clarifying the confusion: a practical framework for evaluating outdoor development programmes for managers', *Management Education and development*, (23): 106–22.

Daniels, K., and Macdonald, L. (2005), *Equality, Diversity and Discrimination: A student text*. London: CIPD.

Davidson, M. J., and Burke, R. J. (1994), *Women in Management: Current Research Issues*, London: Paul Chapman.

Davidson, M. J., and Cooper, C. L. (1992), *Shattering the Glass Ceiling: The Woman Manager*, London: Paul Chapman Publishing.

Dawson, M. (2005), 'Raising awareness of the benefits of diversity at ING', *Human Resource Management International Digest*, (13)2: 20–1.

Dawson, S., Winstanley, D., Mole, V., and Sherval, J. (1995), *Managing in the NHS. A Study of Senior Executives*, HMSO, London.

de Chernatony, L., Harris, F., and Dall'Olmo Riley, F. (2000), 'Added value: its nature, roles and sustainability', *European Journal of Marketing*, (34)1–2: 39–56.

Dewey, J. (1925), 'Experience and nature', The Paul Carus Foundation Lectures 1, Chicago: Open Court Publishing Company.

Dicken, P. (2003), *Global Shift: Reshaping the Global Economic Map in the 21st Century*, London: Sage.

Dixon, N. M. (1990), 'The relationship between trainee responses on participation reaction forms and post-test scores, *Human Resource Development Quarterly*, (1): 129–37.

Donaldson. T., and Dunfee, T. W. (1999), 'When ethics travel: the promise and peril of global business ethics', California Management Review.

Dopson, S., and Stewart, R. (1989), *Widening the Debate of Public and Private Sector Management*, management research paper, Templeton College, Oxford.

Doremus, P., Keller, W., Paily, L., and Reich, S. (1998), *The Myth of the Global Corporation*, Princeton, NJ: Princeton University Press.

Dowling, P. J., and Welch, D. E. (2004), *International Human Resource Management: Managing People in a Multinational Context*, 4th edition, Thomson Learning.

Doyle, M. E., and Smith, M. K. (2001), 'Classical leadership', *The Encyclopedia of Informal Education* http://www.infed.org/leadership/traditional_leadership.htm.

Dreher, G. F., and Cox, T. H. (1996), 'Race, gender and opportunity: a study of compensation attainment and the establishment of mentoring relationships', *Journal of Applied Psychology*, (81)3: 297–308.

Driver, M. J. (1982), 'Career concepts: a new approach to career research', in R. Katz (ed.), *Career Issues in Human Resource Management*, Englewood Cliffs: Prentice Hall.

Du Toit, A. (2006), 'Making sense through coaching', *Journal of Management Development*, (26)3: 282–91.

Dubin, P. (1962), *Human relations in administration*, Englewood Cliffs, New Jersey: Prentice Hall.

Dulewicz, V., and Higgs, M. (1999), 'Can emotional intelligence be measured and developed?', *Leadership and Organization Development Journal*, (20)5: 242–52.

Dulewicz, V., and Higgs, M. (2000), 'Emotional intelligence: A review and evaluation study', *Journal of Managerial Psychology*, (15)4: 341–72.

Eagley, A. H., and Johnson, B. T. (1990), 'Gender and leadership style: a meta-analysis', *Psychological Bulletin*, (108): 233–56.

Earley, P. C., and Mosakowski, E. (2002), 'Linking cultures and behaviour in organisations: suggestions for theory development and research methodology', in F. Dansereau, and F. J. Yammarino (eds), *Research in Multi-level Issues, Vol. 1: The Many Faces of Multi-level Issues*, San Francisco, CA: Elsevier Science.

Earley, P. C., and Mosakowski, E. (2004), 'Cultural intelligence', *Harvard Business Review*, October: 139–46.

Easterby-Smith, M. (1994), *Evaluating Management Development, Training and Education*. Aldershot: Gower.

Easterby-Smith, M. (1994), *Evaluating Management Development, Training and Education*, 2nd edition, Aldershot: Gower.

Easterby-Smith, M., Malina, D., and Yuan, L. (1995), 'How culture-sensitive is HRM? A comparative analysis of practice in Chinese and UK companies', *International Journal of Human Resource Management*, (6)1: 31–59.

Edwards, T., and Rees, C. (2006), *International Human Resource Management Globalization, National Systems and Multinational Companies*, Harlow: FT Prentice Hall.

Elkington. J. (1987), *The Green Capitalists, Industries search for environmental excellence*, London: Gollancz.

Equal Opportunities Commission (2006), 'Facts about women and men in Great Britain 2006, accessed www.eoc.gov.uk 25 November 2009.

Eraut, M. (1994), *Developing professional knowledge and competence*, London: Routledge Falmer.

Eraut, M. (2004), 'Informal Learning in the workplace', *Studies in Continuing Education*, (26)2: 247–73.

Eschbach, D. M., Parker, G. E., and Stoeberl, P. A. (2001), 'American repatriate employees' retrospective assessments of the effects of cross-cultural training on their adaptation to international assignments', *International Journal of Human Resource Management*, 12(2): 270–87.

Escover, J. L. (1994), 'The value measure', *Management Decision*, (32)1: 12–14.

Evans, P., Pucik, U., and Barsoux, J. L. (2002), *The Global Challenge: Frameworks for International Human Resource Management*, Boston, MA: McGraw-Hill.

Fagenson, E. A. (1989), 'The mentor advantage: perceived career/ job experiences of protégés versus non-protégés', *Journal of Organisational Behaviour*, (10)4: 309–20.

Fang, T. (2003), 'A critique of Hofstede's fifth national culture dimension', *International Journal of Cross-cultural Management*, (3)3: 337–68.

Festinger, L. (1957), *A theory of cognitive dissonance*, Evanston: Row, Peterson and Company.

Fiedler, F. E. (1967), *A Theory of Leadership Effectiveness*, New York: McGraw-Hill.

Fink, G., Kolling, M., and Neyer, A. K. (2005), 'The cultural standard method', EI Working Paper C2, Vienna: University of Vienna.

Finkelstein, S., Hambrick, D., and Cannella, A. A. (2008), *Strategic Leadership: Theory and Research on Executives, Top Management Teams, and Boards*, Oxford: Oxford University Press.

Fitzgerald, C. (1997), 'The MBTI and leadership development: Personality and leadership reconsidered in changing times', cited in I. B. Myers, M. H. McCauley, N. L. Quenk, and A. L. Hamer (2003), *MBTI Manual: A guide to the Development and Use of the Myers-Briggs Type indicator*, USA: C

Forret, M. L., Turban, D. B., and Dougherty, T. W. (1996), 'Issues facing organizations when implementing formal mentoring programmes', *Leadership and Organization Development Journal*, (17)3: 28–31.

Fox, S. (1997), 'From Management education and development to the study of management learning', in *Management Learning*, J. Burgoyne, and M. Reynolds (eds), London: Sage.

French, R. (2007), *Cross-cultural Management in Work Organisations*, London: CIPD.

Fricker, J. (1991), 'Training for change: an investment in people', in *Handbook of Training and Development*, Aldershot: Gower.

Fujimoto, Y., Hartel, C. E. J., Hartel, G. F., and Baker, N. (2000), 'Openness to dissimilarity moderates the consequences of diversity in well-established groups', *Asia-Pacific Journal of Human Resources*, (38)3: 46–61.

Fukuyama, F. (1993), *The End of History and the Last Man*, New York: Penguin.

Furnham, A. (1995), 'The relationship of personality and intelligence to cognitive style and achievement', in D. H. Saklofske, and M. Zeidnewr (eds), *International Handbook of Personality and Intelligence*, New York: Plenum Press.

Furnham, A., Dissou, G., Sloan, P., and Chamorro-Premuzic, T. (2007), 'Personality and intelligence in business people: a study of two personality and two intelligence measures', *Journal of Business Psychology*, (22): 99–109.

Gagné, R. M. (1966), *The conditions of learning*, New York: Holt, Rinehart and Winston.

Galagan, P. (1987), 'Between two trapezes', *Training and Development Journal*, (41)3: 40–8.

Gelfand, M. J., Nishii, L. H., and Raver, J. L. (2007), 'On the nature and importance of cultural tightness/looseness', *Journal of Applied Psychology*, (91)6: 1225–44.

Giberson, T. R., Resick, C. J., and Dickson, M. W. (2005), 'Embedding leadership characteristics: an examination of homogeneity of personality and values in organizations', *Journal of Applied Psychology*, (90)5: 1002–10.

Giddens, A. (1990), *The Consequences of Modernity*, Cambridge: Polity Press.

Glynn, C., and Holbeche, L. (1998), *The Management Agenda*, Roffey Park Management Institute.

GMAC Global Relocation Services, Windham International (2000), 'Global relocation trends: 2000 survey report', New York: GMAC Global Relocation Services, Windham International.

Goleman, D. (1996), *Emotional Intelligence: Why It Can Matter More than IQ*, London: Bloomsbury Publishing.

Goleman, D. (1997), 'Beyond IQ: developing the leadership competencies of emotional intelligence', Paper presented at the 2nd International Competency Conference, London, October.

Goleman, D. (1998), *Working with Emotional Intelligence*, New York: Bantam Books.

Goodwin, N. (1998), 'Accountability; environment; leadership; management structure; National Health Service; professionalism', *Journal of Management in Medicine*, (12): 21–32.

Goold, M., Campbell, A., and Alexander, M. (1994), *Corporate-level strategy: creating value in the multibusiness company*, New York: John Wiley and Sons.

Gormley, D. (1996), 'Letters to the editor: managing diversity', *Harvard Business Review*, (177) Nov–Dec, cited in C. Harvey and J. Allard (2002), *Understanding and Managing Diversity: Readings, Cases and Exercises*, New Jersey: Prentice Hall.

Gosling, J., and Mintzberg, H. (2004), 'The education of practicing managers', *Sloan Management Review*, (45)4: 19–22.

Goss, D. (1994), *The Principles of Human Resource Management*, London: Routledge.

Graen, G. B., and Hui, C. (1999), 'Transcultural global leadership in the 21st century: challenges and implications for development', in W. Mobley, M. J. Gessner, and V. Arnold (eds), *Advances in Global Leadership*, Stamford, CT: JAI Press.

Graham, A. K., Morecraft, J. D. W., Senge, P. M., and Sterman, J. D. (1992), 'Model-supported case studies in management education', *European Journal of Operational Research*, (59): 151–66.

Grant, B. Z., and Kleiner, B. H. (1997), 'Managing diversity in the workplace', *Equal Opportunities International*, (16)3: 26–32.

Green, K. (1999), 'Offensive thinking', *People Management*, (5)8: 27.

Grey, C., and French, R. (1996), 'Rethinking management education', in R. French and C. Grey (eds), *Rethinking management education*, London: Sage.

Grey, C. (2002), 'What are business schools for? On silence and voice in management education', *Journal of Management Education*, (26): 496–513.

Grinder, J., and Bandler, R. (1983). *Reframing: Neurolinguistic programming and the transformation of meaning*, Moab, UT: Real People Press.

Grossman, R. J. (2000), 'Is diversity working?', *HR Magazine*, (45)3: 46–50.

Guest, D. (1987), 'Human Resource Management and industrial relations', *Journal of Management Studies*, (24)5: 503–21.

Guest, D. (2006), quoted in Warren, C. (2006), 'Curtain call', *People Management*, 23 March.

Guest, D., and King, Z. (2005), 'Management development and career management', in S. Bach (ed.), *Managing Human Resources: Personnel Management in Transition*, 4th edition, Oxford: Blackwell.

Gunz, H. (1989), *Careers and corporate culture: managerial mobility in large corporations*, London: Blackwell.

Hall, E., and Moseley, D. (2005), 'Is there a role for learning styles in personalized education and training?', *International Journal of Lifelong Education*, (24)3: 243–55.

Hamblin, A. C. (1974), *Evaluation and Control of Training*, Maidenhead: McGraw-Hill.

Hamilton, T. A., and Cooper, C. (2001), 'The impact of outdoor management development (OMD), programmes', *Leadership and Organization Development Journal*, (22)7: 330–40.

Handy, C. (1976), *Understanding Organizations*, London: Penguin Books.

Handy, C. (1989), *The Age of Unreason*, London: Business Books.

Handy, C., Gow, I., Gordon, C., Randlesome, C., and Moloney, M. (1987), *The Making of Managers*, London: National Economic Development Office.

Harris, H., Brewster, C., and Sparrow, P. (2003), *International Human Resource Management*, London: CIPD.

Harrison, R (2005) *Learning and Development*, 4th edition, London: CIPD.

Harrison R. (2009), *Learning and Development*, 5th edition, London: CIPD.

Harvey, C., and Allard, J. M. (2002), *Understanding and Managing Diversity, Readings, Cases and Exercises*, New Jersey: Prentice Hall.

Hautala, T. M. (2006), 'The relationship between personality and transformational leadership', *Journal of management Development*, (25)8: 777–98.

Hay, M. (2008), 'Business schools: a new sense of purpose', *Journal of Management Development*, (27)4: 371–8.

Hayes, J., and Allinson, C. W. (1988), 'Cultural differences in the learning styles of managers', *Management International Review*, (25): 75–80.

Headlam-Wells, J. (2004), 'E-mentoring for aspiring managers', *Women in Management Review*, (19)4: 212–18.

Heinrich, K. T. (1995), 'Doctoral advertisement relationships between women', *Journal of Higher Education*, (66): 447–69.

Hersey, P., Blanchard, K., and Johnson, D. (2001), *Management of Organizational Behaviour: Leading Human Resources*, London: Prentice Hall.

Herzberg, F. I. (1972, revised 1987), 'One more time: How do you motivate employees?', *Harvard Business Review*, (65)5, Sep–Oct 1987: 109–20.

Higgs, M. (1996), 'Overcoming the problems of cultural differences to establish success for international management teams', *Team Performance Management: an International Journal*, (2)1: 36–43.

Hills, A. (2009), 'Succession planning—or smart talent management?', *Industrial and Commercial Training*, (41)1: 3–8.

Hirsh, S. K., and Kummerow, J. M. (1990), *Introduction to Type in Organizations*, European English version, Oxford: Oxford Psychologist Press.

Hirsh, W. (2000), *Succession planning demystified*, Brighton: Institute for Employment Studies.

Hirsh, W., and Bevan, S. (1988), 'What makes a manager? In search of a language for management skills', Institute of Manpower Studies Report No. 144, University of Sussex: Institute of Manpower Studies.

Hirsh, W., and Carter, A. (2002), *New Directions in Management Development*, Brighton: Institute for Employment Studies.

Hirst, P., and Thompson, G. (1999), *Globalisation in Question: The International Economy and the Possibilities of Governance*, Cambridge: Polity Press.

Hite, M., and MacDonald, K. S. (1995), 'Gender issues in management development', *Journal of Management Development*, (14)4: 5–15.

Hoeksema, L. H., Van de Vliert, E., and Williams, A. R. T. (1997), 'The interplay between learning strategy and organizational structure in predicting career success', *The International Journal of Human Resource Management*, (8)3: 307–27.

Hoffer, E. (1973), *Reflections on the Human Condition*, New York: Harper and Row.

Hoffman, B. J., and Frost, B. C. (2006), 'Multiple intelligences of transformational leaders: an empirical examination', *International Journal of Manpower*, (27)1: 37–51.

Hofstede, G. (1980), *Culture's Consequences: International Differences in Work-Related Values*, London: Sage Publications.

Hofstede, G. (1983), 'Dimension of national cultures in fifty countries and three regions', in J. B. Deregowski, S. Dziurawiec, and R. C. Annis (eds), *Explications in cross-cultural psychology*, Lisse, Netherlands: Swets and Zeitlinger.

Hofstede, G. (1991), *Cultures and Organizations: Software of the Mind*, London: McGraw-Hill.

Hofstede, G. (2001), *Culture's Consequences*, Thousand Oaks, CA: Sage.

Hofstede, G. (2003), 'What is culture? A reply to Baskerville', *Accounting, Economy and Society*, (28)(i): 811–13.

Hofstede, G. (with G. J. Hofstede), (2005) *Cultures and Organizations: Software of the Mind*, 2nd edition, New York: McGraw-Hill.

Hofstede, G., and Bond, M. (1988), 'The Confucius connection: from cultural roots to economic growth!', *Organizational Dynamics*, (16)4: 5–21.

Holbeche, L. (2008), 'Realising leadership development potential', *Impact: Quarterly update on CIPD policy and research*, (24), August.

Holbeche, L. (2001), *Aligning Human Resources and Business Strategy*, Butterworth Heinemann.

Holbeche, L. (2002), *Aligning Human Resources and Business Strategy*, Butterworth Heinemann.

Holden, N. J. (2002), *Cross-cultural Management: A Knowledge Management Perspective*, Harlow: FT/Prentice Hall.

Holman, D., Pavlica, K., and Thorpe, R. (1997), 'Rethinking Kolb's theory of experiential learning in management education', Management Learning, London: Sage.

Holman, D., (2000), 'Contemporary models of management education in the UK', *Management Learning*, (31)2: 197–217.

Holton, E. F., III, Bates, R. A., and Ruona, W. E. A. (2000), 'Development of a generalized learning transfer system inventory', *Human Resource Development Quarterly*, (11)4: 333–59.

Holton, E. F. (1996), 'The flawed 4-level evaluation model', *Human Resource Development Quarterly*, (7): 5–21.

Holton, E. F., and Naquin, S. (2005), 'A critical analysis of HRD evaluation models from a decision-making perspective', *Human Resource Development Quarterly*, (16)2: 257–80.

Honey, P., and Mumford, A. (1986), *Using Your Learning Styles*, Maidenhead: Honey Publications.

Honey, P., and Mumford, A. (1992), *Manual of Learning Opportunities*, Maidenhead: Honey Publications.

Honey, P., and Mumford A. (1986), *A Manual of Learning Styles*, Maidenhead: Honey Publications.

Honey, P., and Mumford, A. (1996), *A Manual of Learning Styles*, 3rd edition, Maidenhead, Honey Publications.

Hopkins, M. M., and Bilimoria, D. (2008), 'Social and emotional competencies predicting success for male and female executives', *Journal of Management Development*, (27)1: 13–35.

House, R. J., Javidan, M., and Dorfman, P. (2001), 'The GLOBE Project', *Applied Psychology: An International Review*, (50)4: 489–505.

House, R., Javidan, M., and Hanges, P. (2002), 'Understanding cultures and implicit leadership theories across the globe: an introduction to project GLOBE', *Journal of World Business*, (37)1, Spring: 3–10.

Howell, W. S. (1982), *The empathic communicator*, Minnesota: Wadsworth Publishing Company.

Huczynski, A., and Buchanan, D. (2007), *Organizational Behaviour: An Introductory Text*, Harlow: Pearson Education.

Huntingdon, S. P. (2002), *The Clash of Civilizations and the Remaking of World Order*, New York: The Free Press.

Huselid, M. A. (1995), 'The impact of Human Resource Management on turnover, productivity and corporate financial performance', *Academy of Management Journal*, (38): 365–72.

Ibarra, H. (1992), 'Homophily and differential returns: sex differences in network structure and access in an advertising firm', *Administrative Sciences Quarterly*, (37): 422–47.

Illeris, K. (2004), 'A model for learning in working life', *Journal of Workplace Learning*, (16)8: 431–41.

Institute of Business Ethics www.ibe.org.uk.

Irvine, D., and Wilson, J. P. (1994), 'Outdoor management development: reality or illusion?', *Journal of Management Development*, (13)5: 25–37.

Jackson, T. (2004), *International HRM: A Cross-cultural Approach*, London: Sage.

Jansen, P., and Van der Velde, M. (2001), 'A typology of management development', *Journal of Management Development*, (20)2: 106–20.

Jensen, M. C., and Meckling, W. H. (1976). 'Theory of the firm: managerial behavior, agency costs and ownership'

Johnson, G., and Scholes, K. (1998), *Exploring Techniques of Analysis and Evaluation in Strategic Management*, London: Prentice Hall.

Johnson, G., and Scholes, K. (2002), *Exploring Corporate Strategy*, 6th edition, London: Prentice Hall.

Jones, G. R., George, J. M., and Hill, C. W. L. (2000), *Contemporary Management*, 2nd edition, Boston, MA: McGraw-Hill.

Jung, C. G. (1923), *Psychological Types*, London: Routledge.

Kakabadse, A., and Myers, A. (1994), 'Qualities of top management: comparison of European manufacturers', Cranfield School of Management Paper, Cranfield.

Kandola, R., and Fullerton, J. (1998), *Diversity in Action: Managing the Mosaic*, London: IPD.

Kanter, R. M. (1977), *Men and Women of the Corporation*, New York: Basic Books.

Kaplan, R. S., and Norton, D. P. (1996), *Translating Strategy into Action: the Balanced Scorecard*, Boston, MA: Harvard Business School Press.

Kayes, C. D. (2007), 'Conclusion: institutional barriers to experiential learning revisited', in M. Reynolds and R. Vince (eds), *The Handbook of Experiential Learning and Management Education*, Oxford: Oxford University Press.

Kearns, P. (2005), *Evaluating the ROI from learning*, London: CIPD.

Kelley, R., and Caplan, J. (1993), 'How Bell Labs creates star performers', cited in V. Dulewicz and M. Higgs, (2000), 'Emotional intelligence: a review and evaluation study', *Journal of Managerial Psychology*, (15)4: 341–72.

Kendall, E. (1998), *Manual Supplement MBTI Step 1*. California: C

Kersley, B., Alpen, C., Forth, J., Bryson, A., Bewley H., Dix, G., and Oxenbridge, S. (2006), *Inside the Workplace*, London: Routledge.

Kets de Vries, M. F. R. (1996), 'Leaders who make a difference', *European Management Journal*, (14)5: 486–93.

Keuning, D. (1998), *Management: A Contemporary Approach*, London: Pitman.

Kiersey, D., and Bates, M. (1973), *Please Understand Me II*, 3rd edition, Del Mar, CA: Prometheus Nemesis.

King, Z. (2004), *Career management—a guide*, London: CIPD.

Kirkpatrick, D. L. (1998), *Evaluating Training Programs: The Four Levels*, 2nd edition, San Fransisco: Berrett-Koehler.

Kirkpatrick, D. L. (1983), 'Four steps to measuring training effectiveness', *Personnel Administrator*, November: 19–25.

Kirwin, C., and Birchall, D. (2006), 'Transfer of learning from management development programmes: testing the Holton model', *International Journal of Training and Development*, (10)4: 252–68.

L. (1961), *Variations in Value Orientations*, Evanston,

sophy: Ethics and Politics from Aristotle to MacIntyre,

Coaching in Organizations, London: CIPD (Research

nson, R. A. (1998), *The Adult Learner*, USA:

national Management, Maidenhead: McGraw-Hill.
Apes, International Library of Psychology,

ing, Englewood Cliffs, Prentice Hall.
tler, R. (1994), 'Strategic management development
to assess and develop managerial competencies', in
ting Learning, London: Routledge and Oxford

arning: Experience as a Source of Learning and
NJ: Prentice Hall.
arning: Experience as a Source of Learning and
NJ: Prentice Hall.
rations Rule the World, West Hartford, CT: Kumarian

hevsky, S. (2002), 'Introduction: cultural relativism and
ehaviours', *International Journal of Cross-cultural*

nager, New York: Free Press.
why transformation efforts fail', *Harvard Business*
Review

Kram, K. E. (1985), *Mentoring at Work: Developmental Relationships in Organizational Life*, Scott, Foresman and Co.

Kreitner, R., and Kinicki, A. (2001), *Organizational Behaviour*, New York: McGraw-Hill.

Lammers, C. J., and Hickson, D. J. (eds) (1979), *Organisations Alike and Unlike*, London: Routledge and Kegan Paul.

Lancaster, L., and Stillman, D. (2002), *When Generations Collide: who they are, why they clash, how to solve the generational puzzle at work*, New York: Harper Collins.

Laurent, A. (1986), 'The cross-cultural puzzle of international Human Resource management', *Human Resource Management*, (25)1: 91–102.

Lave, J., and Wenger, E. (1991), *Situated Learning: Legitimate Peripheral Participation*, Cambridge: Cambridge University Press.

Lawrence, G. (1995), *People types and tiger stripes*, Florida, FLA: Center for Application of Psychological Type, Inc.

Lee, M. (1994, 1997), 'The developmental approach: a critical reconsideration', in J. G. Burgoyne, and M. Reynolds (eds), *Management Learning: Integrating Perspectives in Theory and Practice*, London: Sage Publications.

Levinsor, M., Price, C. R., Munden, K. J., and Solley, C. M. (1962), *Men, Management and Mental Health*, Cambridge, MA: Harvard University Press.

Liff, S., and Dale, K. (1994), 'Formal opportunity, informal barriers: black women managers in a local authority', *Work, Employment and Society*, (8)2: 177–98.

Linehan, M. (2001), 'Networking for female managers' career development: empirical evidence', *Journal of Management Development*, (20)10: 823–9.

Loden, M. (1996), *Implementing Diversity*, Boston, MA: McGraw-Hill.

Long, J. W. (1984), 'The wilderness lab', *Training and Development Journal*, (38)5: 59–69.

Lyons, S., Duxbury, L., and Higgins, C. (2005), 'Are gender differences in basic human values a generational phenomenon?', *Sex Roles*, (53)9–10: 763–8.

Mabey, C. (2002), 'Mapping management development practice', *Journal of Management Studies*, (39)8: 1139–60.

Mabey, C., and Terry, R. (2007), 'The manager in the mirror', *People Management*, (13)14, 12 July: 38–40.

Mabey, C., and Ramirez, M. (2004), *Developing Managers: A European Perspective*, London: Chartered Management Institute.

Mabey, C., and Salaman, G. (1995), *Strategic Human Resource Management*, Oxford: Basil Blackwell.

Macdonald, K. M. (1995), *The Sociology of the Professions*, Thousand Oaks, CA: Sage.

MacIntyre, A. (1988), *Whose Justice? Which Rationality?*, University of Notre Dame Press.

Maitland, A. (2006), 'Le patron, der chef and the boss', *Financial Times*, 9 January.

Major, D. A., Turner, J. E., and Fletcher, T. D. (2006), 'Linking proactive personality and the Big Five to motivation to learn and development activity', *Journal of Applied Psychology*, (91)4: 927–35.

Management Today, (2008), 'The trouble with women', 28 February 2008, accessed 29 November 2009.

Mankin, D. (2009), *Human Resource Development*, Oxford: Oxford University Press.

Manning, T., Pogson, G., and Morrison, Z. (2008), 'Interpersonal influence in the workplace, Part one: an introduction to concepts and a theoretical model', *Industrial and Commercial Training*, (42)2: 87–94.

Margerison, C. (1991), *Making Management Development Work: Achieving Success in the 90s*, Maidenhead: McGraw-Hill.

Marsick, V. J., and Volpe, M. (1999), 'The nature and need for informal learning', *Advances in Developing Human Resources*, (1)1: 1–9.

Marsick, V. J., and Watkins, K. E. (1997), 'Lessons from informal and incidental learning', in J. Burgoyne and M. Reynolds (eds), *Management Learning: Integrating Perspectives in Theory and Practice*, London: Sage.

Marton, F., and Ramsden, P. (1988), 'What does it take to improve learning?', in P. Ramsden (ed.), *Improving Learning: New Perspectives*, London: Kogan Page.

Maslow, A. H. (1943), 'A theory of human motivation', *Psychological Review*, 50(4): 370–96.

May, G. D., and Kruger, M. J. (1988), 'The manager "within"', *Personnel Journal*, (67)2: 59–65.

Mayo, A. (2002), *Creating a Learning and Development Strategy*, London: CIPD.

McCall, M. W., Jr, and Lombardo, M. M. (1983), *Off the track: Why and how successful executives get derailed*, Greenboro, NC: Center for Creative Leadership.

McCauley, C. D., and Moxley, R. S., Jr. (1996), 'Developmental 360: how feedback can make managers more effective', *Career Development International*, (1)3: 15–19.

McCauley, C. D., Ruderman, M. N., Ohlott, P. J., and Morrow, J. E. (1994), 'Assessing the developmental components of managerial jobs', *Journal of Applied Psychology*, (79)4: 544–60.

McClelland, D. (1961), 'Methods of measuring human motivation', in J. W. Atkinson (ed.), *The Achieving Society*, Princeton, NJ: D. Van Nostrand.

McClelland, D. C. (1975), *Power—The Inner Experience*, New York: Irnington Publishing.

McCrea, R. R., and Costa, P. T., Jr. (1989), 'Reinterpreting the Myers-Briggs Type Indicator® from the perspective of the Five-Factor Model of personality', *Journal of Personality*, (57)1: 17–40.

McEnrue, M. P. (2002), 'Managerial skills teaching; ten questions and twelve answers', *Journal of Management Education*, (26): 648–72.

McEnrue, M. P., Groves, K. S., and Shen, W. (2007), 'Emotional intelligence development: leveraging individual characteristics', *Journal of Management Development*, (28)2: 150–74.

McGill, I., and Brockbank, A. (2004), *The Action Learning Handbook: powerful techniques for education, professional development and training*, London: Routledge Falmer.

McPhail, K. J. (2002), 'The nursing profession, personality types and leadership', *Leadership in Health Services*, (15)1: vii–x.

Mead, R., and Andrews, T. G. (2009), *International Management Culture and Beyond*, Wiley-Blackwell.

Mead, R. (2005), *International Management Cross-cultural Dimensions*, Blackwell Publishing.

Megginson, D. (1996), 'Planned and emergent learning—consequences for development', *Management Learning*, (27)4: 411–28.

Megginson, D., and Whitaker, V. (2007), *Continuing Professional Development*, 2nd edition, London: CIPD.

Mercer, (2006), Study of Chinese Managers' Competencies.

Mercer, (2008), 'Staying Ahead of the Curve: Leadership Practices in China'.

Mercer, (2008), Attraction and Retention in China.

Michaels, E., Handfield-Jones, H., and Axelrod, B. (1998), 'The war for talent', *McKinsey Quarterly*, (3): 44–57.

Miettinen, R. (2000), 'The concept of experiential learning and John Dewey's theory of reflective thought and action', *International Journal of Lifelong Education*, (19)1: 54–72.

Miller, L., Rankin, N., and Neathey, F. (2001), *Competency Frameworks in UK Organizations*, London: CIPD.

Millmore, M., Lewis, P., Saunders, M., Thornhill, A., and Morrow, T. (2007), *Strategic Human Resource Management: Contemporary Issues*, Essex: Pearson Education Ltd.

Mintzberg, H. (1973), 'Strategy making in three models', *California Management Review*, (16)2: 44–53.

Mintzberg, H. (2004), *Managers Not MBAs*, London: FT Prentice Hall.

Mintzberg, H. (2005), *Managers Not MBAs: A Hard Look at the Soft Practice of Managing and Management Development*, San Francisco: Berret-Koehler Publishers.

Mintzherg, H. (1980), *The Nature of Managerial Work*, Englewood Cliffs, NJ: Prentice Hall.

Modood, T., Berthoud, R., and Lakey, J. (1997), *Ethnic Minorities in Britain: Diversity and Disadvantage*, London: Policy Studies Institute.

Moon, J. A. (2004), *A Handbook of Reflective and Experiential Learning: Theory and Practice*, London: Routledge Falmer.

Moore, S. (1999), 'Understanding and managing diversity among groups at work: key issues for organisational training and development', *Journal of European Industrial Training*, (23)4–5: 208–17.

Morgan, W. (2009), *Management History: Text and Cases*, Routledge.

Morris, J. (1991), 'Action learning: the long haul', in J. Prior (ed.), *Handbook of Training and Development*, London: Gower.

Morrison, A. (2000), 'Developing a Global Leadership Model', *Human Resource Management*, (39)2–3: 117–31.

Mullins, L. J. (2007), *Management and Organizational Behaviour*, London: FT/Prentice Hall.

Mumford, A. (1987), 'Using reality in management development', *Management Education and Development*, (18)3: 223–43.

Mumford, A. (1991a), 'Effectiveness in management development', in J. Prior (ed.), *Handbook of Training and Development*, London: Gower.

Mumford, A. (1991b), 'Learning in action', *Personnel Management*, July.

Mumford, A. (1995a), 'Four approaches to learning from experience', *Industrial and Commercial Training*, (27)8: 12–19.

Mumford, A. (1995b), *Learning at the Top*, Maidenhead, McGraw-Hill.

Mumford, A. (1995c), 'Putting learning styles to work: an integrated approach', *Industrial and Commercial Training*, (27)8: 28–35.

Mumford, A. (1996), 'Could do better', *People Management*, 24 October: 27.

Mumford, A. (1997), *Management Development: Strategies for Action*, 3rd edition, London: CIPD.

Mumford, A., and Gold, J. (2004), *Management Development :Strategies for Action*, 4th edition, London: CIPD.

Murtha, T. P., Lenway, S. A., and Bagozzi, R. P. (1998), 'Global mind-sets and cognitive shift in a complex multinational corporation', *Strategic Management Journal*, (19): 97–114.

Myers, I. B., and Myers, P. B. (1980), *Gifts Differing*, Palo Alto, CA: Consulting Psychologists Press Inc.

Myers, I. B., McCauley, M. H., Quenk, N. L., and Allen, L. H. (2003), *MBTI Manual, A Guide to the Development and Use of the Myers-Briggs Type Indicator®*, 3rd edition, USA: Consulting Psychologists Press Inc.

Myers, K. D., and Kirby, L. A. (2000), *Introduction to Type Dynamics and Development: Exploring the Next Level of Type*, Mountain View, CA: Consulting Psychologists Press Inc.

Neary, D., and O'Grady, D. (2000), 'The role of training in developing global leaders: a case study at TRW Inc.', *Human Resource Management*, (39)2–3: 185–93.

Neary, P., and Lucks, S. (2005), 'How external factors help staff to get the most out of development centres', *People Management*, (11)9: 44.

Needle, D. (2004), *Business in Context*, London: Thomson.

Nemetz, P. L., and Christensen, S. L. (1996), 'The challenge of cultural diversity', *Academy of Management Review*, (21)2: 434–63.

Newton, R., and Wilkinson, M. J. (1994), 'When the talking is over: using action learning', *Management Development Review*, (7)2: 9–15.

Nielsen, K. (2009), 'A collaborative perspective on learning transfer', *Journal of Workplace Learning*, (21)1: 58–70.

Noe, R. A. (2008), *Employee Training and Development*, 4th edition, USA: McGraw-Hill International.

Nonaka, I., and Takeuchi, H. (1995), *The Knowledge-Creating Company: how Japanese companies create the dynamics of innovation*, Oxford: Oxford University Press.

Nordvik, H., and Brovold, H. (1998), 'Personality traits in leadership tasks', *Scandinavian Journal of Psychology*, (39)2: 61–4.

Normann, R., and Ramirez, R. (1994), *Designing Interactive Strategy: from value chain to value constellation*, Chichester: John Wiley and Sons.

Northouse, P. G. (2009), *Introduction to leadership concepts and practice*, Sage.

Nyambegera, S., Sparrow, P. R., and Daniels, K. (2000), 'The impact of cultural value orientations on individual HRM preferences in developing countries: lessons from Kenyan organisations', *International Journal of Human Resource Management*, (11)4: 639–63.

O'Dwyer, M., and Ryan, E. (2002), 'Management development—a model for retail business', *Journal of European Industrial Training*, (26)9: 420–9.

O'Neil (2002), in D. Clutterbuck and B. R. Hagins, *Mentoring and Diversity: an international perspective*, Oxford: Butterworth Heinemann.

Office of National Statistics (2008), Social and Vital Statistics Division and Northern Ireland Statistics and Research Agency, Central Survey Unit, Quartely Labour Force Survey, April–June 2008 [computer file] 3rd edition, Colchester, Essor: UK Data Archive [distributor], March 2010. SN: 6013.

Ohmae, K. (1990), *The Borderless World: Power and Strategy in the Interlinked Economy*, New York: Harper.

Olson, R. G. (1967), 'Deontological ethics', In P. Edwards (ed.), *The Encyclopaedia of Philosophy*, London: Collier Macmillan.

Organization Resources Counsellors (2004), 'Worldwide survey of international assignment policies and practices', London and New York: Organization Resources Counsellors.

Osbaldeston, M. (2005), 'Developing your leaders', in CIPD (ed.), *Reflections on the 2005 Training and Development Survey: latest trends in learning, training and development*, London: CIPD. Online survey available at www.cipd.co.uk/onlineinfodocuments/surveys/.

Parekh, B. (2000), *Commission for the Future of Multi-Ethnic Britain*, London: Runnymede Trust.

Parker, C., and Stone, B. (2003), *Developing Management Skills for Leadership*, FT Prentice Hall Pearson Education.

Parsloe, E. (1999), *The Manager as Coach and Mentor*, London: CIPD.

Paton, N. (2003), 'Leadership skills hold Britain back', Guardian Jobs and Money, 22 February.

Pedersen, P. (1999), 'Intercultural understanding: finding common ground without losing integrity', in D. Christie, D. Wagner, and D. Winter (eds), *Peace, Conflict and Violence: Peace Psychology for the 21st Century*, Uer Saddle River, NJ: Prentice Hall.

Pedler, M. (ed) (1997), *Action Learning in Practice*, 3rd edition, Aldershot: Gower.

Pedler, M., and Boutall, J. (1992), *Action Learning for Change*, Bristol: NHS Training Directorate.

Pedler, M., Burgoyne, J., and Boydell, T. (1994), *A manager's guide to self-development*, 3rd edition, London: McGraw-Hill.

Pedler, M., Burgoyne, J., and Boydell, T. (2006), *A Manager's Guide to Self-development*, 5th edition, Maidenhead: McGraw-Hill.

Pfeffer, J. (1998), *The Human Equation: Building Profit by Putting People First*, Cambridge, MA: Harvard Business School Press.

Phillips, J. (1996), 'Measuring ROI: the fifth level of evaluation', *Technical and Skills Training*, April 10–13.

Phillips, J. J. (1991), *Handbook of Training Evaluation and Measurement Methods*, 2nd edition, Houston, Texas: Gulf Publishing.

Phillips, J. J. (2003), *Return on Investment in Training and Performance Improvement Programs*, 2nd edition, Oxford: Butterworth Heinemann.

Phillips, T. (2007), 'The Age of Difference', speech made on BBC radio, December. Accessed transcript 11 November 2009.

Piaget, J. (1963), 'The attainment of invariants and reversible operations in the development of thinking', *Social Research*, (30): 283–99.

Pilbeam, S., and Corbridge, M. (2006), *People Resourcing: HRM in Practice*, Harlow: FT/Prentice Hall.

Polanyi, M. (1966), *The Tacit Dimension*, London: Routledge and Kegan Paul.

Pool, S., and Pool, B. (2006), 'A management development model: measuring organizational commitment and its impact on job satisfaction among executives in a learning organization', *Journal of Management Development*, (26)4: 353–69.

Porter, M. (1980), *The Competitive Advantage of Nations*, London: Macmillan.

Porter, M. E. (1985), *Competitive Advantage*, New York: Free Press.

Porter, M. E. (1980), *Competitive strategy: techniques for analyzing industries and competitors*, New York: Free Press.

Poulet, R. (1997), 'Designing effective development programmes', *Journal of Management Development*, (16)6: 428–37.

Powell, G. N. (1990), 'One more time: do female and male managers differ?', *Academy of Management Executive*, (4)1: 68–75.

Powell, G. N. (1988), *Women and Men in Management*, London: Sage.

Powell, G. N. (ed.) (1999), *Handbook of Gender and Work*, London: Sage Publications.

Powell, G. N., Butterfield, D. A., and Parent, J. D. (2002), 'Gender and managerial stereotypes: have the times changed?', *Journal of Management*, (28): 177–93.

Prahalad, C. K., and Hamel, G. (1990), 'The core competence of the corporation', *Harvard Business Review*, (68)3: 79–91.

Preskill, H., and Torres, R. T. (1999), *Evaluative Inquiry for Learning in Organizations*, Thousand Oaks, California: Sage.

PricewaterhouseCoopers (2008), '11th annual global CEO survey: key HR issues arising (http://www.pwc.com/gx/en/ceo-survey/pdfs/11th_ceo_survey.pdf accessed 17.9.09).

Quelch, J. (2005), 'A new agenda for business schools', *The Chronicle*, (52)15: B19.

Quinn, R. R., Fraerman, S. R., Thompson, M. P., and McGrath, M. R. (2003), *Becoming a Master Manager: A Competency Framework*, USA: Wiley.

Ragins B. R. (2002), 'Understanding diversified mentoring relationships: definitions, challenges and strategies', in D. Clutterbuck and B. R. Hagins, *Mentoring and Diversity: An International Perspective*, Oxford: Butterworth Heinemann.

Ragins, B. R. (1989), 'Barriers to mentoring: the female manager's dilemma', *Human Relations*, (42)1: 1–22.

Ragins, B. R., and Cotton, J. L. (1991). 'Easier said than done: gender differences in perceived barriers to gaining a mentor', *Academy of Management Journal*, (34)4: 939–51.

Ragins, B. R., and Cotton, L. J. (1999), 'Mentor functions and outcomes: a comparison of men and women in formal and informal mentoring relationships', *Journal of Applied Psychology*, (84)4: 529–50.

Ragins, B. R., and McFarlin, D. (1990), 'Perception of mentor roles in cross-gender mentoring relationships', *Journal of Vocational Behaviour*, (37): 321–39.

Rapoport, R., and Rapoport, R. N. (1980), 'Balancing work, family and leisure: a triple helix model', in C. B. Derr (ed.), *Work, Family and the Career*, New York: Praeger.

Rawls, J., (1971), *A Theory of Justice*, Belknap.

Rayner, C., and Adam-Smith, D. (2009), *Managing and Leading People*, London: CIPD.

Reid, M., Barrington, H., and Brown, M. (2004), *Human Resource Development: Beyond Training Interventions*, London: CIPD.

Rentz, J. O., and Reynolds, F. D. (1991), 'Forecasting the effects of an aging population on product consumption: an age-old-period-cohort framework', *Journal of Marketing Research*, (28): 355–60.

Revans, R. (1980), *Action Learning*, London: Blond.

Revans, R. W. (1978), 'Action learning takes a healthy cure', *Education and Training*, Nov–Dec: 1–3.

Revans, R. W. (1998), *ABC of Action Learning*, London: Lemos and Crane.

Reynolds, M., and Vince, R. (2007), *The Handbook of Experiential Learning and Management Education*, Oxford: Oxford University Press.

Reynolds, J., Caley, L., and Mason, R. (2002), *How Do People Learn?* London: CIPD.

Reynolds, M. (1998), 'Learning styles: a critique', *Management Learning*, (28)2: 115–33.

Reynolds, M., and Trehan, K. (2003), 'Learning from difference', *Management Learning*, (34)2: 162–80.

Reynolds, M., and Vince, R. (2004), *Organizing Reflection*, Farnham: Ashgate.

Richardson, G. B. (1972), *The Organisation of Industry*, *Economic Journal*, (82): 327.

Riding, R., and Rayner, S. (1998), *Cognitive Styles and Learning Strategies: Understanding Style Differences in Learning and Behaviour*, Great Britain: David Fulton Publishers.

Rigg, C., and Trehan, K. (2008), 'Critical reflection in the workplace: is it just too difficult?', *Journal of European Industrial Training*, (32)5: 374–84.

Riggio, R. E., and Reichard, R. J. (2008), 'The emotional and social intelligences of effective leadership', *Journal of Managerial Psychology*, (23)2: 169–85.

Ring and Perry (1985), Academy of Management Review, Vol 10, Number 2.

Robinson, G. (1991), 'Management development and organization development', in J. Prior (ed.), *Handbook of Training and Development*, London: Gower.

Robinson, W. L. (1974), Title unknown, *Personnel Journal*, (53)7: 538–9.

Rosete, D., and Ciarrochi, J. (2005), 'Emotional intelligence and its relationship to workplace performance outcomes of leadership effectiveness', *Leadership and Organization Development Journal*, (26)5: 388–99.

Ross, R., and Schneider, R. (1992), *From Equality to Diversity: a Business Case for Equal Opportunities*, London; Pitman Publishing.

Rotter, J. B. (1954), *Social Learning and Clinical Psychology*, New York: Prentice Hall.

Rousseau, D. M. (1989), 'Psychological and implied contracts in organisations', *Employee Responsibilities and Rights Journal*, (2): 121–39.

Routledge, C., and Carmichael, J. (2007), *Personal Development and Management Skills*, London; CIPD.

Russ-Eft, D., and Preskill, H. (2005), 'In search of the holy grail: return on investment evaluation in human resource development', *Advances in Developing Human Resources*, (7)1: 71–85.

Rutherford, S. (2001), 'Any difference? An analysis of gender and divisional management styles in a large airline', *Gender, Work and Organization*, (8): 326–45.

Salaman, G., and Butler, J. (1994), 'Why managers won't learn', in C. Mabey and P. Iles (eds), *Managing Learning*, London: Routledge, in association with the Open University.

Sarbanes-Oxley Act of 2002: http://www.aicpa.org/info/Sarbanes_oxley.

Sathe, V. (1985), *Culture and Related Corporate Realities: text, cases and readings on organisational entry, establishment and change*, Homewood, IL: Irwin.

Schein, E. (1978), *Career Dynamics: matching individual and organizational needs*, Reading, MA: Addison Wesley.

Schein, E. (1988), *Organizational Psychology*, 3rd edition, London: Prentice Hall.

Schein, E. H. (1985), *Organisational Culture and Leadership*, San Francisco, CA: Jossey-Bass.

Schein, E. H. (1965, 1980), *Organisational Psychology*, Englewood Cliffs, NJ: Prentice Hall.

Schein, V. E. (1976), 'Think manager—think male', *Atlanta Economic Review*, March–April: 21–4.

Schein, V. E., Mueller, R., Lituchy, T., and Liu, J. (1996), 'Think manager—think male: a global phenomenon?', *Journal of Organisational Behaviour*, (17)1: 33–41.

Schewe, C. D., and Meredith, G. E. (1994), 'Digging deep to delight the mature adult consumer', *Marketing Management*, (3): 20–35.

Schneider, B., Smith, D. B., and Goldstein, H. W. (2000), 'Attraction–selection–attrition: towards a person-environment psychology of organizations', in W. B. Walsh, K. Craik, and R. H. Price (eds.), *Person-Environment Psychology: New Directions and Perspectives*, Mohwah, NJ.: Erlbaum.

Schneier, R. (1997), 'People value added: the new performance measure', *Strategy and Leadership*, March/April: 14–19.

Scholte, J. A. (2000), *Globalisation: A Critical Introduction*, London: Macmillan.

Schöön, D. (1983), *The Reflective Practitioner*, New York: Basic Books.

Schöön, D. (1987), *Educating the Reflective Practitioner: Toward a new design for teaching and learning in the professions*, San Francisco: Jossey-Bass.

Schuman, H., and Scott, J. (1989), 'Generations and collective memories', *American Sociological Review*, (54): 359–81.

Schunk, D. (2004), *Learning Theories: An Educational Perspective*, Uer Saddle River, NJ: Pearson.

Schutz, A. (1967), *The phenomenology of the social world* (translated by G. Walsh and F. Lehnert from 1932 original), Evanston: Northwestern University Press.

Schwartz, S. H. (1992), 'Universals in the content and structure of values: theoretical advances and empirical tests in 20 countries', in M. Zanna (ed.), *Advances in Experimental Social Psychology*, (25), New York: Academic Press.

Scullion, H. (1993), 'Creating international managers: recruitment and development issues', in P. Kirkbridge (ed.), *Human Resource Management in Europe: Perspectives for the 1990s*, London: Routledge.

Senior, B., and Fleming, J. (2006), *Organizational Change*, 3rd edition, Harlow: FT Prentice Hall.

Seanen-Jarvela, R. (2005), 'Internal evaluation of a management development initiative: a public sector case', *Journal of Management Development*, (24)1: 45–56.

Seibert, K. W. (1999), 'Reflection in action: tools for cultivating on-the-job learning conditions', *Organizational Dynamics*, Winter 2005 54–65.

Shapiro, D. L., Furst, S. A., Spreitzer, G. M., and Von Glinow, M. A. (2002), 'Transnational teams in the electronic age: are team identity and high performance at risk?', *Journal of Organizational Behaviour*, (23): 455–67.

Simmonds, D. (2003*), Designing and Delivering Training*, London: CIPD.

Sitkin, A., and Bowen, N. (2010), *International Business Challenges and Choices*, Oxford.

Sloman, M. (2003), *Training in the Age of the Learner*, London: CIPD.

Smith, P. J., Salder-Smith, E., Robertson, I., and Wakefield, L. (2007), 'Leadership and learning: facilitating self-directed learning in enterprises', *Journal of European Industrial Training*, (31)5: 324–35.

Smola, K., and Sutton, C. (2002), 'Generational differences: revisiting generational work values for the new millennium', *Journal of Organizational Behavior*, (23): 363–82.

Sparrow, P. (1992), 'Building human resource strategies around competencies: a lifecycle model', Manchester: Manchester Business School, Working paper No. 235.

Sparrow, P. R. (2006), 'International management: some key challenges for industrial and organisational psychology', in G. Hodgkinson and J. K. Rod (eds), *International Review of Industrial and Organizational Psychology*, (21), Chichester: Wiley.

Sparrow, P. R., and Wu, P. C. (1998), 'How much donational value-orientations really matter? Predicting HRM preferences of Taiwanese employees', *Employee Relations: the International Journal*, (20)1: 26–56.

Sparrow, P., and Hiltrop, J. M. (1994), *European Human Resource Management in Transition*, Hemel Hempstead: Prentice Hall.

Sparrow, P., Brewster, C., and Harris, H. (2004), *Globalizing Human Resource Management*, London: Routledge.

Spender, D. (1980), *Man Made Language*, London: Routledge.

Spilsbury, M., and Campbell, M. (2009), 'In a nutshell: assessing progress towards making the UK a world leader in skills, employment and productivity by 2020', UK commission for Employment and Skills—Ambition 2020.

Stein, S. J., Papadogiannis, P., Yip, J. A., and Sitarenios, G. (2008), 'Emotional intelligence of leaders: a profile of top executives', *Leadership and Organization Development Journal*, (30)1: 87–101.

Stewart, R. (1976), *Contrasts in Management*, London: McGraw-Hill.

Stewart, R. (1976), *Managers and their jobs: a study of similarities and differences in the ways managers spend their time*, London: Macmillan.

Stogdill, R. M. (1974), *Handbook of Leadership: a survey of the literature*, New York: Free Press.

Straangard, F. (1981), *NLP made visual*, Copenhagen: Connector.

Summerfield, C., and Babb, P. (eds) (2003), 'National Statistics trends, No. 33, The Stationery Office, London.

Super, D. (1984), 'Career and life development', in Brown, D., Brooks, L., and Associates (eds), *Career choice and development*, San Francisco: Jossey-Bass.

Super, D. E. (1970), *Work Values Inventory*, Boston, MA: Houghton Mifflin.

Suutari, V., and Brewster, C. (2003), 'Repatriation: empirical evidence from a longitudinal study of careers and expectations among Finnish expatriates', *International Journal of Human Resource Management*, (14)7: 1132–51.

Suutari, V., and Viitala, R. (2008), 'Management development of senior executives: methods and their effectiveness', *Personnel Review*, (37)4: 375–92.

Swanson, D. R. (2002), 'Diversity programs: attitude and realities in the contemporary corporate environment', *Corporate Communications: an International Journal*, (7)4: 257–68.

Tajfel, H., and Turner, J. (2004), 'An integrative theory of intergroup conflict', in M. J. Hatch and M. Schultz (eds), *Organizational Identity: A Reader*, Oxford: Oxford University Press.

Tamkin, P., Yarnall, J., and Kerrin, M. (2003), *Kirkpatrick and Beyond: A review of models of training evaluation*, IES Report 392, Brighton: IES; available online at www.employment-studies.co.uk/pdflibrary/rw39.pdf.

Tayeb, M. (2004), *International Human Resource Management: A Multinational Company Perspective*, Oxford: Oxford University Press.

Tayeb, M. H. (1988), *Organisations and National Culture*, London Sage.

Taylor, E. B. T. (1871/1924), *Primitive Culture*, Gloucester, MA: Smith.

Taylor, F. W. (1911), *The Principles of Scientific Management,* Harper and Brothers: New York.

Ten Dam, H. W. (1986), 'Beyond organization development', *Leadership and Organization Development Journal*, (7)5: 8–15.

Tennant, C., Boonkrong, M., and Roberts, P. A. (2002), 'The design of a training programme measurement model', *Journal of European Industrial Training*, (25)5: 230–40.

Thomas, D.A. (1999), 'Beyond the simple demographic-power hypothesis: how blacks in power influence white-mentor–black-protégé developmental relationships', in A. Murrell, F. J. Cosby, and Ely R. J. (eds.), *Mentoring Dilemmas: Developmental Relationships within a multicultural Organizations*, Lawrence Erlbaum.

Thomas, D. A. (1989), 'Mentoring and irrationality: the role of racial taboos', *Human Resource Management*, (28): 279–90.

Thomas, D. A. (1990), 'The impact of race on managers' experiences of developmental relationships', *Journal of Organizational Behaviour*, (11): 479–92.

Thomas, D. A., and Ely, R. J. (1996), 'Making differences matter: a new paradigm for managing diversity', *Harvard Business Review*, (68): 107–16.

Thompson, E. R., and Phua, F. T. (2005), 'Are national traits applicable to senior firm managers?', *British Journal of Management*, (16)1: 59–68.

Thompson, J., and Martin, F. (2005), *Strategic Management: Awareness and Change*, 5th edition, London: Thomson.

Thomson, A., Mabey, C., Storey, J., Gray, C., and Iles, P. (2001), *Changing Patterns of Management Development*, Oxford: Blackwell.

Thurley, K., and Widenius, H. (1989), *Towards European Management*, London: Pitman.

Treacy, M., and Wiersema, F. (1996), *Discipline of Market Leaders: choose your customers, narrow your focus, dominate your market*, London: Harper Collins.

Triandis, H. C., Dunnette, M. D., and Hough, L. M. (eds), (1994), *Handbook of Industrial and Organizational Psychology*, Palo Alto, CA: Consulting Psychologists Press.

Trompenaars, F. (1993), *Riding the Waves of Culture: understanding cultural diversity in business*, London: Economist Books.

Truss, K., Soane, E., Edwards, C. Y. L., Wisdom, K., Croll, A., and Burnett, J. (2006), *Working Life: Employee Attitudes and Engagement 2006* (research report), London: CIPD.

Ulrich, D. (1997), *Human Resource Champions: the next agenda for adding value and delivering results*, Boston, MA: Harvard Business School Press.

Ulrich, D., and Brockbank, W. (2005), *The HR value proposition*, Boston, MA: Harvard Business School Press.

Ulrich, D., and Brockbank, W. (2007), *HR: The Value Proposition*, Harvard Business School Press.

Van der Sluis-den Dikken, L., and Hoeksema, L. H. (2001), 'The palette of management development', *Journal of Management Development*, (20)2: 168–79.

Van Rensburg, T., and Prideaux, G. (2006), 'Turning professionals into managers using multisource feedback', *Journal of Management Development*, (25)6: 561–71.

Veale, D. J., and Wachtel, J. M. (1996), 'Mentoring and coaching as part of a human resource development strategy: an example at Coca-Cola Foods', *Management Development Review*, (9)6: 19–24.

Verdonschot, S. G. M. (2006), 'Methods to enhance reflective behaviour in innovation processes', *Journal of European Industrial Training*, (30)9: 670–86.

Vinnecombe, S., and Bank, J. (2002), *Women with Attitude*, London: Routledge.

Vroom, V. H., and Yetton, P. W. (1973), *Leadership and Decision Making*, Pittsburgh: University of Pittsburgh Press.

Vygotsky, L. S. (1978), *Mind in society: the development of higher psychological processes*, Cambridge, MA: Harvard University Press.

Waldman, D. A., Atwater, L. E., and Antonioni, D. (1998), 'Has 360 degree feedback gone amok?', *Academy of Management Executive*, (12)2: 86–94.

Warr, P., Bird, M., and Rackham, N. (1978), *Evaluation of Management Training*, London: Gower.

Warren, C. (2006), 'Curtain call', *People Management*, 23 March: 24.

Watson, S. (2008), 'Where are we now? A review of management development issues in the hospitality and tourism sector: implications for talent management', *International Journal of Contemporary Hospitality Management*, (20)7: 758–80.

Watson, S., and Vasilieva, E. (2007), 'Wilderness thinking: a novel approach to leadership development', *Development and Learning in Organizations*, (21)2: 10–13.

Watson, T., and Harris, P. (1999), *The Emergent Manager*, London: Sage.

Weber, M. (1964), *The Theory of Social and Economic Organization*, New York: The Free Press.

Wellner, A. (2000), 'How do you spell diversity?', *Training*, (37)4: 34–8.

Wenger, E. (1998), *Communities of practice: learning, meaning and identity*, Cambridge: Cambridge University Press.

Whates, P. (2006), *Business Ethics and the 21st Century Organisation*, London: BSI.

Whetten, D., Cameron, K., and Woods, M. (2000), *Developing Management Skills for Europe*, FT Prentice Hall Pearson Education.

Whiteley, J. (2004), 'Creating behavioural change in leaders', *Industrial and Commercial Training*, (36)4: 162–5.

Whitley, R. (2000), *Divergent Capitalisms: The Social Structuring and Change of Business Systems*, Oxford: Oxford University Press.

Whitmore, J. (1996), *Coaching for performance*, 2nd edition, London: Nicholas Brealey.

Whittington, R. (1993), *What Is Strategy and Does It Matter?* 2nd edition, Cengage Learning.

Wiethoff, C. (2004), 'Motivation to learn and diversity training: application of the theory of planned behaviour', *Human Resource Development Quarterly*, (15): 263–83.

Wiley, C. (1996), 'Training programmes that equip managers to deal with a diverse workforce', *Equal Opportunities International*, (15)1: 22–31.

Williamson, O. E. (1975), *Markets and Hierarchies: Analysis and Antitrust Implications*, New York: The Free Press.

Willmott, H. (1994), 'Management education: provocation to a debate', *Management Learning*, (5)1: 105–36.

Wilson, B. (2008), 'Hidden dragons, *People Management*, 7 August, London: CIPD.

Wilson, J. P.(ed.) (2005), *Human Resource Development: Learning and Training for individuals and organisations*, London: Kogan Page.

Wiltsher, C. (2005), 'Fundamentals of adult learning', in J. P. Wilson (ed.), *Human Resource Development*, 2nd edition, London: Kogan Page.

Woodall, J., and Winstanley, D. (1998), *Management Development: Strategy and Practice*, Oxford: Blackwell.

Workplace Employment Relations Survey (2004), London: Department for Trade and Industry, Economic and Social Research Council, Advisory Conciliation and Arbitration Service, Policy Studies Institute.

www.cipd.co.uk.

www.i-l-m.com/research-and-comment/2515.aspx.

Yeung, A., and Ready, D. (1995), 'Developing leadership capabilities of global corporations: a comparative study in eight nations', *Human Resource Management*, 3404: 529–47.

Yoe, R. (2003), 'The tangibles and intangibles of organisational performance', *Team Performance Management: An International Journal*, (9)7–8, 199–204.

Yorks, L. (2005), *Strategic Human Resource Development*. USA: South-Western, part of Thomson Corporation.

Yuki, G. (1999), 'An evaluation of conceptual weaknesses in transformational and charismatic leadership theories', *Leadership Quarterly*, (10): 285–305.

Yuki, G. (2006), *Leadership in Organizations*, London: Prentice Hall.

Yuki, G. A. (1994), *Leadership in Organisations*, 3rd edition, Englewood Cliffs, NJ: Prentice Hall.

Zaccaro, S. J., Harding, F. D., Mumford, A., Jacobs, T. O., and Fleishman, E. A. (2000), 'Leadership skills for a changing world solving complex social problems', *The Leadership Quarterly*, (11): 11–35.

Zemke, R., Raines, C., and Filipczak, B. (2000), *Generations at Work: managing the clash of veterans, boomers, Xers and nexters in your workplace*, New York: AMACOM.

Zysman, J. (1996), 'The myth of a "global" economy: enduring national foundations and emerging regional realities', *New Political Economy*, 1/2: 157–84.

Index